Ocmulgee River User's Guide

NEAR GA. 316, YELLOW RIVER,
GWINNETT COUNTY

Ocmulgee River User's Guide

Joe Cook

GEORGIA RIVER NETWORK GUIDEBOOKS

Published in Cooperation with Altamaha Riverkeeper, Yellow River Water Trail, Ocmulgee River Water Trail, and South River Watershed Alliance

The University of Georgia Press Athens

A Wormsloe
FOUNDATION
nature book

GEORGIA RIVER NETWORK GUIDEBOOKS

Athens, Georgia 30602
www.ugapress.org

Designed by Omega Clay
Set in 9/11.5 Quadraat OT by Kaelin Chappell Broaddus
Printed and bound by Reliance Printing
The paper in this book meets the guidelines for permanence
and durability of the Committee on Production Guidelines
for Book Longevity of the Council on Library Resources.

Most University of Georgia Press titles are available from popular e-book vendors.

Printed in China
25 24 23 22 21 P 5 4 3 2 1

Library of Congress Cataloging-in-Publication Data

Names: Cook, Joe, 1966– author.
Title: Ocmulgee River user's guide / Joe Cook.
Description: Athens : The University of Georgia Press, 2021. | Series: Georgia river network guidebooks | "Published in Cooperation with Altamaha Riverkeeper, Yellow River Water Trail, Ocmulgee River Water Trail, and South River Watershed Alliance."
Identifiers: LCCN 2020032182 | ISBN 9780820358901 (paperback)
Subjects: LCSH: Boats and boating—Georgia—Ocmulgee River. | Outdoor recreation—Georgia—Ocmulgee River. | Ocmulgee River (Ga.)—Guidebooks.
Classification: LCC GV776.G42 O363 2021 | DDC 797.109758/5—dc23
LC record available at https://lccn.loc.gov/2020032182

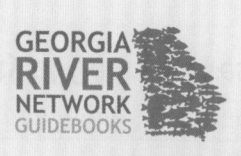

Contents

Acknowledgments

The information gathered in this book was developed from numerous sources, including interviews with local residents, historians, outfitters, scientists, and river lovers.

During the writing of this book I drew information from the following publications: *Pioneer Days along the Ocmulgee* by Fussell M. Chalker; *Running the River: Poleboats, Steamboats, and Timber Rafts on the Altamaha, Ocmulgee, Oconee, and Ohoopee* by Carlton A. Morrison; *The Natural Communities of Georgia* by Leslie Edwards, Jonathan Ambrose, and L. Katherine Kirkman; *Sherman's Horsemen: Union Cavalry Operations in the Atlanta Campaign* by David Evans; *Canoeing and Kayaking Georgia* by Suzanne Welander and Bob Sehlinger; *Historical Record of Macon and Central Georgia* by John C. Butler; *Gwinnett: A Little above Atlanta* by Elliott E. Brack; *A History of DeKalb County, 1822–1900* by Vivian Price; *A History of Rockdale County* by Margaret G. Barksdale, E. L. Cowan, and Frances King; *History of Newton County* by the Newton County Historical Society; "Chronological Summary of the Laws of the State of Georgia: Free Passage of Fish" a report compiled by Bill Frazier; *Georgia Game and Fish*, July 1969; *History of Jasper County* by the Jasper County Historical Foundation; *Monroe County, Georgia: A History* by the Monroe County Historical Society; *History of Pulaski and Bleckley Counties, Georgia, 1808–1956* compiled by the Hawkinsville Chapter of the Daughters of the American Revolution; *Atlanta and Its Environs* by Franklin M. Garrett; *History of Dodge County* by Addie Davis Cobb; *Gwinnett County, Georgia: Families, 1818–2005* by Bill Baughman, Walter Freeman, Scott Holtzclaw, Alice McCabe, and Pam Stenhouse; *History of Gwinnett County, Georgia* by James Flanigan; *Water Powers of Georgia* by the Geological Survey of Georgia (published in 1896, 1908 and 1921); *The Live Oak Soapstone Quarry, DeKalb County* by Daniel T. Elliott; *Statistics of the State of Georgia (1849)* by George White; *Lamar Archaeology: Mississippian Chiefdoms in the Deep South* edited by Mark Williams and Gary Shapiro; *The Courthouse and the Depot: The Architecture of Hope in the Age of Despair* by Wilber W. Caldwell; *Georgia Place-Names* by Ken K. Krakow; *Placenames of Georgia: Essays by John Goff* edited by Frances Lee Utley and Marion R. Hemperley; numerous reports written by the secretary of war for Congress between the 1870s and 1920s; multiple issues of the *Georgia Historical Quarterly*, published by the Georgia Historical Society; *The History of the 72nd Indiana Volunteer Infantry of the Mounted Lightning Brigade* by Benjamin F. McGee; and *Wayfarers in Walton: A History of Walton County, Georgia* by Anita B. Sams.

Important online resources included Newspapers.com, which archives copies of the *Atlanta Constitution* and the *Macon Telegraph*; the Georgia Archives, www.georgiaarchives.com, for historic county maps; Georgia Historic Newspapers at the Digital Library of Georgia, www.gahistoricnewspapers.galileo.usg.edu, with archived copies of the *Jackson Herald*, the *Hawkinsville Dispatch*, and many other newspapers; the New Georgia Encyclopedia, www.georgiaencyclopedia.com; and web pages of the Georgia Department of Natural Resources and Georgia's Environmental Protection Division, www.gadnr.org.

Additionally, many people and organizations lent their experience, stories, and assistance to this project, including Deborah Shepherd, Johnny Waits, Dorinda Dallmeyer, Ray Lambert, Wes Hollingsworth, Chris Skelton, Chris Nelson, Maurine McCleskey, David Maughon, Darrell Huckaby, Jerry McCollum, Steve Brown, Kathleen O'Neal, Jared Godin, Scott Taylor, Kit Carson, and Mark Wilson.

Compiling this book involved traveling every mile of the rivers, on foot, by car, and, most especially, by canoe, from the headwaters of the South, Yellow, and Alcovy Rivers to the Ocmulgee's confluence with the Oconee. Many friends and family members assisted me in this endeavor, accompanying me on paddle trips and providing shuttle service and other support. These included Kit and Mary Carson, Cary Baxter, Chris Thompson, Mark Wilson, Tom and Suzanne Welander, Ramsey Cook, Rena Peck, Vincent Payne, Keith and Lisa Haskell, Scott Taylor of Three Rivers Outdoors, Bill and Susan Atkinson, Laura Kemp, and Fletcher Sams. Invaluable support and information was provided by Mark Wilson with the Yellow River Water Trail, Jackie Echols with South River Watershed Association, Kit Carson with the Ocmulgee River Water Trail, and Fletcher Sams and Jen Hilburn with Altamaha Riverkeeper.

Special thanks to the groups that funded the production of this book, especially the Peyton Anderson Foundation of Macon, the Yellow River Water Trail, and the Ocmulgee River Water Trail. This project originated in a March 2018 meeting on the banks of the Ocmulgee in Hawkinsville, at which Hugh Lawson, John Bembry, and Randy Coody listened patiently to the idea of a comprehensive guide to the Ocmulgee River system. Thanks to their interest and support, the book received its legs.

Map Legend

- ★ Point of Interest
- ◎ Shoal/Rapid
- Fish Weir
- ⊗ Water Intake/Discharge
- • River Mile Marker
- ■ River Gauge
- — Dam
- Campground
- Marina
- ⊙ Outfitter
- Take Out/Launch Site
- Public Land

The map on the next page provides an overview of the length of the river, detailing sections covered on the individual maps later in this book. The legend above explains the symbols used on the maps.

Lawrenceville
Dacula
Annistown
Monroe
Athens
Atlanta
Alcovy Trestle
Rockbridge
Milstead
Covington
Atlanta-DeKalb
Panola
Porterdale
20
Factory Shoals
Peachstone
Allen's Bridge
Snapping Shoals
Jackson Lake
Lamar Mill
Dame's Ferry
Amerson
Macon
Bond Swamp
Warner Robins
Dublin
16
Oaky Woods
Hawkinsville
Pulaski
Wilcox
Abbeville
The Forks
Dodge
Jacksonville
Ben Hill
Lumber City
Albany
75

Ocmulgee River User's Guide

NEAR PANOLA SHOALS, SOUTH RIVER,
DEKALB COUNTY

Introduction

BLACK-CROWNED NIGHT HERON, OCMULGEE RIVER, TELFAIR COUNTY

With the exception of the Flint River, which is born in southwestern Atlanta and is almost immediately piped beneath Hartsfield-Jackson Atlanta International Airport, no Georgia river is born of more compromised beginnings than the Ocmulgee.

Unlike Georgia rivers such as the Chattahoochee, Savannah, and Coosa, which begin their journeys to the sea along the flanks of ridges in the relatively pristine confines of national forests, the Ocmulgee rises inside Atlanta's perimeter highway, in a jungle of asphalt and concrete, as the South River. In fact, its headwaters are buried beneath a hazardous waste site. Its other main tributaries—the Yellow and the Alcovy—rise in Atlanta's fast-growing northeastern suburbs of Gwinnett County, and they too have not escaped the impacts of city life. The springs that give rise to both rivers are almost immediately insulted—dammed to create amenity lakes for subdivisions.

If you were to designate a river system that has borne the gamut of Georgia's land-use changes from the colonial period to the present, the Ocmulgee might be your top pick.

In its southernmost reaches, the Ocmulgee saw the longleaf pine forests along its banks harvested from the mid-1800s to early 1900s and the land converted to cotton and peanut fields; across its midsection, where it spills over rapids and shoals at the fall line, it was among the state's first rivers to be dammed and harnessed to produce hydroelectricity; in the late 1800s, its South River headwaters became both Atlanta's first water source and its first sewer. In the early 1900s, significant sections of the Alcovy River were channelized in a misguided effort to restore to production frequently flooded agricultural land, and by the late 1900s, those same restored lands were swallowed up as Atlanta's suburbs spread unrelentingly—a process that continues into the present.

Change has been forcefully and dramatically thrust on the Ocmulgee and its trio of headwater rivers. Yet despite the degradation that often resulted, the South, Yellow, Alcovy, and Ocmulgee remain highly prized destinations for paddlers, anglers, hunters, and other river users in the heart of Georgia.

The South—perhaps the most maligned river in the state—rises in East Point and flows through the heart of Atlanta, beneath the city's downtown connector highway, and then meanders through DeKalb, Rockdale and Newton Counties, where it spills over rapids at historic mill sites. Along the way, it receives polluted stormwater from the big city and treated discharges from countless sewage plants. Despite this, it serves as a centerpiece for the still-in-development South River Trail, a paved recreational path stretching through Rockdale and DeKalb Counties, and for the South River Water Trail, a boating path running from DeKalb County to Jackson Lake.

To the South's north and east rise the Yellow and Alcovy Rivers, both beginning along the ridge separating the Ocmulgee from the Chattahoochee River system in Gwinnett County.

The Yellow rushes through Gwinnett, tumbling over countless rock outcroppings to create, in the midst of the suburbs, whitewater-paddling hot spots at places such as Sand Shoals and Annistown Falls. So much fun is the paddling that local boosters have established the Yellow River Water Trail, a boating path along most of the Yellow's route through Gwinnett, Rockdale, and Newton Counties.

The Alcovy—the easternmost arm of the Ocmulgee's headwaters—is best known for its slow, braided path through what is considered the northernmost tupelo swamps in Georgia. In stark contrast to the Yellow, with its shoals and rapids, the Alcovy plods slowly through Walton and Newton Counties before finally picking up speed. Its pace reaches a crescendo at picturesque Factory and White Shoals, home to the most formidable whitewater run on the Ocmulgee's three headwater branches. A Newton County park welcomes boaters, tubers, and picnickers to this scenic and historic spot.

Lloyd Shoals Dam, completed in 1911, backs up the water of the South, Yellow, and Alcovy Rivers as Jackson Lake. The three rivers converge about three miles upstream of the dam, and when their joined flows leave the dam's tailrace, the modern Ocmulgee proper is born.

For its first 40 miles, the river rolls over rocks, shoals, and rapids as it descends across the fall line, flanked for a considerable distance by the Chattahoochee-Oconee National Forest and the Piedmont National Wildlife Refuge. In Macon-Bibb County, the recently developed Amerson Park has become a river recreation mecca hosting thousands of kayakers and tubers annually.

Beyond Macon, the Ocmulgee enters Georgia's Coastal Plain where it adopts the winding, sinuous ways of Deep South rivers characterized by cut banks, point sandbars, and countless oxbow lakes and cutoffs. In these haunts, vast stretches of public and private forestland occupy the river's wide floodplain, lending the river a wild and remote atmosphere. In fact, the Ocmulgee corridor south of Macon holds the only known population of black bears in Georgia outside the North Georgia mountains and the Okefenokee Swamp.

The Bond Swamp National Wildlife Refuge and the Georgia wildlife management areas along the river, including Echeconnee Creek, Oaky Woods, Ocmulgee, Horse Creek, Flat Tub, and Bullard Creek, protect tens of thousands of acres and

ALLIGATOR, OCMULGEE RIVER, BEN HILL COUNTY

create a paradise for hunters and anglers pursuing deer, wild hogs, waterfowl, and alligators.

These public lands, in combination with some 225 miles of unfettered river from Juliette Dam to the Ocmulgee's confluence with the Oconee near Lumber City, provide excellent opportunities for multiday boating trips. Primitive campsites can be made on wide sandbars. The potential for this kind of recreation is part of the impetus for a multijurisdictional effort by local governments and other stakeholders to develop and promote the Ocmulgee River Water Trail. For the adventurous, the Altamaha River awaits beyond the Ocmulgee, flowing free for another 137 miles to Georgia's coast.

The Altamaha basin—including its Ocmulgee and Oconee arms—encompasses some 14,000 square miles, nearly a quarter of Georgia's landmass. The Ocmulgee is responsible for draining some 6,100 square miles of that, including all or part of 30 counties with a cumulative population of more than 3.2 million—more than 4 million if you include Fulton County, where the South River begins the system's long journey to the Atlantic Ocean.

The Ocmulgee system is a workhorse for the communities it supports. Its water is used to make bricks and paper. It is harnessed for hydroelectricity at Milstead and Lloyd Shoals Dams. It feeds water to the Georgia Power Company's Plant Scherer in Monroe County, one of the largest coal-fired power plants in the country.

The Ocmulgee and its tributaries are tapped at about 20 locations to provide drinking water, supplying 9 percent of Metro Atlanta's water needs and an average of about 90 million gallons a day to communities such as Covington, Monroe, McDonough, Jackson, Forsyth, Barnesville, and Macon. The river also carries away our waste, assimilating pollution from some 50 municipal and industrial facilities permitted to discharge treated wastewater into it or its tributaries.

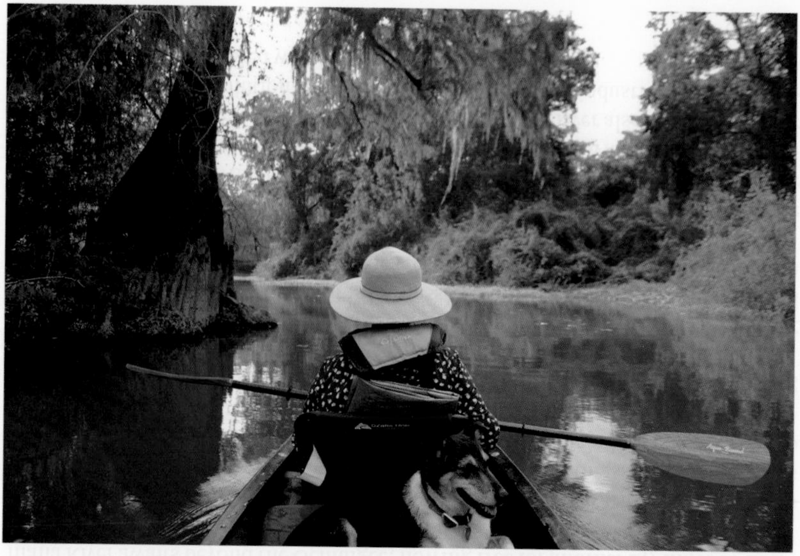

CYPRESS IN SLOUGH, OCMULGEE RIVER, WILCOX COUNTY

Farmers in the Ocmulgee River basin hold nearly 2,600 state permits to draw from surface or groundwater sources to irrigate crops, water livestock, or meet other agricultural needs.

On the nonhuman side, the river hosts 100 species of fish, 85 of which are native to it, as well as 18 native freshwater mussel species, including 7 species found no where else on the planet. This diversity is typical of the region. Researchers estimate that about 75 percent of the country's native fish species are found in southeastern rivers, along with more than 90 percent of all mussel and crayfish species. To put this into perspective, the Ocmulgee basin, with some 500 river miles (including the South, Yellow, and Alcovy) holds almost three times as many native fish species (85) as does the Pacific Northwest's Columbia River (31), which runs for more than 1,200 miles.

Like all the state's rivers, the Ocmulgee has played a central role in Georgia's history. Archaeological research at places such as the Ocmulgee Mounds National Historic Park in Macon-Bibb County trace human occupation of the river valley back more than 17,000 years. It is from those original inhabitants that the river gets its name. "Ocmulgee," in the language of the Creek Indians, means "where water boils up."

Somewhere along the Ocmulgee—though no one is certain exactly where—in 1540, Hernando de Soto, his army, and accompanying Catholic priests became the first Europeans to encounter the native people of the area. We can trace our region's long love affair with barbecue to the hogs the Spaniards brought with them, but the diseases de Soto's men brought wreaked havoc on the native people.

For a short time in the early 1800s, the Ocmulgee was Georgia's frontier—the barrier separating the Creek Nation to the west from the young United States to the east. It was during these years that pole boat captains began using the phrases "bow white" and "bow Injun" to direct their crews to push their boats east or west as they plied the waters of the Altamaha River system. Those commands persisted into the 1900s and the heyday of timber rafting on the Ocmulgee.

For more than a century, from the early 1800s to the early 1900s, the Ocmulgee was, more than anything, the primary avenue of commerce in Central Georgia. The city of Macon grew up around the river trade in the 1820s as pole boats hauling tens of thousands of pounds of goods made the trip to Darien and, amazingly, back upstream, powered only by a crew of men armed with long poles.

Macon celebrated the arrival of the Ocmulgee's first steamboat in 1829, and for the next 80 years the river—and its ever-changing path and unpredictable levels—did battle with men intent on taming and training it into a reliable waterway for steamboats. Though the state and federal governments spent hundreds of thousands of dollars in the effort, the river was unrelenting. Remnants of the battle, in the form of curious lines of 100-year-old wooden posts and rock weirs, can be seen at numerous sites.

By the mid-20th century, the U.S. Army Corps of Engineers had conceded defeat. Concluding that the Altamaha-Ocmulgee system could be made navigable only by a series of locks and dams, the corps drew up plans for what would have been a multi-billion-dollar public works effort. That proposal wasn't abandoned until the 1970s. Yet it was not the most ambitious of the proposals made for the Ocmulgee. In the late 1800s, the federal government sponsored surveys of the river with the intention of forging an inland passage of canals and locks that would connect the Mississippi River drainage to rivers of the Atlantic Coast via the Tennessee River.

While these surveys were under way, hardscrabble farmers and industrial-scale logging operations in South Georgia were clearing the vast longleaf pine forests surrounding the Ocmulgee and floating the logs downriver in massive rafts to Darien. At the peak of the river's log-rafting days, in 1900, Darien shipped out 116 million board feet of lumber. The era both transformed the landscape of South Georgia, converting virtually all the longleaf forests to farmland, and left an indelible impression on the culture of the region—one that persists today and is preserved in the novels and writings of Georgia authors such as Brainard Cheney and Janisse Ray.

In the upper reaches of the Ocmulgee and along its three headwater tributaries, the rivers were harnessed to power gristmills, sawmills, and textile mills and later to produce electricity, giving communities in Fulton, DeKalb, Gwinnett, Rockdale, and Newton Counties flour, cornmeal, and the area's first industries. Examples of this activity are scattered throughout the basin: at the preserved and restored Freeman's Mill on the Alcovy River in Gwinnett County, at Snapping Shoals on the South River, and at turn-of-the-century textile mill towns such as Milstead and Porterdale on the Yellow River.

The dam-building era reached its peak in 1911 with the construction of Lloyd Shoals Dam and the creation of Jackson Lake. When completed, it was the highest dam east of the Mississippi, and it was the largest reservoir in Georgia until after the 1940s. It electrified local communities, but also led to an outbreak of malaria as the backwaters spread over former farmland. Today, only Lloyd Shoals and Juliette Dams, located 19 miles downstream of Lloyd Shoals, still block the Ocmulgee's path.

Of the Ocmulgee's headwater rivers, the South River is blocked by one dam. The Yellow's headwaters are dammed to create an amenity lake for a subdivision in Gwinnett County, and a circa-1970 flood-control dam blocks its path before it reaches Rockdale and Newton Counties, where once-impressive falls were dammed around 1900 to power textile operations in Milstead and Porterdale. The dam and adjoining mill buildings at Porterdale, now redeveloped into residences, preserve a picture of a Georgia mill village from the mid-20th century. The Alcovy, like the Yellow, had its very headwaters dammed—in the 1950s to create a series of commercial recreational fishing lakes. Beyond Crowe's Lakes, however, the Alcovy flows free with the exception of the small dam at Freeman's Mill—now a Gwinnett County park.

Perhaps the greatest impact on the Ocmulgee River basin, however, has been Atlanta's unrelenting growth since the Civil War.

The South River, flowing eastward across the southern edge of Atlanta's downtown area, has borne the brunt of it, and in its history is a metaphor for the resilience of Ocmulgee River system as a whole. One of the South River's tiny headwater tributaries was dammed in 1874 to create Atlanta's first public water supply—what is now known as Lakewood. Not long after, flows from the city's first flush toilets were directed to the South River via rudimentary sewer lines, and for the next 100 years the South became almost synonymous with sewage. Modern sewage treatment plants weren't built in Atlanta until the 1930s, and even then the city's growing population outpaced their capacity.

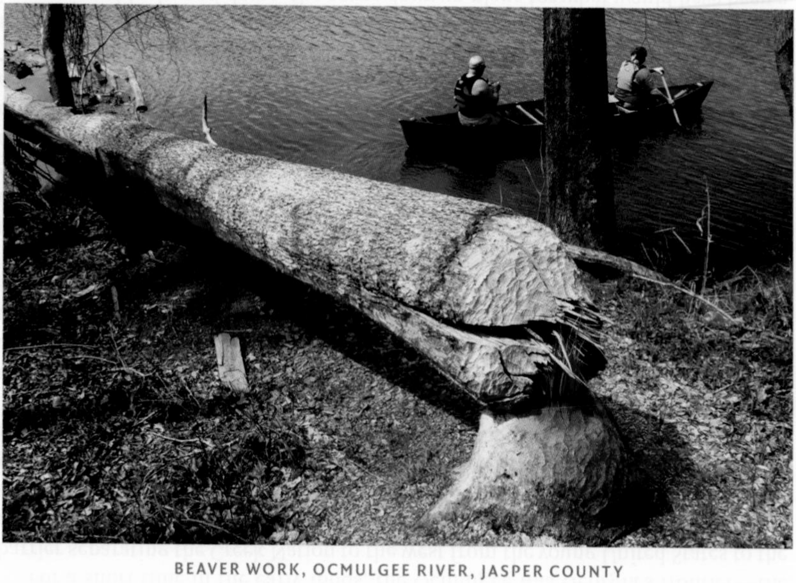

BEAVER WORK, OCMULGEE RIVER, JASPER COUNTY

In the 1950s, DeKalb County's Panola Shoals—the site of a 19th-century textile mill—became known as "Soap Shoals" because of the head-high flotillas of suds that collected beneath the sloping falls. The aeration caused by the falls, combined with high nutrient levels from treated wastewater and chemicals from wastewater treatment plants upstream, created the phenomenon.

Today, while most of Metro Atlanta's sewage is treated, the South remains plagued by sewer overflows caused when water from heavy rains infiltrates sewer lines. At places in Fulton and DeKalb Counties, signs still warn residents to keep out of the water. Since 2010, DeKalb County has been under a federal-court-ordered consent decree requiring the county to spend hundreds of millions of dollars to upgrade its sewer infrastructure, but progress has been slow. Completion dates scheduled for 2020 have been pushed back five years.

Meanwhile, stormwater from the highly urbanized landscape—20 percent of the South River's headwaters area is covered by concrete, asphalt, or rooftops—further degrades the river. Litter that washes into or is dumped into the river is ubiquitous. In places, giant flotillas of plastic bottles cover the river from bank to bank; at other locations, discarded car tires virtually carpet the river bottom.

Yet there is hope for this river, which is vitally important to Atlanta's growth but maligned by those that depend on it. Thanks to sewer upgrades, its health has steadily improved in recent decades. The completion of remaining projects will further eliminate sources of pollution, and initiatives led by the City of Atlanta to redirect stormwater so that it soaks into the ground rather than rushing off streets and parking lots directly into streams will help heal the South.

Citizen groups like the South River Watershed Association have in recent years focused public attention on the river, sponsoring river cleanups and paddle trips, and advocating for the South River Water Trail, a recreational boating trail stretching through DeKalb, Rockdale, and Newton Counties.

Like other Georgia rivers that were degraded and neglected and then protected and restored, the South is on the cusp of that same transformation. Should you venture onto the South after exploring it first in this book, you will be pleasantly surprised. The beauty is still there, awaiting rediscovery at places such as Albert Shoals and Peachstone Shoals, and when you go, you will be part of the story of another Georgia river being revived.

That is essentially the story of the Ocmulgee River system. Though heavily abused for the past 200 years, it has proved resilient. Its beauty is tarnished in places, but far, far from gone. With help from those who depend on it, use it, fall in love with it, and protect it, further restoration will occur—perhaps even the removal of obsolete dams, the elimination of plastic pollution, and the return of longleaf pine habitat.

That process starts when we venture onto its waters.

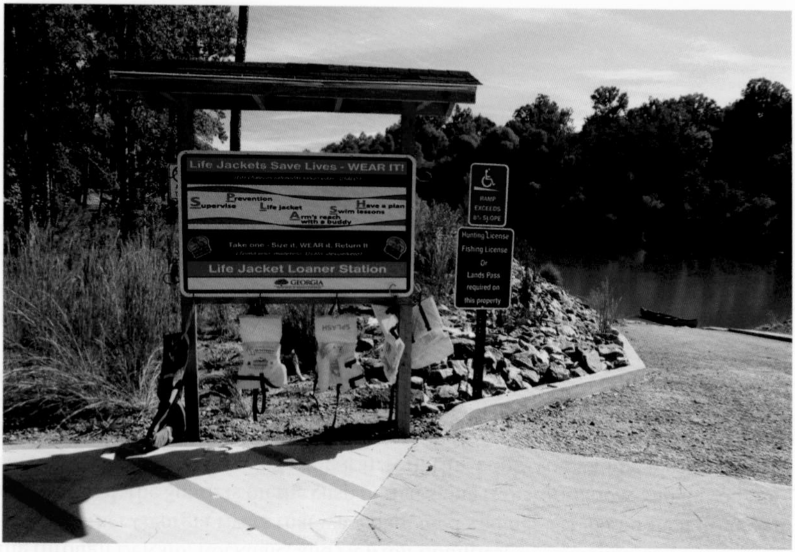

SCUFFLE BLUFF LANDING, OCMULGEE RIVER, TELFAIR COUNTY

Safety

Like all rivers, the Ocmulgee is not without its dangers. Rivers are unforgiving of our carelessness. Being properly prepared for your excursion and abiding by safe boating practices (including state boating laws) will reduce your risk of mishaps and keep you coming back to the river time after time.

Wear Your Life Jacket

This is the number 1 rule of boating safety. PFDs—personal flotation devices—are known as life jackets for a reason: they save lives. Wear a PFD or run the risk of being DOA. Georgia law requires that all vessels have at least one U.S. Coast Guard–approved Type I, II, III, or V PFD for each person on board. Type V PFDs, however, are acceptable only when worn and securely fastened. Children under the age of 10 must wear a life jacket at all times on a moving vessel.

Though state law doesn't require it, wearing your life jacket at all times is the best practice.

Know Your Boat

Whether you are in a canoe, kayak, paddleboard, or motorized boat, know how to operate your vessel. Canoe and kayaking classes are taught by numerous organizations. The Georgia Canoeing Association, www.gapaddle.com, teaches regular classes on paddling and boating safety. Additionally, the American Canoe Association, www.americancanoe.org, is an excellent resource for online boating safety information.

The Georgia Department of Natural Resources, www.gadnrle.org/boating-rules-regulations, provides extensive information on safety practices in motorized vessels. Operators of motorized vessels born on or after January 1, 1998, must complete a boating-education course approved by the GADNR before operating such a vessel.

Know the River and Prepare for Your Trip

If you are reading this, you have taken the first step toward a safe river trip—know the section of river that you plan to travel, and understand its unique dangers. For example, portions of all four rivers covered in this guidebook, the South, Yellow, Alcovy and Ocmulgee, include Class II–III rapids that can be hazardous, and as river levels rise, those risks increase. River gauges should be consulted when planning a trip. Trips during high flows should be attempted only by paddlers with strong whitewater-paddling skills. Do not attempt river sections that are beyond your skill level. Additionally, the Ocmulgee and its tributaries are home to several dams that can create potential hazards: Snapping Shoals Dam on the South River, Milstead and Porterdale Dams on the Yellow, and Juliette Dam on the Ocmulgee are all lowhead dams. These obstacles should be portaged. River users should never attempt to paddle over or through these obstacles, because of the dangerous hydraulics created at the base of these dams. Leave your trip itinerary with someone who can notify authorities if you don't return as planned. Remember, what you take on the trip is all that you will have available if you need to rescue yourself. Carry appropriate food, water, clothes, and rescue equipment. While no section of the Ocmulgee is far from "civilization," expect the unexpected and plan accordingly.

Wear the Right Clothes

Wear the appropriate clothes to protect from sun, heat, rain, and cold. Cold water is especially dangerous, since extended contact with it can lead to hypothermia and even death. During cool weather, dress in layers of clothing made of synthetic fabrics such as polypropylene, nylon, neoprene, and polyester fleece. Always bring extra clothing protected in a waterproof container. When temperatures are below 60 degrees Fahrenheit or when combined air and water temperatures are below 120 degrees Fahrenheit, wear a wet suit or dry suit. Waterproof shoes, socks, and gloves are also recommended. Always wear secure-fitting river shoes to protect your feet. Helmets should always be worn when paddling whitewater.

Watch for Other Boaters

This safety practice is especially important on the river's whitewater sections and on Jackson Lake, where paddlers are likely to encounter motorized-boat traffic. On reservoirs, paddlers should stay close to the shore and avoid main channels whenever possible. Waves created by motorboats are best navigated by turning the bow (nose) of the boat into the wave rather than taking the wave broadside. When paddling at night, a white light must be shown toward oncoming traffic. On whitewater sections (and in other locations where navigational hazards exist), paddlers should confirm that downstream boaters are clear of the rapid or obstacle before proceeding.

BOATER'S CHECKLIST

- ☐ A Spare Paddle . . . because paddles break and motors die
- ☐ Hat or Helmet . . . hat for sun protection or warmth and a helmet whenever paddling whitewater
- ☐ Whistle or Signaling Device . . . three sharp blows on a whistle are a universal distress signal
- ☐ Throw Bags (Ropes) and Other Rescue Gear . . . especially important in whitewater
- ☐ "River" Knife . . . a safely and easily accessible knife can save a life when entangled in a rope or other hazards
- ☐ Bilge Pump or Bailer . . . because holes in boats do happen
- ☐ Extra Clothing in a Dry Bag . . . dry clothes keep you warm; wet clothes, not so much.
- ☐ Sunscreen
- ☐ Compass and Map
- ☐ First-Aid Kit
- ☐ Matches in a Waterproof Container
- ☐ Small Boat Repair Kit with Duct Tape

Boating Etiquette

Practice No-Trace Travel

Practicing no-trace travel is simple: leave your route in such a condition that those who come behind you will not know that someone had passed before them. Never litter and always pack out trash (including the trash of those less considerate).

Conduct all toilet activity at least 200 feet from any body of water. Bury your waste in a cathole 6–8 inches deep or pack it out. Be conscious of private property and do not conduct your toilet activity in someone's backyard.

Additionally:

- Avoid building campfires, except in established fire rings or in emergencies.
- Minimize impacts to the shore when launching, portaging, scouting, or taking out.
- Examine, but do not touch, cultural or historic structures and artifacts.
- Leave rocks, plants, and other natural objects as you find them.
- Do not disturb wildlife.

Respect Others

The Ocmulgee and its tributaries are traveled by many people, and many others make their homes along it. Always be respectful of other river users and riverfront property owners. Poor behavior by some river users can lead to increased regulation and fees, limitations on access, and damage to the environment. Nearly all property along the Ocmulgee and its tributaries is privately owned. Islands within the river are also pri-

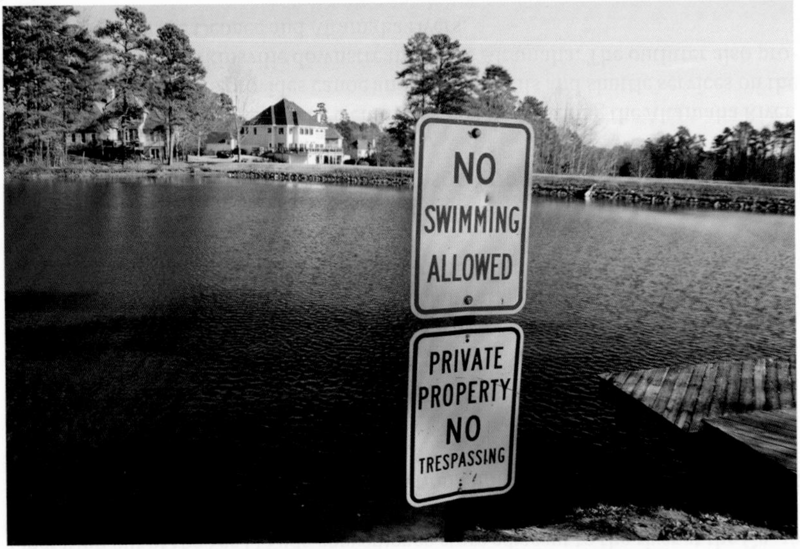

CROWE'S LAKE, ALCOVY RIVER, GWINNETT COUNTY

vate property. While Georgia law allows boaters the right of passage on navigable streams, the law does not extend the right to travel on private property. Remain in the river channel, except in cases where you know public land exists or where you know that property owners allow boaters access.

Additionally:

- Know and obey all rules and regulations.
- Be courteous and polite when communicating with others.
- Avoid interfering with the recreational activities of others.
- Never engage in loud, lewd, or inappropriate behavior.
- Take care to avoid paddling near areas of heightened security.
- Control pets or leave them at home.
- Do not operate your vessel while under the influence of alcohol or drugs. Georgia law prohibits operating both motorized and nonmotorized vessels while under the influence of alcohol or drugs.

A Note on Parking at Launch Sites and Take Outs

While many popular launch and take out sites have designated parking areas or pull-offs on rights of way, some river-access locations identified in this guide do not have developed and designated, or even adequate, parking. Care should be taken when parking vehicles and unloading boats. Avoid parking on roadsides wherever possible.

Outfitters

Several private outfitters provide services on the Ocmulgee and on Jackson Lake, offering boat rentals, parking, shuttles, and other services. These businesses are listed here as well as in the chapters covering the river sections where they commonly operate.

JACKSON LAKE

Jackson Lake Rentals

770-713-7069, www.jacksonlakerentals.com

Operating from Berry's Boat Dock, Berry Dendry provides pontoon boat rentals and ski tube rentals.

OCMULGEE RIVER

Ocmulgee Outdoor Expeditions

Macon, Ga. 478-733-3386, www.ocmulgeeoutdoorexpeditions.com

Operating in Middle Georgia with a focus on the Ocmulgee River between Lloyds Shoals Dam and downtown Macon, Ocmulgee Outdoor Expeditions provides canoe and kayak rentals and regularly organizes special paddling events. It provides shuttle service to all access points north of Macon and, by prior arrangement, as far south as Hawkinsville.

Ocmulgee Adventures

54 Ga. Hwy. 16 W., Monticello, Ga. 31064, 770-504-9272

Operating out of the Sac O Suds convenience store adjacent to the river at the Ga. 16 bridge between Jackson and Monticello, Ocmulgee Adventures provides kayak and tube rentals and shuttle service on the sections immediately downstream of Lloyd Shoals Dam.

$10 Tubing

2552 North Pierce Ave., Macon, Ga. 31204, 844-386-8823, www.rivertubing.com

Operating out of Macon-Bibb County's Amerson Park, $10 Tubing provides tube rentals for the 2-mile float between the park's two boat landings.

Three Rivers Outdoors

612 McNatt Falls Rd., Uvalda, Ga. 30473, 912-594-8379, www.explorethreerivers.com

Located near the confluence of the Ocmulgee and Oconee along the Altamaha River, Three Rivers Outdoors provides canoe and kayak rentals and shuttle services on the Ocmulgee from Hawkinsville downstream to the Altamaha. The outfitter also provides service on the Oconee and Altamaha rivers.

How to Use This Book

Each chapter presents a portion of the river that can generally be paddled in a canoe, kayak or other nonmotorized vessel within a single day and provides essential information about the estimated length of the run (in hours and miles), the water levels necessary for the journey to be attempted, the location of current water-level information, and directions to launch and take out sites. Alternative launch sites and take out sites are noted where available. The largest portion of each chapter presents, by distances (in miles) and GPS coordinates, points of interest along the river. Mileage markers begin at the mouth of the river with Mile O and extend upriver to the river's source. The map accompanying each chapter is intended for use as a reference while on the river. For that reason, all the maps are oriented from upstream to downstream rather that from north to south, and they present only the most important roads for reference. Drivers should use, in conjunction with the written directions to launch and take out sites, road maps or a GPS.

FISHING NEAR STATHAM SHOALS, OCMULGEE RIVER,
WILCOX COUNTY

An Ocmulgee River Fishing Primer

Passing through a variety of habitats spanning the Piedmont and Coastal Plain regions of the state, the Ocmulgee River is home to 100 fish species, including 85 native ones. While only a handful of these are considered sport fish, the Ocmulgee River system's fishing opportunities are abundant, with nearly 500 miles of mainstem rivers and more than 4,000 acres of reservoir habitat in Jackson Lake. In addition, countless oxbow lakes and sloughs along the lower Ocmulgee are legendary fishing holes: the world-record largemouth bass was caught on one in 1932.

South, Yellow, and Alcovy Rivers

During the mid-20th century, before the era of massive U.S. Army Corps of Engineers impoundments such as Lake Allatoona and Lake Lanier, anglers looked to small commercial fishing lakes, and the Upper Ocmulgee, with its proximity to Atlanta, was for a time a hotbed of these fishing holes. Lake Lucerne near Snellville, Norris and Gaines Lakes near Lithonia, Lake Rockaway near Conyers, and Crowe's Lake near Lawrenceville catered to anglers who might pay $1 a day for the right to fish from the banks or more for a boat rental. While these impoundments still exist, today they are primarily amenity lakes for subdivisions and not generally open to the public.

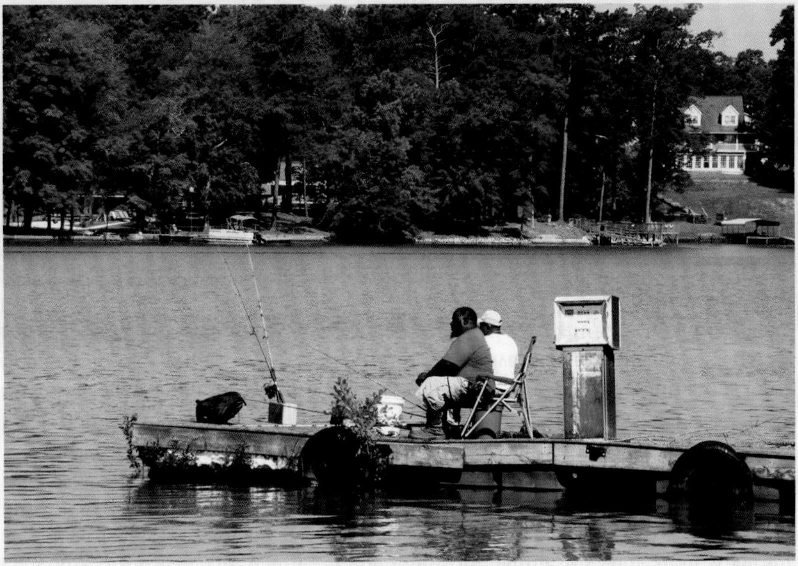

WALKER MARINA, JACKSON LAKE, NEWTON COUNTY

But those willing to get on the moving rivers of the Ocmulgee's headwaters are generally rewarded. The fishing is good and the fishing pressure light. Caution should be exercised because each arm of the Ocmulgee's headwaters comes with significant Class II–III rapids. Anglers should be aware of these obstacles when planning float trips on the South, Yellow, or Alcovy.

For those who prefer bank fishing, the choices are more limited. On the South River, public access can be found at Panola Shoals in DeKalb County, Panola Mountain State Park, and Rockdale County's Lorraine Park as well as at numerous locations along the South River Trail. On the Yellow River, Gwinnett County's Yellow River Park and Porterdale's Yellow River Park and Cedar Shoals Park are the best bets for bank fishing. On the Alcovy, anglers can use Gwinnett County's Freeman's Mill Park and Harbins Park as well as Newton County's Factory Shoals Park.

The South River's fishing hot spot is at Snapping Shoals in the early spring. The lowhead dam blocks crappie and migrating white, hybrid, and striped bass moving up river from Jackson Lake. Live minnows or plastic jigs work on crappie, which arrive below the dam in February and March. White, hybrid, and striped bass show up later in March and April and can be lured with live minnows as well as roostertails, small crankbaits, spinners, and two-inch curly-tailed plastic grubs. Similarly, the Yellow River downstream of the Porterdale Dam tends to gather the same species in the early spring. On the Alcovy, the hot spot is the base of the big falls at Factory Shoals Park.

Upstream of these obstacles, the mostly free-flowing rivers are home to the usual sport fish: bass, bream, crappie, and catfish, but don't expect trophies. The smaller rivers produce smaller fish, so when fishing the Ocmulgee's headwater streams, go light and small. Light rods and reels—and even fly rods—make catching the smaller fish more fun, and with smaller lures, you can cast for bream, bass, and crappie simultaneously. Look to the deeper holes for the largest fish. Catfish, which also inhabit these deep holes, can be caught on worms and livers.

Of the Ocmulgee's three headwater arms, the Alcovy is the least accessible and least navigable, but for those same reasons, the fishing pressure on it is light. For adventurous souls willing to paddle into the strainer-choked sections of the river to access the tupelo and bottomland swamps in Walton and Newton Counties, the fishing can be excellent.

Jackson Lake

Spanning over 4,750 acres, Jackson Lake was once known for its trophy largemouth bass. The nitrogen and phosphorus coming downriver from Metro Atlanta's wastewater treatment plants created a nutrient-rich lake and thus bigger bass. But as phosphorus has been eliminated from the wastewater stream, the trophy bass in Jackson have become fewer. The lake record, a 14-pound, 7-ounce largemouth, dates to 1986.

That said, there are still plenty of big fish in the lake. Largemouth and spotted bass dominate, but the Georgia Department of Natural Resources (GADNR) regularly stocks the lake with hybrid and striped bass. Catfish, bream, and crappie round out Jackson's offerings.

TURTLE CREEK MEADOWS POND, ALCOVY RIVER, GWINNETT COUNTY

For bass, look to the deeper water, especially where structure or shallower shelves intersect with deep drop-offs. Crankbaits and jigs are effective on largemouths; spotted bass will take smaller crankbaits and spinning lures. The GADNR reports that October to February is the time to land larger bass on Jackson Lake, but the fishing is good throughout the spring and summer too.

Casting along the shoreline using topwater lures can be effective early in the morning during the summer months, but as the water warms, the bass go deeper and tend to feed on points along the edges of shallow and deep water. That is when plastic worms on a Carolina or Texas rig or a jig 'n pig fished along the bottom can entice strikes.

Stocked striped bass are another top-tier predator in the lake. If you can find schools of shad, you will find the stripers feeding on them. In the early morning, stripers can often be seen striking shad on the lake's surface in the main channel of the rivers. Under these conditions, topwater lures can be effective. Otherwise, trolling live gizzard shad or crankbaits through the schools can produce strikes. The cool, deep water near Lloyd Shoals Dams is a good place to start. Average fish are in the 5-pound range but 18-pounders are not uncommon.

Night fishing is the best bet for landing one of the lake's big catfish. Channel, blue, and flathead catfish dominate, and they get large: 20-pounders are caught regularly. The lake records for blue catfish (46 pounds, 7 ounces), flathead catfish (63 pounds, 11 ounces), and channel cats (16 pounds, 10 ounces) were set between 2016 and 2018.

Cut shad, liver, and live bait fished on the bottom of the lake, especially in the deep holes found along old creek- and riverbeds, produce the best chances. One note: flathead catfish like rocky substrates and hard river bottoms. Indian Fishery, Barnes, and Lemon Shoals, noted in the chapter covering the Yellow River, likely provide the preferred habitat for flatheads.

Jackson Lake is noted also for its redear sunfish, bluegill, and redbreast fishing. The late spring and early summer is the time to hit the lake for these panfish. Live baits like worms and crickets are effective, as are ultralight spinning tackle. To find the fish, look for structure along the shoreline, including docks, blowdowns, and weeds. When they begin bedding, you can find them by looking for their circular beds on sandy bottoms in shallow water.

Crappie are abundant on the lake, and April is prime crappie time. Casting around docks, where the fish hide in the shade, or trolling lines along old creek channels are the most common techniques. Small jigs, crankbaits, and live minnows are effective. For larger crappie, those pushing two pounds, try fishing the deeper water near the dam.

Upper Ocmulgee

Of all the fishing spots in the Ocmulgee system, the section from Lloyd Shoals Dam to Macon is perhaps the most dynamic. The very diverse habitats found here create homes for a host of game fish. Frequent shoals on the Upper Ocmulgee preclude trips by most large motorized vessels, making this a great section for wading or kayak/canoe fishing.

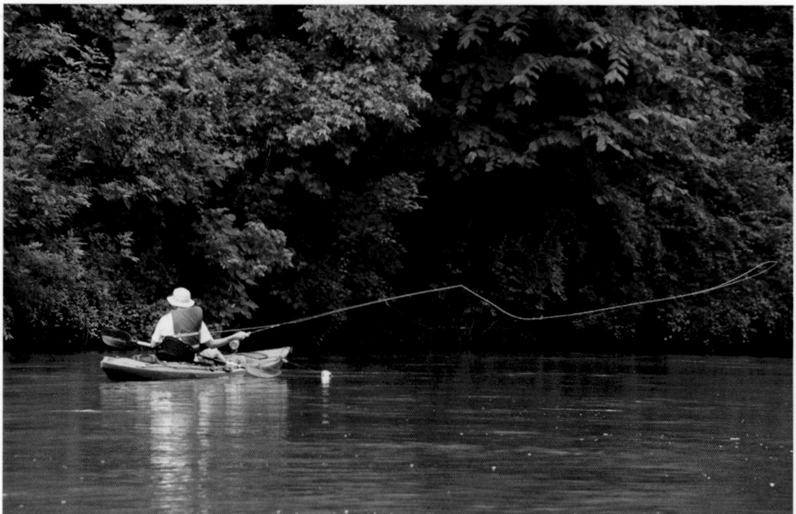

FLY-FISHING, OCMULGEE RIVER, BUTTS COUNTY

The six miles below Lloyd Shoals Dam, with four public access points, are an especially popular section to fish, but remoter sections downstream provide similar habitats with less fishing stress.

The king of the Upper Ocmulgee is the shoal bass. Stocked during the 1970s, the fish now have a "finhold" in the numerous shoals and rapids in the 40 miles between Lloyd Shoals Dam and Macon. Using light tackle and even fly rods makes it even more fun to catch these intense fighters, though if your intent is to land a trophy shoalie of five pounds or more, larger tackle and larger lures are in order.

Spinner baits, poppers, plastic worms, and minnow lures are effective on traditional rods and reels. Fly fishermen should consider woolly buggers. Shoalies tend to be most active in the spring and fall, and are best caught by casting in moving water. They will lie in wait in eddies below shoals and rapids looking for bait to flush through on the fast-moving water.

Again, wading or casting from a canoe or kayak is the best way to access the habitat of shoal bass.

Shoals are also the habitat of redbreasts. Small spinners and poppers are effective, as are crickets in areas of swift to moderate current.

Bluegill and redear fishing is especially good immediately downstream of Lloyd Shoals Dam. While bluegill can be caught on the same artificial lures used for redbreast, redear are best landed by using worms fished on the river bottom.

The two dams in this stretch tend to congregate fish at their bases during spring migration runs. Thus, striped bass and hybrids—along with American shad—can be caught in abundance in the tailrace waters of Lloyd Shoals Dam and beneath the lowhead dam at Juliette from March through May.

The Ocmulgee's shad average about 2 pounds, whereas the stripers and hybrids average 4–8 pounds, and larger stripers come in at up to 30 pounds. Choose your tackle based on your target. Shad can be caught on light tackle and even fly rods. Pair the light tackle with small jigs, and the fly rod with small fly streamers. Larger tackle and lures will be needed for bass, with live shad or large jigs being the top choices.

Largemouth and spotted bass are also abundant on the Upper Ocmulgee. For largemouth bass, look to the slack water along riverbanks where there are deadfalls or other structure. Plastic worms, spinner baits, and topwater baits can be effective. Spotted bass can be found in areas with moderate currents and can be caught using the same techniques used to land shoalies and largemouth.

Lower Ocmulgee

No fishing guide to the Lower Ocmulgee would be complete without mention of the world-record largemouth bass caught by George Perry on Montgomery Lake in 1932. The 22-pound, 4-ounce fish remains legendary, but it is far from the only lunker pulled from the waters of the Lower Ocmulgee. Invasive flathead catfish have found a home in the Ocmulgee. The river's rod-and-reel record is a 59-pounder caught near Hawkinsville in 2002; in 2009, that was surpassed by a 103-pounder caught on a trotline near Bonaire.

STRAINER, OCMULGEE RIVER, HOUSTON COUNTY

For sure, the Lower Ocmulgee grows some large ones. From Macon south, catfish, largemouth bass, and bream are the top sport fish.

The Lower Ocmulgee's catfish like the deep holes found opposite point sandbars on the outside bends of the river's many oxbows. Look to woody debris that creates eddies and resting places for fish. An ideal strategy is to cast from an upstream sandbar into the deep water along the steep banks. Use weights to keep the bait on the river bottom. Live bream work best for the biggest predators—flathead catfish. Channel and blue catfish will strike live bream as well; cut bait, chicken livers, and worms are also effective. Nighttime and early morning from March through September are the best times to land large catfish.

Redbreast, bluegills, and redears can be taken on the Ocmulgee. Crickets and worms are the best baits. Using a bobber and weight, place the bait near the bottom of the river. For bluegills and redears, look along the riverbanks where structure creates eddies and slack water. Oxbow lakes and sloughs off the main channel are excellent haunts for these fish as well.

Though redbreast numbers have declined because of the introduction of flathead catfish, they can still be found on the Lower Ocmulgee. But look to faster-moving water. Crickets fished on the river bottom, as well as spinner baits, are good choices to lure redbreasts.

Though it has been nearly 90 years since the world-record largemouth bass was caught along the Ocmulgee, big fish remain. The GADNR reports occasional landings of largemouths of 7–10 pounds from the river, caught on a variety of artificial lures. The choice of lure will depend on the water. In low water when the river is running clear, Texas rigs with plastic worms and jigs dropped below the water's surface are most effective. When the river is up and muddy, anglers have success using buzz baits and showier topwater plugs to lure the fish from their hiding places. Like sunfish, largemouths will be found in the slack water created by woody debris along the shoreline; the river's oxbow lakes, sloughs, and eddies below sandbars also provide largemouth habitat.

Access to the Lower Ocmulgee is generally excellent. Public boat ramps are spaced 10–15 miles apart from Macon to Lumber City, and state and federal lands provide direct public access to the river in multiple locations.

One of the more unusual fishing techniques seen on the Lower Ocmulgee is used to land mullet, a marine fish that travels far up Georgia's coastal rivers and is often spotted making impressive leaps out of the water. Prized for their tasty meat and roe, mullets are best caught by submerging a salt block and a chum bag filled with a farm feed like rabbit chow in the eddy of a sandbar. This attracts the fish, which can then be caught using simple cane poles fitted with small hooks baited with pieces of red wiggler worms.

For additional and updated information about fishing trends on the Ocmulgee River and Jackson Lake, visit the GADNR website, www.georgiawildlife.com/fishing-forecasts. The Georgia River Fishing website, www.georgiariverfishing.com, is an excellent resource for additional information about fishing the South, Yellow, and Alcovy Rivers.

Remember: to fish in Georgia, all anglers must first obtain a state fishing license. Licenses can be purchased online at https://gooutdoorsgeorgia.com.

MOUNTAIN LAUREL AND BOULDERS, DEKALB COUNTY

SOUTH RIVER

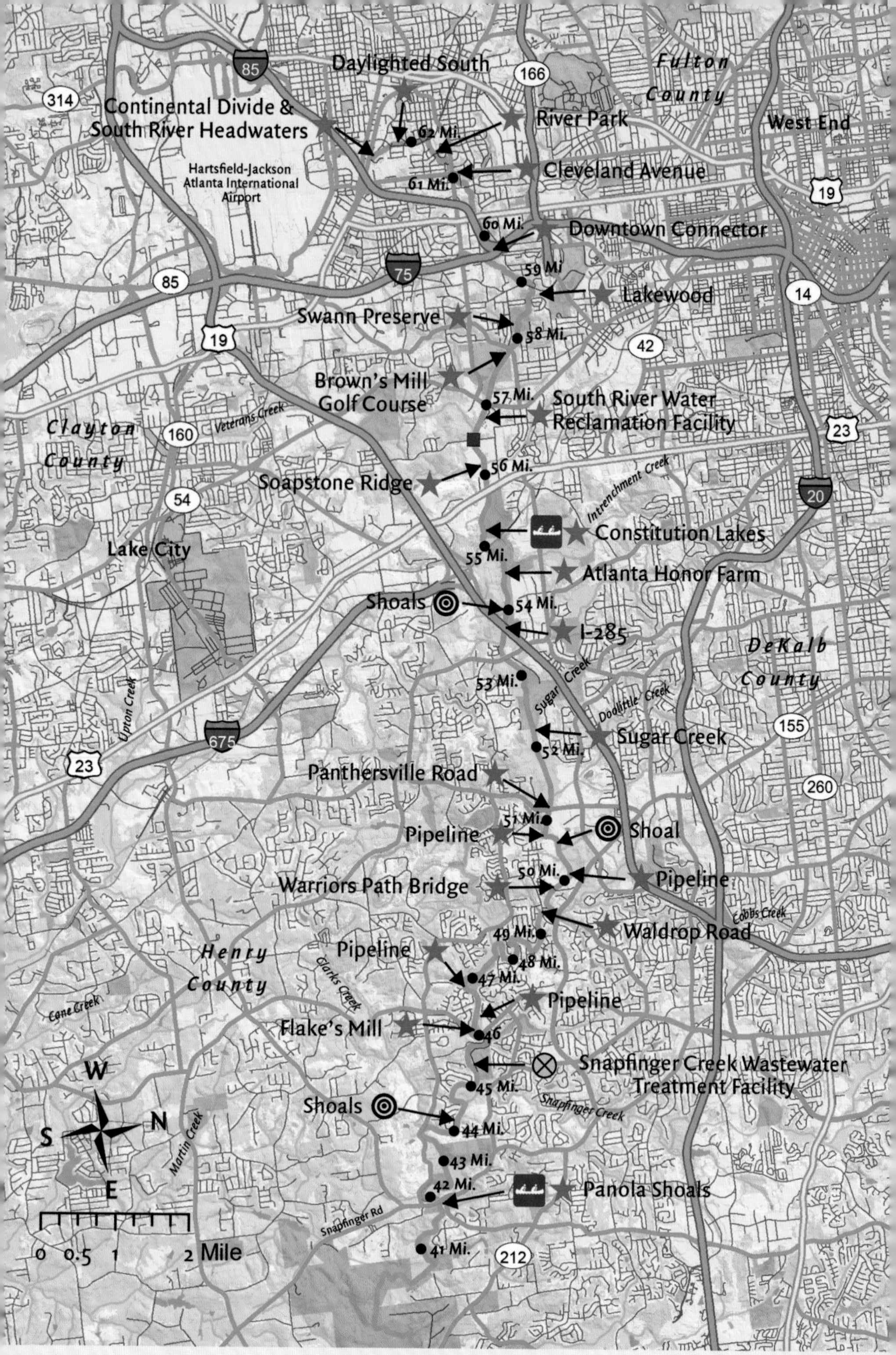

Daylighted South
Fulton County
Continental Divide & South River Headwaters
River Park
West End
62 Mi.
Hartsfield-Jackson Atlanta International Airport
Cleveland Avenue
61 Mi.
60 Mi.
Downtown Connector
59 Mi
Lakewood
Swann Preserve
58 Mi.
Brown's Mill Golf Course
57 Mi.
South River Water Reclamation Facility
Veterans Creek
Clayton County
56 Mi.
Soapstone Ridge
Intrenchment Creek
Constitution Lakes
55 Mi.
Lake City
Atlanta Honor Farm
Shoals
54 Mi.
I-285
DeKalb County
53 Mi.
Sugar Creek
Doolittle Creek
Upton Creek
Sugar Creek
52 Mi.
Panthersville Road
51 Mi.
Pipeline
Shoal
50 Mi.
Warriors Path Bridge
Pipeline
Cobbs Creek
49 Mi.
Waldrop Road
Pipeline
Henry County
48 Mi.
Clarks Creek
47 Mi.
Cane Creek
Pipeline
Flake's Mill
46
Snapfinger Creek Wastewater Treatment Facility
45 Mi.
Shoals
Snapfinger Creek
44 Mi.
Martin Creek
43 Mi.
42 Mi.
Panola Shoals
Snapfinger Rd
0 0.5 1 2 Mile
41 Mi.
W
S
N
E

Atlanta-DeKalb

Length 20 miles (Headwaters to Snapfinger Road). The headwaters to Moreland Avenue section is not considered navigable and flows mostly through private property. But some public property and public trails exist along or near the river and are noted in the Points of Interest section of this chapter. The river is marginally navigable from Moreland Avenue to Snapfinger Road, but expect numerous strainers requiring portages. The section also includes numerous shoals, including Class III Panola Shoals.

Time 5–8 hours (Moreland Avenue to Snapfinger Road)

Minimum Level Flows of at least 20 cubic feet per second and a gauge height of 3 feet at the Forest Park Road bridge are generally sufficient to provide a navigable channel from Moreland Avenue to Snapfinger Road, but travelers should be prepared for frequent strainers and deadfall on this narrow, winding river through an urban landscape.

River Gauge The nearest river gauge is located in the middle of this section at Forest Park Road: https://waterdata.usgs.gov/ga/nwis/uv/?site_no=02203655&PARAmeter_cd=00065,00060,00062,00010.

Trailhead The first 6 miles of the South River flow through a heavily urbanized landscape and through mostly private land, so following the river's path on foot is not possible; however, several public parks along its route provide glimpses of the river as it winds through industrial areas, business districts, and in-town Atlanta neighborhoods. Riverview Park, located less than a mile from where the river first emerges, provides views, though no access to the river, since it is fenced for health and safety reasons. The river also flows through publicly owned Swann Preserve and Brown's Mill Golf Course. Along the golf course's perimeter, the short Southtowne Trail passes over the river on a footbridge. Downstream of Moreland Avenue, Constitution Lakes, a DeKalb County wildlife preserve, provides access to the river, and portions of the PATH Foundation's South River Trail follow the river's course near Georgia State University–Perimeter College at Panthersville Road and at Panola Shoals and Snapfinger Road.

DIRECTIONS TO HEADWATERS The South River originates along a nondescript ridge separating the Ocmulgee River basin from that of the Chattahoochee and Flint Rivers. The ridge generally follows the current route of the Norfolk Southern Railroad and Main Street in East Point. With many of its smallest headwaters rivulets piped and covered, the South first emerges into daylight near the intersection of Norman Berry Drive and Calhoun Avenue. From exit 75 (Sylvan Rd.) on I-85 southbound, travel south on Sylvan Road 0.3 mile. Turn right on Willingham Drive and proceed 0.6 mile. Turn right on Norman Berry Drive and travel 0.5 mile. Turn left on Calhoun Avenue. Here, the South River emerges from pipes beneath Calhoun Avenue.

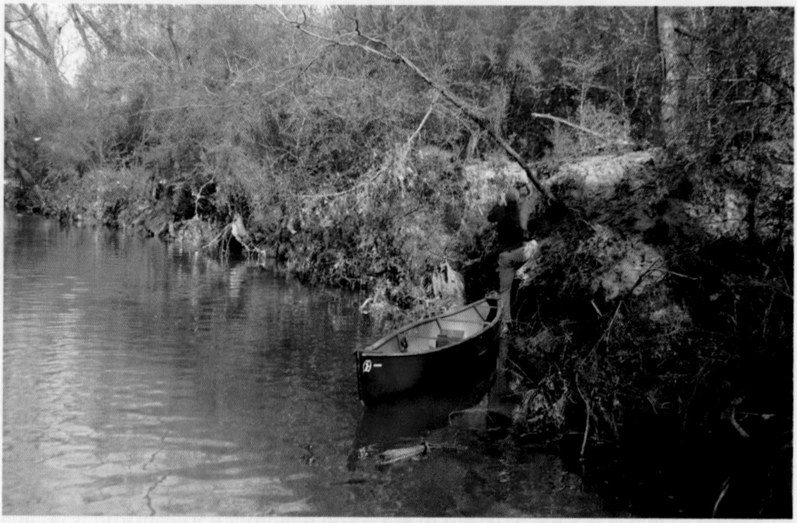

LAUNCHING AT CONSTITUTION LAKES PARK, DEKALB COUNTY

Launch Site For those wishing to explore the South's urban path through Atlanta in boats, Moreland Avenue is probably the uppermost access point, but here the river is narrow and shallow, prone to being blocked by strainers, and, frankly, not terribly inviting because of the tremendous volume of trash that it carries from the urban landscape. Compromised water quality from legacy pollution sources in the river's headwaters, stormwater runoff, and sewage overflows further diminish the attractiveness of this paddle path. There is no developed access here and no parking, but it is possible to access the river from the right-of-way and launch beneath the bridge. Parking is available at the Constitution Lakes Trailhead, located 0.3 mile from the Moreland Avenue bridge over the river. It is also possible to park at Constitution Lakes, carry your boat to the river along Doll's Head Trail leading south toward the river, and launch from the riverbank. Again, there is no developed launch site on the river.

DIRECTIONS From exit 53 (Moreland Ave.) on I-285, go north on Moreland Avenue 0.8 mile to the river. To reach the Constitution Lakes trailhead parking area, continue 0.1 mile beyond the river, turn right on South River Industrial Boulevard, and then immediately right into the entrance road to Constitution Lakes.

Take Out Site The take out site is located on river left downstream of Snapfinger Road and Panola Shoals, a Class III shoal beneath the bridge. A sandbar slopes up to the parking area at the Panola Shoals Trailhead, providing access to the South River Trail.

DIRECTIONS From the launch site, travel south on Moreland Avenue 1.7 miles. Turn left on Cedar Grove Road and proceed 2.0 miles to Bouldercrest Road. Turn right and travel 0.9 mile to the intersection of Panthersville Road and Bouldercrest.

Bear right on Bouldercrest, continuing 0.8 mile to Linecrest Road. Turn left and proceed 2.9 miles to River Road. Turn right and proceed 2.8 miles to Snapfinger Road. Turn left and travel 0.3 mile to Panola Road. Turn right; South River Trail parking will be on right.

Alternative Take Out Sites Take outs at Bouldercrest Road, Panthersville Road, Waldrop Road, and Flakes Mill Road create trips of 2, 4, 6, and 10 miles, respectively, but there are no developed take out sites or parking areas at these locations. If you are accessing the river via private property rather than rights-of-way, permission must be sought. Scout take outs before your journey to ensure that you will have suitable access and parking.

Outfitters No outfitters operate on this section of river.

Description Probably no other river in Metro Atlanta is more maligned than the South. While restoration of the polluted Chattahoochee River from the mid-1900s to the present is well documented, the South has suffered in anonymity. The South became Atlanta's original sewer in the late 1800s as the first flush toilets in the city coursed to it. Today, it still receives a heavy load of treated wastewater and, sadly, untreated sewage when storms cause sewer lines to overflow. The redheaded stepchild of Atlanta's rivers, it is still waiting for the restorative actions that have helped transform the Chattahoochee downstream of Atlanta. Even from its beginnings, it is insulted. A hazardous waste site at the river's very headwaters leaches toxic chemicals into the river and causes it to turn an otherworldly, milky turquoise color as it leaves its East Point birthplace. As it crosses heavily urbanized areas, the river carries a disturbing load of plastic and other trash. Car bumpers, shopping carts, and

DISCOLORED SOUTH RIVER AND TRIBUTARY, FULTON COUNTY

mattresses litter its banks in places. Beauty can still be found, but make no mistake, the South is still waiting for the attention and restoration it has long deserved—a sadly ironic position for a river that in addition to being Atlanta's first sewer was also the city's first developed water source.

Points of Interest

MILE 62.6 (33.666416, −84.424325) **Continental Divide & South River Headwaters.** Here the South has its inauspicious start. The Norfolk Southern Railroad and Central Avenue just to the south parallel the ridge that separates the Flint River watershed from the South's drainage basin. In fact, if you walk due south from this location 900 feet, crossing the railroad, Central Avenue, and Willingham Drive, you will step into the tiny Flint River as it winds its way east and south, bound for pipes that will take it beneath Hartsfield-Jackson Atlanta International Airport. Though nondescript, the rise of land followed by Central Avenue serves as the eastern continental divide. Rain falling on the south side of this ridge, at about 1,000 feet above sea level, is bound for the Flint River and ultimately the Gulf of Mexico; that falling on the north face of the ridge will flow downhill to the South, Ocmulgee, and Altamaha Rivers before finally reaching the Atlantic Ocean east of Darien. Unfortunately for the South, the land that gives rise to the river is heavily industrialized and is home to two hazardous waste sites that contribute polluted groundwater to the river. Though these sites have been listed on the state's inventory of hazardous waste sites since the 1990s, full and complete cleanups of the sites have never been conducted by the owners of the properties. Among the toxins documented at these sites are lead, cadmium, arsenic, mercury, and antimony. Evidence of this pollution persists for miles downstream as the South flows an unusual, milky turquoise color. In 2019, the city of East Point secured U.S. Environmental Protection Agency Brownfields Program grants to assess some of the city's contaminated sites for possible remediation and redevelopment.

MILE 62.2 (33.671543, −84.426728) **Daylighted South.** Having had most of its spring-fed rivulets piped and covered by urban development, the South emerges at this point to begin looking like a stream, though unnatural in color and largely lifeless. It parallels Norman Berry Drive for 0.3 mile before descending to the east beneath the road named in honor of the organizer and onetime president of the East Point Chamber of Commerce who died in 1960.

MILE 61.5 (33.678609, −84.423315) **River Park.** Perhaps nothing illustrates the plight of the South River in this area more vividly than East Point's River Park. Featuring a playground and picnic tables, the park is bisected by the river. Anywhere else, the waterway might be the centerpiece of this kind of small neighborhood park; instead, tall fences prevent access to the river and a sign reads: Danger / Do Not Play in Creek. The turquoise wash continues to color the river here.

LITTER AT CLEVELAND AVENUE, FULTON COUNTY

MILE 61.0 (33.681421, −84.417393) Cleveland Avenue.

MILE 59.7 (33.685895, −84.399300) Downtown Connector. Here the South River flows beneath the south split of Atlanta's Downtown Connector, an 8-mile-long superhighway that carries the combined traffic of I-75 and I-85. Originally built in the 1940s through the 1950s with just four lanes, it has grown into a major artery with as many as 16 lanes. Originally designed to move long-distance motorists rapidly through the city, it has become a critical and often clogged roadway for local trips. As Atlantans moved from the city center to the suburbs during the latter half of the 20th century, dependence on automobiles and the connector increased while use of the city's bus and streetcar system declined. In the early 1970s, Atlanta mayor Sam Massel and other progressives sought relief from the state legislature in the form of a 1¢ sales tax that, if approved by voters, would fund construction of a rapid rail system known as MARTA. This was no easy task, for in 1971 the rural-dominated General Assembly was no friend of the big city. Nevertheless, Massel prevailed. When the legislature greenlit the MARTA sales tax, Massel responded by sending a cadre of young women dressed in pink hot pants to the Capitol to present legislators with keys to the city and invitations to a lunch at city hall. Later that year, Massel famously flew over Atlanta's traffic-snarled connector in a helicopter and, armed with a bullhorn to project his voice to motorists stuck in traffic, urged them to approve the 1¢ sales tax at the polls in November. They did. Unfortunately for Atlanta commuters, voters in outlying counties such as Cobb and Gwinnett never approved the funding. Many historians place the blame on race relations and the mass exodus of Atlanta's white residents to the burgeoning suburbs. Though suburban commuters would benefit from rail transit, many feared it would invite Atlanta's black residents to the suburbs. Princeton University history professor Kevin M. Kruse, author of *White Flight: Atlanta and the Making of Modern Conservatism*, told *Atlanta Magazine* in 2012: "The more you think about it, Atlanta's transportation infrastructure was designed as much to keep people apart as to bring people together." In 2019, the connector remained clogged, and rail transit still did not extend to outlying counties. The connector carries up to 437,000 vehicles daily.

MILE 58.7 (33.693635, −84.388972) **Lakewood.** About three-quarters of a mile upstream on a tributary once known as Poole's Branch (now Perkerson Creek) sits Lakewood Park, site of Atlanta's original waterworks. It is a property that closely follows the arc of Atlanta's evolving culture and economy since the Civil War. In 1874, the city built a 350-foot-long, 35-foot-high dam to turn the branch into a lake, but within two decades the city had outgrown the source; so in 1893, Atlanta tapped the Chattahoochee River. The former water-supply lake and surrounding land then became Lakewood Park, a popular amusement area for turn-of-the-century Atlantans. It featured picnic areas, harness races, dance pavilions, and, beginning in 1896, an amusement ride called "Shooting the Chutes." The ride consisted of a large wooden ramp with metal rails that sent small boats and their riders plummeting down the ramp and skipping across the surface of the lake. Originally part of the Cotton State Exposition at Piedmont Park, the ride was moved to Lakewood following the close of the exposition in 1895. The following year, Lakewood Park advertised in the *Atlanta Constitution*: "Now open every day and night. Music afternoons and evenings. Two elegant pavilions overlooking the lake . . . Only white people admitted." By 1901, the park was hosting 50,000 visitors annually in a city of 89,872 people. Later, in 1915, the area became the site of the Southeastern Fair, held annually through 1975. By the late 1930s, the harness-racing track had made the transformation from horses to stock cars, and Lakewood Speedway became the haunt of the fastest drivers among North Georgia's bootleggers. By the late 1970s, however, the fairgrounds and its rides, including the legendary wooden roller coaster the Greyhound, had fallen into disrepair. In 1979, the Greyhound was demolished during the filming of a scene for the movie *Smokey and the Bandit II*. Fittingly, in the 21st century the fairgrounds and the original Southeastern Fair exhibition halls have been transformed into a 300,000-square-foot movie production facility, a product of Georgia's favorable tax credits for movie and TV production, which were first enacted in 2002. Only New York and California host more film and TV productions than does Georgia. Nearby Lakewood Amphitheater, upholding a tradition of musical performances in the park dating to the late 1800s, began hosting concerts in its 19,000-seat venue in 1989.

MILE 58.2 (33.690551, −84.382007) **Swann Preserve.** The PATH Foundation's Southtowne Trail spans the river on a bridge in the midst of this 57-acre nature preserve owned by the city of Atlanta. The trail runs 1.3 miles from Lakewood Avenue at South Bend Park to Bromack Drive. Continuing east on Bromack Drive, it connects with portions of the Southtowne Trail surrounding Brown's

Mill Golf Course via another footbridge over the river. The preserve is named in honor of the property's original owners. The Trust for Public Land brokered the sale in 2002.

MILE 57.8 (33.688118, −84.376990) **Brown's Mill Golf Course.** Here the river passes beneath the PATH Foundation's Southtowne Trail a second time as it courses through Brown's Mill Golf Course, a city of Atlanta–operated public golf course. The 18-hole course was completed in 1970. It was designed by George Cobb, who famously designed the par-three course at Augusta National, home of the Masters Golf Tournament. Cobb had a hand in the construction of more than 100 courses over his career, starting with one he built during his stint in the U.S. Marine Corps. Knowing that he was an avid golfer, his superiors assigned him the task of building a course for Camp Lejeune in North Carolina. From those beginnings, Cobb built a career developing golf courses. Members of the Brown family were among the original settlers of this area, in the early 1800s, and many of them are buried on a ridge overlooking the river downstream. Early settlers harnessed the fall of the river in milling enterprises, and as late as 1896, 15 mills still operated on the South River, grinding corn and flour, ginning cotton, powering saws, and producing leather goods.

MILE 56.8 (33.680793, −84.362287) **South River Water Reclamation Facility.** On river left is a city of Atlanta sewage treatment facility originally constructed in 1936 with funds provided by the federal Works Progress Administration as part of a $6 million overhaul of Atlanta's inadequate sewer system. The city's sewage disposal problem was so bad, according to a story published in a 1938 issue of the *Engineering News-Record*, that a onetime Atlanta mayor described his city as "an island practically surrounded by sewage." The South River plant, designed to treat up to 6 million gallons a day, was one of three such facilities; more than 50 miles of sewer lines helped alleviate the city's sewage problem in the 1930s. But as the city grew, its sewer troubles resurfaced. By the 1990s, millions of gallons of untreated sewage were spilling into the South River from the city's aging sewer system. The city's practice of funneling stormwater to its sanitary sewer lines aggravated the problem. Not until the late 1990s did Atlanta fully address its sewer problem, and then only because of a lawsuit brought by Chattahoochee Riverkeeper. That legal action led to a consent decree and some $4 billion worth of sewer improvements, including a 1.7-mile-long, 14-foot-wide tunnel bored 170 feet underground to collect and store stormwater and sewage for treatment at this plant. The tunnel runs from Macon Avenue to this point. That project—with a price tag of $109 million—was a little more costly than the original WPA-built plant. The facility, however, does not discharge its effluent into the diminutive South. Instead, the treated wastewater is pumped nearly 15 miles to the larger Chattahoochee River, which is more capable of assimilating the treated water.

MILE 56.1 (33.680298, −84.351628) **Soapstone Ridge.** Rising above the river's floodplain to the south is Soapstone Ridge, a place that tells the story of trash left by humans from the Late Archaic period to the present. Archaeologists who excavated the site in 1986 determined that Native Americans quarried the ridge for soapstone, which they used in making vessels, pipes, ornaments, and other items between 1500 and 600 BC. The finished pieces were traded throughout the eastern half of North America. Most of the artifacts found at the site were the discarded remains of carved bowls—trash pieces left at the numerous manufacturing sites identified on the ridge. That study was sponsored by Waste Management of North America, which began operating its Live Oak Landfill at the site in the 1980s. Through 2004, the landfill accepted millions of tons of Atlanta's trash annually, entombing within its cells hundreds of thousands of late 20th-century plastic vessels that archaeologists will likely marvel over some 3,000 years from today. About three years after its closure, the landfill took on new life as an energy recovery system. The decomposing organic matter in the landfill releases massive amounts of methane. In fact, in 2014 landfills contributed 20 percent of the total methane emissions in the United States. Now, methane from the site is collected, processed, and sent to the natural gas pipeline grid. The site produces some 1,500 megawatt-hours of gas daily.

MILE 55.3 (33.678875, −84.337020) **Constitution Lakes.** On river left is this DeKalb County park with hiking trails featuring unique folk art installations created by park visitors from the trash and debris that collected on the urban site during the past century. The park's namesake lakes are the result of excavations performed by the South River Brick Company from the early 1890s until about 1910 as the company dug for the clay needed to produce its bricks. The company played a role in one of the more infamous periods of Georgia's history.

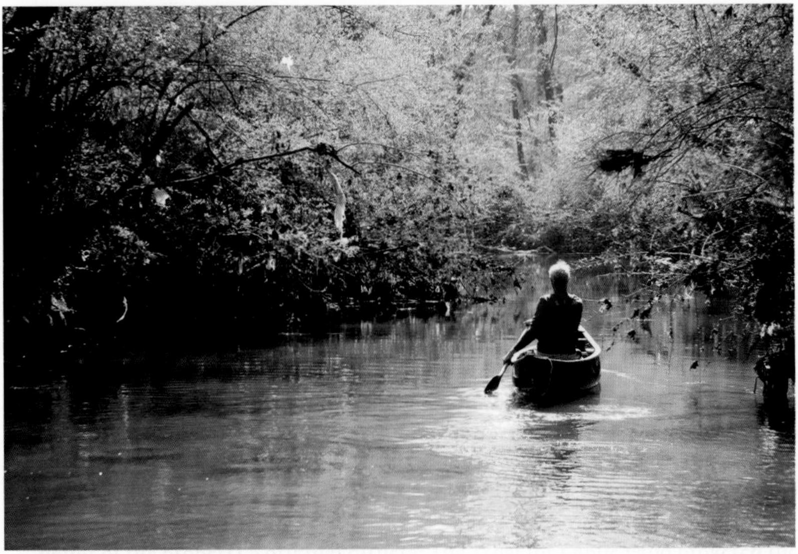

NEAR CONSTITUTION LAKES PARK, DEKALB COUNTY

Following the Civil War, the financially strapped state found it beneficial to lease its prisoners to private companies rather than spend tax money to house and feed them. The system deprived free laborers of jobs and imposed on the convicts an inhumane form of incarceration. Most convicts were, in fact, former slaves, and they soon discovered that the convict-leasing system was more brutal than antebellum slavery: as slaves, they had been property worth preserving, but as convicts, if injured or killed, they could be easily replaced. It was by this method of labor that the fictional Scarlett O'Hara in Margaret Mitchell's novel *Gone with the Wind* restored her family's fortune in the lumber business following the Civil War. Although the South River Brick Company employed free labor, its primary competition, the Chattahoochee Brick Company, took advantage of convict leasing. In 1897, the issue came to a head in Atlanta when the city council proposed an ordinance requiring that all city contractors use materials made by free labor. In council chambers, the two brick companies squared off. Said J. M. Stephens of South River: "There's no doubt that an effort is being made by the convict labor brick men to freeze the free labor brick men out of the market by cutting prices." James W. English, a former Atlanta mayor and the owner of the Chattahoochee Brick Company, countered: "Say the convict labor has reduced the price of brick on an average of $4 a thousand, then on the 100,000,000 bricks furnished to Atlanta, we have made a saving to the people of $400,000. Who got the benefit of this? Surely not the Chattahoochee company." A week later, a city committee killed the proposed ordinance. The South River Brick Company was eventually pushed out of business.

English and his company kept churning out bricks until the late 20th century. In fact, the company produced some of the bricks used in the construction of Atlanta's Olympic Stadium for the 1996 summer games. One of the ingredients for those bricks was incinerated biosolids from the city of Atlanta's R. M. Clayton wastewater treatment plant, leading to one of the great ironies of those games: as Carl Lewis leaped to gold in the long jump, spectators from around the world sat on Atlanta's processed excrement. Though English is remembered as one of the fathers of Atlanta's rise from the ashes after the Civil War, his wealth was gained from a brutal system. In 1897, English's companies controlled 1,206 of Georgia's 2,881 convicts. The Georgia General Assembly voted to end the prisoner-lease system in 1908 after hearing testimony from guards at the brick furnaces that told of regular whippings and even murders of convict laborers.

The 125-acre Constitution Lakes Park was purchased by Atlanta as part of the consent decree the city reached in a federal Clean Water Act lawsuit brought by Chattahoochee Riverkeeper in the late 1990s. The decree required the city to preserve property to improve the health of the city's urban streams.

MILE 54.5 (33.681876, −84.326867) Atlanta Honor Farm. On both sides of the river here from 1920 until 1965, the federal government operated an experimental prison that came to be known as the Honor Farm. The original farm property spread over more than 1,000 acres of bottomland bisected by the South. The idea was to employ those convicted of minor crimes as farm laborers to produce food for the nearby full-security federal penitentiary while providing rehabilitation and job training for the prisoners. By the 1940s, the farm was producing half the food eaten by the penitentiary's 2,000 inmates. In 1946, the farm grew 33 varieties of vegetables and produced 2.5 million pounds of food, along with more than 200,000 pounds of pork and 115,000 gallons of milk, some of which was used to produce cheese. Peaches, apples, grapes, and berries rounded out the farm's products. During this time, about 90 prisoners worked the unfenced, unguarded farm. Perhaps the farm's most famous prisoner was Earl Carroll, a producer and director of some 60 Broadway shows and musicals from the 1920s to the 1940s. Known as the "troubadour of the nude" for the revealing costumes his showgirls wore, he found himself imprisoned on account of nudity (and perjury). During a Prohibition-era party, he entertained guests by producing a tub containing a nude woman bathing in illicit liquor. Federal authorities learned of the incident when it was reported in a New York City newspaper, the editor of which had attended the soiree. Under questioning, Carroll was caught in a lie, charged with perjury, and sent to the farm for six months. Newspapers reported breathlessly on his prison experience: "The man who once was one of Broadway's gayest figures has attained a goal jealously sought by inmates—a goal which besides furnishing the freedom of a good sized model farming community, provides opportunity for shortening one's sentence. His health was reported to have shown marked improvement since he entered the prison on a stretcher June 8 . . . after suffering a nervous breakdown."

Intrenchment Creek flows into the river here, and about a mile upstream of its mouth sits the Intrenchment Creek sewage treatment plant. Completed in the 1910s, the facility was among Atlanta's first modern treatment facilities. After 100 years on the job, the plant is expected to be decommissioned in the 2020s, with its flow piped to the city's South River Water Reclamation Facility.

MILE 54.0 (33.681160, −84.318603) Shoals.

MILE 53.8 (33.680342, −84.314872) I-285. This 64-mile perimeter highway carries at this location about 150,000 vehicles daily. First included on state highway planning maps in the 1950s, I-285 was constructed between 1958 and 1969. Beneath the bridge is a series of small shoals.

MILE 52.2 (33.683449, −84.289733) Sugar Creek. On river left, this creek, which drains much of East Atlanta, joins the South. From its confluence, the PATH Foundation's South River Trail extends almost a mile to Doolittle Creek and the Georgia State University–Perimeter College campus. This portion of the South River Trail runs east from the campus for 5.2 miles along the river and Sugar Creek and provides views of the river along the route.

MILE 51.1 (33.684540, −84.272602) Panthersville Road. Just downstream of this bridge is a pipeline that creates a navigational hazard. At lower water levels, it is possible to limbo beneath it; at higher levels, a portage may be required. A second pipe about 100 yards farther downstream requires the same attention.

PORTAGING PIPELINE, DEKALB COUNTY

MILE 50.8 (33.683269, −84.266515) Pipeline. This elevated water and sewer infrastructure pipe creates a navigational obstacle that requires either a limbo or a portage.

MILE 50.6 (33.685433, −84.264781) Shoal.

MILE 50.1 (33.686905, −84.257104) Pipeline. Like those just upstream, this pipe will need to be bypassed via portage or limbo.

MILE 49.8 (33.683549, −84.254507) Warriors Path Bridge.

MILE 49.3 (33.680717, −84.249368) Waldrop Road. At this bridge on March 6, 1981, a DeKalb County fireman spotted the body of 13-year-old Curtis Walker snagged on a log in the river below the bridge. Walker was one of at least 29 black children, youth, and adults who were murdered between 1979 and 1981, a series of crimes that came to be known as Atlanta's Missing and Murdered Children cases. The murders attracted national attention, and Congress allocated more than $3 million to provide investigators to find the killer and to fund youth activity programs to help protect the city's children. Meanwhile, Sammy Davis Jr. and Frank Sinatra hosted a benefit concert at the Atlanta Civic Center that raised more than $148,000 to aid in the investigation. Three months after the concert, a 23-year-old Georgia State University dropout named Wayne Williams was arrested for the murder of two adult victims. In February 1982 he was convicted of those crimes and sentenced to life in prison. Most of the remaining murders were attributed to Williams, though he never stood trial for them. To this day, he maintains his innocence, and because much of the evidence used to convict him was circumstantial, many believe that he was not the man responsible. During the affair, the killer used Atlanta's rivers as a favored disposal spot for the bodies, and it was a stakeout along a bridge over the Chattahoochee River that ultimately led to Williams's arrest. There is a small shoal directly beneath the bridge.

MILE 46.8 (33.663684, −84.235870) Pipeline. During normal to low flows, this elevated water and sewer infrastructure pipe is easy to paddle beneath. At higher flows, portages may be necessary. Approach with caution.

MILE 46.2 (33.664483, −84.225740) Pipeline. Less elevated than the one just upstream. During normal to low flows, this elevated water and sewer pipe is easy to paddle beneath. At higher flows, portages may be necessary.

MILE 46.1 (33.665582, −84.224232) Flake's Mill. From this bridge downstream for the next 1,000 feet, the river descends over small shoals that mark the site of this mill. Remains of previous iterations of the Flakes Mill Road Bridge can also be seen in this stretch of river. A 1903 survey of the river noted this mill as having a six-foot-high dam in operation with a total fall of 12 feet. From the Civil War through 1921, T. J. Flake was an influential leader in DeKalb County. He served on the county commission while also farming some 1,000 acres and operating this gristmill. In an 1895 report to Congress, Flake reported that he produced 266 pounds of cotton per acre along the river in 1891–1892, at a cost of about 8¢ a pound. Cotton prices were likewise about 8¢ a pound, so the crop was not profitable. But he and his sons eventually found a cash cow in the South River, harnessing it to produce electricity for Lithonia and Conyers around the turn of the century as the Panola Light and Power Company. In 1912, the company turned a profit of $2,904, the equivalent of $76,000 today. T. J. Flake, however, was far from the first person to harness the river. Russell W. Garr milled corn and wheat here in 1840, and Eli J. Hulsey owned and operated the mill until 1884, when Flake took ownership.

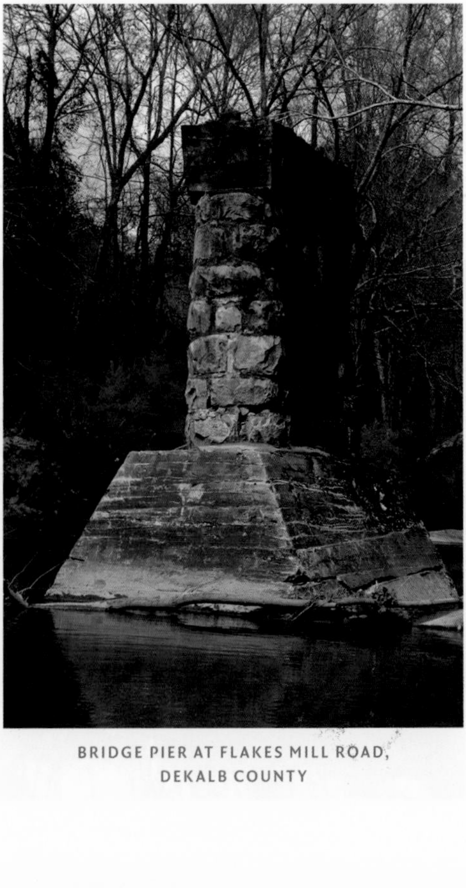

BRIDGE PIER AT FLAKES MILL ROAD, DEKALB COUNTY

Four years after Flake's death in 1921, milling here stopped altogether when the shoals were blasted by the Honor Farm in an effort prevent flooding and better drain bottomlands for cultivation at the federal prison.

MILE 45.4 (33.662813, −84.217257) Snapfinger Creek Wastewater Treatment Facility. On river left is the discharge point for this DeKalb County sewage treatment plant, which processes up to 36 million gallons of wastewater a day (MGD). It is part of the county's aging and beleaguered sewer system. In 2010, DeKalb County entered into a consent decree with the U.S. Environmental Protection Agency and Georgia's Environmental Protection Division that forces the county to address chronic sewer overflows and spills into the South River. Among the projects undertaken is a $215 million expansion of this facility that will enable it to treat up to 54 MGD. From 2012 to 2017, the county identified nearly 900 spills in which untreated sewage entered the county's streams or rivers. Expanding Snapfinger's capacity is but one solution. The largest number of spills is caused when fats, oils, and grease build up in sewer lines and create backups. As part of the consent decree, DeKalb has bolstered its program of cleaning of sewer lines and embarked on an public education campaign urging homeowners and businesses not to flush cooking oils, animal fats, dairy products, and a host of other common food items down the sink. In the half mile below the discharge, the river flows over several small shoals.

MILE 44.1 (33.658857, −84.204836) Shoals. This shoal marks the beginning of a series of seven small but picturesque Class I shoals that the river spills over during the next half mile.

MILE 41.9 (33.653500, −84.187585) Panola Shoals. As much a waterfall as a shoal, this rapid can be portaged on river right beneath the Snapfinger Road bridge. At appropriate water levels, the rapid is runnable by those with adequate whitewater experience. The route on river right involves a long, sloping 100-foot-long slide over a smooth rock ending in a large wave at the bottom of the descent. The route on river left involves a more abrupt and precipitous drop followed by another set of smaller shoals. Because this is the site of a former dam that powered a large cotton mill, rebar embedded in rock may be encountered. Any descent should be scouted and undertaken with caution. Beyond the shoals, the river settles out next to a massive sandbar adjacent to the South River Trail and parking area.

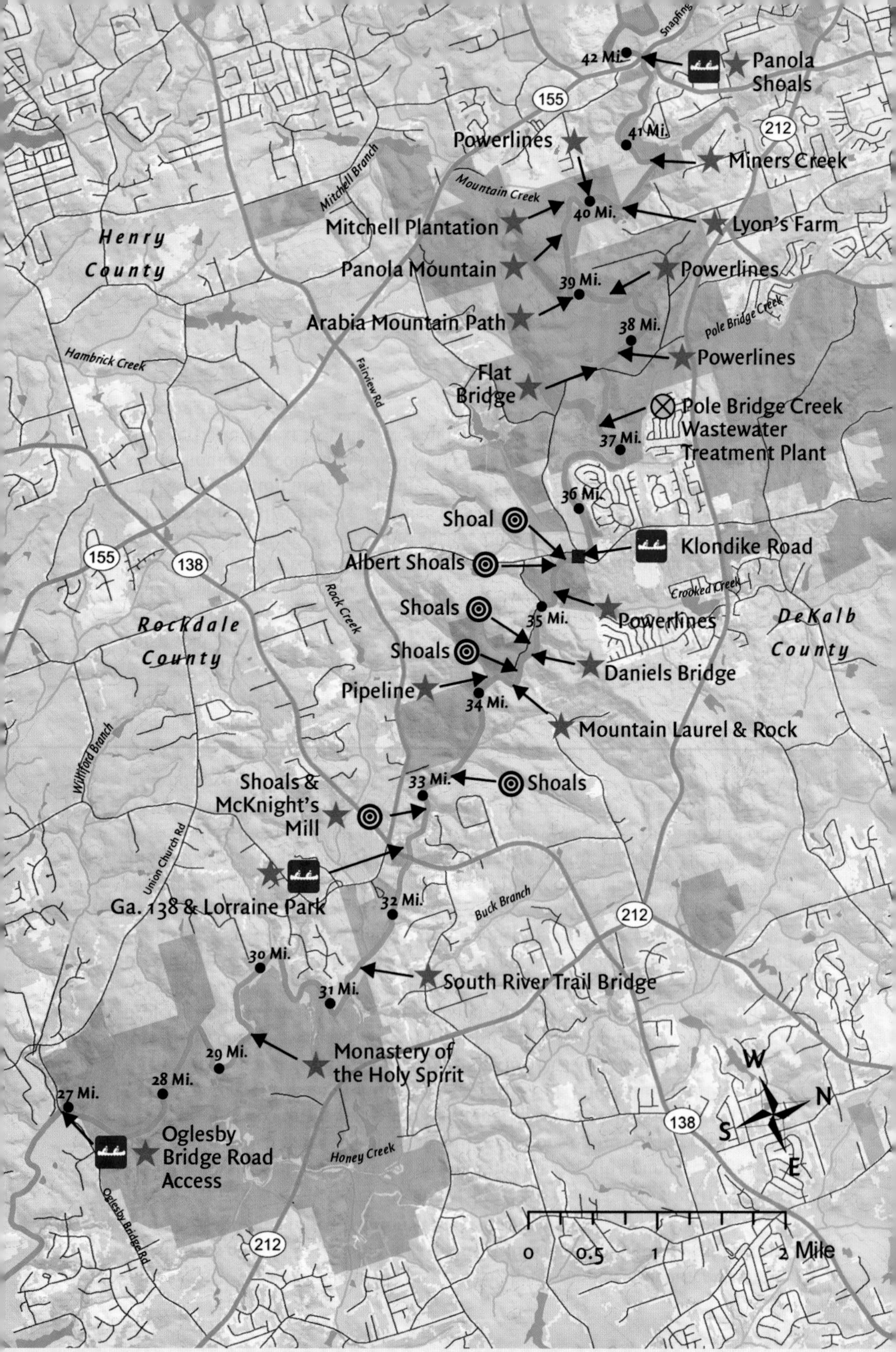

Panola Shoals
42 Mi.
Snapfinger
155
212
Powerlines
41 Mi.
Miners Creek
Mitchell Branch
Mountain Creek
40 Mi.
Mitchell Plantation
Lyon's Farm
Henry County
Panola Mountain
Powerlines
39 Mi.
Arabia Mountain Path
38 Mi.
Pole Bridge Creek
Hambrick Creek
Fairview Rd
Powerlines
Flat Bridge
Pole Bridge Creek Wastewater Treatment Plant
37 Mi.
36 Mi.
Shoal
Klondike Road
155
138
Albert Shoals
Rock Creek
Crooked Creek
Shoals
35 Mi.
Powerlines
Rockdale County
DeKalb County
Shoals
Daniels Bridge
Pipeline
34 Mi.
Mountain Laurel & Rock
Williford Branch
Shoals & McKnight's Mill
33 Mi.
Shoals
Union Church Rd
Ga. 138 & Lorraine Park
32 Mi.
Buck Branch
212
30 Mi.
South River Trail Bridge
31 Mi.
29 Mi.
Monastery of the Holy Spirit
28 Mi.
27 Mi.
W
N
S
E
138
Oglesby Bridge Road Access
Honey Creek
Oglesby Bridge Rd
212
0
0.5
1
2 Mile

Panola

Length 15 miles (Snapfinger Road to Oglesby Bridge Road)

Class I–III

Time 6–9 hours

Minimum Level Levels above 150 cubic feet per second (cfs) at the Klondike Road gauge should be sufficient to run Albert Shoals and other shoals along this section of the South. As flows exceed 1,000 cfs, the difficulty and dangers associated with Albert Shoals increase; caution should be exercised.

River Gauge The nearest river gauge is located at Klondike Road in the middle of this section: https://waterdata.usgs.gov/ga/nwis/uv/?site_no=02204070&PARAmeter_cd=00065,00060,00062,00010.

Launch Site The launch site is from a wide sandbar on the north side of the river adjacent to the Panola Shoals parking area for the South River Trail.

DIRECTIONS From exit 68 (Wesley Chapel Rd.) on I-20, go south on Wesley Chapel Road 0.3 mile. Turn left on Snapfinger Road and proceed 4.5 miles. Turn left on Panola Road and travel 0.1 mile to the entrance of the parking area on the right.

Take Out Site As of May 2020, there was no developed take out site at this location, but in April 2020, Rockdale County secured a state grant to develop a public boat launch on river left just upstream of the bridge. Until the access is developed, the river is accessible via a trail leading from a sandbar to the road on the upstream and east side of the bridge.

DIRECTIONS From the launch site, return to Snapfinger Road. Turn left and proceed 5.4 miles. Turn left on Ga. 138 and travel 0.8 mile. Turn right on Union Church Road and proceed 4 miles. Turn left on Oglesby Bridge Road and proceed 0.6 mile to river. The access is on the east and upstream side of the bridge.

Alternative Take Out Sites Klondike Road, the Rockdale River Trail (DeCastro Trailhead), and Lorraine Park, a Rockdale County Park located at Ga. 138, can be used to create trips of 6, 7, and 9 miles, respectively. The Klondike Road take out avoids the Class II–III Albert Shoals, and the Rockdale River Trail take out allows whitewater enthusiasts to paddle the short 1-mile run of Albert Shoals between Klondike Road and the Rockdale River Trail. At Lorraine Park, there is no developed river access, but parking and picnic areas are available.

DIRECTIONS TO THE KLONDIKE ROAD TAKE OUT SITE From the launch site, turn right on Panola Road and travel 1.4 miles to Ga. 212. Turn right and proceed 3.7 miles. Turn right on Klondike Road and proceed 1.1 miles to the undeveloped parking area and launch site on the left before crossing the bridge. To access the DeCastro Trailhead downstream of Albert Shoals, continue across the bridge for 0.1 mile.

Turn left on Union Church Road and proceed 0.4 mile to Daniels Bridge Road. Turn left and proceed 0.1 mile to the trailhead parking on the left. From the trailhead parking, it is a 0.4 mile walk to a steep and undeveloped take out on river right, located just beyond the powerline cut along Daniels Bridge Road. While it is possible to park vehicles temporarily at this site for loading boats, it is best to use the trailhead parking area for long-term parking.

Outfitters No outfitters operate on this section of the river.

Description As tributaries add their flow to the South, pollution from the Metro Atlanta area becomes less concentrated. The river descends through the Arabia Mountain National Heritage Area, 64 square miles of public and private lands featuring many significant natural and cultural sites connected by the river and a series of recreational paths. From Panola Shoals nearly to Oglesby Bridge Road, the river is paralleled by PATH Foundation recreational trails that cross the river on footbridges twice. Much of the property along the riverbanks is publicly owned, including the 1,600-acre Panola Mountain State Park, which features the area's most pristine granite monolith. In tandem with the recreational amenities and cultural and natural resources encompassed by the heritage area, the South River Water Trail is part of an outdoor recreation mecca that attracts thousands of visitors each year. The river is home to a rich history as it alternates between long stretches of flatwater and numerous, sometimes challenging shoals. With continued improvements to wastewater management and attention to eliminating polluted stormwater runoff, the health of the South in this section should improve, increasing its draw as a paddling destination.

Points of Interest

MILE 41.9 (33.653500, −84.187585) Panola Shoals. These shoals, along with the bottomland surrounding the river here, have been harnessed and cultivated since the 1800s. In the 1840s, Charles Latimer took ownership of several hundred acres here, including "Flat Shoals," and developed Panola Plantation. A leader in the early history of DeKalb County, he is noted for having operated Decatur's first store; in 1860, a DeKalb grand jury urged the community leader to build a bridge over the river at Flat Shoals or else "remove the obstructions" that were hampering the ford there.

Charles is best known as the father of Rebecca Latimer Felton, who went on to fame as the first woman to serve in the U.S. Senate. Rebecca married William Felton, a widower 12 years her senior. They met when she was the valedictorian at Madison Female College and he was the commencement speaker. Ultimately, the pair formed a dynamic political force in post–Civil War Georgia. Felton was elected to Congress in 1874, with his wife as campaign manager, a position that did not go unnoticed by conservative newspaper editors. The *Thomasville Times* noted: "We sincerely trust that the example set by Mrs. Felton will not be followed by Southern ladies. Let the dirty work of politics be confined to

PANOLA SHOALS, DEKALB COUNTY

men . . . There is a higher, nobler, purer sphere for women; let her fill it." From her days aiding her husband in Washington until her death in 1930, she was a significant, and in light of today's sensibilities, a complicated, political force. A progressive, she played key roles in Georgia's women's suffrage movement and the effort to end Georgia's convict-leasing system. Her presumed liberal political stances prompted opponents to accuse her of attempting to "re-Africanize the South" after Reconstruction ended. And though she considered slavery an "evil," she was unapologetic about her belief in white supremacy. In one speech, she endorsed the lynching of black men. In calling for women's voting rights after the Georgia General Assembly failed to ratify the Nineteenth Amendment, she complained, "The manifest preference of certain Georgia legislators for giving the franchise to Negro men over intelligent white women will become an incentive in years to come to vote against such misfits." Yet her work to end convict leasing was a direct benefit to thousands of black men and women incarcerated in brutal conditions. Her ascension to the U.S. Senate was the result of purely political motivations on the part of Governor Thomas Hardwick. In 1922, when the sitting senator Thomas E. Watson died in office, Hardwick was responsible for appointing a replacement until a special election could be held. Coveting the Senate seat for himself, he wanted his appointment to be someone who would not challenge him in the special election, so he chose the 87-year-old Felton. He also felt that the appointment might win him votes from recently enfranchised women. Felton served just two days in the Senate, but in her only address to the body, she predicted: "When the women of the country come in and sit with you, though there may be but very few of them in the next few years, I pledge you that you will get ability, you will get integrity of purpose, you will get exalted patriotism and you will get unstinted usefulness." In addition to being the first woman to serve in the Senate, she was also the last former slave owner to serve in the body. It was ten more years before a woman was elected to the Senate.

In the late 1800s, Robert M. Clarke took ownership of much of the Panola Plantation property, and beginning in 1866, he harnessed the shoals to power two cotton mills: Oglethorpe Manufacturing and Panola Manufacturing. In 1874, the river turned nearly 6,000 spindles at the mills, providing employment for 150 people and producing some 40,000 pounds of yarn monthly. By 1875, a spur rail line ran from Panola to Atlanta daily. *Atlanta Constitution* reports from the era document the challenges of operating the mills and maintaining the 25-foot-high milldam. In 1876, a flood wiped out the milldam, and production stopped for three days. In 1879, fire destroyed the Panola Manufacturing mills along with the adjacent grist and sawmill, costing Clarke more than $75,000 in losses. In the 1880s, Clarke and other mill owners on the South River filed lawsuits against the city of Atlanta because, they claimed, the city's waterworks dam and reservoir on the river's headwaters were causing low flows and diminishing their ability to operate. Finally, in 1893 another fire destroyed the Panola cotton mills. In 1905, the Panola Light and Power Company transformed the old milldam into a hydropower plant and began providing electricity to Lithonia and later to Conyers. In the latter half of the 20th century, as pollution from Atlanta and DeKalb County's sewer system increased, the shoals came to be known as "Soap Shoals" because of the massive flotillas of foam generated as the polluted and nutrient-rich water splashed over the falls.

Adjacent to the large sandbar on river left is a parking area for the South River Trail, a recreational path that stretches both upstream and downstream, ultimately connecting to other trails leading to Panola Mountain State Park and Arabia Mountain National Heritage Area. Much of the property on the north side of the river from here to DeKalb County's Pole Bridge Wastewater Treatment Plant is owned by the state or DeKalb County—a distance of almost 5 miles.

MILE 40.7 (33.651159, −84.174168) Miners Creek. On river left is an 83-acre parcel of land owned by DeKalb County through which passes the South River Trail. Archaeological digs here have turned up potsherds with designs that date occupation of the site by Native Americans to the Woodland period, roughly from 1000 BC to AD 900.

MILE 40.2 (33.645592, −84.170113) Lyon's Farm. On river left here about 700 feet from the river sits a farmhouse and outbuildings dating to the 1820s. The property, now owned by DeKalb County and bisected by the South River Trail and the Arabia Mountain Path, was owned by the Lyon family from the 1820s until 2006. In 2018, DeKalb County began stabilizing and restoring the historic structures on the site. Joseph Emanuel Lyon received the property in 1790 as reward for his service during the Revolutionary War. Originally a British soldier, he was captured by Patriots in Pennsylvania, took an oath of allegiance, and joined the Continental Army. During his service, he was gravely wounded at the Battle of Cowpens, an injury that resulted in the loss of one arm. He moved his family to the South River in the early 1820s, and family members recall stories of encounters with Native Americans during those initial years. By 1860, the farm was a thriving plantation operated by Joseph's son, George, who owned some 17 slaves at the outbreak of the Civil War. The family continued to farm the property into the 1970s. The house is considered one of the oldest in DeKalb County and the longest continually occupied by the same family. Near Lyon's Farm is Flat Rock Cemetery, where numerous slaves are interred. It is considered one of the only intact slave cemeteries in the state. On river right at this location, the Panola Mountain State Park property begins; it extends on the south side of the river some 4 miles downstream.

NEAR LYON'S FARM, DEKALB COUNTY

MILE 40 (33.643221, −84.172382) Powerlines.

MILE 39.8 (33.641127, −84.172515) Mitchell Plantation. On river right is Mountain Creek, which flows through the Panola Mountain Golf Course. Long before the property was a golf course, it was the plantation of William Mitchell, who settled on the land in the 1830s. This was the Mitchell clan that produced Margaret Mitchell, the Pulitzer Prize–winning author of *Gone with the Wind*.

MILE 39.5 (33.639040, −84.168780) Panola Mountain. On river right beyond the riverside rock outcroppings, this 946-foot-high monadnock (isolated mountain) rises more than 250 feet above the river and the surrounding terrain. Similar to its cousins Stone Mountain and Arabia Mountain to the north, it is a granite monolith, but Panola's granite, unlike the stone from those other sites, was never suitable for large-scale commercial use. Consequently, the 100-acre mountain has been preserved in a relatively pristine state, leading to its designation as a national natural landmark. It is home to rare plants like elf orpine (*Diamorpha smallii*); pool sprite (*Amphianthus pusillus*), listed as threatened by the federal government; and black-spored quillwort (*Isoetes melanospora*), listed as endangered. All three depend on the shallow, flat-bottomed pools of water found in depressions on Panola Mountain and other granite outcrops. Elf orpine, with its bright red foliage and tiny white flowers, which strongly contrast with the gray granite that surrounds it, puts on its eye-popping show each April. Pool sprite, an annual, sports small five-lobed flowers on the surface of these pools in mid-March. Reproducing through spores, the flowerless black-spored quillwort is conspicuous for its slender, spongy, spiky leaves, 1–3 inches long, which grow in the pools only when enough water is available, usually in the spring. The mountain is part of Panola Mountain State Park and is accessible only by guided hikes led by park rangers. The park encompasses 1,635 acres and includes 25 miles of hiking trails, a bouldering area, an archery range, Alexander Lake (for fishing and boating), picnic shelters, campsites, and an interpretive center. 2620 Highway 155 SW, Stockbridge, Ga. 30281, 770-389-7801, www.gastateparks.org/PanolaMountain

MILE 39.0 (33.638714, –84.160790) Arabia Mountain Path. This bridge is part of the Arabia Mountain Path, a network of paved recreational trails extending 33 miles southeast to northeast from the Monastery of the Holy Spirit to Stonecrest Mall. The trails take travelers to numerous sites of cultural and natural significance within the Arabia Mountain National Heritage Area, including historic homesteads, abandoned quarry sites, and, of course, the granite monoliths at Panola and Arabia Mountains. More information about the Arabia Mountain trails system can be found at www.arabiaalliance.org

MILE 38.8 (33.641609, –84.159010) Powerlines.

MILE 37.9 (33.640820, –84.152051) Powerlines.

MILE 37.6 (33.638738, –84.150814) Flat Bridge. The remains of Flat Bridge partially span the river here. From the 1800s, this was an important river crossing, and the bridge remained in use through the late 1970s. Johnny Waits, founder and president of the nearby Flat Rock Archives, recalls crossing the one-lane bridge as a young man and can recount the river's transformation during his lifetime: "We didn't play in it or fish in it much because it was always filthy. We used to see foam 20 feet high (at Panola Shoals). Thank God we don't see that anymore. It looks much cleaner than it used to. I'll be glad when people can get back in it."

MILE 37.3 (33.636505, –84.143800) Pole Bridge Creek Wastewater Treatment Plant. On river left here is the discharge from this sewage treatment plant, which has a capacity of 40 million gallons per day. DeKalb County owns more than 450 acres here, including about 2 miles of riverfront stretching from here upstream.

MILE 35.5 (33.630150, –84.128520) Klondike Road.

MILE 35.4 (33.628588, –84.128586) Shoal.

MILE 35.3 (33.627224, –84.128235) Albert Shoals. These Class II–III shoals extend more than 1,000 feet over a series of ledges, including a significant 5-foot drop on river right. The best course through the obstacle is to begin on far river right and then work through a series of ledges to far river left, where a shallow,

FLAT BRIDGE, DEKALB COUNTY

rocky run finishes the descent. This route avoids the high ledge on river right at the base of the shoals. The shoals were the site of a gristmill operated by J. S. McLendon in the late 1800s and early 1900s. A 1902 U.S. Geological Survey report describes the shoals as having a fall of 16.8 feet over a distance of 2,100 feet. The shoals can be accessed via the Rockdale River Trail, a 9.5-mile paved recreational trail that parallels the river from Panola Mountain State Park to the Monastery of the Holy Spirit. Where the trail travels beneath a powerline cut, the river is visible to the north, with Albert Shoals located just upstream of the powerlines.

MILE 35.2 (33.625946, −84.125073) Powerlines.

MILE 34.7 (33.622273, −84.118984) Shoals.

MILE 34.6 (33.621398, −84.118471) Daniels Bridge. The impressive stone piers here mark the location of Daniels Bridge, a span dating to the 1800s and noted on river surveys from the early 1900s.

MILE 34.5 (33.619543, −84.116826) Shoals.

MILE 34.3 (33.618608, −84.115277) Mountain Laurel & Rock. On river left here is a noteworthy rock outcropping with dump-truck-size monoliths rising above the river, flanked by banks of mountain laurel. The blooms are particularly striking in early May.

MILE 34.1 (33.616960, −84.117005) Pipeline.

MILE 33.2 (33.607841, −84.106713) Shoals.

MILE 32.9 (33.605158, −84.103447) Shoals & McKnight's Mill. Over the next 700 feet, the river spills over a pair of significant ledges—the last one dropping about 3 feet. The Georgia Department of Agriculture described this section of the river in an 1885 report: "The river at the dam here is 200 feet wide with 12 feet fall." In this vicinity during the late 1800s stood McKnight's Mill. The abundance of water-powered milling operations on the South River and its tributaries during the 1800s is hard to fathom. The same 1885 report notes that all the major streams feeding the South also powered mills: "The five counties through which the South River flows in 1880 had in population 106,599," with "75 flour and grist mills, 43 saw mills, four paper mills, four furniture factories, seven foundries and machine shops and seven cotton mills."

SHOALS NEAR MCKNIGHT'S MILL, ROCKDALE COUNTY

MILE 32.5 (33.601733, −84.098201) Ga. 138 & Lorraine Park. On the south side of the Ga. 138 bridge is this small Rockdale County park, which features the Rockdale River Trail and picnic areas. The lack of a boat launch at this riverfront park is indicative of the troubling state of the South River, which for years has been accurately perceived as a polluted water body. Failing sewer systems in Atlanta and DeKalb County have been the primary culprits, and high fecal bacteria levels have caused virtually the entire length of the South from its headwaters to Jackson Lake to be included on the state's list of polluted streams. The state has also issued a fish consumption advisory for bluegill, buffalo, and largemouth bass caught in the river, because of unhealthy levels of polychlorinated biphenyls (PCBs). PCBs, manmade chemicals and probable carcinogens, were used in the production of electric transformers, oil-based paint, fluorescent-light ballasts, hydraulic systems, and adhesives and tapes from 1929 until 1979, when they were banned. PCBs persist for years in the environment, accumulating in large fish and ultimately in humans that eat the fish. Consuming contaminated fish is the primary exposure pathway for humans; dermal contact with contaminated river sediments is not considered as serious a threat to human health. No single source has been identified as the main contributor to the South's PCB contamination; scientists suspect that the chemicals entered the river through stormwater runoff from the urban environment and sewage overflows. In recent years, the South River Watershed Alliance (SRWA) has been instrumental in advocating for the establishment of a South River Water Trail, and as improvements have been made to sewer systems upstream, more boaters are taking to the river. In fact, Rockdale County emergency personnel in 2019 began installing mile markers along the river to aid in identifying the location of boaters during emergencies. A boat launch at Lorraine Park is part of the SRWA master plan for its water trail.

MILE 31.5 (33.592319, −84.086803) South River Trail Bridge. This 520-foot steel footbridge is part of the 33-mile system of recreational trails along the South River that connect the Monastery of the Holy Spirit, Panola Mountain State Park, and the Arabia Mountain National Heritage Area. Completed in 2014, it was then the largest bridge installed on the PATH Foundation trail system. The PATH Foundation, a nonprofit organization organized in 1991, has worked for the past three decades to establish recreational trails in Metro Atlanta. The Silver Comet Trail and the Arabia Mountain Trail system are among the organization's shining stars. Eb McBrayer, PATH's founder, was inspired to advocate for recreational trails during a harrowing bike ride along Atlanta's busy Ponce De Leon Avenue en route to Stone Mountain Park. Now, three decades after that ride, a 19-mile walking-cycling path extends from downtown Atlanta to the park, and users have to ride on surface streets for only a small portion of the way.

MILE 29.5 (33.578906, −84.083040) Monastery of the Holy Spirit. On river left here is a high bluff filled with mountain laurel. It marks the beginning of some 2,000 acres of land owned by the Monastery of the Holy Spirit, a Trappist monastery established in 1944. The monastery is home to some 35 monks, who, in addition to leading a contemplative life focused on prayer and worship, work in a variety of enterprises on the campus. They operate a bakery specializing in fruitcakes and fudge; a stained-glass studio; a garden center focused on bonsai plants, tools, and accessories; and in the woods bordering the South River, a conservation burial ground. The monastery's 70-acre Honey Creek Woodlands offers "green" burial services for all faiths. Simply put, green burials are burials done the old-fashioned way. Bodies interred at Honey Creek Woodlands are not embalmed. They are either placed in a shroud or a biodegradable container and buried just three feet deep, allowing the natural decomposition process to return the body to soil. Many families opt to identify the graves with living markers such as trees or wildflowers, rather than traditional stone tablets. Green burials have the added advantage of keeping embalming chemicals, including formaldehyde (a probable carcinogen), from leaching into soil and groundwater. The monastery hosts visitors daily, offering daily services in the Abbey Church and self-guided tours of the grounds, along with a visitor center and store.

MILE 26.9 (33.455553, −83.931914) Oglesby Bridge Road Access. On river left is property that in 2020 was slated for development into a public river access park by Rockdale County. The 1.8-acre parcel was initially secured through the efforts of Jackie Echols and the South River Watershed Alliance to further develop the South River Water Trail. The SRWA purchased the land and donated it to Rockdale County for the park.

27 Mi.
28 Mi
Honey Creek
Airline Rd
26 Mi.
Oglesby Bridge Rd
Big Cotton Indian Creek
25 Mi.
Deer Run Lake
20
Walnut Creek
23 Mi.
Rockdale County
212
Big Cotton Indian Creek
21 Mi.
24 Mi.
Shoal
20 Mi.
22 Mi.
Henry County
Shoals
19 Mi.
Peachstone Shoals
20
Ola Rd
18 Mi.
212
Walnut Creek Water Reclamation Facility
17 Mi.
Butler Bridge Rd
Sampson Creek
16 Mi.
South East River Sand
Honey Creek
Freeman Creek
15 Mi.
Butler Bridge
14 Mi.
212
13 Mi.
Powerlines
Bethany Rd
River Rd
Creek
12 Mi.
Snapping Shoals
W
N
S
E
11 Mi.
Newton County
81
Ga. 81
0
0.5
1
2 Mile
10 Mi.

Peachstone

Length 16 miles (Oglesby Bridge Road to Ga. 81)

Class I–II

Time 6–9 hours

Minimum Level Levels above 300 cubic feet per second at the Ga. 81 gauge should provide sufficient flows to allow boaters to navigate the shoals on this section.

River Gauge The nearest river gauge is located at Ga. 81 at the end of this section: https://waterdata.usgs.gov/ga/nwis/uv/?site_no=02204520&agency_cd=USGS.

Launch Site In 2020, Rockdale County was slated to begin development of a public boat launch here. Until its completion, access is via a footpath on the north and upstream side of the bridge through property owned by the South River Watershed Alliance.

DIRECTIONS From exit 82 (Ga. 20) on I-20, travel south on Ga. 20 6.2 miles. Turn right on Oglesby Bridge Road and proceed 4 miles to the river. The best access is on the north and upstream side of the bridge.

Take Out Site There is no developed take out site at this location, but it is possible to use the right-of-way along Ga. 81. The best access is on the north and downstream side of the Ga. 81 bridge, where a rugged path leads from the river to parking along the right-of-way.

DIRECTIONS From the launch site, return on Oglesby Bridge Road 2.1 miles to Ga. 212 (Scott Hwy.). Turn right and proceed 2.2 miles. Turn right on Ga. 20 / Ga. 212 and continue on Ga. 212 proceed 5.7 miles. Turn right on Ga. 81 and travel 0.1 mile and pull off on left.

Alternative Take Out Site The right-of-way at Ga. 20 may be accessed to create a 5-mile trip. There is no developed river access at this location.

DIRECTIONS From the launch site, travel west on Oglesby Bridge Road 0.6 mile. Turn left on Airline Road and proceed 1.3 miles. Turn left on Kelleytown Road and travel 2.2 miles. Turn left on Ga. 20 and proceed 0.7 mile to the river.

Outfitters No outfitters operate on this section of river.

Description This 16-mile run meanders along the border between Henry, Rockdale, and Newton Counties, fast-growing suburban Atlanta communities. Though it skirts many subdivisions along its route, the river corridor remains mostly undeveloped. Flatwater predominates, but beginning at Peachstone Shoals at Ga. 20, for about 2 miles the river spills over numerous shoals, including one challenging ledge that drops more than 3 feet. The rich history along the paddle path includes 19th-century mill sites and several Civil War sites.

Points of Interest

MILE 24.4 (33.542780, −84.052756) Deer Run Lake. On river left is the outfall of Deer Run Lake, a large amenity lake surrounded by the Deer Run and Deer Forest subdivisions. Rockdale, like other Metro Atlanta counties, has experienced tremendous growth during the past four decades. The county's 2018 population of 90,312 is nearly three times larger than the county's population in 1980. With this growth have come more homes, more businesses, and more concrete and asphalt, all of which degrade the health of area streams and rivers. Since less rainwater soaks into the ground, more of it washes off built surfaces, carrying pollutants directly to streams. In large portions of the South River watershed, more than 10 percent of the land area is covered by impervious surfaces (buildings, roadways, parking lots, and other hard surfaces that prevent rain from soaking into the ground). Studies have shown that when impervious surfaces cover as much as 10 percent of the land draining to a stream, stream health declines. When hard surfaces cover 25 percent or more of the land, streams usually cannot support aquatic life.

MILE 23.2 (33.530272, −84.050953) Shoal.

MILE 21.7 (33.526340, −84.044460) Peachstone Shoals. These shoals begin just upstream of the Ga. 20 bridge and continue some 1,000 feet beneath the bridge and beyond as the river descends over several river-wide ledges. The falls here attracted early industrialists, and at the time of the Civil War, Pearsall's Mill, a gristmill, stood beside the river here. That mill met its end on August 21, 1864,

NEAR OGLESBY BRIDGE, ROCKDALE COUNTY

PEACHSTONE SHOALS, HENRY COUNTY

one of many property casualties during a Union cavalry raid south of Atlanta intended to cut railroad supply lines to Confederate troops defending the city. Some 4,000 Union cavalry passed over the river here that day on a bridge adjacent to the mill as they moved north, fleeing Confederates whom they had fought a day earlier at the Battle of Lovejoy's Station. In passing the bridge, the cavalry set fire to the mill, and once across the river, set ablaze the bridge, along with three other South River bridges, to slow down their pursuers. For the soldiers, the bridge was a welcome sight. Earlier in the day, the 4,000 men, their mounts, wagons carrying wounded soldiers, and pack animals were forced to ford the rain-swollen Big Cotton Indian Creek just to the south. One soldier and at least 50 mules and horses drowned. As recounted in David Evans's *Sherman's Horsemen: Union Cavalry Operations in the Atlanta Campaign*, Private John Nourse described the scene: "As soon as they (pack mules) reached the swift current they would roll over and down the stream they went. Generally all we could see was four legs sticking up out of the water kicking vigorously." The crossing was so arduous that Union brigadier general Hugh Judson Kilpatrick ordered the abandonment of a prized cannon. It was disabled and tossed in the creek. In the 1940s, a Civil War cannon was, in fact, recovered from the creek.

After the war, Charles Thornton Zachry, a former Confederate colonel, returned to Henry County and took possession of the Peachstone Shoals property, developing a gristmill, sawmill, and cotton gin powered by the river. By 1883, a textile mill with 129 looms was also operating here. Zachry served several terms in the Georgia Senate in the 1880s and 1890s. An *Atlanta Constitution* profile of the politician in 1890 portrayed him as a hero of the Civil War: "He came home from the war to his desolate home with his spirit undimmed and his courage unfaltering . . . The old fashioned southern gentleman is a type of aristo-

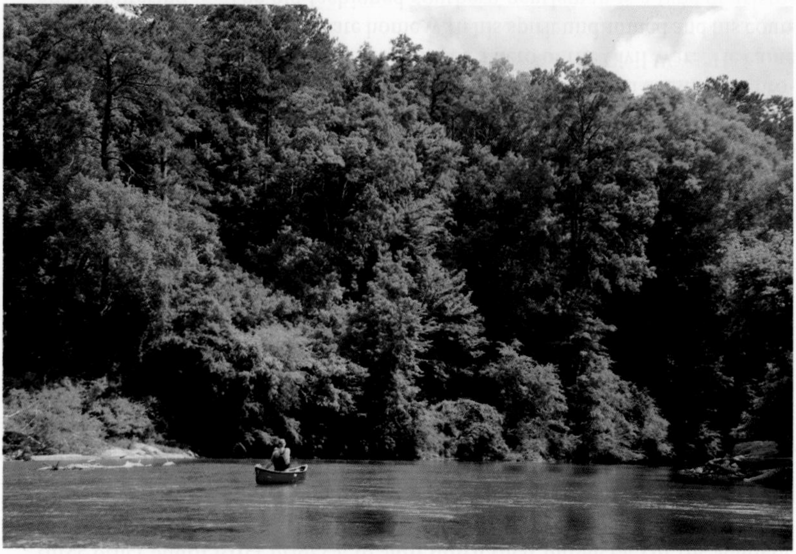

NEAR BIG COTTON INDIAN CREEK, HENRY COUNTY

cratic manhood that is fast going out before the utilitarian ideas of the present day . . . He has given his best energies toward the up building and prosperity of his country." Zachry's home, known as The Castle Mound, stood on a rise overlooking the river here. He died in 1906.

MILE 20.5 (33.514750, −84.054455) Big Cotton Indian Creek. On river right, this large tributary contributes its flow. In the past, it also likely contributed to the formation of the cut-off and oxbow here. Maps from the early 1900s show a large oxbow south of here, but by the mid-20th century the river had carved a new channel, cutting off the oxbow. Significant flows from Big Cotton Indian Creek running headlong into the river's eastern bank likely accelerated the process. A rocky shoal now interrupts this cut-through, and the oxbow is only navigable at high water levels. Big Cotton Indian Creek played a significant role in the development of Henry County, since dams on it provided the first electricity for McDonough and surrounding communities in the early 1900s. Archaeological digs in the 1960s revealed several Native American burial sites between Big Cotton Indian Creek and the South River. Early surveyors bestowed on this creek the Anglicized translation of the Native American word "panola" (cotton)—which, of course, is the same name assigned to the mountain and shoals up river. A large sandbar on river left sits opposite the upstream mouth of the oxbow.

MILE 19.4 (33.517603, −84.046918) Shoals. An odd pile of rocks in the middle of the river marks the beginning of about 1,000 feet of shoals, culminating in a precipitous ledge and a 3-foot fall that makes a good surf spot for whitewater enthusiasts. It is also one of the most scenic views on this section of river.

MILE 16.4 (33.494691, −84.033342) Walnut Creek Water Reclamation Facility. On river right is the mouth of the creek that lends its name to the adjacent Henry County sewage treatment plant. The county's Walnut Creek facility treats up to 8 million gallons of sewage daily through a land application system. The sewage receives primary treatment, is pumped to two holding ponds capable of storing some 80 million gallons, and then is sprayed on some 1,000 acres of forested land, where nature completes the treatment process. Land application systems differ from traditional wastewater treatment plants in that they do not discharge directly into a water body, instead allowing the wastewater to soak into the ground. This method of treatment, which prevents the direct discharge of pollutants into local water bodies, was a popular alternative in Metro Atlanta during the 1970s and 1980s, but as Georgia's population has grown, so has the demand for drinking water. Thus, in recent years there has been a trend away from land application systems to facilities that discharge highly treated wastewater directly into rivers and streams. The Henry County Water Authority maintains some 450 miles of sewer lines servicing many of the 225,000 residents of the county. The authority and county own much of the next five miles of riverfront on the Henry County side of the river, stretching almost to Ga. 81—some 1,900 acres.

MILE 15.5 (33.496581, −84.023333) South East River Sand. At mid-river is a dredge boat, and on river left is the accompanying operation, which produces sand, one of the world's most commonly mined materials. Georgia's Environmental Protection Division permits more than 60 sand-dredging operations on Georgia's water bodies. In a typical day, South East River Sand produces 400–

SOUTH RIVER SAND COMPANY, NEWTON COUNTY

500 tons of sand at this location. In Atlanta, you might find South River sand in the landscaping around Mercedes Benz Stadium or at Zoo Atlanta, which uses it in some of its animal enclosures. Before South East River Sand began operations, Ray Lambert, a longtime member of the board of the Georgia Department of Natural Resources, operated a dredge at multiple locations on the South River from the 1980s until 2012, a period when state and local authorities began enforcing state laws to prevent erosion and sedimentation at land development sites. "After those started to be in place, we saw a dramatic reduction in the sand and silt put into the river," Lambert recalled. "It hurt my business, but at least the land wasn't washing into the river any more. We saw better than anyone the good that was coming from erosion control." When streams and rivers carry excessive dirt from upstream land disturbances, the health of those water bodies and the creatures that live in them decline.

MILE 14.9 (33.497603, −84.015222) Butler Bridge. This historic bridge location dates to antebellum days. The last bridge here carried traffic into the late 1970s before being abandoned. Jim Miles, in *Civil War Ghosts of Central Georgia and Savannah*, records a fanciful tale of the haunting of this location by 10 Union soldiers who were reportedly captured and hanged near the bridge during the Civil War: "A local legend said if someone went there on a dark night and sang 'Dixie,' the bodies of the executed men would appear, dangling from oak trees." Wes Hollingsworth, a retired Henry County firefighter, provided the story to Miles and insisted that as a teenager, he and friends had had a paranormal experience at the bridge: "You could see the blue in their clothes," he said. No war records support the claim that 10 Union soldiers were executed here, but Union and Confederate soldiers did pass through the area between July and November 1864.

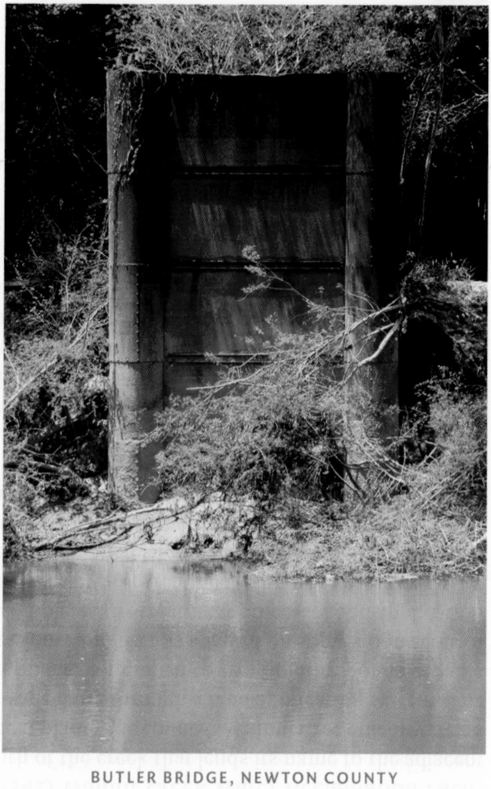

BUTLER BRIDGE, NEWTON COUNTY

Another Civil War tale, told by an eyewitness and recorded in a 1933 issue of the *Atlanta Constitution*, is likely valid and underscores the importance of South River bridges during that conflict. During a Union cavalry expedition that came to be known as Kilpatrick's Raid, horsemen fleeing pursuing Confederate soldiers were desperate to get north of the South River and stop their enemy's pursuit by destroying the South's bridges. Once the main force had crossed at the Peachstone Shoals bridge and then destroyed it, the cavalry moved up and down the South River to locate and destroy other bridges, including Butler's. It was during these maneuvers that eight-year-old Joseph A. McCord and his father, William S. McCord, encountered Union soldiers. The younger McCord recounted the story to the Atlanta newspaper in the waning years of his life: "We were living at the time in the Snapping Shoals district. There had been an engagement between Federal and Confederate troops one afternoon in 1864 not far from our vicinity. The Federal troops, known as Kilpatrick's division, were a part of Sherman's raiders. By sunrise the next morning they had reached our house and invited themselves to breakfast. They became angered with my father, because he was unable to tell them the location of Butler's Bridge, and started to hang him, going so far as to fasten the rope on a limb and put the noose around his neck. After reciting his service in the War of 1812 in which he served the Union forces against the British, his own temper flared up and he concluded what he had to say with 'now, damn you, hang!'" The soldiers let the elder McCord live, but ultimately did locate and destroy Butler's Bridge, securing their escape to Union lines north of Atlanta. Beginning in the late 1980s, Ray Lambert, who, as mentioned above, operated a sand dredge on the river in this area, dismantled and removed a steel bridge dating from the early 1900s that had collapsed into the river. The steel bridge supports can still be seen on either bank of the river.

MILE 12.7 (33.488405, −83.984174) Powerlines.

MILE 10.5 (33.484616, −83.958069) Ga. 81. A bridge has spanned the river at Snapping Shoals since the mid-1800s, and many versions have been destroyed and built over the last 160 years. During the Civil War, the span here was set ablaze by Union cavalry escaping Confederate pursuers during Kilpatrick's Raid. In 1873, a $750 contract was awarded to build a bridge here. In 1883 the bridge was washed away in a flood. In 1902 the *Atlanta Constitution* reported on another freshet: "The bridge at Snapping Shoals, one of the heaviest bridges in the county, was completely destroyed." In 2020, the Georgia Department of Transportation began replacing a late-1940s span.

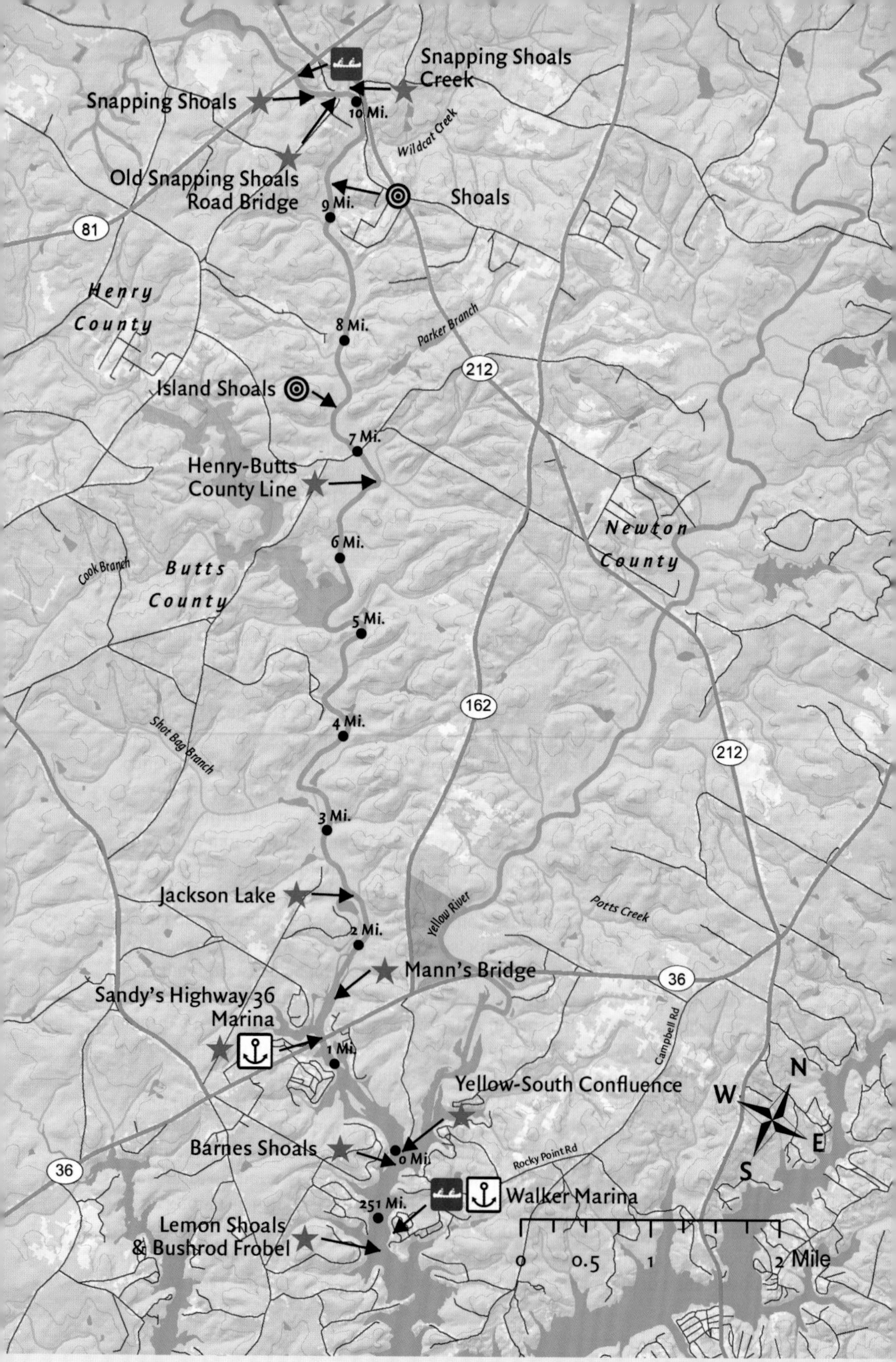

Snapping Shoals Creek
Snapping Shoals
10 Mi.
Wildcat Creek
Old Snapping Shoals Road Bridge
Shoals
9 Mi.
81
Henry County
8 Mi.
Parker Branch
212
Island Shoals
7 Mi.
Henry-Butts County Line
Newton County
6 Mi.
Cook Branch
Butts County
5 Mi.
162
4 Mi.
Shot Bag Branch
212
3 Mi.
Jackson Lake
Yellow River
Potts Creek
2 Mi.
Mann's Bridge
36
Sandy's Highway 36 Marina
Campbell Rd
1 Mi.
Yellow-South Confluence
N
W
E
S
Barnes Shoals
0 Mi.
Rocky Point Rd
36
Walker Marina
251 Mi.
Lemon Shoals & Bushrod Frobel
0
0.5
1
2 Mile

Snapping Shoals

Length 11 miles (Ga. 81 to Walker Marina on Jackson Lake)

Class I–II

Time 5–7 hours

Minimum Level Levels above 300 cubic feet per second at the Ga. 81 gauge provide enough water to float Snapping Shoals. Downstream of Snapping Shoals, the river is navigable at flows below this level.

River Gauge The nearest river gauge is located at Ga. 81 at the beginning of this section: https://waterdata.usgs.gov/ga/nwis/uv/?site_no=02204520&agency_cd=USGS.

Launch Site There is no developed launch site at this location, but there is a rugged path that leads to the river on the north and downstream side of the Ga. 81 bridge. Parking is limited to the shoulder of the road or at businesses located just north of the river and within a short walking distance.

DIRECTIONS From the intersection of Ga. 81 and Ga. 212 south of Porterdale, travel south on Ga. 81 about 600 feet. The pull-off is on left, and the river can be accessed via path from this pull-off.

Take Out Site The take out site is at Walker Marina, a private boat ramp and marina on Jackson Lake. Parking fees may apply.

DIRECTIONS From the launch site, return to Ga. 212. Turn right and proceed 7.8 miles to the roundabout at the intersection with Ga. 36. Turn right on Ga. 36 (first turn out of the roundabout) and proceed 0.5 mile. Turn left on Campbell Road and proceed 1.7 miles. Bear to the right on Rocky Point Road and proceed 1.2 miles. Turn left on Lang Road and travel 0.7 mile to Walker Marina.

Alternative Take Out Sites To avoid the mostly flatwater paddling below Snapping Shoals, whitewater enthusiasts can use an undeveloped take out site along Old Snapping Shoals Road. Also, a boat ramp at Sandy's Highway 36 Marina upstream of the confluence of the South and Yellow Rivers eliminates the final 1.7 miles of lake paddling.

DIRECTIONS TO OLD SNAPPING SHOALS ROAD From the Ga. 81 launch site, travel south on Ga. 81 0.7 mile. Turn left on River Road and proceed 0.6 mile. Turn left on Old Snapping Shoals Road and proceed 0.5 mile. River will be on the left.

Outfitters Although no outfitters operate on this section of river, Jackson Lake Rentals rents boats for use on the lake.

Jackson Lake Rentals, 770-713-7069, www.jacksonlakerentals.com.

Barry Dendy provides pontoon boat rentals and ski tube rentals with pickup at Berry's Boat Dock.

Description This section's first 2,000 feet start out with a roar of Class I–II whitewater below Snapping Shoals Dam, but the final 10 miles are mostly a flatwater paddle ending in several miles of lake paddling as the South River spreads out behind Lloyd Shoals Dam on the Ocmulgee. What the river lacks in shoals it makes up for in scenery. The route is mostly wooded and undisturbed until lakefront homes begin encroaching on the corridor as the river transforms into Jackson Lake. Hawks, ospreys, blue and green herons, and ducks are common on this run.

Points of Interest

MILE 10.3 (33.484115, −83.953441) Snapping Shoals. The lowhead dam here marks the beginning of nearly a half mile of continuous whitewater—a descent of some 20 feet over a distance of about 2,000 feet. During low flows—500 cubic feet per second or less—it is possible to paddle up to the dam and drop your boat below the three-foot-high obstacle. At higher flows, the dam should be portaged on river right to access a series of Class II ledges. At high water levels, the course becomes more challenging. At low to moderate levels, the best course is to follow the chutes immediately below the dam, moving toward far river right to run the most significant rapid. This rapid should be scouted for strainers, which sometimes block the channel.

Perhaps no other location along the South River has done more to shape this portion of Newton and Henry Counties. Milling operations began here in the early to mid-1800s, and by the mid-20th century, waterpower was responsible for electrifying the dark, rural, back-road farms of the area. Following the Civil War, a number of men attempted to turn a profit by harnessing the river's power,

SNAPPING SHOALS, NEWTON COUNTY

most notably Josiah Bosworth. During the 1870s and early 1880s, Bosworth operated flour mills on the site, but newspaper records of the early 1880s indicate a man tilting toward insolvency, desperately searching for investors to expand the use of the South's waterpower. He advertised repeatedly in the *Atlanta Constitution* in 1881, seeking "manufacturers or capitalists desiring to invest in water power or milling property." In 1883, raging floodwaters almost cost him his life when the boat carrying him capsized in the shoals. He was rescued by his blacksmith, but his finances could not be saved. He owed creditors some $28,000, and in 1884 the property was sold at auction. Around 1895, H. A. DeLoach took ownership of the Snapping Shoals mills, and by the turn of the century he was running South River Mills, an operation than included a sawmill, cotton gin, and flour mill. The *Jackson Progress Argus* gushed over DeLoach: "If you want to find a genius in milling and a man with the snap and vim to do the right thing at the right time and in the right way you can find all in the person of Mr. DeLoach."

Throughout the early 20th century, Snapping Shoals was a popular destination for camping outings, fish fries, and other gatherings. In 1936, President Franklin D. Roosevelt's Rural Electrification Administration (REA) lent $90,000 to transform the mechanical power at Snapping Shoals into hydroelectric power. That loan set in motion the Snapping Shoals Power and Light Company and the construction of 90 miles of powerlines providing electricity to 270 customers in the surrounding area. Within four years, the hydro plant was serving 1,450 customers, dramatically changing farm life in Newton, Henry, and Rockdale. The onset of power prompted one local landowner (and investor in the Snapping Shoals Power and Light Company), E. V. Ellington, to subdivide 115 acres near

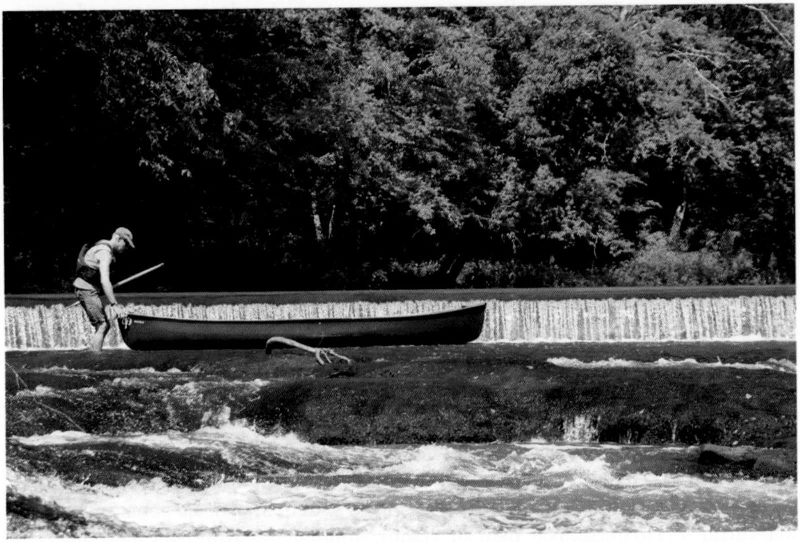

SNAPPING SHOALS DAM, NEWTON COUNTY

the dam into house lots, promising electrified "summer resorts" overlooking a "fisherman's paradise" at Snapping Shoals. By 1950, 80 percent of U.S. farms had been provided electricity thanks to the REA.

The turbines at Snapping Shoals continued generating electricity into the 21st century, powering the work of an aluminum die casting manufacturer into the 1970s. In 1976, the property was purchased by Thomas Brothers Hydro, Inc., which put the river to work producing ice and powering a machine shop where, appropriately, the company manufactures and repairs hydropower turbines. Production of electricity was halted around 2010 following a protracted and contentious legal battle between Thomas Brothers and neighboring Henry County over Hoke and Mike Thomas's 2004 proposal to raise the old milldam to create a 26.2-billion-gallon public water-supply reservoir on the river and increase the hydroelectric capacity of the Thomases' plant. At the same time, the Henry County Water Authority (HCWA) was planning an "off-stream" reservoir on nearby Tussahaw Creek. The competing plans and an HCWA effort to purchase properties adjacent to the Thomases' dam and hydro plant saw the two parties lock horns in court—a battle that was ultimately decided in the HCWA's favor and resulted in Thomas Brothers ceasing hydropower operations at the facility. Though the generators have been silenced, Thomas Brothers Hydro, Inc., still produces and repairs turbines in the buildings that once housed the Snapping Shoals powerhouse. In recent years, the South River Watershed Alliance and others have advocated for the dam to be breached or removed to improve fisheries and recreational access to Snapping Shoals.

MILE 10.2 (33.485321, –83.951499) Old Snapping Shoals Road Bridge. On either side of the river are the stone piers that once supported a circa-1900 steel bridge spanning the river. In March 1902, the *Atlanta Constitution* reported that the bridge at "Snapping Shoals, one of the heaviest in the county, was completely destroyed" in a major flood that took out numerous other bridges in Newton County. The current steel bridge, undoubtedly, replaced the bridge described in this report.

MILE 10.1 (33.485861, –83.950713) Snapping Shoals Creek. The name of this creek, which drains large portions of Newton and Rockdale Counties, and the identically named shoals on the South River have a colorful history. The research of Ken Krakow, author of *Georgia Place-Names*, suggests that the name is derived either from the sound of the water rolling over the rapids or from a Native American fish trap located here, from which fish could be pitched or "snapped" from the shallow waters. More colorful origin stories involve the tale of a Native American who missed the opportunity to shoot a deer near here when his flintlock musket failed to fire. Upon pulling the trigger, he heard only a snap. Finally, a June 1893 story in the *Atlanta Constitution* makes the claim that Captain Thomas Weaver, while hunting for deer along the river here in 1813, encountered the same problem with his rifle, and "from this small incident Snapping Shoals got its name."

MILE 9.2 (33.475950, –83.947048) Shoals.

OLD SNAPPING SHOALS ROAD BRIDGE, NEWTON COUNTY

MILE 7.4 (33.455553, −83.931914) Island Shoals. From the 1800s, this was the site of a dam and gristmill. When it was advertised for sale in 1884, it was described as a 47-acre tract containing "one very fine grist mill, with four runs of stone, a regrind and purifier, four dwelling houses, a blacksmith shop and ginhouse." A 1901 U.S. Geological Survey of the river notes this spot as the site of "Haley's Mill, a new roller flour mill on the west side of the river, operated from a canal which starts at the upper end of the shoals and gives a head of 10 feet." The surveyors noted a fall of 14 feet over a distance of nearly a half mile. A 1908 survey notes the Island Shoals Bridge spanning the river downstream of the milling operations. Little evidence of this industry remains, except for remnants of the steel bridge on river left at the powerline cut. The shoals are limited to small riffles, and there is no visible evidence of the namesake island.

MILE 6.7 (33.450708, −83.922459) Henry-Butts County Line. On river right is a significant sandbar, and just downstream is the boundary separating these two counties. Butts County—a name some would call "unfortunate"—was created in 1825 from portions of Henry and Monroe Counties. In 2003, Don Earnhart, a radio personality in Jackson, started a campaign to change the county's name, providing as support the fact that no local businesses at that time included "Butts" in their name: "What are we going to have? 'Butts Cleaners, we get the stains out?'" Earnhart's campaign ultimately died, but not before attracting national media attention. *CBS News* noted that no other county in the country is named "Butts." Butts County was named to honor Samuel Butts, a Virginian who moved to the area in the early 1800s and was killed in 1814 while serving in

SANDBAR, BUTTS COUNTY

the Georgia Militia during the Creek Indian War. The South and Ocmulgee form the northern and eastern border of the county for the next 23 miles.

MILE 2.4 (33.410423, −83.898980) Jackson Lake. Though the current slows farther upstream, a slough on river left confirms this is Jackson Lake's backwaters. Lloyd Shoals Dam, completed by the Georgia Power Company in 1911, created what was at the time the state's largest reservoir, and with Atlanta and DeKalb County's failing sewer systems sending millions of gallons of untreated sewage downstream, the lake became known as one of the state's most polluted reservoirs. Recent strides in wastewater management in the metro area have improved the lake's health, but floating trash remains a significant problem for lake users. In 2019, DeKalb County announced it would fully fund the installation of a $400,000 floating litter trap upstream on the South River. The announcement came in response to a long-running effort by the Jackson Lake Association and the South River Watershed Alliance that raised more than $115,000 from private donors for such a device. DeKalb County's decision freed up those funds for use in the installation of additional traps on the South and Yellow Rivers.

MILE 1.5 (33.399410, −83.895537) Mann's Bridge. In February 1921, this bridge (only portions of its steel skeleton remain) was the scene of one of the most horrific murders in Georgia history. Once exposed, the story laid bare the widespread and illegal practice of peonage on Georgia farms, a system that kept many blacks in virtual slavery well into the 20th century. In the years following the Civil War, thousands of former slaves found themselves jailed for violating so-called black laws, which required black men be employed. An idle black man was sure to be incarcerated. With no means to post bail or pay their fines, these men languished in jail unless a "benefactor" paid their fine. Such a benefactor would then take the freed prisoner and require him to work off the fine on a plantation. Common practice was to keep the men in debt slavery indefinitely. Such was the case on the plantation of John Williams in Jasper County. When federal investigators, who were tipped off to the illegal activity, paid Williams a visit and asked pointed questions of Williams and his black workers, Williams panicked. Fearing discovery, he systematically killed 11 of his workers, forcing his black foreman, Clyde Manning, to commit the murders. The first two to die were chained together, weighted with sacks of rocks around their necks, and forced over the rail of Allen's Bridge into the Yellow River, a mile to the east on Ga. 36. The third, Harry Price, died here. Having watched his friends forced into the brown water of the Yellow moments earlier, Price understood his fate when Williams stopped his car on this bridge and ordered him out. Price willingly went to the edge, saying, "Don't throw me over. I'll get over." He paused and muttered, "Lord have mercy," before leaning over the edge and plunging to his death. The completion of Lloyd Shoals Dam a decade earlier had widened and deepened these rivers, making them, to Williams's line of thinking, ideal places to dispose of bodies. Two more met a similar fate in the Alcovy arm of the lake the next evening. When the bodies were discovered, the trail ran back to Williams and Manning, who were both arrested for murder. In that era, the murder of black men was not usually noted in newspapers, but the heinous nature of these crimes attracted both national attention and the attention of prominent progressive white Atlantans, who paid not only for the defense of Manning but

MANN'S BRIDGE, NEWTON COUNTY

SWIMMING, BUTTS COUNTY

also for additional attorneys to assist the local prosecutor in seeking the conviction of Williams. At a trial in Covington, an all-white jury found Williams guilty of murder. The verdict marked the first time since 1877 that a southern white man was convicted of first-degree murder of a black man or woman. Even more compelling was the fact that he was convicted primarily on the testimony of a black man. While newspapers hailed the justice wrought in the Newton County Courthouse, and Governor Hugh Dorsey issued an antipeonage proclamation, little changed. Peonage persisted, and it would be 45 years before another white man was convicted of murdering a black man in the South. Perhaps the most revealing incident of the virulent racism of that era was a letter from Williams's pastor in Monticello, published in the *Atlanta Constitution*. Far from defending Williams, the pastor called for justice. Yet in the same breath, he attacked the press for vilifying Jasper County as a den of peonage and murder. The man of the cloth concluded that Williams would get a "fair and impartial trial by a set of twelve men of the old Anglo-Saxon strain of blood, unmixed by any foreign element whatsoever, and I know of no better people on earth."

MILE 1.2 (33.395183, –83.894182) Sandy's Highway 36 Marina. Just upstream and on river right is a private boat ramp and marina that can be used as a take out or launch site. User fees may apply. The Ga. 36 bridge just downstream was completed in 2016 at a cost of $4 million.

MILE 0.0 (33.388255, –83.877222) Yellow-South Confluence. Here the South River meets the Yellow River and the Ocmulgee is officially formed. The Alcovy contributes its flow to the Ocmulgee just down the lake. Maps dating to the early 1800s show the South as the South Branch of the Ocmulgee, and the historian

John Goff attributed this designation to Georgia's earliest settlers and explorers, who often called the westernmost branch of a river the "south branch," even if the river flowed through land to the west of other branches. Late 19th-century maps drawn by the U.S. Army Corps of Engineers, along with newspaper accounts from the same time period, refer to the stream as both the South and the "Welawnee River."

MILE 251.4 (33.387168, −83.877230) Barnes Shoals. Just below the confluence of the South and Yellow Rivers and before the impoundment of Jackson Lake, the free-flowing Ocmulgee spilled over Barnes Shoals here. An 1876 U.S. Army Corps of Engineers Survey described the now submerged shoal this way: "The last shoal on the river (Ocmulgee), Barnes', is just at the junction of the South and the Yellow rivers and is utilized for a grist mill The head of the shoal is on both streams and just at the junction of the two is a rock ledge crossing both and forming an almost perfect dam with deep water above it. The width of the South river is about 325 feet, that of the Yellow river about 275 feet, and that of the Ocmulgee about 500 feet." A precipitous fall, Barnes Shoals dropped nearly 12 feet over a distance of just 500 feet.

MILE 250.7 (33.378196, −83.873472) Lemon Shoals & Bushrod Frobel. Submerged near here is another of the Ocmulgee's original shoals. It is described in an 1876 U.S. Army Corps of Engineers survey: "At Lemon shoal . . . a natural rock dam extends almost entirely across the river leaving an opening of about 50 feet called Bull Sluice." Colonel Bushrod Frobel, a West Point graduate, Confederate veteran, and noted engineer in post–Civil War Georgia, was responsible for traveling the river and surveying it for the corps in 1876. A dreamer of big dreams and clearly a river man, as a U.S. congressman he attempted to secure appropriations to build a canal connecting the Mississippi River to rivers draining to the Atlantic Ocean. He also tried to sell the city of Atlanta on a plan to dig a 75-mile canal from the Chattahoochee north of Atlanta to the city center. The canal would power industrial facilities by day, and at night, when the mills shut down, the water would be diverted to a massive sewage tunnel beneath the city. The diverted flows would carry the waste to the Chattahoochee downstream of Atlanta. More than 100 years later, such tunnels have in fact been constructed, though the sewage is now treated before being released into the river.

YELLOW RIVER PARK, GWINNETT COUNTY

YELLOW RIVER

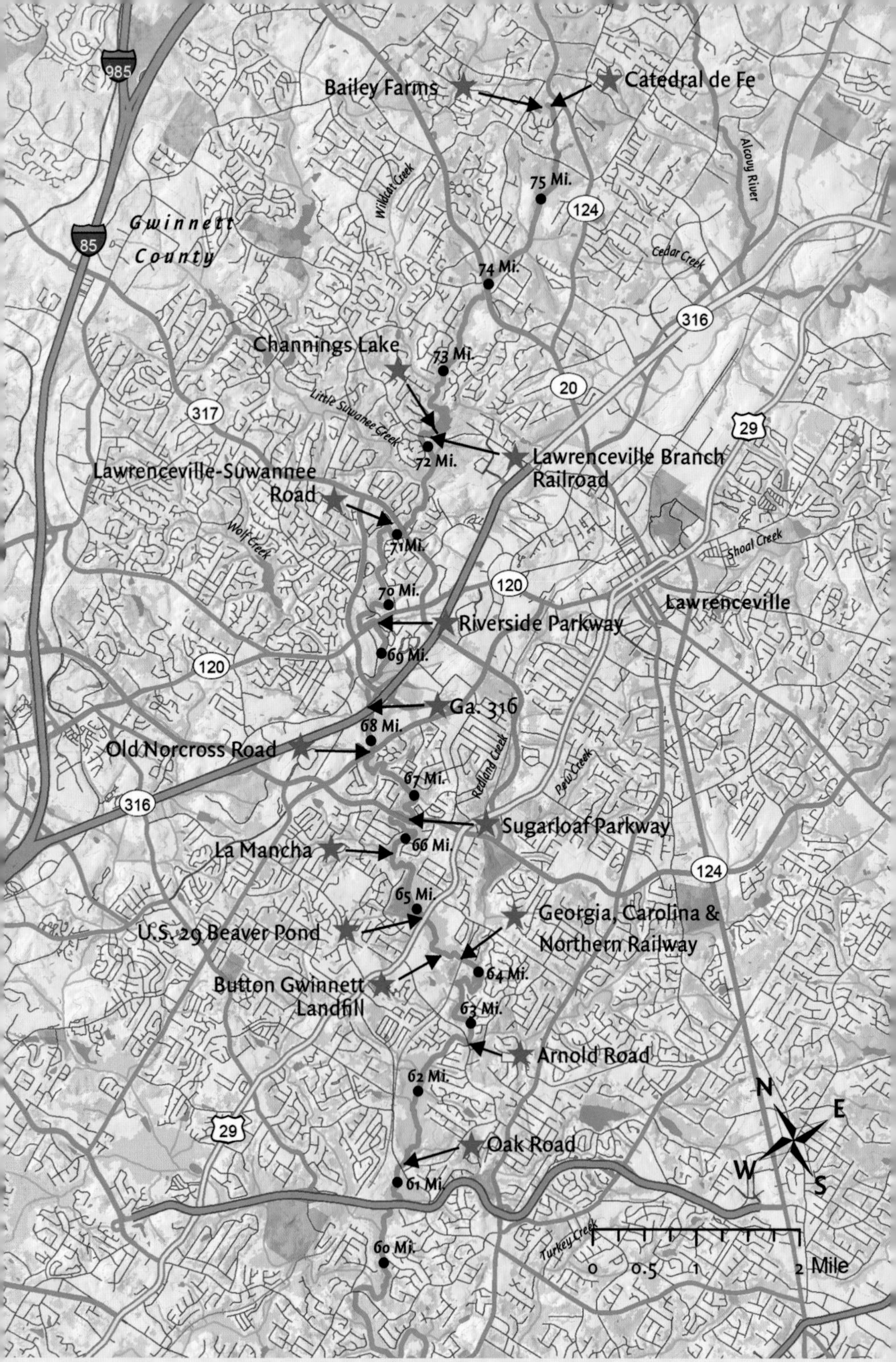

Bailey Farms
Catedral de Fe
Alcovy River
Wildcat Creek
75 Mi.
Gwinnett
County
Cedar Creek
74 Mi.
Channings Lake
73 Mi.
Little Suwanee Creek
72 Mi.
Lawrenceville Branch
Railroad
Lawrenceville-Suwannee
Road
Wolf Creek
Shoal Creek
71 Mi.
70 Mi.
Lawrenceville
Riverside Parkway
69 Mi.
Ga. 316
68 Mi.
Old Norcross Road
Redland Creek
Pew Creek
67 Mi.
Sugarloaf Parkway
La Mancha
66 Mi.
65 Mi.
Georgia, Carolina &
Northern Railway
U.S. 29 Beaver Pond
64 Mi.
Button Gwinnett
Landfill
63 Mi.
Arnold Road
62 Mi.
N
E
W
S
Oak Road
61 Mi.
Turkey Creek
60 Mi.
0
0.5
1
2 Mile

Lawrenceville

Length 15 miles (Headwaters to Oak Road)
Class Unnavigable (foot, bike, vehicle travel only)
Time Not applicable
Minimum Level Not applicable

River Gauge The nearest river gauge is located at Killian Hill Road, downstream of this section: https://waterdata.usgs.gov/ga/nwis/uv/?site_no=02206500&agency_cd=USGS.

Trailhead The first 15 miles of the Yellow River are generally unnavigable, and because the full length of this section flows almost entirely through private land, foot travel is prohibited without permission from landowners. This run of the river is best explored from public roads, via bicycle or automobile. But there are accessible lands, both public and private, along the route where travelers can experience the river.

DIRECTIONS The Yellow's origins are found amid the suburban sprawl of Gwinnett County. The river rises in the Bailey Farms subdivision, located off Ridge Road. From exit 115 (Ga. 20) on I-85, travel south on Ga. 20 1.5 miles. Turn left on Old Peachtree Road and proceed 0.6 mile. Turn right on Prospect Road and travel 1.3 miles. Turn right on Ridge Road and proceed 0.3 mile to the entrance to Bailey Farms, on the left.

DIRECTIONS TO OAK ROAD (LAUNCH SITE FOR NEXT SECTION) From the entrance to the Bailey Farms subdivision, turn left on Ridge Road and proceed 1.5 miles. Turn left on Ga. 20 and proceed 3.5 miles to East Pike Street in Lawrenceville. Turn right, travel 0.4 mile, and then bear left on U.S. 29 (Lawrenceville Hwy.). Continue on U.S. 29 for 4.8 miles. Turn left on Huff Road and proceed 1.2 miles. Turn left on Gloster / Oak Road and proceed 0.6 mile to the river.

Outfitters No Outfitters operate on this section of the river.

Description The upper reaches of the Yellow River are surrounded by Gwinnett County's urban sprawl. In fact, its headwaters are dammed to create an amenity pond in the Bailey Farms subdivision. From these beginnings, it winds between residential developments, beneath no less than 13 bridges and past a former landfill. Not considered navigable above Oak Road, its corridor is mostly flanked by private property, making bridge crossings the only publicly accessible locations. It is best explored on foot, bicycle, or vehicle.

Points of Interest

MILE 76.0 (34.018885, −83.968446) Bailey Farms. This neighborhood was billed as a swim, tennis, and lake community when developed in the late 1990s. Its centerpiece is a 1.4-acre lake created by a dam located less than 700 feet from the Yellow's origins. It can be seen from the community pool and tennis area along Bailey Farms Drive.

MILE 75.8 (34.018596, −83.965803) Catedral de Fe. It is perhaps fitting that the Yellow River's origins in Gwinnett County run along the property of this Spanish-language church, for during the past several decades this booming suburban Atlanta county has become one of the state's most ethnically diverse communities. In 1970, Gwinnett was home to 72,000 residents, almost all of them white. In 2019, Gwinnett's population was around 900,000, about 55 percent of it white. Some 25 percent of Gwinnett residents were born outside the United States, and in 2017 residents of Norcross and Loganville elected their first nonwhite mayors, respectively, an African American and a Cuban American. The Yellow's beginnings, at about 1,200 feet above seal level, sit in what might be considered a birthing suite for Georgia rivers. Within 1.5 miles of this location, on slopes draining to the east and south, are the origins of the Apalachee River (a tributary of the Oconee) and the Alcovy River (which joins the Yellow and South rivers at Jackson Lake). Two miles north is Ivy Creek, a stream that ultimately flows to the Chattahoochee River to the west.

BAILEY FARMS LAKE, GWINNETT COUNTY

MILE 72.3 (33.987734, −84.007010) Channings Lake. The second of 4 dams still standing on the mainstem of the Yellow River, this small dam was constructed in 1970 under the auspices of the Gwinnett County Resource Conservation and Development Council (RC&D) and is one of 12 dams in the county built for flood control between 1965 and 1973. This era of small-dam building was funded largely through the Food and Agriculture Act of 1962. For Gwinnett County in the 1960s, this meant an opportunity, as one *Atlanta Constitution* report from the era framed it, "to effect an orderly transition form rural to urban life" and avoid "unplanned growth." Gwinnett's farms were beginning to disappear and suburban growth was accelerating. Ironically, the program paying for small watershed dams was geared primarily to prevent the flooding of farmers' bottomlands along the Yellow and other streams. Thus, at a time when the county's farms were disappearing, federal funding became available to assist those farms. Nationally, in fact, some farmers were being paid by the federal government not to plant crops, a point not lost on critics of the program. Said George Bagby, director of Georgia's Game and Fish Commission, in 1969: "It just doesn't make sense. We are paying people to take land out of production on the one hand and draining land and destroying fish and wildlife to provide more farmland on the other—all at the expense of the taxpayer."

In the 21st century, taxpayers are still footing the bill for these structures, which now protect homes and businesses, many of them built on the flood-prone farmland the dams were originally intended to safeguard. In 2008, some $3 million in federal funds were used to rehabilitate this aging dam. At the time, some 90 homes were at risk from a catastrophic dam failure. Proponents of the spending argue that the dams and reservoirs prevent millions of dollars in property losses during floods and thus raise property values around the lakes. Opponents argue that the dams fragment the river system and destroy habitat for fish and other aquatic wildlife. Land-use ordinances that prevent building in flood-prone areas would be more cost-effective, they argue. This dam was originally known as Yellow River Watershed Dam No. 15, and its impoundment was eventually named Harris Lake in honor of Lloyd Harris, who was the original director of the Gwinnett County RC&D Council. Now it is also called Channings Lake, a nod to the nearby subdivision of the same name, which was developed in the early 1990s.

MILE 72.1 (33.986666, −84.008207) Lawrenceville Branch Railroad. Where traffic on Collins Hill Road now rushes over the Yellow, locomotives of this railroad, which connected Lawrenceville to the Atlanta and Charlotte Air Line Railroad in Suwannee, once chugged across a trestle. Completed in 1881, the railroad operated until 1920. At that time, the 10-mile run from Lawrenceville to Suwannee took about 40 minutes—about the time it would take a modern traveler to cover the distance in an auto during Metro Atlanta's rush hour.

MILE 71.1 (33.978044, −84.020133) Lawrenceville-Suwannee Road.

MILE 69.5 (33.968819, −84.031395) Riverside Parkway.

MILE 68.5 (33.959004, −84.038409) Ga. 316. Aside from I-85 running north-south through Gwinnett County, perhaps no other roadway personifies the county's tremendous growth after 1970. When first built, in 1960, it was just a short highway connecting I-85 to Lawrenceville, but in the final three decades of the 20th century, it was extended west to east across the county, ultimately connecting Atlanta to Athens and the University of Georgia. In 2004, the roadway prompted local governments in Gwinnett, Barrow, Oconee, and Clarke Counties to band together as the Georgia Bioscience Joint Development Authority, an effort to attract high-paying, high-tech jobs to the area. In 2012, the development authority began branding the roadway as "Georgia's Innovation Corridor."

MILE 67.9 (33.953854, −84.041095) Old Norcross Road.

MILE 66.6 (33.944878, −84.042669) Sugarloaf Parkway.

MILE 65.7 (33.940099, −84.046093) La Mancha. Here the river runs between the La Mancha and La Mancha Quail Hollow subdivisions, which were built in the mid to late 1970s—about the same time Gwinnett and Georgia's leaders were beginning to address two of the ill effects of rapid land development—erosion and the subsequent movement of dirt and mud into the state's waterways. Excessive sediment can choke the life out of streams, covering the cobbled creek bottoms, the habitat of the aquatic insects that form the basis of the riverine food chain. In 1972, Gwinnett County became the first local governing body in the state to adopt a soil erosion and sedimentation ordinance. Three years later, the Georgia General Assembly adopted a statewide law mandating that developers use practices such as silt fences, rock dams, sediment ponds, and natural buffers along streams to stem the flow of mud from construction sites into the state's drinking-water sources. In addition to degrading the health of streams and aquatic wildlife, excessive sediment drives up the costs of treating drinking water from those polluted streams. Sediment from construction sites, road-building projects, and other land-disturbing activities remains one of the leading causes of water pollution in Georgia.

MILE 64.9 (33.930540, −84.046054) U.S. 29 Beaver Pond. On the north side of Lawrenceville Highway adjacent to the river is a massive beaver pond and wetlands area. The 52-acre parcel, which flanks the river for nearly a half mile, was donated to the county in the 1980s. This is a good place to view a beaver lodge. While beavers that inhabit rivers tend to build burrows in riverbanks, wetland beavers construct large dome-shaped lodges that rise above the surface of the surrounding water. The entrances to this lodge are found underwater. Like Channings Lake, the man-made flood-control reservoir upstream, these beaver-dammed wetlands hold water and help prevent flooding downstream. The difference is that the beaver's handiwork didn't cost taxpayers anything.

MILE 64.5 (33.925018, −84.046040) Button Gwinnett Landfill. Within 150 feet of the west bank of the river here is a covered, graded, and terraced mountain of trash. The Button Gwinnett Landfill operated from the 1960s until 1999, taking in as much as 400 tons of trash daily in the late 1990s. Like many older landfills, it includes cells that were not lined with membranes to prevent landfill leachate from draining into groundwater. In the late 1980s, tests showed unsafe lev-

AT U.S. 29, GWINNETT COUNTY

els of contaminants in both groundwater and the river. State efforts to prevent pollution from landfills weren't initiated until 1972; nearly two decades of piecemeal legislation on solid waste culminated in 1990 when the General Assembly adopted the Comprehensive Solid Waste Management Act. Now virtually all of Georgia's municipal solid waste is disposed of in lined landfills with leachate and methane collection systems, and operators are required to monitor groundwater for contaminants. But many landfills, like Button Gwinnett, are located directly adjacent to rivers. State law now prevents the development of landfills within the 100-year floodplain surrounding the state's rivers and streams. According to statistics compiled by the state, each Georgian tosses more than five pounds of trash in landfills daily. This includes some 2.6 million tons of recyclable materials having an estimated value of more than $300 million.

MILE 64.2 (33.923194, –84.043509) Georgia, Carolina & Northern Railway. Now part of the CSX rail system, this railroad, built between 1887 and 1892, connected Atlanta to near Charlotte, North Carolina. When it opened, the new road was a great convenience for Atlanta travelers. The *Atlanta Constitution* noted the year it was completed: "It is a quick trip to Athens now that the Georgia, Carolina and Northern railway links the two cities . . . it being but a two hours ride."

MILE 62.8 (33.913016, –84.048928) Arnold Road.

MILE 61.1 (33.902749, –84.068274) Oak Road. According to a survey by the *Washington Post* of the most popular street names in each state, "Oak" is the second-commonest roadway name in Georgia, which has 401 streets named Oak. Though the live oak is the official state tree, "Dogwood" (408) surpasses "Oak" as the leader in street names. "Pine," "Park," and "Williams" round out the top five.

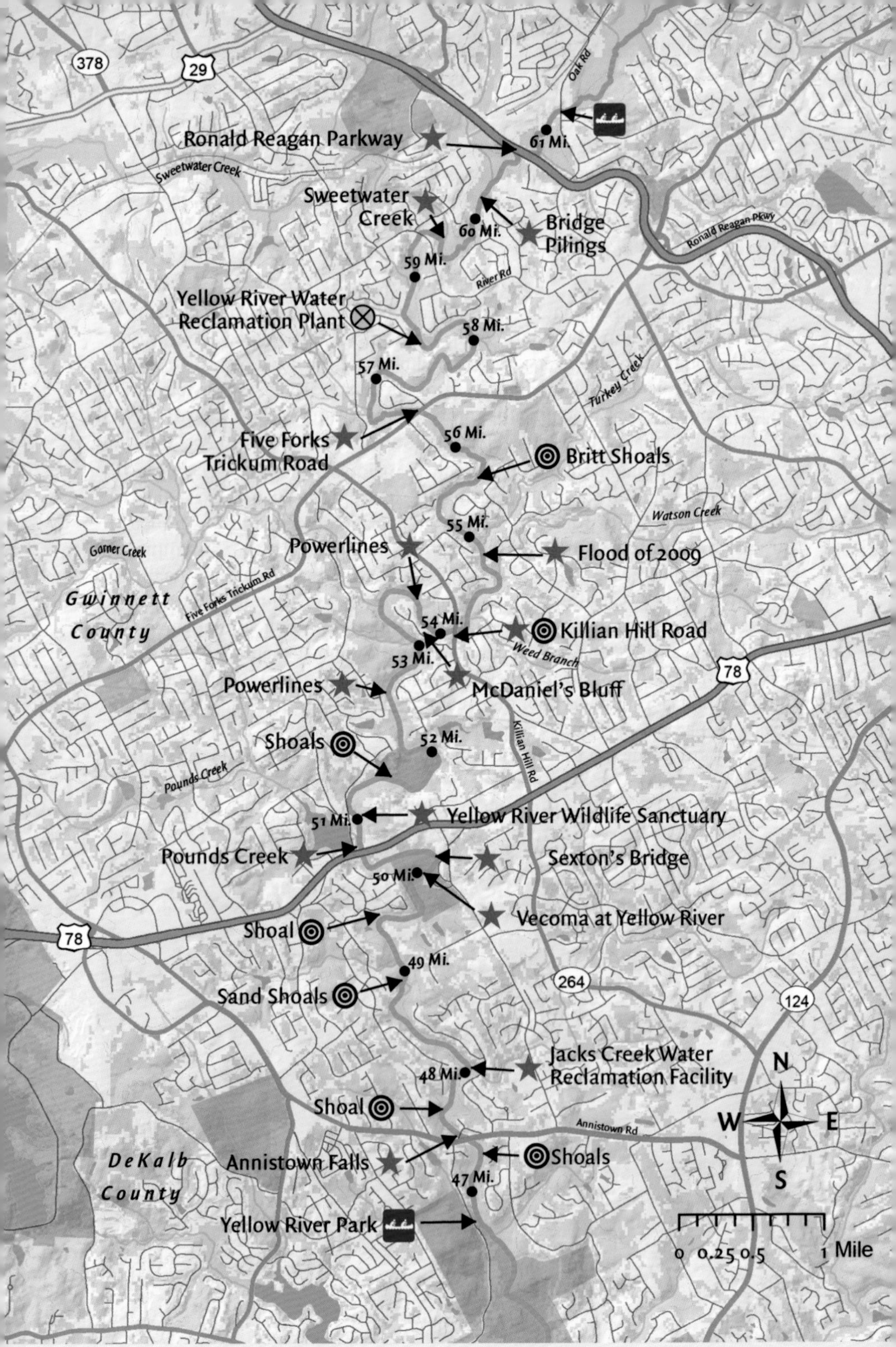

378
29
Oak Rd
61 Mi.
Ronald Reagan Parkway
Sweetwater Creek
Sweetwater Creek
60 Mi.
Bridge Pilings
Ronald Reagan Pkwy
59 Mi.
River Rd
Yellow River Water Reclamation Plant
58 Mi.
57 Mi.
Turkey Creek
Five Forks Trickum Road
56 Mi.
Britt Shoals
Watson Creek
55 Mi.
Powerlines
Flood of 2009
Garner Creek
Gwinnett County
Five Forks Trickum Rd
54 Mi.
Killian Hill Road
Weed Branch
53 Mi.
78
Powerlines
McDaniel's Bluff
52 Mi.
Shoals
Killian Hill Rd
Pounds Creek
51 Mi.
Yellow River Wildlife Sanctuary
Pounds Creek
Sexton's Bridge
50 Mi.
Vecoma at Yellow River
Shoal
78
49 Mi.
264
Sand Shoals
124
Jacks Creek Water Reclamation Facility
48 Mi.
N
Shoal
W
E
Annistown Rd
DeKalb County
Annistown Falls
Shoals
S
47 Mi.
Yellow River Park
0 0.25 0.5 1 Mile

Annistown

Length 14 miles (Oak Road to Yellow River Park)

Class I–III

Time 6–8 hours

Minimum Level Water levels of 6 feet and 200–300 cubic feet per second (cfs) at the Killian Hill Road gauge are generally necessary to render this section navigable. High flows can create dangerous water levels at this section's whitewater runs, located between U.S. 78 and Yellow River Park, which hold two Class II–III obstacles. For whitewater paddlers, optimal flows are 350–850 cfs for this section, though higher levels can be run. The urbanized nature of the Upper Yellow River watershed means that water levels can fluctuate wildly. Stream gauges should be consulted before embarking on any trips, and major obstacles should be scouted before running.

River Gauge The nearest river gauge is located at Killian Hill Road, in the middle of this section: https://waterdata.usgs.gov/ga/nwis/uv/?site_no=02206500&agency_cd=USGS.

Launch Site Oak Road lacks both parking and a developed launch site, but it is possible to access the river via the right-of-way at the bridge. Paddlers must seek permission from property owners before accessing the river from private property.

DIRECTIONS From exit 104 on I-85 (Pleasant Hill Rd.) travel east on Pleasant Hill Road 2.9 miles to the Ronald Reagan Parkway exchange. Use the right lane to enter Ronald Reagan Parkway and then travel 1.5 miles to the Bethesda Church Road exit. After exiting, turn left on Bethesda Church Road and proceed 0.5 mile. Turn right on Winn Drive and proceed 0.8 mile. Turn right on Gloster Road and proceed 0.3 mile, cross the railroad tracks, and continue hard right on Oak Road 0.6 mile to the river. The best access is along the right-of-way on the south side of the river.

Take Out Site The take out site is located within Gwinnett County's Yellow River Park and requires a 0.4-mile carry to parking areas in the park. Alternatively, it is possible to park your vehicle along Juhan Road while loading your boat. This reduces the carry to about 200 feet. Cars should not be parked at this location long term.

DIRECTIONS From Oak Road Bridge, travel south on Oak Road 2.5 miles. Turn right on Highpoint Road and proceed 2.6 miles. Turn right on Ga. 124 and travel 2.8 miles. Turn right on Annistown Road and proceed 1.0 mile. Turn left on Juhan Road and proceed 0.9 mile to the entrance of Yellow River Park, on the left. The closest parking to the take out is in the parking area for the pedestrian trail.

Alternative Take Out Sites The river is crossed by six roads in this 13-mile run, and launching from them allows for trips of various lengths. Access at U.S. 78, though undeveloped, is popular because it provides the closest access to the whitewater between this bridge and Yellow River Park downstream. It also enables pad-

STRAINERS, GWINNETT COUNTY

dlers floating from upstream to avoid these obstacles. Access at other bridge crossings is also undeveloped. If you are accessing the river via private property rather than rights-of-way, permission must be sought. Take outs should be scouted before your journey to ensure suitable access and parking.

DIRECTIONS TO U.S. 78 From Oak Road Bridge, travel south on Oak Road 2.5 miles. Turn right on Highpoint Road and proceed 1.6 miles. Turn right on U.S. 78 and proceed 2.9 miles to the bridge. There is no developed parking area at this site.

Description Small and intimate, the navigable sections of the Yellow River in Gwinnett County offer some of the best whitewater in the Atlanta area, though long stretches of flatwater must be crossed to access the rapids. And although it passes through the heart of Gwinnett's suburban sprawl and residential development, the river corridor maintains a mostly wild appeal. Cross-river strainers commonly clog the upper portions of the run, but downstream of Killian Hill Road the path becomes more open and the shoals more numerous. Two sets of Class II–III rapids culminate in 7-foot-high Annistown Falls, an obstacle that is best portaged except for those with adequate whitewater-paddling experience. Immediately below the falls and Annistown Road Bridge, the river descends over Class II rapids and then for the next half mile an almost continuous run of Class I shoals. The river corridor is rich in cultural history, and at many sites the remains of historic bridges, mills, and dams can still be seen.

Points of Interest

MILE 60.6 (33.899061, −84.073489) Ronald Reagan Parkway. According to the Ronald Regan Presidential Library, only three places in Georgia are named in honor of the fortieth president, who defeated Georgia's Jimmy Carter in the 1980 election. Upon learning of the parkway bearing his name, Reagan, as was his habit, recalled an anecdote. He told the story of a small Irish town from which his ancestors came naming the town pub in his honor: "I'm very proud of that pub and I know what an honor is it. But I must admit when I thought of something being named after me, I was thinking more along the lines of a building or highway!"

MILE 60.1 (33.894172, −84.077407) Bridge Pilings. Here are the remains of a bridge. It is likely that this bridge carried a road in the early and mid-20th century that ran from the Bethesda Church community to the north across the river here to Five Forks to the southeast. The bridge is noted on 1938 Gwinnett County maps.

MILE 59.5 (33.889896, −84.081844) Sweetwater Creek. This large tributary, which enters on river right, significantly contributes to the Yellow's flow. In late 2019 when an angler landed an invasive snakehead fish on a pond in the Sweetwater Creek watershed, it set off alarm bells among Georgia's wildlife managers. It was the first time the invasive fish, native to Asia and Africa, had been reported in a water body in Georgia. In 2002, the federal government banned the trade in snakehead fish because of the damage they can cause to native fish pop-

NEAR RONALD REAGAN PARKWAY, GWINNETT COUNTY

ulations. The long, slim snakeheads, which have dorsal fins running the lengths of their bodies and grow up to three feet long, reproduce at a high rate, and they can outcompete native fish such as bass and bream. The voracious predators can crawl like snakes on land and survive out of the water for several days. Georgia Department of Natural Resources wildlife officials were uncertain how the fish came to inhabit the pond, but immediately called on anglers to be on the lookout for the fish and kill and freeze any that they might land.

MILE 58.5 (33.880323, −84.083888) Yellow River Water Reclamation Plant. On river right is the discharge from this sewage treatment plant operated by Gwinnett County. Built in the early 1980s, the facility was extensively renovated and upgraded between 2006 and 2012, at a cost of about $245 million. That modernization expanded the facility's capacity to 22 million gallons a day and helped eliminate the need for five smaller wastewater treatment facilities on tributaries to the Yellow. Each of the large round structures visible from the river is capable of holding 20 million gallons of sewage. The construction of each tank required a delivery from one concrete truck every 2 minutes for 14 hours. Since the plant is surrounded by subdivisions on all sides, one goal of the redesign was to eliminate the offensive odors that naturally plague sewage treatment plants. Enclosed tanks, air scrubbers, and the use of ultraviolet disinfection rather than chlorine have helped turn a facility that was a pariah into a mostly benign neighbor. The state-of-the-art facility also includes a LEED-certified Gold operations building and a system for capturing methane gas and converting it to renewable energy. The Yellow wraps around the 130-acre site for more than a mile.

MILE 56.4 (33.873965, −84.083928) Five Forks Trickum Road. In the 1800s, this was the site of a critical bridge over the Yellow, connecting Lawrenceville to Stone Mountain and Atlanta. It was also the site of the Yellow River post office, established in 1846 by Thomas P. Hudson. During the Civil War and the Union Army's occupation of Atlanta, this area fell victim to a Union foraging expedition. Throughout September and October 1864, the Union forces occupying Atlanta periodically ventured into the surrounding countryside to acquire food for soldiers and livestock. Near the community of Yellow River, members of the local home guard, known as the Hudson Guards, attacked the foragers before retreating across the bridge and attempting to burn it. The Union cavalry pursued the Confederates across the still-usable bridge into Lawrenceville and discovered on the east side of the river abundant forage. There they loaded 300 wagons with corn. The Union colonel J. S. Robinson reported of the expedition: "I found here a productive country and had no difficulty in loading the entire train (of wagons) . . . On the following day my brigade . . . returned without accident to its encampment at Atlanta . . . My brigade secured about 6000 bushels of corn besides the usual amount of provisions and other promiscuous articles." It was also likely at this bridge that Major Charles Henry Smith of the Confederate Army tied a rock around court documents pertaining to treason files that the Confederacy was prosecuting and sank them in the river. Major Smith went on to fame as Bill Arp, the celebrated humorist and columnist for the *Atlanta Constitu-*

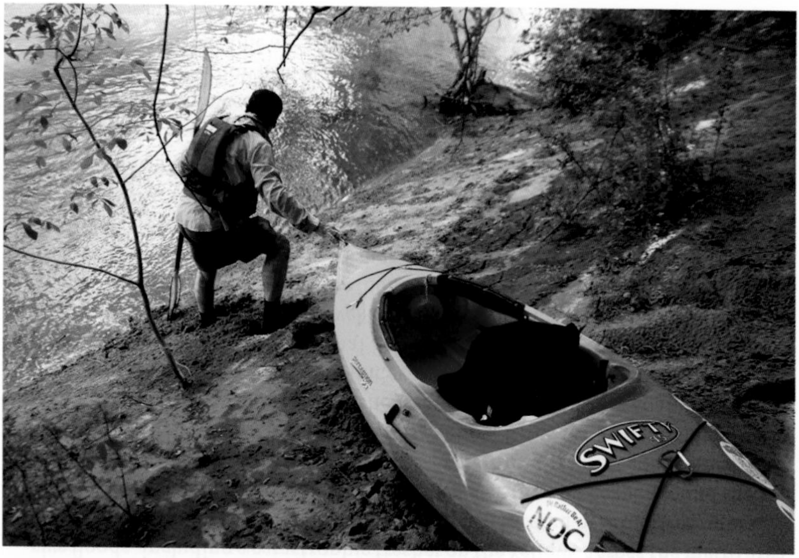

LAUNCH AT FIVE FORKS TRICKUM ROAD, GWINNETT COUNTY

tion during the late 1800s. In the years following the Civil War, a seven-foot-high dam was constructed on the river here, diverting water to a gristmill operated by the Simmons family. The millpond became the baptismal pool for the nearby Yellow River Baptist Church, established in 1871. The original Yellow River post office building and the circa-1840s Hudson-Nash home have been saved and now form the heart a Gwinnett County park dedicated to preserving the history of the Yellow River community, located 0.6 mile east of the river here. This spot on the river is also considered the uppermost launch site of the Yellow River Water Trail, a 53-mile recreational boating trail stretching from here to Jackson Lake that is being developed by the nonprofit Yellow River Water Trail in cooperation with local governments.

MILE 55.6 (33.867666, −84.076639) Britt Shoals. These Class I shoals occupy a picturesque bend in the river. From here downstream to Killian Hill Road, several small shoals break up the flatwater. The Hugh Britt Jr. family settled in the Five Forks area in the 1830s and ultimately spawned a slew of Britts, who now populate the area. One of best-known Britts was William Clifford, the great-grandson of Hugh Jr., who in 1930 came to teach at Snellville's school. In 1931 when a summer hailstorm destroyed the cotton crop, Britt encouraged local families to plant vegetables, promising that he would have a cannery up and running at the school by harvest time, thus enabling the community to preserve their harvest for consumption during the winter. With a donation of 10,000 cans from Sears, Roebuck and assistance from the Red Cross, the cannery helped feed local families during the height of the Great Depression. In 1932, the community cannery put

BRITT SHOALS, GWINNETT COUNTY

up 50,000 containers of fruits and vegetables and became a model followed by other communities across the state and beyond. William Clifford Britt served as principal of Snellville High School from 1945 to 1956, and today W. C. Britt Elementary School in Snellville bears his name.

MILE 54.9 (33.860506, −84.076122) Flood of 2009. In September 2009, as much as 20 inches of rain fell on parts of Atlanta in less than 24 hours, spawning massive floods, including a catastrophic freshet on the Yellow. Across the metro area, nearly 17,000 homes were flooded, including two located here on river right. The flood was unlike any previous one in part because the landscape around the Yellow had changed so dramatically in the preceding three decades. Since more than 70 percent of the land in the Upper Yellow River watershed is developed, stormwater coursed directly into the river rather than slowly soaking into the ground, as it would have done on undeveloped land. The Yellow peaked at 16,500 cubic feet per second (cfs); normal flows in September are 257 cfs. The predictable results were higher flood levels. Structures that previously would have been safely outside the floodplain were inundated. Following the flood, federal, state, and local agencies redrew flood maps to reflect the changed landscape, and Gwinnett County purchased and demolished the flood-damaged homes here.

MILE 54.1 (33.853269, −84.078444) Killian Hill Road. Just upstream of Killian Hill Road is a low river-wide ledge that makes a good surfing spot. The bridge soaring high above the river here was completed in 2013, four years after historic floods overflowed the circa-1960 bridge. Historically, the bridge spanning the river here was known as McDaniel's Bridge. William McDaniel moved to this area in 1823 and became a leader in the community that grew into Lilburn.

MILE 53.8 (33.853984, −84.082737) McDaniel's Bluff. Downstream of Killian Hill Road, the river runs headlong into a high bluff fronted with overhanging rock formations.

MILE 53.7 (33.855694, −84.083310) Powerlines.

MILE 52.6 (33.846839, −84.086329) Powerlines.

MILE 51.6 (33.838810, −84.085584) Shoals. Over the next 200 feet, the river spills over a series of four small ledges.

MILE 51.0 (33.834862, −84.089399) Yellow River Wildlife Sanctuary. On river left here is a wildlife sanctuary that has been a fixture along the river since 1983, when Art Rilling moved his Stone Mountain Game Ranch to this location. The ranch, which had been housed at Stone Mountain Park from 1962 until 1982, made its home at this location for more than 30 years, displaying as many as 600 wild, exotic, and domestic animals in a petting-zoo environment. After running afoul of U.S. Department of Agriculture inspectors and coming under fire from activists with the People for the Ethical Treatment of Animals, the ranch shut its gates in 2017. In 2019, the ranch reopened under new ownership as the Yellow River Wildlife Sanctuary, with improved enclosures and habitats for the animals. Among the ranch's most famous residents was General Beauregard Lee, a groundhog that each February 2 drew a crowd to the ranch intent on discovering whether they would enjoy an early spring or six more weeks of winter. Through the years, according to Rilling, General Lee's predictions enjoyed a 94 percent accuracy rating.

SHOALS AT YELLOW RIVER PARK, GWINNETT COUNTY

The Groundhog Day tradition has its origins in European folklore. In Old World cultures, February 2 was celebrated as the midway point between the winter and spring solstices, and because it was traditionally the time when ewes gave birth to their lambs, it became known as Imbolc—"ewe's milk." For Europeans, it was a time of expectancy and new life in the midst of the harsh winter. In time, Christian church leaders appropriated the holiday into their spiritual calendar as the fortieth day after the birth of Jesus. European tradition held that if on February 2 a hedgehog emerged to sunny skies, six more weeks of winter were in store, but if the day was overcast, an early spring could be expected. German immigrants living in Pennsylvania, finding no hedgehogs there, substituted the groundhog, and they are said to be the first to have used this method of weather prediction in the United States during the 1800s.

Groundhogs are, in fact, commonly seen along Georgia rivers, since they tend to inhabit the ecotones where woodlands give way to open spaces. When the game ranch closed, General Lee was moved to the Dauset Trails Nature Center in Butts County, where he continues to predict the weather each February. In keeping with the exotic animals that have lived along the river here through the years, the riverbank along the game ranch is crowded with English ivy and bamboo, exotic plants that create "deserts" in which native plants cannot survive.

MILE 50.8 (33.832403, −84.089119) Pounds Creek. This tributary on river right drains 40-acre Lake Lucerne. It was originally built by Alvin Phillips and his wife, Allene, in the late 1930s and named Possum Lake for the abundance of opossums they encountered there. An Atlanta businessman, Phillips built the lake and his lakeside home as a rural retreat and a business venture. At a time when the big federal reservoirs were a decade or more away from completion, there was a demand for private lakes offering fishing for $1 a day. The Phillipses provided boats for rent and, later, rustic cabins, placing classified ads in Atlanta newspapers asking, "Have you seen the sun set across beautiful Possum Lake?" During the 1940s, a youth hostel on the shores welcomed junior and senior high students from Decatur and Atlanta schools, and *Atlanta Constitution* fishing reports through the 1960s routinely included big catches from Possum Lake, including a 53-pound catfish in 1949. Some four years later, the dam failed, creating a roar of crashing water and earth. Mrs. Phillips's description of the catastrophe reflects the fears of the day. She told the *Atlanta Constitution*: "I thought it was either a tornado or the Russians." The dam was rebuilt, and a decade later the Phillipses' land had been purchased, subdivided, and offered for sale by Suburban Developments, Inc., which advertised "waterfront living at its best" around the "sparkling, spring-fed" lake. But the "possum" moniker was gone. As one longtime resident noted in a Lake Lucerne Estates Civic Club history, the developers decided it would be difficult to sell fine houses on a lake named after the much-maligned marsupial. Today, the lake is surrounded by acres of suburban neighborhoods.

MILE 50.2 (33.831534, −84.080138) Sexton's Bridge. Before the 1930s and the construction of Ga. 10 / U.S. 78 upstream, the road between Snellville and Stone

Mountain crossed the river on this bridge, the stone pier of which still stands on river left. For Jim Cofer, the historian and author of *200 Years of Snellville History*, this location holds vivid memories. His father, Wendell Cofer, as a youngster found in this bridge a way to earn a bit of money when the river rose. During the late 1920s, the road leading to the bridge would become inundated. Though still passable by vehicles, the danger lay in keeping the vehicle on the raised roadway above the adjoining floodplain. For a nickel a car, Wendell would walk in front of the drivers, directing them safely to the bridge. Later, the rural mail carrier and Baptist minister returned to this spot to employ hand-cranked telephone magnetos in a highly effective method of electrofishing. "I can remember him coming home with a 100 pounds of catfish squirming in a bag," Jim recalled. "Of course, that was highly illegal." The U.S. 78 bridge upstream is the take out for those wishing to avoid the whitewater downstream.

MILE 50.1 (33.830162, −84.081407) Vecoma at Yellow River. On river left here, bride-and-groom sightings are not uncommon. Vecoma is a wedding and events facility that has operated on this site since the 1990s, but the story of Vecoma stretches back much further. In 1927, Cotton and Venie Mather built a 6-sided cabin made entirely of stone and wood taken from the property and named it Vecoma (mashing together the first two letters of each their first names and surname). Mather, who operated a successful furniture store chain in Georgia, South Carolina, and Florida, was a noted world traveler. By 1939, when commercial air travel was still in its infancy, Mather had logged 63,000 miles, including a transatlantic flight on the ill-fated *Hindenburg* zeppelin after attending the

UNKNOWN RUINS AT SAND SHOALS, GWINNETT COUNTY

1936 Summer Olympics in Berlin. For all his travels, the Yellow River was his and his wife's escape from the bustle of Atlanta. The foundation and chimney of the original cabin are still part of the landscape on the property.

MILE 49.5 (33.825789, −84.085709) Shoal. This ledge, about two feet high, spans the width of the river and is best run on river right.

MILE 48.9 (33.820105, −84.083431) Sand Shoals. Noted in a 1903 U.S. Army Corps of Engineers river survey, the name given to these shoals may be misleading, for there is more rock than sand here, creating a formidable set of challenging Class II–III rapids. The river drops an estimated 14 feet over a span of about 700 feet. The run begins with a 4-foot ledge with recovery pool, followed by a 3-foot ledge and another recovery pool. Below the second ledge, the river splits around an island. The left-hand route spills over a precipitous rock garden at the head of the island, bends around to a short ledge on the island's flank, and then flows through a series of small shoals at the island's tail. Flows of 350–850 cubic feet per second (cfs) are recommended for these shoals. The river-right route around the island is impassable at low-to-normal water levels, but at flows approaching 1,000 cfs, paddlers will be forced right. At such flows, numerous ledges at Sand Shoals can create dangerous hydraulics. Scouting this rapid is recommended. On river right below the second ledge is a stand of stacked stone, likely the remains of a bridge noted on late 19th-century maps. No records indicate the existence of a mill here after that time, but the same surveyors that named this Sand Shoals in 1903 noted that they made a "chisel mark on large rock opposite old mill," suggesting that at some time during the 1800s the power of this shoal was harnessed.

MILE 48.1 (33.811643, −84.075401) Jacks Creek Water Reclamation Facility. On river left here is a sign noting the outfall of one of Gwinnett County's sewage treatment plants. It was closed in 2012 with the completion of the expanded Yellow River WRF upstream. This project, in tandem with the closing of four small facilities discharging into the Yellow, has significantly improved the health of the river by reducing incidents of bacterial pollution.

MILE 47.7 (33.807575, −84.078302) Shoal. This shoal warns of the impending Annistown Falls, located about 1,000 feet downstream.

MILE 47.5 (33.805155, −84.075923) Annistown Falls. Here a rock ledge about six feet high runs diagonally from river right upstream to the north, creating this significant Class III rapid. It should be scouted before running, and attempted only by those with adequate whitewater-paddling experience. The best location for scouting is on the right bank where a rock outcropping slopes gently to the river above the falls. This is also the best portage route, but in high water this portage and scouting location can become inundated. Accessing this portage route means ferrying across the river directly above the falls.

Human history here dates back more than 1,000 years. Archaeological studies conducted in 1998 revealed a natural-rock outcrop or shelter where Native American ceramics were found, along with circular-shaped depressions carved into the walls of the shelter. The finds suggested that humans occupied the spot

ANNISTOWN FALLS SHOALS, GWINNETT COUNTY

between AD 1000 and 1400. When European settlers arrived, they wasted no time in harnessing the falls, and a succession of families used the power of the river to grind corn and wheat, including the Ballards, Steadmans, and Holts. By the late 19th century, the river was powering a sawmill that produced 150,000 board feet of lumber and 40,000 shingles annually. Come the turn of the century, an 11-foot-high dam diverted water to power a cotton mill, but by 1908, a fire had destroyed the mill, and operations at these falls ceased. Rebar protruding from rocks along the falls is the only obvious visual evidence of this lengthy history of manufacturing. Annistown was named by C. J. Haden, who took ownership of the mill operations in 1897 and bestowed the name to honor his wife or his daughter. In early references, it is spelled "Annestown." By portaging around the falls, paddlers can run a set of Class II ledges stretching from beneath the Annistown Road bridge about 150 feet downstream. The first ledge is best run on far river left adjacent to the bridge pier. A series of waves follows, leading to the second ledge, which is best run along the centerline of the river. The second ledge has a strong hydraulic that can be dangerous at high water levels.

MILE 47.3 (33.803506, −84.073832) Shoals. Downstream for the next 0.4 mile is an almost continuous section of fast-moving water and shoals, culminating in a small ledge where the river enters Gwinnett County's Yellow River Park. The take out for this section is located on river right—a flat, sloping rock outcropping that leads to footpaths and Juhan Road. To avoid a 0.2-mile carry to the parking area in the park, boats can be carried along footpaths a short distance to the shoulder of Juhan Road and loaded on vehicles there. The parking area is a 0.2-mile walk downstream along Juhan Road or along walking paths in the park.

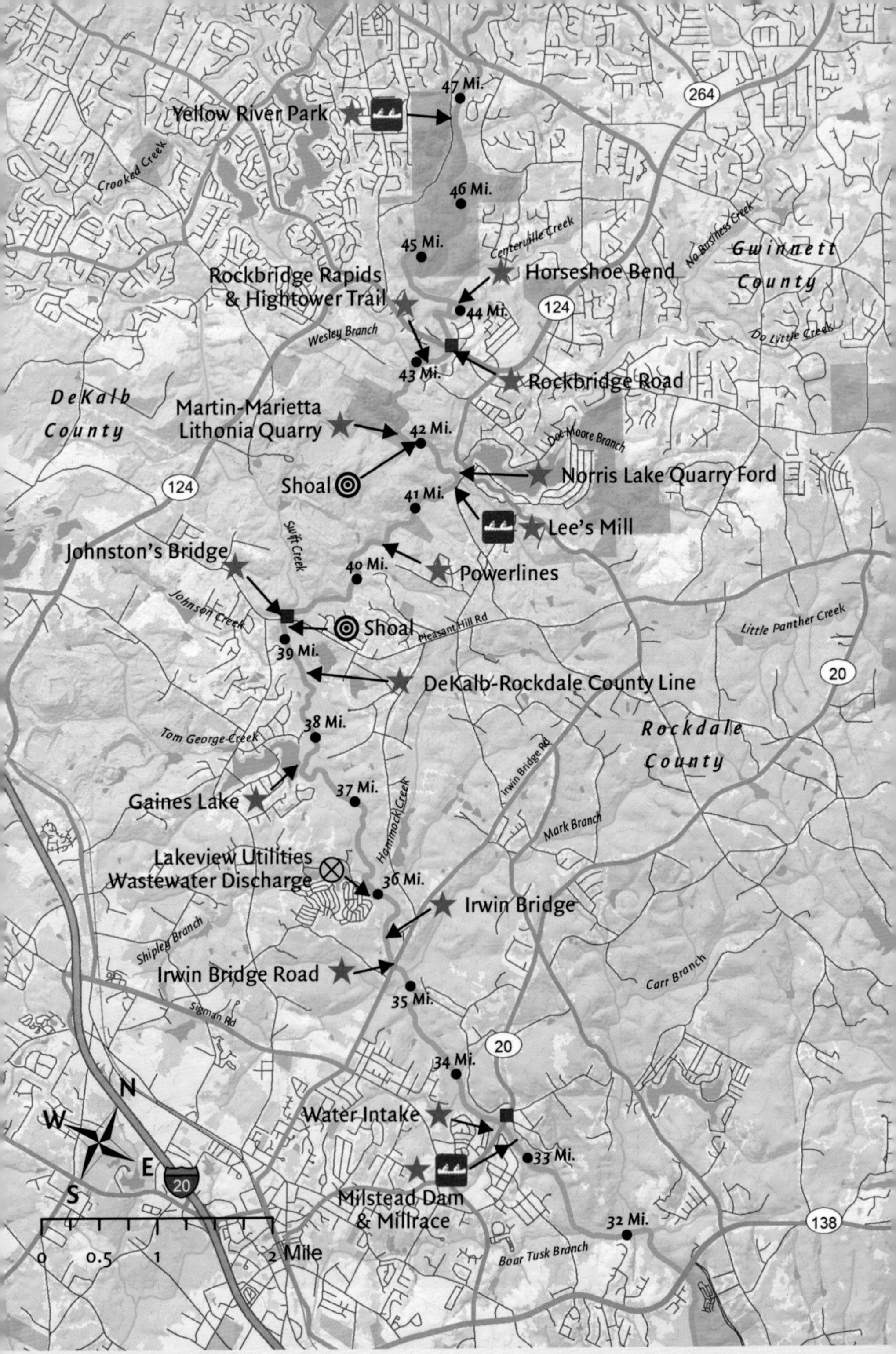

47 Mi.
264
Yellow River Park
Crooked Creek
46 Mi.
45 Mi.
Centerville Creek
No Business Creek
Gwinnett
County
Rockbridge Rapids
& Hightower Trail
Horseshoe Bend
44 Mi.
124
Wesley Branch
Do Little Creek
43 Mi.
Rockbridge Road
DeKalb
County
Martin-Marietta
Lithonia Quarry
42 Mi.
Doe Moore Branch
Norris Lake Quarry Ford
124
Shoal
41 Mi.
Lee's Mill
Johnston's Bridge
Swift Creek
40 Mi.
Powerlines
Johnson Creek
Shoal
Pleasant Hill Rd
Little Panther Creek
39 Mi.
20
DeKalb-Rockdale County Line
38 Mi.
Tom George Creek
Rockdale
County
Irwin Bridge Rd
37 Mi.
Gaines Lake
Hammock Creek
Mark Branch
Lakeview Utilities
Wastewater Discharge
36 Mi.
Irwin Bridge
Shipley Branch
Irwin Bridge Road
Carr Branch
35 Mi.
Sigman Rd
20
34 Mi.
N
W
E
S
Water Intake
33 Mi.
20
Milstead Dam
& Millrace
32 Mi.
138
0
0.5
1
2 Mile
Boar Tusk Branch

Rockbridge

Length 15 miles (Yellow River Park to Milstead Dam)
Class I
Time 7–9 hours
Minimum Level Water levels of 1.4 feet and 80 cubic feet per second at the Lithonia / Pleasant Hill Road gauge are adequate to render this section navigable. The urbanized nature of the Upper Yellow River watershed means that water levels can fluctuate wildly. Stream gauges should be consulted before embarking on any trips, and major obstacles should be scouted before running.

River Gauges Three river gauges are located in this section: at Ga. 124 (Rockbridge Rd.): https://waterdata.usgs.gov/ga/nwis/uv/?site_no=02207120&PARAmeter_cd=00065,00060,00062,00010; at Pleasant Hill Road: https://waterdata.usgs.gov/ga/nwis/uv/?site_no=02207220&PARAmeter_cd=00065,00060,00062,00010; and at Ga. 20 at Milstead: https://waterdata.usgs.gov/ga/nwis/uv/?site_no=02207300&PARAmeter_cd=00065,00060,00062,00010.

Launch Site The launch site is located about 0.2 mile from the parking lot for the pedestrian trail in Gwinnett County's Yellow River Park. But boats can be dropped off on the side of Juhan Road where a walking trail crosses the road about 0.2 mile north of the pedestrian-trail parking area in the park. After unloading and transporting boats about 200 feet down the trail toward the river, visitors can return their cars to the trail parking area.

DIRECTIONS From the intersection of U.S. 78 and East Park Boulevard, travel south on East Park Boulevard 0.1 mile, continuing straight on to Rockbridge Road. Continue 0.5 mile to the intersection with West Park Place Boulevard. Continue straight on Rockbridge Road 0.8 mile to the intersection with North Deshon Road. Continue straight to Annistown Road and follow it for 1.2 miles. Turn right on Juhan Road and proceed 0.8 mile to the entrance and park on the left.

Take Out Site The take out site is located on river right upstream of Milstead Dam. A moderately sloped bank meets the river directly in front of the millrace entering the Milstead hydropower operation. Parking is along Main Street upstream of the take out. The dirt road leading into the mill ruins and hydro plant are private and sometimes gated.

DIRECTIONS From Yellow River Park, return to Juhan Road and turn left. Proceed 0.8 mile. Turn left on South Rockbridge Road and travel 0.7 mile to Ga. 124 (Rockbridge Rd.). Turn left and proceed 1.1 miles. Turn right on Norris Lake Road and travel 1.0 mile. At Norris Lake, turn right and continue on Norris Lake Road 1.5 miles. At Pleasant Hill Road, continue straight to Humphries Road, proceeding 1.6 miles. Turn right on Irwin Bridge Road and travel 0.3 mile. Turn left on Mt. Zion / Almand Road and travel 1.0 mile to Ga. 20. Turn right and proceed 1.9 miles. Turn left on Main Street in Milstead and proceed 0.1 mile to the dirt road on the left. Park outside the gate along Main Street.

Alternative Take Out Sites Rockbridge Road, Pleasant Hill Road, and Irwin Bridge Road cross the river in this section, providing trips of 3, 7, and 11 miles, respectively. There are no developed take out sites or parking areas at these locations. If you are accessing the river via private property rather than rights-of-way, permission must be sought. Take outs should be scouted before your journey to ensure suitable access and parking. Additionally, an undeveloped Yellow River Water Trail take out site along Norris Bridge Road can be used to create a 5-mile journey.

DIRECTIONS TO THE NORRIS LAKE ROAD TAKE OUT From Yellow River Park, return to Juhan Road and turn left. Proceed 0.8 mile. Turn left on South Rockbridge Road and travel 0.7 mile to Ga. 124 (Rockbridge Rd.). Turn left and proceed 1.1 miles. Turn right on Norris Lake Road and travel 1.0 mile. At Norris Lake, turn right, proceed about 0.1 mile, and look for the footpath to the river, on the right.

Description Although multiple tributaries contribute their flow, the Yellow doesn't expand much in size below Yellow River Park. It remains narrow, shaded, and intimate; cross-river strainers are not uncommon. Periodic shoals interrupt a mostly flatwater journey. The cultural history along the river spans thousands of years, from the Native American ford at "Rock Bridge" to a series of small commercial fishing lakes flanking the river and dating to the mid-20th century. Those havens for anglers are now amenity lakes for the residential developments that cropped up during the latter half of the 20th century as the growth of the suburbs gobbled up land in Gwinnett, DeKalb, and Rockdale Counties. Mill sites dating to the 1800s are also notable.

Points of Interest

MILE 46.8 (33.797442, −84.073874) Yellow River Park. From the launch site, this Gwinnett County park stretches for nearly two miles downriver, including a 1.5-mile stretch in which the park encompasses both banks of the river. With 691 acres of undisturbed land, the park is known as one of Gwinnett's remaining natural escapes. Used primarily for passive recreation, the park holds 12 miles of biking, hiking, and equestrian trails. During the past 40 years, Gwinnett has become almost synonymous with urban sprawl. Between 1970 and 1980, the county more than doubled in size, to 166,903 people. Since then another 800,000 people have been added, and today it still consistently ranks among the fastest-growing counties in the country. A 2004 University of Georgia analysis of tree cover showed that between 1991 and 2005, the county lost 15 percent of its tree canopy. It was during this explosive growth that the county's public utilities department abandoned a plan to build a sewage treatment plant here, and the parks and recreation department took over management of the land.

YELLOW RIVER PARK, GWINNETT COUNTY

MILE 44.0 (33.777186, −84.061165) Horseshoe Bend. Even in Georgia's Piedmont region, where rivers tend to be kept in their courses by the hard, rocky underlying rock, rivers will, over time, change course. Such is the case here, where a cut-through formed, isolating an oxbow bend on river left. Maps show this oxbow in existence during the mid-20th century.

MILE 43.5 (33.773052, −84.058431) Rockbridge Road. Just upstream of the modern Ga. 124 / Rockbridge Road are these stone piers, evidence of an earlier iteration of this historic river crossing. Originally, Hightower Trail, a Native American path, crossed the river near here (perhaps on the rock outcroppings located above the island 0.3 mile downstream). By the mid-1800s, a proper bridge had been established here; though built of wood, it borrowed the name of the natural rock "bridge" used by Native Americans. During its early years, the bridge funneled travelers to this location, and a notorious tavern did business nearby. One account described the clientele thus: "Men of all classes, especially the fun lovers, the dissolute, the bullies among the fighters, the gamblers and the drunkards of which there were many. As the population increased, this place became a regular knock-down drag-out black eye and bloody nose resort" (Vivian Price, *History of DeKalb County, Georgia, 1822–1900*).

During the Civil War, Rockbridge played an important role in a Union cavalry raid aimed at destroying railroad bridges over the Yellow and Alcovy Rivers near Covington. On the evening of July 21, 1864, Union horsemen crossed Rockbridge and descended on the plantation of Thomas Maguire, who documented the intrusion in his diary: "At 12 or 1 o'clock the Yankees came here in force. Knocked us up. The house was soon filled with thieving Yankees, robbed us of nearly everything they could carry off. Broke open all our trunks, drawers, etc. and carried off the keys. They must have practiced roguery from their childhood up, so well they appeared to know the art." The Yankees, for their part, were impressed with what they found along the Yellow. One Union soldier described the landscape as the "finest and best country we had seen in the whole South . . . fine plantations, large mansions, everything indicating wealth and prosperity." Indeed, Thomas Maguire was successful at his Promised Land home and plantation. Maguire had grown the homestead, established in the 1820s, into a plantation of some 900 acres worked by 26 slaves. Among the items lost to the Yankees, enumerated by Maguire in official filings with Gwinnett County, were 600 pounds of bacon, valued at $2,400, and 12 bales of cotton, valued at $6,000. But his most valuable possessions were the 4 slaves that left with the Union soldiers—valued at $13,000. Margaret Mitchell is said to have used details in Maguire's diary to help her craft *Gone with the Wind*.

In the 1920s, Maguire's Promised Land home and a portion of the original plantation were purchased by the Livseys, a family of African American descent, who soon established a thriving African American community centered on the former plantation. In 2016, Gwinnett County purchased the historic Promised Land home, intending to restore the home and use it to tell the story of the Maguire and Livsey families. The home is located less than a mile east of the river on Anderson Livsey Lane.

MILE 43.1 (33.769506, −84.061027) Rockbridge Rapids & Hightower Trail. Though the modern Rockbridge crossings were built 0.3 mile upstream, if you were a Native American traveling on foot, this site, where an island splits the river and a long narrow rock outcropping extends almost to the east bank, would likely have kept your feet drier than the crossings upstream. Today, the "rockbridge" and island force the river east and west. The west or right channel should be avoided, since it narrows to a sizable waterfall that is often choked with strainers. The left channel offers a fun ride over a 3-foot ledge. Be mindful of the boat-swamping rock just below the ledge. Another set of small shoals must be navigated at the tail of the island.

A half mile due east of here is the Anderson family cemetery, which serves as the final resting place of Thomas Maguire. Maguire, owner of the Promised Land plantation, noted above, married into the Anderson family—twice. He first married Jane Anderson, but after bearing three children, Jane developed blood poisoning after scratching here leg on a pin in her clothing while dismounting her horse. A year after her death, her sister, Elizabeth, at the age of 17 became Maguire's new bride. She raised her sister's three children and gave birth to eight more. The depredations inflicted by Union soldiers on the Maguire and Anderson families during the Civil War did not end with the encounter in July 1864. Upon breaking camp in Atlanta to head for Savannah in November of that year, Union soldiers again visited Promised Land. This time they burned the plantation's stables, barn, gin house, and other buildings while Maguire and family hid in nearby woods. They did, however, spare the house,

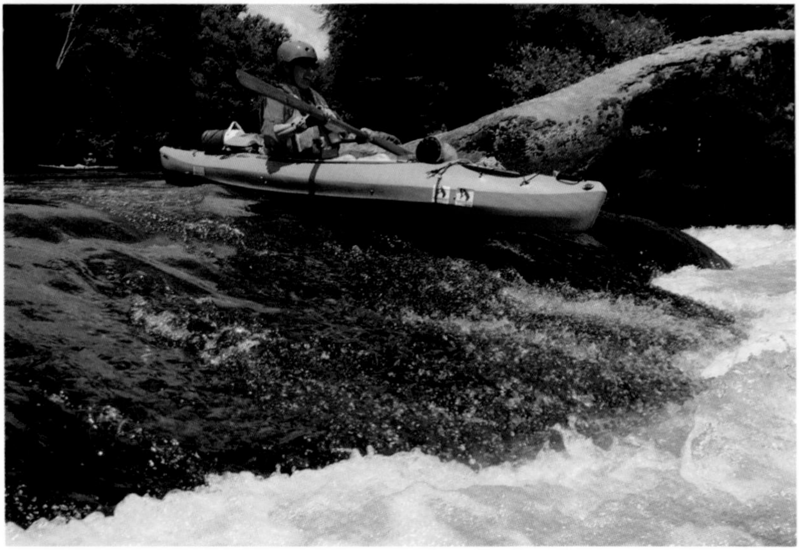

ROCKBRIDGE RAPID, DEKALB COUNTY

which still survives. Though Maguire may have never known it, the goods taken from his plantation did ultimately "sting" the Union soldiers. David Evans, in *Sherman's Horsemen: Union Cavalry Operations in the Atlanta Campaign*, recounts the story of a beehive that soldiers likely took from Promised Land during their July raid: "They had wrapped it in a rubber blanket or poncho and were taking turns balancing the load . . . on their saddles. This worked well until the cover suddenly slipped off (on one unfortunate cavalryman) . . . As the bees began buzzing around his head, he unceremoniously dumped the hive in the middle of the road . . . Horses reared and bucked wildly . . . Before their fury was spent, the enraged insects stung a horse to death and nearly stampeded the whole regiment."

MILE 42.3 (33.760267, –84.059271) Martin-Marietta Lithonia Quarry. On river right is an impressive outcropping of Lithonia gneiss, reminiscent of the landscapes of nearby Stone Mountain and Arabia Mountain. Beyond the outcropping is the Martin-Marietta Lithonia Quarry (formerly Consolidated Quarries), a site that has operated continuously since 1929, producing crushed stone and other aggregate that finds its way into construction projects across the region. The geology of the area runs deep—both literally and figuratively. Nearby is the "city of stone," Lithonia, which borrows its name from the Greek "lithos," meaning stone. Lithonia's golden age of quarrying was around 1900. In 1919, 12 quarries were in operation in the area, mostly excavating stone for paving blocks and curbs. In the 1940s, the miners found a new use for gneiss: as an additive in chicken feed. It turns out that finely crushed stone added to chicken feed provides the birds with important minerals and aids in their digestion. Today, numerous quarries still operate in the Lithonia area.

MILE 42.1 (33.760410, −84.055960) **Shoal.** This is a river-wide, gently sloping granite slide with a large outcropping of rock on river right, adjacent to and below the slide. It is a good place to take a break.

MILE 41.6 (33.759522, −84.049278) **Norris Lake Quarry Ford.** Beneath the surface of the river here is a curious wooden structure that likely dates to the late 1930s, when Clarence Norris began constructing the dam for his commercial fishing lake, which opened in 1941 to much fanfare. At the time, Norris was a well-known angler, having created a stir by showing off a massive Lake Burton bass in downtown Atlanta. Read the headline in the *Atlanta Constitution* in May 1940: "10 ½ Pound Bass, Biggest of 1940, Causes a Traffic Jam Here." When the 175-acre lake opened, Norris offered 20 boats for rent and even provided a snack boat that delivered soft drinks, sandwiches, and cigarettes to anglers. Throughout the 1940s, the lake was regularly noted in *Constitution* fishing reports. By the early 1950s, homesites were being offered for sale around the impoundment on Doc Moore Branch. Newspaper ads lured prospective homeowners with lots for $295: "The developers welcome the many who will be eager to establish for themselves a cottage, home or hideaway, featuring fresh, clear beaches, boating, fishing, nature study or good-old-fashioned lazing around." Today, Norris Lake is a residential community of some 900 homes. Norris's fishing paradise was likely facilitated by that curious wooden structure on the river bottom here—and the presence of Consolidated Quarries on the opposite side of the river. To build his dam, Norris needed rocks, and lots of them. Rather than paying to have the rock trucked nearly 5 miles on roads, it is likely that Norris instead constructed this river ford, allowing rock to be transported a mere mile to his dam site.

NORRIS LAKE QUARRY FORD, DEKALB COUNTY

MILE 41.5 (33.758192, −84.048304) Lee's Mill. On river left at this small shoal is a large rock outcropping that slopes to the river and leads to a path that empties out on Norris Lake Drive. This spot serves as a Yellow River Water Trail access point and can be used to create a 5-mile trip from Yellow River Park. The site also marks the location of Lee's Mill, built around 1838 by Zachary Lee. In 1863, after Lee's death, Zadock Baker took ownership of the milldam and mill, and by 1871 he was embroiled in a court battle with his neighbor, Thomas Maguire, over the operation of the mill. Baker's rebuilding of Lee's aging milldam caused water levels upstream on No Business Creek to rise, flooding portions of Maguire's property. Maguire brought suit, seeking $5,000 in damages. The case ultimately came before the Georgia Supreme Court, which ruled that a mill operator has the right to repair and rebuild an existing dam so long as it is built to the same height as the original. Interestingly, Baker argued that Maguire's land flooded, when it had not previously done so, because No Business Creek had been severely filled with soil (eroding from Maguire's fields). Poor soil-management practices did, indeed, plague Georgia farms and rivers during the late 1800s and early 1900s. Topsoil washing off the hilly fields of Georgia's rolling Piedmont terrain filled local streams and rivers, limiting the carrying capacity of the water bodies and contributing to the flooding of bottomlands. During the early 20th century, this problem led to extensive federally and state-funded programs to dredge and straighten creeks and rivers. Baker's Mill was still in operation in 1885, when a U.S. Department of the Interior report described it as having a fall of "9 or 10 feet and a pair of stones" (for grinding corn and wheat).

SHOALS AT LEE'S MILL, DEKALB COUNTY

ROCK OUTCROPPING, DEKALB COUNTY

MILE 40.4 (33.747238, −84.054989) Powerlines.

MILE 39.3 (33.734087, −84.061750) Johnston's Bridge. Just upstream of the present-day Pleasant Hill Road bridge are the remains of its predecessor. In the late 1800s, the crossing here was known as Johnston's Bridge.

MILE 39.1 (33.732527, −84.060599) Shoal.This shoal sits beneath the powerline easement crossing the river here.

MILE 38.7 (33.728959, −84.0549620) DeKalb-Rockdale County Line. Here the river leaves DeKalb County after coursing through the eastern edge of the county for just 4.5 miles. DeKalb, formed in 1822 from parts of Gwinnett, Henry, and Fayette Counties, was named in honor of Baron Johann DeKalb, a French solider of German descent who traveled to America as a secret agent of the French government to assess the mood of the colonists in the years leading up to the Revolution. His snooping attracted the attention of the British, who had him arrested on suspicion of spying. After his arrest and release, he returned to France to report on the growing dissatisfaction of the American colonists, and that report ultimately played a role in France supporting the fledgling nation. DeKalb returned to America with the marquis de Lafayette and battled the British in South Carolina, where he died in 1870 after being wounded 11 times in the Battle of Camden. When George Washington later visited DeKalb's grave, he reportedly said, "So there lies the brave DeKalb, the generous stranger who came from a distant land to fight our battles and to water with his blood the tree of our liberty. Would to God he had lived to share its fruits."

MILE 37.7 (33.719054, –84.048524) Gaines Lake. On river right here is the outfall from a reservoir known up until the 1960s as Gaines Lake, one of several private commercial fishing lakes constructed in the early to mid-20th century along the Yellow River. Through the late 1950s, it catered to Atlanta-area anglers seeking an escape from the big city. By the early 1960s, owners were giving up the lure of lures and bass for more lucrative uses of the lake. By 1963, developers had changed the name to Lake Capri and advertised "Live Carefree at Capri" on home lots surrounding "170 acres of cool spring water." The Lake Capri Homeowners Association now maintains the neighborhood's three lakes and boasts of the popularity of the midcentury-modern-style houses surrounding the lakes.

MILE 36.0 (33.709793, –84.029523) Lakeview Utilities Wastewater Discharge. On river right is this discharge from a small wastewater treatment plant servicing a mobile home community known as Lakeview Estates, which surrounds Lake Rockaway. Like Gaines, Norris, and Opossum Lakes upstream, Lake Rockaway was originally a private commercial fishing lake catering to Atlanta-area anglers in the mid-20th century. During the 1940s, S. W. Galloway hosted gala events for organizations such as the Atlanta Fly and Bait Casting Club while renting cabins and boats to turn a profit on his lake. A 1941 visitor noted in the *Atlanta Constitution*'s outdoor page the quality of Galloway's clientele: "He will not allow carousing, which means that he will always have more decent folks than he can take care of. We need more such places in Georgia." Alas, Galloway may have rolled over in his grave at what became of Lake Rockaway. Beginning in the early 1960s, property around the lake was marketed as "Trailer Acres" and "Lakeview Mobile Homes Estates" and billed as "Georgia's Newest Mecca for Modern Mobile Home Living." Through the 1970s, the community held strong, offering multiple recreational amenities and a clubhouse, but in the 1980s, as renters began to outnumber mobile home owners, the community declined, becoming a notorious high-crime area. Attracted by low rents, Hispanic immigrants moved to Lakeview Estates, and in 2010 they made up more than 80 percent of the nearly 2,700 residents. Though community programs have attempted to organize residents to revitalize the area, it remains one of Rockdale County's high-crime neighborhoods. The small sewage plant that services the community discharges up to 158,000 gallons of treated wastewater into the river daily. It is operated by PoyntSource Solutions, a company run by the family of Randy Poynter, the former chairman of the Rockdale County Commission and onetime candidate for lieutenant governor. He died unexpectedly in 2002, and afterward commissioners named the county's new water-supply reservoir in his honor.

MILE 35.5 (33.705444, –84.025305) Irwin Bridge. The remains of this historic bridge can be seen on both banks of the river. These piers carried traffic on Irwin Bridge Road during the mid-20th century, but they did so at the peril of motorists. During the 1940s and 1950s, this aging bridge delayed the paving of Irwin Bridge Road for some two decades because funds were not available to replace it. (The county did not want to pave the road until the bridge was replaced.) In the early 1960s, a new bridge was built just downstream, leading to a blacktop road and the end of dust and mud. But the elevation of that early-1960s bridge proved too low when floods in 2009 topped it. In 2011, that bridge was razed, and the current bridge was built several feet higher than the original.

MILE 35.3 (33.703097, −84.022455) Irwin Bridge Road.

MILE 33.4 (33.692420, −83.997337) Water Intake. On river right, just upstream of the Ga. 20 bridge, is the defunct water intake for the city of Conyers. The city pulled water from the Yellow here until the early 1990s, when Rockdale County and Conyers began purchasing water from neighboring Gwinnett County. Today, the region's water needs are provided by Rockdale County's Randy Poynter Reservoir on Big Haynes Creek, which meets the Yellow some 6 miles downstream. In 2019, no communities withdrew drinking water directly from the Yellow.

MILE 33.2 (33.691228, −83.994203) Milstead Dam & Millrace. Here the river is blocked by this 15-foot-high dam, which diverts much of the river's flow to a millrace on river right, sending water to the Milstead Hydroelectric Plant, operated by Enel North America, a power provider that specializes in wind, solar, geothermal, and hydroelectric facilities. The textile mills on this section of the river closed in 1960, but the circa-1920s water turbine that once powered them still produces up to 800 kw of electricity, which is sold to Snapping Shoals EMC, a local electric cooperative that services areas of Rockdale, Newton, and Henry Counties. Use caution when approaching this lowhead dam. It should not be approached when the river is flowing over the top of the dam. After passing beneath the Ga. 20 bridge, stay on river right to access the take out adjacent to the

VIEW FROM MILSTEAD DAM, ROCKDALE COUNTY

entrance to the millrace. The take out for this section is a grassy, sloping bank on river right, adjacent to the gates to the millrace. There is no easy portage route around the dam. While it is possible to portage on river left, once below the dam, normal-to-low water levels make this a difficult endeavor, requiring a series of portages over shallow shoals and rock outcroppings, with limited opportunities to float a boat for the next 0.4 mile. At high flows, the run below the dam becomes a formidable Class II–III whitewater course that should be scouted and attempted only by those with adequate whitewater-paddling skills. It is also possible to portage through the old mill site by following the dirt road and sewer easement 0.4 mile downstream.

MILSTEAD MILLRACE, ROCKDALE COUNTY

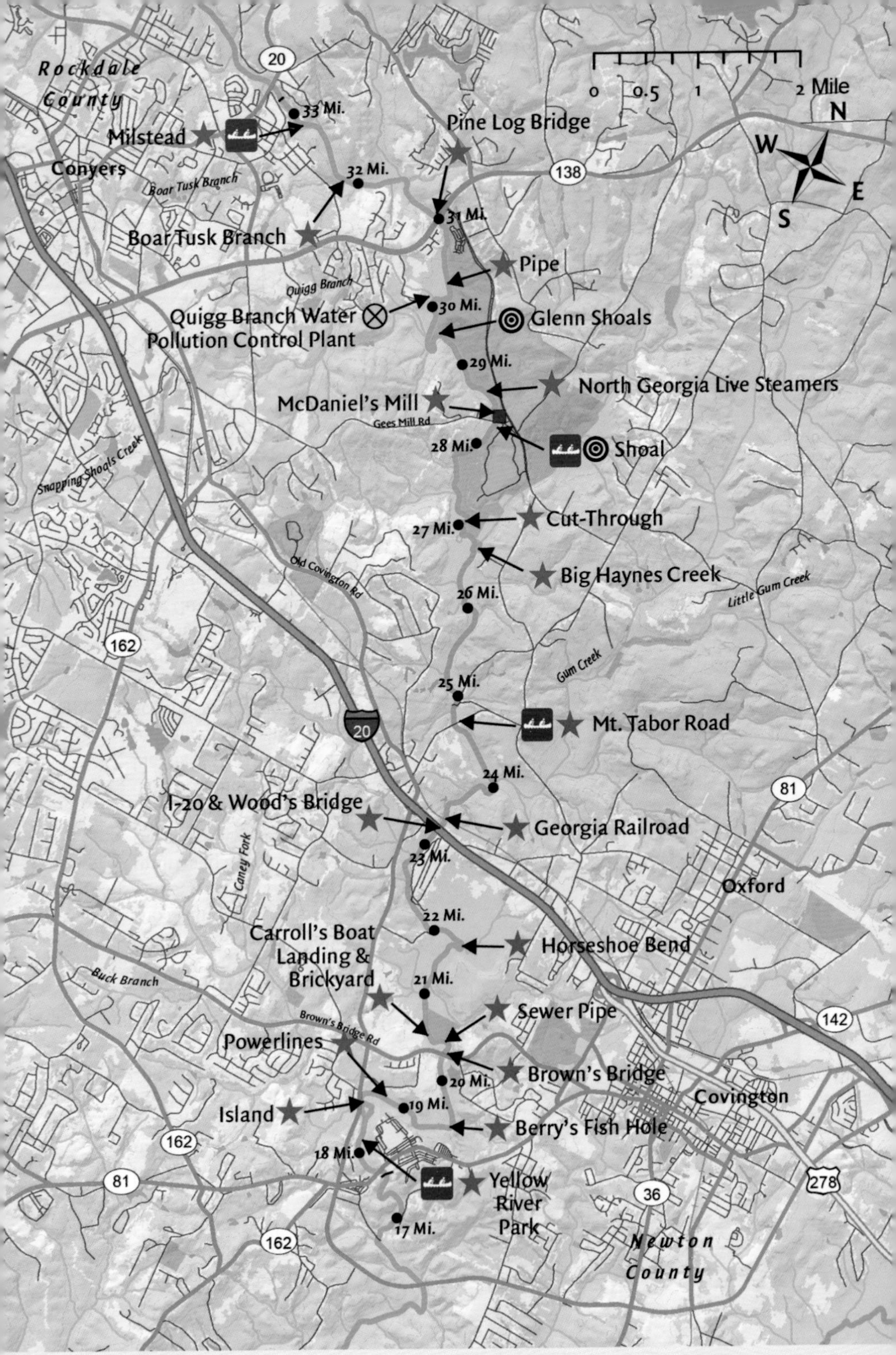

Rockdale County
20
0 0.5 1 2 Mile
N
W
E
S
33 Mi.
Milstead
Pine Log Bridge
Conyers
32 Mi.
Boar Tusk Branch
138
31 Mi.
Boar Tusk Branch
Pipe
Quigg Branch
30 Mi.
Quigg Branch Water Pollution Control Plant
Glenn Shoals
29 Mi.
North Georgia Live Steamers
McDaniel's Mill
Gees Mill Rd
28 Mi.
Shoal
Snapping Shoals Creek
Cut-Through
27 Mi.
Big Haynes Creek
Old Covington Rd
26 Mi.
Little Gum Creek
162
Gum Creek
25 Mi.
20
Mt. Tabor Road
24 Mi.
81
I-20 & Wood's Bridge
Georgia Railroad
23 Mi.
Caney Fork
Oxford
22 Mi.
Carroll's Boat Landing & Brickyard
Horseshoe Bend
21 Mi.
Buck Branch
Sewer Pipe
Brown's Bridge Rd
142
Powerlines
Brown's Bridge
20 Mi.
Covington
Island
19 Mi.
Berry's Fish Hole
162
18 Mi.
81
Yellow River Park
278
36
17 Mi.
162
Newton County

Milstead

Length 15 miles (Milstead Dam to Yellow River Park in Porterdale)
Class I
Time 7–9 hours
Minimum Level Water levels of 100 cubic feet per second at the Milstead / Gees Mill Road gauge are necessary to render this section navigable. The urbanized nature of this Upper Yellow River watershed means that water levels can fluctuate wildly. Stream gauges should be consulted before embarking on any trips, and major obstacles should be scouted before running.

River Gauge The nearest river gauge is located at Gees Mill Road in the middle of this section: https://waterdata.usgs.gov/ga/nwis/uv/?site_no=02207335&PARAmeter_cd=00065,00060,00062,00010.

Launch Site The launch site located below the Milstead powerhouse is not easily accessible. While the road leading to the powerhouse is often open, the gate is generally closed after daylight. Vehicles should not be left on the mill property without first making arrangements with caretakers on site. In general, park vehicles near Ga. 20 and walk 0.4 mile to the launch site, located along a Rockdale Water Resources sewer easement. It is possible to drive to the end of the mill road at the powerhouse, unload boats, and carry them 0.2 mile farther downstream to an undeveloped launch along a gently sloping sandbank. Alternatively, it is possible to launch above the dam, paddle across the river, and portage around the dam to run the shoals below. Low water levels will render this stretch of shoals below the dam unnavigable. High water flows can create a challenging whitewater run of Class II–III rapids.

DIRECTIONS From I-20 at Ga. 138 in Conyers, proceed north on Ga. 138 1.5 miles. Turn left on Sigman Road and proceed 1.4 miles. Turn right on Ga. 20 and proceed 0.6 mile to Main Street. Turn right and proceed 0.1 mile and then bear left onto the dirt road that enters the Milstead property. Proceed 0.3 mile to the dead end at the powerhouse. A sewer easement continues down a steep slope and parallels the river for 0.2 mile to the launch site. The sewer line easement is not accessible by vehicle.

Take Out Site The take out site is located on river left at Yellow River Park in Porterdale with a canoe and kayak launch and a parking area.

DIRECTIONS From Main Street at Ga. 20 in Milstead, turn left on Ga. 20 and return 0.6 mile to Sigman Road. Turn left and continue 1.4 miles to Ga. 138. Turn right and proceed 1.5 miles to the entrance ramp to I-20 eastbound. Follow the freeway 5.5 miles to exit 88 (Crowell Rd.). Turn right at the exit, following Crowell Road 3.8 miles. Turn left on Ga. 81 and proceed 0.6 mile. In downtown Porterdale, turn left on Hemlock Street and proceed 0.3 mile to the entrance of Yellow River Park, on the left. Follow the park road to the parking area at the river launch.

SHOAL AT GEE'S MILL ROAD, ROCKDALE COUNTY

Alternative Take Out Sites The river is crossed by Ga. 138, Gees Mill Road, Mt. Tabor Road, and Brown Bridge Road. Taking out at these sites offers trips of 2, 5, 8 and 13 miles, respectively. Only Mt. Tabor Road includes a Yellow River Water Trail developed parking area and a moderately improved boat-launch area. There is an access point on public land about 1,000 feet downstream of Gees Mill Road on river left within the Georgia International Horse Park, but this site is undeveloped. At the other sites, if you are accessing the river via private property rather than rights-of-way, permission must be sought. Take outs should be scouted before your journey to ensure suitable access and parking.

DIRECTIONS TO THE MT. TABOR ROAD TAKE OUT From Main Street at Ga. 20 in Milstead, turn left on Ga. 20 and return 0.6 mile to Sigman Road. Turn left and continue 3.6 miles. Turn left on Old Covington Road and proceed 2.4 miles. At the stop sign, continue straight on Almon Road 1.1 miles. Turn left on Mt. Tabor Road and travel 0.9 mile to the entrance to the parking area on the right.

Outfitters No outfitters operate on this stretch of the river.

Description Leaving behind the big shoals at Milstead, the river flattens and slows as it winds to Porterdale and the river's next dam-and-shoal complex. Still, interspersed between long stretches of flatwater are a few Class I shoals. Along the way, the Yellow passes by the Georgia International Horse Park, site of the equestrian events during the 1996 Summer Olympic Games, and beneath I-20 and the historic Georgia Railroad Bridge, site of an important skirmish during the Civil War. While the reaches upstream of Mt. Tabor Road are lightly traveled, because of limited access at Milstead, the run from Mt. Tabor to Porterdale has, in the early stages of development of the Yellow River Water Trail, become a popular paddling destination.

Points of Interest

MILE 32.8 (33.689996, −83.988490) Milstead. The launch site for this section is at the base of the 0.4-mile run of Long Shoals—a descent of nearly 60 feet and one that rivals other popular southern whitewater destinations. But because of diversions to the hydroelectric plant, the main channel is mostly barren and dry except during periods of high flows. With such a fall, it is not surprising that early settlers quickly harnessed these shoals. By 1871, a dam was diverting water to power a sawmill, paper mill, and gristmill. At the turn of the century, Frank D. Milstead established the Milstead Manufacturing Company, a sprawling mill that produced yarn and cotton duck fabric until 1960. In its heyday, the company employed as many as 1,000 workers, and Milstead was the quintessential mill town. The company built and maintained the houses, stores, doctor's office, water system, school, community gymnasium (including a bowling alley), swimming pool, baseball fields, tennis courts, and a golf course. Today, all that is left of this massive textile operation overlooking Long Shoals is the millrace and powerhouse, along with the foundations of the former mill buildings.

MILE 32.2 (33.685857, −83.978757) Boar Tusk Branch. This creek on river right is notable as one of the primary tributaries draining the town of Conyers, and because its name harks back to the time some 500 years when Hernando de Soto brought hogs to America during his travels through what would become Georgia and neighboring states. Since then, feral hogs have firmly established themselves. While nearly half the population of feral hogs is found in the South, the tusked creatures can now be found in 31 of the 50 states.

LONG SHOALS AT MILSTEAD, ROCKDALE COUNTY

MILE 31.1 (33.687478, −83.96237) Pine Log Bridge. While the concrete and steel Ga. 138 bridge now carries traffic over the Yellow, in the 19th century several stout pine stringers supported the bridge that spanned the river here. So notable were the massive logs that the bridge and road came to be known as Pine Log. The name lives on in Conyers's Pine Log Road and Pine Log Park.

MILE 30.4 (33.680236, −83.955449) Pipe. Depending on the river's water level, this water-sewer infrastructure pipe can create a navigational hazard and should be approached with caution. At low water levels, it is possible to slide beneath it. At higher levels, a portage over the pipe is necessary. River left generally provides the best portage opportunities.

MILE 30.1 (33.676660, −83.956403) Quigg Branch Water Pollution Control Plant. On river right here is the discharge from this facility, which is permitted to pump up to 6 million gallons of treated sewage a day into the river. It is the largest of Rockdale County's five wastewater treatment plants. In 2017, the county received a $22.6 million state grant to build a new treatment facility that will eliminate three smaller, aging facilities. Keeping water and sewer infrastructure on pace with population growth has been a consistent challenge for fast-growing metro communities like Rockdale County. In 2018, the county had a wastewater treatment capacity of 10 million gallons daily (MGD), but population projections suggest that by 2050, the county will need to expand its capacity to 22 MGD.

MILE 29.4 (33.673486, −83.952896) Glenn Shoals. At this bend and 0.6 mile below are a pair of shoals identified in turn-of-the-century surveys of the Yellow. Though the shoals were noted for the potential to generate up to 386 horsepower, it appears that neither was ever developed. The shoals borrow the name of the John Wingfield Glenn family, which farmed the land surrounding the river here in the mid-1800s. In her book *I Remember, I Remember*, Layona Glenn, John's daughter (born in 1866), recalled a harrowing childhood event in which the river would have taken a younger sibling had it not been for the heroics of the family dog, Don: "One day when the Yellow River was high, we began to throw sticks in the water so this dog could jump in and bring them out. The baby fetched a huge stick nearly as big as he was, and proceeded to drag it toward the water. Suddenly the bank caved in beneath his little feet. Into the river he went! 'Get him, Don!' I screamed . . . I screamed again and again. Don jumped instantly, seized the child by the shoulder of his little shirt and held his blond head above the water. Don swam strongly, towing his precious load. [We] followed along the river bank, until . . . I waded out to meet Don and take his burden from him."

MILE 28.6 (33.669867, −83.941635) North Georgia Live Steamers. On river left, on land that is part of the Georgia International Horse Park, is this park for miniature-train enthusiasts. The property features nearly a mile of miniature railroad track, where model train enthusiasts can operate their one-eighth-size steam locomotives. Engines can weigh up to 2,500 pounds and, depending on the model, can haul up to 50 people. The International Horse Park hosted the equestrian events during the 1996 Olympic Games, and now hosts everything

GLENN SHOALS, ROCKDALE COUNTY

from human steeplechases to the annual Conyers Cherry Blossom Festival. The site also features 8 miles of mountain bike trails, 15 miles of horseback trails, and a golf course. In the late 1980s, local governments purchased the 1,139-acre site for a sewage land-application system. That proposed use never materialized, giving rise to its development as a horse park. The park property extends nearly 2 miles upstream and downstream of this location.

MILE 28.4 (33.667773, −83.938651) McDaniel's Mill. A 1903 survey of the Yellow River notes McDaniel's Dam at this site, a 6-foot-high dam that diverted water to the millrace on river right. Later known as Gee's Mill, the mill stands on a portion of the original Glenn family plantation. Layona Glenn, in her autobiographical book *I Remember, I Remember*, published in 1969 when she was 103, called the mill Bald Rock Mill: "The wheel ran our sawmill and turning lathe, where the furniture was made, and the mill that ground our flour." Though all that remains of the operation are the race and the foundation, the adjacent house dates to the 1850s. The tailrace of the mill empties into the river downstream of Gee's Mill Road.

MILE 28.3 (33.666831, −83.937949) Shoal. Located directly downstream of Gee's Mill Road bridge, the shoal can create sizable waves at the right water level. Beyond the shoal on river left is an undeveloped access point on property of the Georgia International Horse Park. This public property includes a parking area near the access point that may be used when the park is not hosting large events.

MILE 27.1 (33.652939, −83.934991) Cut-Through. Here the river has cut a new path through a small oxbow, forming a small island on river left.

MILE 26.7 (33.650799, −83.931634) Big Haynes Creek. Some six miles up this significant tributary of the Yellow lies Randy Poynter Reservoir, which serves as the drinking-water supply for Rockdale County. The construction of the lake was approved by county voters in 1989, but like many water-supply projects in the metro area, it took more time and money to build than originally expected. It cost $24 million to build, three times the original projected cost. In 1998, when county commissioners celebrated its completion, they brought in a bald eagle, representing the county's freedom from having to purchase water from neighboring counties, and an owl, representing the "wisdom" of the county's voters for supporting the project. In recent years, many communities have shown wisdom by investing in water conservation and water efficiency measures, which are considered more cost-effective means of extending local water supplies than building new water-supply reservoirs. These measures, coupled with slowed growth, have forestalled the need for several new reservoirs in the Metro Atlanta area.

MILE 24.8 (33.628368, −83.920722) Mt. Tabor Road. A parking area, an information kiosk, and a slightly improved launch and take out site mark this road crossing as a Yellow River Water Trail site. This site, maintained by Newton County, has become one of the more popular launches on the Yellow River Water Trail, since it provides access to a gently flowing, easy-to-paddle 7-mile section of river ending at Porterdale's Yellow River Park. Pilings for the original Mt. Tabor Road bridge can be seen 0.2 mile upstream.

MILE 23.3 (33.616462, −83.914647) Georgia Railroad. The Georgia Railroad has spanned the Yellow River here since the late 1830s. During the Civil War, the bridge played a strategic role in the Union Army's siege of Atlanta. On July 22, 1864, Union cavalry raiders with orders to destroy the bridge and cut the Confederate Army's supply lines from Augusta encountered a handful of local old men and boys defending the 555-foot span. The encounter did not end well for the home guard. "Ancient muzzle loaders and shotguns were no match for forty or fifty veteran troopers with Spencers [rifles]," writes David Evans in *Sherman's Horseman: Union Cavalry Operations in the Atlanta Campaign*. "The first exchange killed a white-haired old man named Brown. The others simply ran away. Crossing to the east bank, the Yankees set fire to the wagon bridge and trestle, a large flour mill a short distance downstream and the house of the mill operator, Albert B. Torrence." Brigadier General Kenner Garrard reported to Sherman two days later that his men had destroyed not only the bridge, but also 6 miles of railroad, and had set fire to depots in Conyers and Covington, 2,000 bales of cotton, and a Confederate hospital. Some 200 slaves followed the army to safety north of Atlanta. This cavalry raid and others left the Confederates defending Atlanta with only one supply route, which led south toward Macon. The stone piers of a former bridge date to before 1890. That year, Lieutenant Thomas Rees with the U.S. Army Corps of Engineers described them: "The Georgia Railroad Bridge . . . is a Howe truss deck bridge, about 350 feet long in three spans . . . The two piers are of stone and about 30 feet high." Today the rail is part of the CSX rail system.

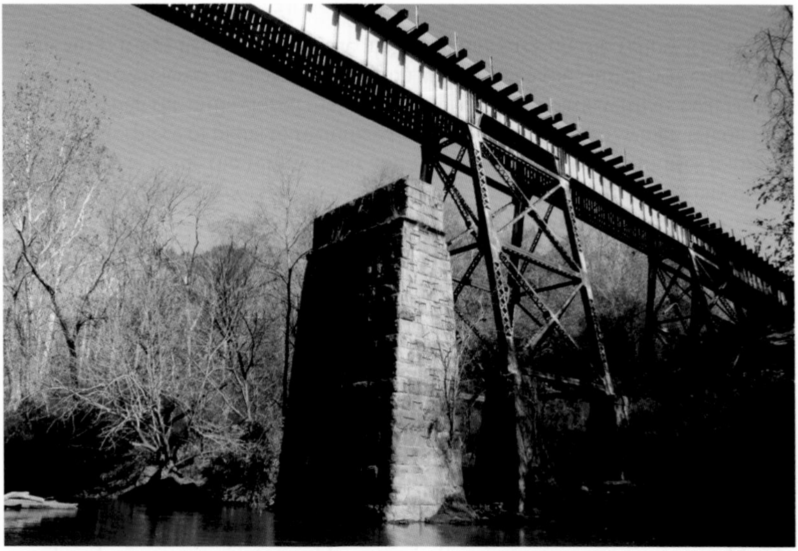

GEORGIA RAILROAD BRIDGE, NEWTON COUNTY

MILE 23.2 (33.614760, −83.914837) I-20 & Wood's Bridge. Now spanned by this six-lane highway and an accompanying two-lane access road, the transportation infrastructure at this spot appeared much differently in 1890. During a river survey conducted that year, Lieutenant Thomas Rees of the U.S. Army Corps of Engineers described Wood's Bridge (the pilings of a later iteration of that bridge can be seen just downstream) this way: "Just below the railroad bridge, is a low, wooden trestle bridge about 150 feet long, and is only 3 feet in the clear above low water. The decking is sloping, the upstream side being about 5 inches lower that the downstream side. It was found that high bridges were invariably carried away during freshets, and low sloping bridges are now usually built . . . so that when the water rises high enough to bring down logs . . . the bridges will be entirely covered and floating objects will pass over them without doing any damage." In the fall of 1864, portions of the Union Army crossed the river here en route from Atlanta to Savannah. Having destroyed the wagon bridge and railroad bridge during an earlier cavalry raid, the Union soldiers employed pontoons to span the river.

MILE 21.7 (33.602291, −83.902285) Horseshoe Bend. The wooded bank on river left in this sharp bend conceals extensive wetlands. An 1890 U.S. Army Corps of Engineers river survey notes Hendrick's Spring at this location.

MILE 20.6 (33.589415, −83.900315) Carroll's Boat Landing & Brickyard. From the site of this boat landing and brickyard on river right, workers polled boats loaded with bricks down river to Porterdale for construction of the mills there. The presence of granite, molders sand, and terra-cotta clay along the banks of the river between Porterdale and the Georgia Railroad prompted late 19th-century business boosters in nearby Covington to petition Congress to "improve" the river here, making it navigable for steamboats. In 1889, officers of the Central Ocmulgee Navigation Company wrote to Washington. D.C.: "An appropriation by the General Government of $10,000 would be sufficient to put said stream in good order for small steamers and thereby establish four large industries and add greatly to the value of property along said stream." Representatives from the U.S. Army Corps of Engineers who surveyed the river after this request was made were less than impressed. They estimated it would cost some $1.5 million to "improve" this section of river by building a series of locks and dams to get boats around the shoals at Porterdale. The engineers reported that the Yellow was "not worthy of improvement." Said Lieutenant Thomas Rees in his report: "If there be any prospective benefits arising from such improvements commensurate with that outlay I have been unable to discover them."

MILE 20.4 (33.589790, −83.897163) Sewer Pipe. This piece of Newton County Water and Sewerage Authority infrastructure carries wastewater to the Yellow River Water Reclamation Plant near Porterdale, and at low-to-normal water levels it requires a portage, which is best accomplished along a sandbar on river right.

MILE 20.3 (33.588241, −83.896905) Brown's Bridge. Just upstream of the current Brown's Bridge stand stone piers marking the location of a circa-1890 bridge. On July 22, 1864, Union cavalry under the command of Major General George Stoneman crossed the river on a bridge here en route to Covington and points beyond, with the mission of destroying the Macon railroad, which was resupplying the embattled Confederate troops in Atlanta. Less than two weeks later, after pillaging homes and fields on its way from Covington to Macon, the bulk of Stoneman's force was killed or surrendered during the Battle of Sunshine Church. Some 400 Union soldiers, including Stoneman, were captured in the battle and later marched through Macon, where refugees who had recently had their property taken or destroyed by the raiders jeered. As recounted in David Evans's *Sherman's Horseman: Union Cavalry Operations in the Atlanta Campaign*, one woman called out to Stoneman: "I bet you don't feel as big as you did Saturday morning when your men came into my house."

MILE 19.5 (33.579944, −83.890248) Berry's Fish Hole. This bend, with a piney bluff rising above the river and rock outcroppings extending into the river, is identified on circa-1890 maps.

MILE 18.8 (33.579168, −83.9017810) Powerlines.

MILE 18.6 (33.577044, −83.904881) Island.

MILE 18.2 (33.572692, −83.902261) Yellow River Park. Since 2011, the city of Porterdale has made the Yellow River and the recreational opportunities it affords the centerpiece of plans to revitalize the former textile town, which fell on hard times when the mills closed in the 1970s. Yellow River Park, with its boat launch, is the crown jewel of that revitalization effort. Since the launch was completed, in 2014, it has become one of the most popular sites on the Yellow River Water

Trail. While many paddle downstream from Mt. Tabor Road, others launch from here, paddle upstream against the slack current created by the Porterdale Dam, and then float back to their initial launch. Historically, the land where the park is now situated was used for some interesting purposes. It was for a time the site of a baseball diamond used by Negro League teams. During World War II, prisoners of war were housed on the grounds while they worked in the Porterdale mills. (POWs from the European theater were put to work at many locales throughout Georgia during the war.) Today, it is the site of the annual Yellow River Jam, a music festival and river celebration featuring paddle trips, live music, food and drink vendors, and more. The festival is held each fall. The milldam is located 0.4 mile downstream, just below Main Street. A lowhead dam, it creates dangerous hydraulics at its base and should be portaged. Below the dam is a quarter-mile run of Class II–III rapids.

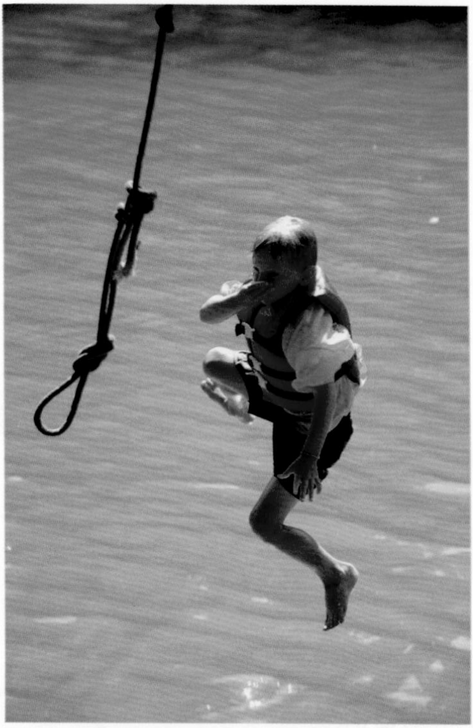

ROPE SWING AT YELLOW RIVER PARK, NEWTON COUNTY

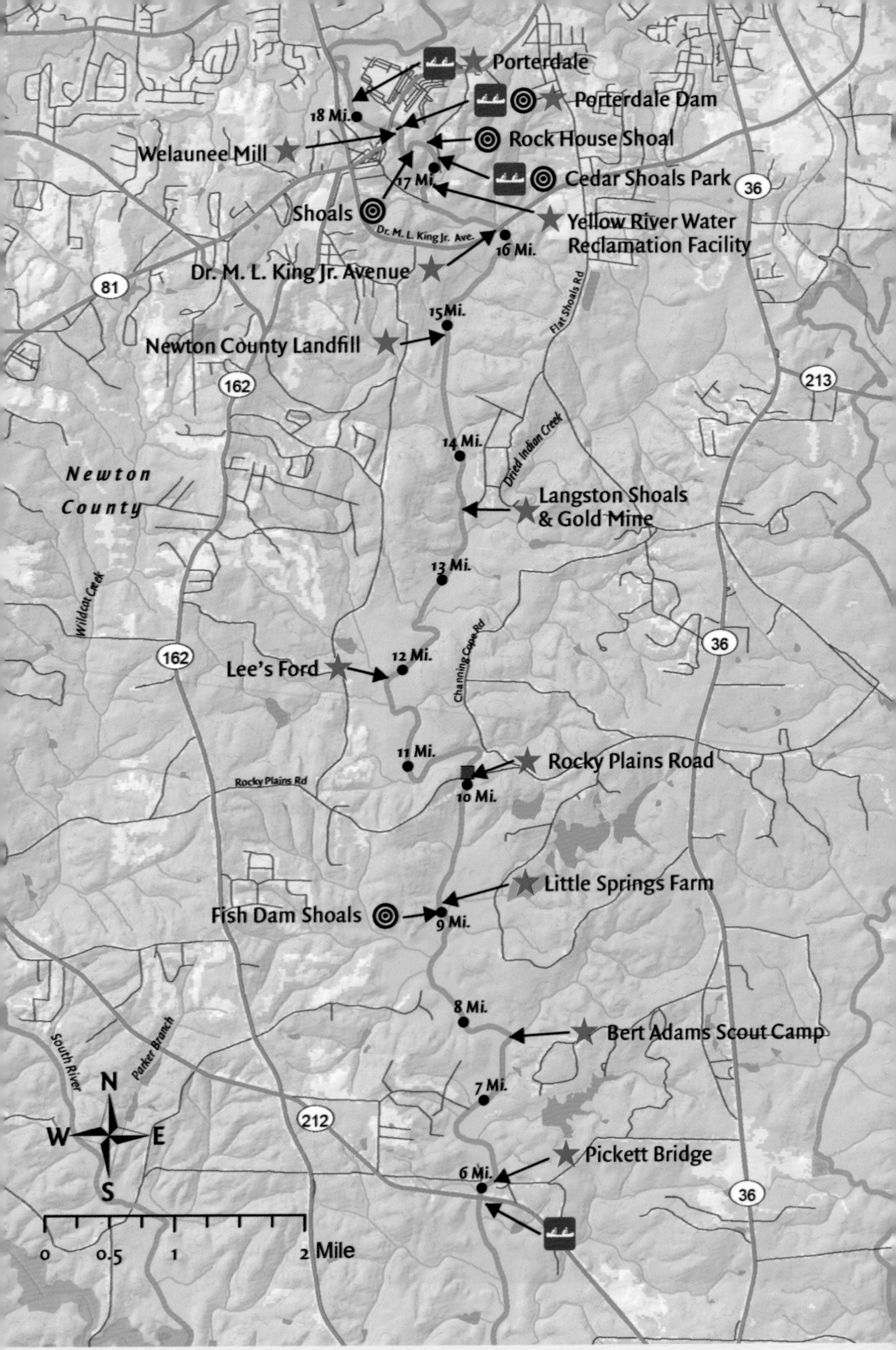
Porterdale
Porterdale Dam
18 Mi.
Rock House Shoal
Welaunee Mill
Cedar Shoals Park
17 Mi.
36
Shoals
Yellow River Water
Reclamation Facility
Dr. M. L. King Jr. Ave.
16 Mi.
Dr. M. L. King Jr. Avenue
81
Flat Shoals Rd
15 Mi.
Newton County Landfill
162
213
Dried Indian Creek
14 Mi.
Newton
County
Langston Shoals
& Gold Mine
13 Mi.
Wildcat Creek
Channing Cope Rd
36
162
12 Mi.
Lee's Ford
11 Mi.
Rocky Plains Road
Rocky Plains Rd
10 Mi.
Little Springs Farm
Fish Dam Shoals
9 Mi.
8 Mi.
Bert Adams Scout Camp
South River
Parker Branch
N
W
E
S
7 Mi.
212
Pickett Bridge
6 Mi.
36
0
0.5
1
2 Mile

Porterdale

Length 11 miles (Yellow River Park in Porterdale to Ga. 212)

Class I–III–IV

Time 5–7 hours

Minimum Level Water levels of at least 400 cfs at the Rocky Plains Road gauge should be sufficient to navigate Cedar Shoals below the dam at Porterdale.

River Gauge The nearest river gauge is located at Rocky Plains Road in the middle of this section: https://waterdata.usgs.gov/ga/nwis/uv/?site_no=02208000&PARAmeter_cd=00065,00060,00062,00010.

Launch Site Because of Porterdale Dam, launching from Yellow River Park is not recommended except for short out-and-back excursions, since the dam lies just 0.4 mile downstream of the park. For whitewater enthusiasts, the city of Porterdale has developed a launch that provides access to the half mile of Class I–IV whitewater run immediately below the dam. Those wishing to avoid these obstacles can launch from Cedar Shoals Park along River Front Road. Launching here provides access to Class I shoals and then 10 miles of flatwater paddling to Ga. 212.

DIRECTIONS From I-20 at exit 88 (Almon/Crowell Road) travel south 3.7 miles. At the stoplight, turn left on Ga. 81 and proceed 0.4 mile to the bridge over the Yellow River. Travel 0.5 mile to reach Hemlock Street; turn left and proceed 0.3 mile to the entrance to Yellow River Park on the left. To access the whitewater run below the dam, paddlers can drop boats on the south side of the bridge adjacent to the dam. Parking is in lots on the opposite side of the river. To access Cedar Shoals Park on River Front Road, continue on Ga. 81 (Main Street) for 0.7 mile beyond Hemlock Street. Turn right on River Front Road and proceed 0.8 mile to the park adjacent to the river.

Take Out Site The take out site is located on river left beneath the Ga. 212 bridge. There is no developed access or parking here, but boaters can access the river via the right-of-way.

DIRECTIONS From Yellow River Park in Porterdale, return to Ga. 81 (Main Street). Turn right and proceed 0.6 mile to Jackson Road (Ga. 162C). Turn left and travel 7.5 miles to Ga. 212. Turn left and proceed 1.8 miles to the bridge. Parking is along the right-of-way on the east side of the bridge.

Alternative Take Out Site As noted above, Cedar Shoals Park provides an alternative take out site for paddlers wishing to travel only the whitewater portions of this section below Porterdale Dam.

Outfitters No outfitters operate on this stretch of the river.

Description This 11-mile run has two distinct characters. For nearly a mile from below Porterdale Dam to the final drop at Cedar Shoals, the river spills over a series of shoals, including some that reach Class IV in difficulty during high water. Beyond these shoals and for the next 10 miles, the river settles into a lazy meander as it makes its way to the backwaters of Jackson Lake. The river corridor is mostly wild and remote, and much of the land along it is preserved as a Boy Scout camp and agricultural land.

Points of Interest

MILE 18.1 (33.572730, –83.902269) Porterdale. This quintessential textile town is rich in history—largely because of its location at Cedar Shoals, an extensive fall and shoals area dropping 90 feet in elevation in less than a mile. The first settlers to secure lots here, in 1821, quickly harnessed the falls, and by 1826 a gristmill, a sawmill, and a blacksmith's shop had been established. By 1855, a chair factory and wool-carding machine had been added. The annual output of these industries amounted to some $16,000, or about $451,000 in 2018 dollars. Not surprisingly, the site attracted the attention of investors. In the 1850s, a Boston-based firm known as the Cedar Shoals Water Power Company was formed to build a textile empire on the Yellow that would rival the one in Lowell, Massachusetts. The pitch to potential investors betrayed the attitude of northerners to the South during that era, and in extolling the low cost of doing business in Georgia, it strikingly resembles modern chamber of commerce pitches to potential businesses: "Our location possesses many advantages . . . The climate is very healthy and attractive—neither excessive heat or cold. Rich southern fruits abound and yield many luxuries very infrequent here (Boston), as well as some impossible to obtain at the North . . . and the necessary expenses of living are but little more than half what they are in Boston or New York . . . We find many of the natives here in the mechanic arts about seventy-five years behind the age, consequently the field is open and large for introduction of all the new and useful improvements of our native State, Massachusetts, in all different departments and branches of art . . . thus making (possible) a New England Colony or City in the heart of the State of Georgia." The northern investors were never able to raise the capital, and operations at Cedar Shoals remained in local hands. During the early 1860s, Hugh McLean took possession of a portion of the Cedar Shoals property and operated a cotton mill on the shoals. In 1864, when the Union Army threatened the area, McLean began flying a British flag over his factory in hope of avoiding the depredations of the invading Yankees. Locals were aroused by this lack of loyalty to the Confederacy, and some, with designs on acquiring the mill, warned McLean of a potential uprising and lynching. Fearing for his life, McLean sold his operation for $60,000 and left town. In fact, the threat of violence was merely a ruse to acquire the business. McLean eventually sued his antagonists to regain his mill, but lost his fight in the Georgia Supreme Court in 1872.

Ultimately, the Cedar Shoals property fell into the hands of Oliver S. Porter, who in 1890 established Porterdale Mills. The massive, 800-foot-long mill build-

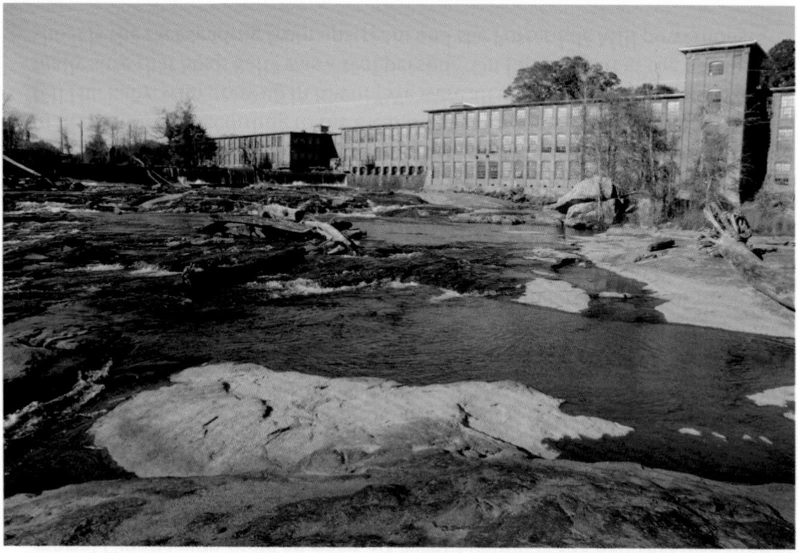

PORTERDALE MILL AND CEDAR SHOALS, NEWTON COUNTY

ing fronting the river was built in 1899 (from bricks made upriver and floated down on pole boats). Bibb Manufacturing operated the mill throughout the 20th century. During its heyday, Porterdale was a thriving mill town, employing hundreds, most of whom resided in the village of company-owned houses. Producing yarn, twine, and cotton rope, Porterdale was also at one time the world's largest producer of fishing line. Porterdale Mills closed in the 1970s, and the town languished until recently, when city leaders began focusing on redeveloping the community's unique assets. In 2006, the old mill was repurposed and developed, and the river—long the heartbeat of the community—became a focal point of the town's revival, particularly the development of Yellow River Park and its boat launch. The stretch of river between the mill and Cedar Shoals Park is arguably the most scenic stretch of the Yellow, but also among the most difficult to access.

MILE 17.6 (33.570305, −83.896392) Porterdale Dam. This 125-foot-long, 12-foot-high dam dates to the 1800s, but was improved and raised by the Bibb Manufacturing Company in 1900. Through the early 1900s, the dam and powerhouse produced both electrical power and mechanical power, generating some 1,400 horsepower, which ran machines that made cord and fabrics. During the height of its production, 1940–1970, the Porterdale Mill was considered the world's largest producer of twine. Today, the dam no longer generates power, but like the restored mill buildings adjacent to the river, it serves as a powerful historic landmark for local residents.

In 2007, the River Basin Center at the University of Georgia assessed the feasibility of removing the dam; it noted that such a project would likely improve habitat for migratory fish like shad and open up new recreational opportunities. But no extensive efforts to remove the dam have been pursued. In 1967, three young men did attempt to remove the dam. They planned to strap an explosive device consisting of several sticks of dynamite and a timer to an inner tube and float the package downstream to the head of the dam. Instead, the device exploded long before ever reaching the dam, killing one of the men and injuring a second. The blast rattled windows throughout the mill village and could be heard from miles away. Newton County sheriff Henry Odom told the *Atlanta Constitution*: "Their clothes were ripped off them like shreds." One of the accomplices told police they merely wanted to "scare the police," but locals have insisted the trio was angry with the mill's managers and were intent on shutting down the plant by taking out its power source. Sheriff Odom said the dam could have been "ripped apart" had the dynamite reached it. As more is learned about the benefits of removing obsolete dams and restoring free-flowing rivers, it is likely that Porterdale will someday have to wrestle with deciding the fate of its historic dam. A boat launch on river right just below the dam provides access to Porterdale's whitewater run, which descends some 67 feet in elevation in a half mile. Flows of at least 400 cfs at the Rocky Plains gauge are needed to make the shoals navigable. As flows surpass 1,000 cfs, the danger and difficulty of navigating the Class I–IV shoals increases.

MILE 17.5 (33.569316, −83.895933) Welaunee Mill. On river right, adjacent to the roaring shoals below the dam, is this two-story mill building dating to 1920. This mill is located on the site of Phillips Mill, which was the first mill built in Porterdale, in the 1820s. Across the river in the town's preserved Porterdale Memorial Gymnasium (now an open-air event facility) is the bell that was rung at shift changes at Welaunee. During World War II, a local worker saved the bell from being melted down for scrap metal.

MILE 17.3 (33.568017, −83.894125) Shoals.

MILE 17.2 (33.568030, −83.892607) Rock House Shoal. Here the main flow of the river pushes to far right and descends beneath what is locally known as the Rock House, a massive rock outcropping that stretches some 80 feet above the river and includes several footpaths through, under, and around this giant jumble of rocks. The shoal should be run with caution, since undercut rocks await on river right along and at the base of this rapid. Lowell Chambers, who has owned the property since 1993, said that despite its beauty, the location is relatively inaccessible, and Porterdale residents have historically considered it a place of haunts. During the mill village's heyday, parents warned children of Soap Sally, a witch who captured children who stayed out too late, and boiled them down into soap in her cauldron. According to the local historian and newspaper columnist Darrell Huckaby, who grew up in town: "We were all scared to death of her. We were really sure that Soap Sally was a real person." On far river left at the base of this shoal is the race leading from upstream and the Porterdale Mill powerhouse.

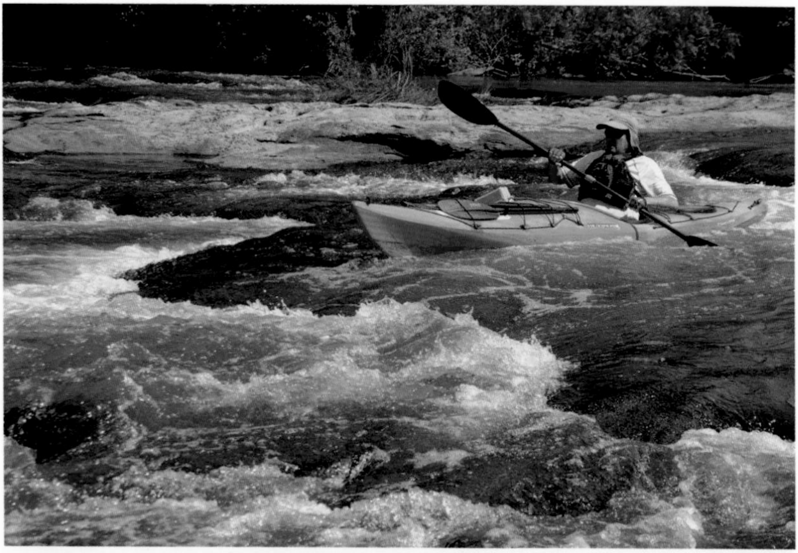

HENRY SHOALS, NEWTON COUNTY

MILE 17.1 (33.566606, −83.890856) Cedar Shoals Park. This park might be more appropriately named "Henry Shoals," since that was the name given to these shoals in the late 1800s. Thomas H. Rees, who surveyed the river for the U.S. Army Corps of Engineers in 1891, described the descent from the Porterdale Dam: "The fall from the level of the mill pool to the pool below the shoals is 41.2 feet in a distance of about one-third of a mile. The water flows in many divided streams, and with many leaps and rapids, down a steep, rocky slope and has hardly recovered its tranquillity at the foot before it is hurried in the same manner over the Henry Shoals, falling 18.8 feet in about a quarter of a mile. There is, therefore, at this point, a total fall of 61 feet in less than a mile." Cedar Shoals Park is a popular destination for tubers and waders. On far river right, between the island and the west bank of the river, once stood what Rees's 1891 survey identified as "Old Variety Works Dam." Henry Shoals extend downriver from the park about 1,000 feet.

MILE 16.8 (33.563749, −83.891681) Yellow River Water Reclamation Facility. On river left beyond Cedar Shoals Park is this Newton County Water and Sewerage facility, which treats about 2 million gallons of sewage daily. Unlike typical riverside sewage-treatment plants, it does not discharge directly into the river. Instead, after initial treatment, the wastewater is pumped a mile to the southeast, where it is sprayed on some 2,400 acres of land; this allows the water to soak into the ground and complete its treatment through natural processes.

MILE 16.1 (33.559474, −83.882364) Dr. M. L. King Jr. Avenue. This 330-foot-long bridge, which carries the Covington Bypass Road, was completed in 1988.

MILE 14.9 (33.547869, −83.888703) Newton County Landfill. On river right is this beleaguered landfill, which for years has vexed county leaders and frustrated advocates working to protect the Yellow River. The problem: an unlined cell at the landfill has contaminated groundwater that inevitably finds its way to the river. In 2018, the Newton County Commission voted to move forward with a $9 million project to excavate the waste and move it to a lined cell.

MILE 13.7 (33.528911, −83.885966) Langston Shoals & Gold Mine. An 1891 U.S. Army Corps of Engineers survey described the shoals here as 800 feet long, with a fall of about 5.5 feet. The surveyors noted a gold mine located on river right that was also documented in a 1909 Geological Survey of Georgia publication: "[This] small placer deposit . . . has been worked for gold at several different times, some mining having been carried on before the Civil War. The deposit, which is quite limited in area, occurs along a small branch and would not probably repay mining operations other than of a very limited character." Opposite the gold mine and downstream slightly is the mouth of Dried Indian Creek. The tributary is said to have gotten its name when an early settler found the dried corpse of a Native American tied to a tree on its bank.

MILE 11.9 (33.510352, −83.894971) Lee's Ford. This historic ford is noted on an 1891 U.S. Army Corps of Engineers river survey.

MILE 10.1 (33.499974, −83.884076) Rocky Plains Road. Before the construction of the Rocky Plains Road Bridge, in the late 1800s this river crossing was known as Flat Shoals Ford, its name taken from a small set of shoals that dropped 4 feet over a distance of about 1,000 feet. By the early 1900s, Flat Shoals Bridge had replaced the ford.

NEAR LEE'S FORD, NEWTON COUNTY

MILE 9.1 (33.485447, −83.887327) Little Springs Farm. On river left is this 2,800-acre cattle farm, which occupies about 2.4 miles of riverfront stretching from Rocky Plains Road downstream. The farm is notable for its former owner, Joachim Herz, who died at the age of 65 in 2008 in a boating accident. Herz, a billionaire heir of a German coffee retailer, came to the United States in the 1970s and bought this farm. The man whom *Forbes* magazine once ranked as the 368th-richest person in the world was known for puttering around the farm on heavy equipment, finding unique rocks, digging them up, and placing them at strategic locations on the property. Though his ties to Germany were still strong, his wish was to be buried on his farm. His grave, marked with an engraved stone from the farm, rests on a knoll overlooking the river. The Joachim Herz Stiftung Foundation still owns the farm; the foundation funds programs supporting education and scientific, medical, and legal research in both Germany and the United States.

MILE 9.0 (33.484947, −83.887192) Fish Dam Shoals. An 1891 U.S. Army Corps of Engineers survey of the Yellow River identifies this as the location of Fish Dam Shoals, suggesting that this was the site of a prehistoric or 19th-century fish trap. Archaeologists have confirmed the existence of 128 fish weirs on Georgia's rivers. The V-shaped rock dams were used to corral and capture fish.

MILE 7.6 (33.471663, −83.877436) Bert Adams Scout Camp. Beginning at this bend, this 1,300-acre Boy Scouts of America camp stretches downstream on river left for nearly two miles. The site has been home to the camp since 1960. It was named in honor of an Atlanta real estate agent who in 1927 helped establish the Atlanta Council's first camp, along the Chattahoochee River. Adams, who died at the age of 47 in 1926, never lived to see the camp that was constructed on the property he had secured. Among other things, the Bert Adams Scout Camp provides opportunities for camping, swimming, hiking, boating, shooting, climbing, and, of course, earning merit badges. There are more than 135 Boy Scout merit badges. Since 1910, only 367 people have earned all them.

MILE 6.1 (33.455948, −83.879745) Pickett Bridge. The remains of Pickett Bridge can be seen on river left here. In the late 1800s, Webb's Bridge spanned the river here.

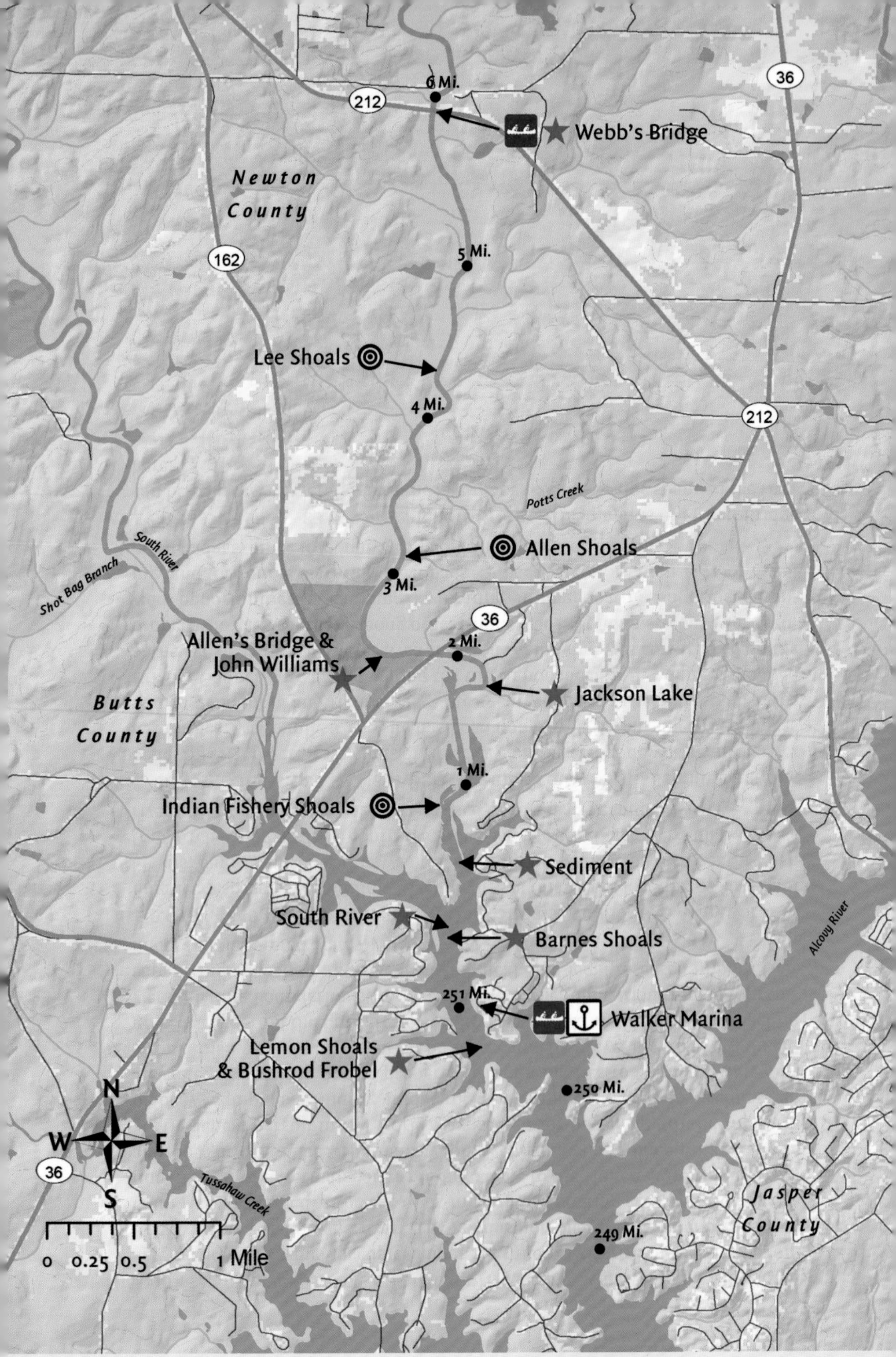
6 Mi.
212
36
Webb's Bridge
Newton
County
5 Mi.
162
Lee Shoals
4 Mi.
212
Potts Creek
Allen Shoals
South River
Shot Bag Branch
3 Mi.
36
Allen's Bridge &
John Williams
2 Mi.
Jackson Lake
Butts
County
1 Mi.
Indian Fishery Shoals
Sediment
South River
Barnes Shoals
Alcovy River
251 Mi.
Walker Marina
Lemon Shoals
& Bushrod Frobel
250 Mi.
N
W
E
S
36
Tussahaw Creek
Jasper
County
249 Mi.
0 0.25 0.5 1 Mile

Allen's Bridge

Length 6 miles (Ga. 212 to Walker Marina on Jackson Lake)

Class I

Time 3–5 hours

Minimum Level This short stretch of river is generally navigable year-round. Flows above 100 cfs at the Rocky Plains gauge should provide sufficient water.

River Gauge The nearest river gauge is located at Rocky Plains Road, upstream of this section: https://waterdata.usgs.gov/ga/nwis/uv/?site_no=02208000&PARAmeter_cd=00065,00060,00062,00010.

Launch Site There is no developed launch site at this location. Parking is limited to the shoulder of the road. If you are accessing the river via private property rather than the right-of-way, permission must be sought from property owners.

DIRECTIONS From the intersection of Ga. 162 and Ga. 212 south of Porterdale, travel southeast on Ga. 212 for 1.8 miles to the bridge over the river. The best access is on the east and downstream side of the bridge.

Take Out Site The take out site is at Walker Marina, a private boat ramp and marina located on Lake Jackson. Parking fees may apply.

DIRECTIONS From the launch site, travel 2.5 miles southeast on Ga. 212 to the roundabout at the intersection with Ga. 36. Turn right on Ga. 36 (the first turn out of the roundabout) and proceed 0.5 mile. Turn left on Campbell Road and proceed 1.7 miles. Bear to the right on Rocky Point Road and proceed 1.2 miles. Turn left on Lang Road and travel 0.7 mile to Walker Marina.

Outfitters Jackson Lake Rentals, owned by Barry Dendy, provides pontoon boat rentals and ski tube rentals with pickup at Berry's Boat Dock.

Jackson Lake Rentals, 770-713-7069, www.jacksonlakerentals.com

Description This flatwater and lake journey takes in the last of the free-flowing Yellow as it spills into the backwaters of Jackson Lake. The riverbanks are wooded, wild, and mostly undeveloped until you reach the backwaters of the lake, where waterfront homes become more numerous.

Points of Interest

MILE 5.9 (33.454300, −83.881018) Webb's Bridge. Now the Ga. 212 bridge, the bridge that spanned the river here in the 19th century was known as Webb's Bridge. Augustus James Webb, a farmer from the Rocky Plains area, and his wife, Talitha Wright, reared eight children in this portion of Newton County between 1846 and 1867.

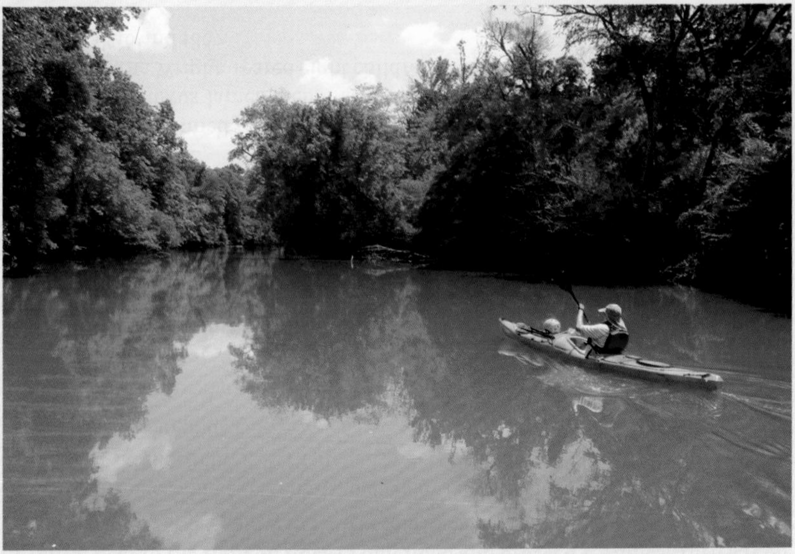

NEAR LEE SHOALS, NEWTON COUNTY

MILE 4.4 (33.433214, −83.879830) Lee Shoals. Though not visible today, these shoals are noted in an 1885 Georgia Department of Agriculture publication as a potential location for developing water-powered industry. They were described as having a fall of 4 feet over a distance of 1,400 feet. It was one Yellow River shoal that never was harnessed; many others on the Yellow and its tributaries certainly were. *The Commonwealth of Georgia: The Country, the People, the Productions* gives a full description of Gwinnett, DeKalb, Rockdale, and Newton Counties, including numerous industries, most of which were powered by water: "The four counties through which the river flows had in 1880 a population of 54,489 . . . There were 233 manufacturing establishments of all kinds . . . producing articles valued at $1,083,252. In addition to these there are . . . the Covington Cotton Mills at Cedar Shoals and the Sheffield Cotton Mills operating 3,160 spindles. Embraced in the manufacturing establishments above are 67 flour and grist mills, 44 saw mills . . . and the Rockdale paper mill is located on Yellow River." Today 1.9 million people live in those same four counties, but with the exception of the Milstead hydropower operation upstream, no power is generated by the river, and no mills still operate.

MILE 3.2 (33.417866, −83.882918) Allen Shoals. Surveys of the river from the 1880s note that this shoal created a drop of 2 feet over a length of 400 feet and was once the site of a mill. The shoals now lie beneath the backwaters of Lake Jackson.

MILE 2.4 (33.409921, −83.883670) Allen's Bridge & John Williams. In February 1921, this bridge (only its supports and a pier remain), then known as Allen's Bridge, was the scene of one of the most horrific murders in Georgia history.

Once exposed, the story laid bare the widespread and illegal practice of peonage on Georgia farms, a system that kept many blacks in virtual slavery well into the 20th century. In the years following the Civil War, thousands of former slaves found themselves jailed, many on charges of vagrancy, for state laws required black men to be employed. An idle black man was sure to be incarcerated. With no means to post bail or pay their fines, these men languished in jail unless a "benefactor" paid their fine. The "benefactor" then took the freed prisoner and required him to work off the fine on the plantation. Common practice was to keep the men in debt slavery indefinitely. Such was the case on the plantation of John Williams in Jasper County. When federal investigators, tipped off to the illegal activity, paid Williams a visit and asked pointed questions of Williams and his black workers, Williams panicked. Fearing he would be discovered, he systematically killed 11 of his workers, forcing his black foreman, Clyde Manning, to commit the murders. The first two to die were chained together, weighted with sacks of rocks around their necks, and forced over the rail of Allen's Bridge. The completion of Lloyd Shoals Dam a decade earlier had widened and deepened these rivers, making them, to Williams's way of thinking, ideal places to dispose of bodies. Another of his men was chained and forced off the bridge over the South River the same night. Two more met a similar fate in the Alcovy arm of the lake the next evening. When the bodies were discovered, the trail ran back to Williams and Manning, who were both arrested for murder. In that era, the murder of black men was not usually noted in newspapers, but the heinous nature of these crimes both attracted national attention and the attention of prominent progressive white Atlantans, who paid not only for the defense of Manning but also for additional attorneys to assist the local prosecutor in seeking the conviction of Williams. At trial in Covington, an all-white jury found Williams guilty of murder. The verdict marked the first time since 1877 that a southern white man was convicted of first-degree murder of a black man or woman. Even more compelling was the fact that he was convicted primarily on the testimony of a black man. While newspapers hailed the justice wrought in the Newton County Courthouse, and Governor Hugh Dorsey issued an antipeonage proclamation, little changed. Peonage persisted, and it was 45 years before another white man was convicted of murdering a black man in the South. Perhaps the most revealing story of the virulent racism of that era was a letter from Williams's pastor in Monticello, published in the *Atlanta Constitution*. Far from defending Williams, the pas-

REMAINS OF ALLEN'S BRIDGE, NEWTON COUNTY

tor called for justice. Yet in the same breath, he attacked the press for vilifying Jasper County as a den of peonage and murder. The man of the cloth concluded that Williams would get a "fair and impartial trial by a set of twelve men of the old Anglo-Saxon strain of blood, unmixed by any foreign element whatsoever, and I know of no better people on earth."

MILE 1.7 (33.407527, −83.874368) Jackson Lake. At this bend, the river begins its spread behind the 1911 Lloyd Shoals Dam. When it was built, the 100-foot-tall dam was among the largest in the United States. It brought electric light to surrounding communities, but for many its construction was more curse than blessing, and in at least one instance, the curse was of biblical proportions. In the years immediately after the filling of the lake, the surrounding land was beset by a plague of frogs. Said one local resident: "I've seen so many frogs on this road out here that you could look down and see the black streak where a car, wagon or something went along and killed them." More troublesome was an outbreak of malaria that was attributed to the expansive lake. Several residents died, and others abandoned their farms and homes to escape the threat. Already angered by being forced to sell their prime farmland along the Yellow, South, and Alcovy Rivers, Newton County residents fought back against the Central Georgia Power Company. A local grand jury indicted the company for failure to clear the reservoir area properly, and other residents sued to have the reservoir drained. A letter to the editor published in the *Covington News* called the dam builders "northern capitalists," railing, "This cruel corporation comes along and takes their [residents'] homes and orders them to move out. Those who have been brave to stay are paying for it with sickness and death. Where does justice and right come in, my people? . . . There is but one remedy. The reservoir must be drained." Of course, it was not. Today the dam continues to generate electricity for Georgia Power. The reservoir, with 135 miles of shoreline and a maximum depth of 98 feet, spreads over more than 4,700 acres of former farmland and forest, hosts hundreds of lakefront homes, and serves as a recreational mecca for the area.

MILE 0.8 (33.397898, −83.877648) Indian Fishery Shoals. Buried beneath the water of Lake Jackson is this shoal, described in 1885 as having a fall of 12 feet over a length of 400 feet. The U.S. Department of Interior reported of the shoal: "At the head of the shoal a natural rock dam extends entirely across the river, with deep water above it. A fall of 11 feet is used by a grist mill on the right bank." The name likely refers to a Native American fish dam, or weir, that probably was used at this location before damming for the mill.

MILE 0.5 (33.393058, −83.876435) Sediment. Here along the mainstem of the Yellow is evidence of the siltation of Jackson Lake in the shallow water and on marshy islands. Like all reservoirs, Jackson Lake is destined, over time, to fill with the soil washed down river from upstream land. Between the completion of the dam in 1911 and 1935, studies showed that the storage capacity of the lake had been reduced by about 12 percent. By 1991, Georgia's Department of Natural Resources estimated that the reservoir had lost more than 40 percent of its original storage capacity because of sediment buildup. Aside from reducing the lake's storage capacity, the sediment can degrade water quality, blocking sunlight from reaching aquatic vegetation and reducing water levels—a combination that can result in higher water temperatures and decreased oxygen levels. The lake has periodically experienced fish kills due to that very deadly combination.

MILE 0.0 (33.387948, −83.877270) South River. Probably no other river in Georgia has been—and continues to be—more maligned than the South. In the 1880s, it became the city of Atlanta's first sewer when workers ditched springs that gives rise to the river, lined it with rocks, covered it, and began piping to it the waste from the city's affluent homes that had flush toilets. By 1890, the city was home to 2,829 flush toilets, many of which emptied directly into the South. More than 100 years later, it still is plagued by sewer leaks and combined sewer overflows during storm events. In recent years, the South River Watershed Alliance has pressured federal and state regulators and local sewage-treatment providers to upgrade sewage collection and treatment systems. These improvements are beginning to pay dividends in improved water quality. From the confluence of the South and the Yellow, the Ocmulgee runs about 252 miles to join the Oconee and form the Altamaha, which winds 137 miles to the Georgia coast at Darien.

MILE 251.4 (33.387168, −83.877230) Barnes Shoals. Before the impoundment of Jackson Lake, the free-flowing Ocmulgee spilled over Barnes Shoals here. An 1876 U.S. Army Corps of Engineers Survey described the now-submerged shoal this way: "The last shoal on the river [Ocmulgee], Barnes', is just at the junction of the South and the Yellow rivers, and is utilized for a grist-mill. The head of the shoal is on both streams, and just at the junction of the two is a rock ledge, crossing both, and forming an almost perfect dam, with deep water above it. The width of the South river is about 325 feet; that of the Yellow river about 275 feet; and that of the Ocmulgee about 500 feet." A precipitous fall, Barnes dropped nearly 12 feet over a distance of just 500 feet.

MILE 250.7 (33.378196, −83.873472) Lemon Shoals & Bushrod Frobel. Submerged near here is another of the Ocmulgee's original shoals. Described in an 1876 U.S. Army Corps of Engineers survey: "At Lemon shoal . . . a natural rock dam extends almost entirely across the river, leaving an opening of about 50 feet, called Bull Sluice." Colonel Bushrod Frobel, a West Point graduate, Confederate veteran, and noted engineer in post–Civil War Georgia, was responsible for traveling the river and surveying it for the corps in 1876. A dreamer of big dreams and clearly a river man, as a U.S. congressman he attempted to secure appropriations to build a canal connecting the Mississippi River to the Atlantic Ocean via the Tennessee and Savannah Rivers. He also tried to sell the city of Atlanta on a plan to dig a 75-mile canal from the Chattahoochee north of Atlanta to the city center. The canal would power industrial facilities by day, and then at night, when the mills shut down, the water would be diverted to a massive sewage-collecting tunnel beneath the city. The diverted flows would carry the waste to the Chattahoochee downstream of Atlanta. More than 100 years later, such tunnels, in fact, have been constructed, though the sewage is now treated before being released into the river.

FREEMAN'S MILL DAM, GWINNETT COUNTY

ALCOVY RIVER

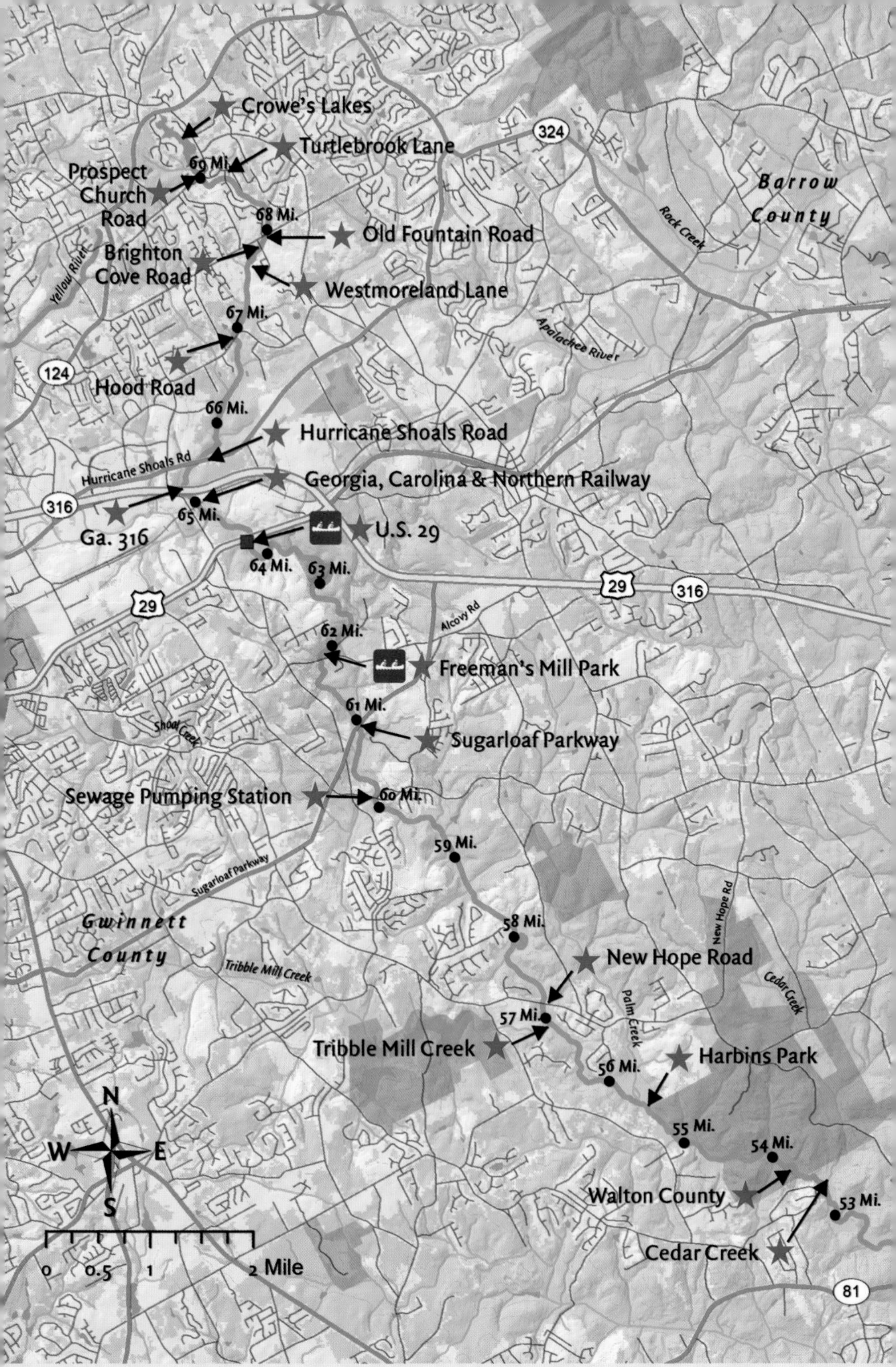
Crowe's Lakes
Turtlebrook Lane
324
69 Mi.
Prospect Church Road
Barrow County
68 Mi.
Old Fountain Road
Rock Creek
Brighton Cove Road
Yellow River
Westmoreland Lane
67 Mi.
Apalachee River
124
Hood Road
66 Mi.
Hurricane Shoals Road
Hurricane Shoals Rd
Georgia, Carolina & Northern Railway
316
65 Mi.
Ga. 316
U.S. 29
64 Mi.
63 Mi.
29
316
29
Alcovy Rd
62 Mi.
Freeman's Mill Park
61 Mi.
Shoal Creek
Sugarloaf Parkway
Sewage Pumping Station
60 Mi.
59 Mi.
Sugarloaf Parkway
58 Mi.
Gwinnett County
New Hope Rd
New Hope Road
Tribble Mill Creek
Cedar Creek
Palm Creek
57 Mi.
Tribble Mill Creek
56 Mi.
Harbins Park
N
W
E
S
55 Mi.
54 Mi.
Walton County
53 Mi.
0
0.5
1
2 Mile
Cedar Creek
81

Dacula

Length 17 miles (Headwaters to Ga. 81)

Class Unnavigable (foot, bike, vehicle travel only). Though most of this section is not navigable, whitewater-paddling enthusiasts can, at proper water levels, run a short, 2-mile section of the river between U.S. 29 and Alcovy Road.

Time Not applicable

Minimum Level For whitewater enthusiasts interested in running the section from U.S. 29 to Alcovy Road, flows of between 200 and 1,000 cfs at the New Hope Road gauge are recommended.

River Gauge A river gauge is located at New Hope Road, in the middle of the headwaters section and downstream of the whitewater run: https://waterdata.usgs.gov/ga/nwis/uv/?site_no=02208150&PARAmeter_cd=00065,00060,00062,00010.

Trailhead The first 16 miles of the Alcovy River are generally unnavigable, and because much of this section flows through private land, foot travel is prohibited without permission from landowners. This run of river is best explored from public roads, via bicycle or automobile. But there are a few accessible public lands along the route, including Freeman's Mill Park and Harbins Park, where travelers can experience the river.

DIRECTIONS TO HEADWATERS The Alcovy River rises along a ridge paralleled by Ga. 124 / Braselton Highway in Gwinnett County. Its headwaters are immediately dammed at Crowe Lakes at the intersection of Brasleton Highway and Terrace Lake Drive. From the intersection of Ga. 20 and Old Peachtree Road, travel east on Old Peachtree 2 miles. Turn right on Braselton Highway and proceed 0.2 mile before turning right into the parking area of the Old Peachtree Village shopping center. Crowe Lakes are visible on the opposite side of the road within the Lakes of Old Peachtree subdivision.

DIRECTIONS TO GA. 81 (LAUNCH SITE FOR NEXT SECTION) From the intersection of Ga. 20 and Ga. 81 in Loganville, travel north on Ga. 81 for 5.7 miles to the river. The best access is along the right-of-way at the corner of Jack Pittman Road on the east (north) side of the bridge.

Launch Site for Whitewater Run (at U.S. 29) There is no developed launch site at this location, but it is possible to access the river via the right-of-way on the north and upstream side of the bridge.

DIRECTIONS From the intersection of Ga. 316 and U.S. 29, travel southwest on U.S. 29 toward Lawrenceville 0.7 mile to river.

Take Out Site for Whitewater Run (at Alcovy Rd.) Gwinnett County's Freeman's Mill Park provides access to the river here.

DIRECTIONS From the launch site, travel 0.4 mile toward Lawrenceville on U.S. 29. Turn left on Cedars Road and proceed 0.4 mile. Cedars Road becomes Rock House Road. At 0.4 mile, Rock House Road bears right and East Rock House Road continues straight. Bear right on Rock House Road and travel 0.7 mile. Turn left on Alcovy Road and proceed 0.5 mile to the entrance to Freeman's Mill Park on the left.

Description The Alcovy's headwaters, like those of its sister streams the South and the Yellow, have been dramatically altered by human activity. Within a mile of the river's beginnings, it is dammed four times to create small ponds that now serve as amenities for residential developments. From there the river weaves between suburban neighborhoods, beneath multiple roads, and past industrial and commercial pockets as it cuts a southeasterly course through Gwinnett County. Though the river is mostly inaccessible and on private land, Gwinnett County's Freeman's Mill Park, home to a historic gristmill, and Harbins Park, with its dozens of miles of recreational trails, provide opportunities to visit and explore the river. In high water, the 2.5-mile section between U.S. 29 and Freeman's Mill Park provides whitewater paddling enthusiasts with a popular run that includes Class II–IV rapids.

Points of Interest

MILE 69.4 (34.031478, −83.952418) Crowe's Lakes. These lakes were formed in 1950 when Grover S. Crowe, the owner of a general store on Braselton Highway, built a series of dams on the Alcovy's headwaters to create several fishing holes. The lakes became a landmark along the Braselton Highway during the later part of the 20th century. Visitors could fish for $1 a day (by the 1980s, inflation had bumped the fee to $2) every day but Sunday, when Crowe closed the lake for use by local churches. "Baptizing and fishing don't go together," he told the *Atlanta Constitution* in 1984. Crowe, who died in 1991, opened his general store in 1925 after he traded a 50-gallon barrel of homemade sorghum syrup for chewing tobacco, snuff, and groceries and then began selling those traded wares. The site of his store, where he sold a wide variety of supplies, including chicken feed and motor oil, is now occupied by a strip mall housing, among other things, a fitness center and a hair and nail salon. On the east side of the lakes runs a ridge that separates the Alcovy-Ocmulgee river basin from the Apalachee-Oconee basin. The spring that gives rise to the Apalachee begins 800 feet to the east of the lakes, on the opposite side of Old Peachtree Road. The waters separated by geology here are rejoined some 300 miles downstream where the Oconee and Ocmulgee unite to form the Altamaha.

MILE 69.0 (34.026654, −83.949183) Prospect Church Road.

MILE 68.7 (34.026611, −83.945095) Turtlebrook Lane.

MILE 67.9 (34.019195, −83.938099) Old Fountain Road.

MILE 67.8 (34.019195, −83.938099) Brighton Cove Road.

MILE 67.6 (34.015249, −83.940598) Westmoreland Lane.

CROWE'S LAKE, GWINNETT COUNTY

MILE 66.9 (34.005153, −83.942739) Hood Road. Between Crowe's Lakes and Hood Road—a distance of less than two miles—the Alcovy is flanked by no fewer than 100 homes as it flows through the heart of suburban Gwinnett County. Between 1970 and 2017, Gwinnett's population swelled from 72,000 to more than 920,000. With that growth has come increased pollution of the area's streams as fields and forests have been replaced by asphalt, concrete, and rooftops. When rains come, stormwater, rather that soaking into the ground, runs off man-made surfaces and courses through stormwater infrastructure directly into the Alcovy. This type of pollution, known as non-point-source pollution, is considered the leading cause of water pollution in Georgia. The impacts of non-point-source pollution are far reaching. Even in low-density residential development in which as little as 12 percent of the land has been converted to hardened surfaces, streams can become polluted. As the density of development increases, stream health deteriorates: bacteria levels increase, water temperatures rise, stream-bank erosion worsens, and insect and fish diversity declines. Gwinnett County property owners pay a stormwater utility fee, in addition to ordinary property taxes, to help fund and implement practices that protect the Alcovy and the county's other streams.

MILE 65.6 (33.988724, −83.948142) Hurricane Shoals Road.

MILE 65.3 (33.984582, −83.950975) Ga. 316.

MILE 64.9 (33.982569, −83.948076) Georgia, Carolina & Northern Railway. The railroad, now part of the CSX rail system, was originally built between 1887 and 1892, connecting Atlanta with Charlotte. In 1896, the 272-mile trip from

Charlotte to Atlanta took around seven hours. In September 2000, a train derailment near here caused the release of some 90,000 gallons of ethylene glycol and methanol, a spill that forced the city of Monroe to shut down its drinking-water intake downstream. Such incidents have prompted many water authorities to initiate interconnections with adjacent water systems in order to provide redundancy in case of similar emergencies.

MILE 64.4 (33.978574, −83.939219) U.S. 29. The 2.5 miles from here to Alcovy Road contain a notable whitewater run for those that like narrow, creek-like runs. The route includes Class II–IV rapids (depending on water levels) and is navigable only during periods of high flows, 200–1,000 cfs, according to Suzanne Welander and Bob Sehlinger's *Canoeing and Kayaking Georgia*. On river right at this location is Gwinnett County's Alcovy Pump Station, a facility that moves the county's sewage through pipes to the F. Wayne Hill Water Resources Center, one of the county's three primary sewage-treatment plants. Sewage-pumping stations are common in Gwinnett County because F. Wayne Hill sits on a rise of land, rather than in bottomland, like most sewage plants. (In the latter case, sewage systems rely on gravity to move waste to treatment facilities.) As Gwinnett County grew in the 1980s, county leaders set aside land along the Yellow River for a major sewage plant, but that property's proximity to houses ultimately made it an undesirable spot for an often odoriferous facility. Legend has it that the county commissioner F. Wayne Hill chose the site of the plant named in his honor after conducting aerial reconnaissance and identifying a site between I-85 and I-985 where few houses existed.

MILE 61.9 (33.963425, −83.926439) Freeman's Mill Park. This property was purchased by Gwinnett County in 2002 with $350,000 provided by the state's Community Greenspace Program, which was established to encourage fast-growing counties like Gwinnett to preserve at least 20 percent of the county's land from development. Milling at the site began in the years following the Civil War and continued until 1986, making it Gwinnett's last operating, and only surviving, water-powered gristmill. In 1880, census data show that the mill churned out 40 barrels of flour, 14,400 pounds of cornmeal, and 54,000 pounds of livestock feed annually. During historic flooding in 2009, the mill was saved by renovations that had recently raised the building 5 feet above its original foundation. Gwinnett took that precaution in part because the river's 100-year floodplain had expanded: intense development surrounding the river had changed the natural landscape and exacerbated flooding events. Some residents during that flood were not so lucky, since floodwaters inundated properties previously thought safe from flood hazards. While the historic mill has been preserved by the county, historic uses of the river at the mill—namely, baptisms—have not endured. For generations, the nearby Alcova Baptist Church conducted baptisms at the mill, but when the county took ownership of the property, those ceremonies ended. Park rules prohibit "swimming, bathing and wading" except in "areas designated for such use." The 10-foot-high milldam does indeed create a hazard, especially during high flows, which can come suddenly following heavy thun-

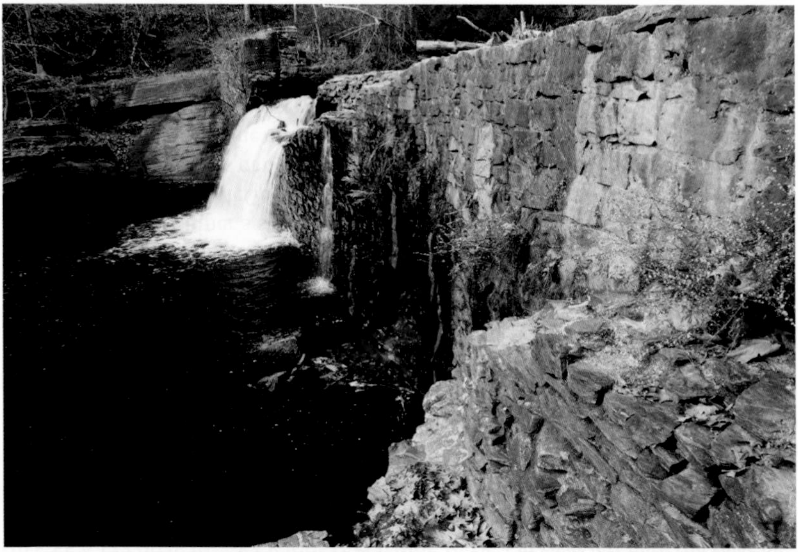

FREEMAN'S MILL DAM, GWINNETT COUNTY

derstorms as large volumes of stormwater run off the surrounding developed landscape. In addition to the restored mill building, with its interactive and interpretive exhibits, the 12-acre park features a playground, a walking trail, and restrooms.

MILE 60.9 (33.953923, –83.920291) Sugarloaf Parkway.

MILE 60.1 (33.944136, –83.917354) Sewage Pumping Station. On river right here is a Gwinnett County Department of Water Resources pumping station. Gwinnett County has an undulating landscape, and therefore some of its 3,000 miles of sewer lines are "force mains." Force mains use pumps to push sewage uphill, and in Gwinnett County there are about 300 miles of force mains, serviced by more than 200 pumping stations like the one here. Traditionally, sewer lines are placed so that gravity can do the work of moving waste. That is why sewage treatment facilities are often located in bottomland along rivers. But Gwinnett County's F. Wayne Hill Water Resource Center sits on a hill, which contributes to the complexity of moving sewage to the facility. The maintenance of smaller pumping stations like this one becomes critical if sewer systems are to function properly. The Brooks Road pumping station moves about 2.3 million gallons of sewage a day.

MILE 57.2 (33.917171, –83.888069) New Hope Road.

MILE 56.9 (33.914490, –83.886689) Tribble Mill Creek. Just upstream on this creek is Gwinnett County's Tribble Mill Park, a 700-acre passive recreation park that features a 100-acre lake surrounded by a 3-mile paved recreational trail, plus 12 additional miles of trails for hikers, bikers, and horseback riders. The park

SHOALS AT BROOKS ROAD, GWINNETT COUNTY

sits on the former site of Tribble Mill, a gristmill located on a precipitous rock outcropping along which the creek flows. Remains of the overshot wheel and milldam can be seen at this popular swimming hole and sliding rock. Upstream of the remains of the mill is the 39-foot-high dam built in 1992 to form Ozara Lake, the centerpiece of the park.

MILE 55.6 (33.903520, −83.870051) Harbins Park. On river left here the river begins skirting this 1,960-acre Gwinnett County park, most of which is preserved in its natural state for passive recreation. The park features more than 4 miles of paved trails as well as 7 miles of equestrian trails, a 13-mile route for mountain bikes, and a 4-mile hiking trail that descends to a rock outcrop overlooking the river. The county finalized purchase of the property in 2003 and opened the trails in 2009. Protection of the Alcovy was one of the reasons for acquiring the property. The park sits amid what in the 1800s was known as the community of Harbins, named for John Harbin, one of the area's early settlers. During the 1840s and 1850s, he served as captain of the local militia district and justice of the peace. During Prohibition, this property was likely the site of a notable bust of a moonshiner's still, which was reported in 1925 in the *Atlanta Constitution*: "Sheriff W. T. McGee and two deputies cut down a 60-gallon still and destroyed 2,000 gallons of beer yesterday in Harbins district. The still was near Alcovy River and when the officers were within about 50 feet of the operators, they made a dive for the icy water, swimming to safety on the other side, but not before they were recognized by the officers. Arrests will be made soon, according to the sheriff."

MILE 53.7 (33.895736, −83.844965)
Walton County. Here, the Alcovy leaves Gwinnett County and passes into Walton County, where it winds south and southwest for more than 22 miles before entering Newton County. In December 1818, Walton was one of seven counties formed following the acquisition of Creek and Cherokee Indian lands. Among the others were Gwinnett and Hall, which form Gwinnett's northern boundary. The three connected jurisdictions were named to honor Georgia signers of the Declaration of Independence—George Walton, Button Gwinnett, and Lyman Hall.

HARBINS PARK, GWINNETT COUNTY

MILE 53.4 (33.893701, −83.839768)
Cedar Creek. Just upstream of the mouth of this creek are the remains of the Hugh Lowe Grist Mill, which dates to the late 1800s. Along the creek in Harbins Park is a massive stacked stone pier associated with the mill and a portion of the earthen millrace that carried water to the mill. The remnant stone walls of the mill building are located in Walton County on adjacent private land.

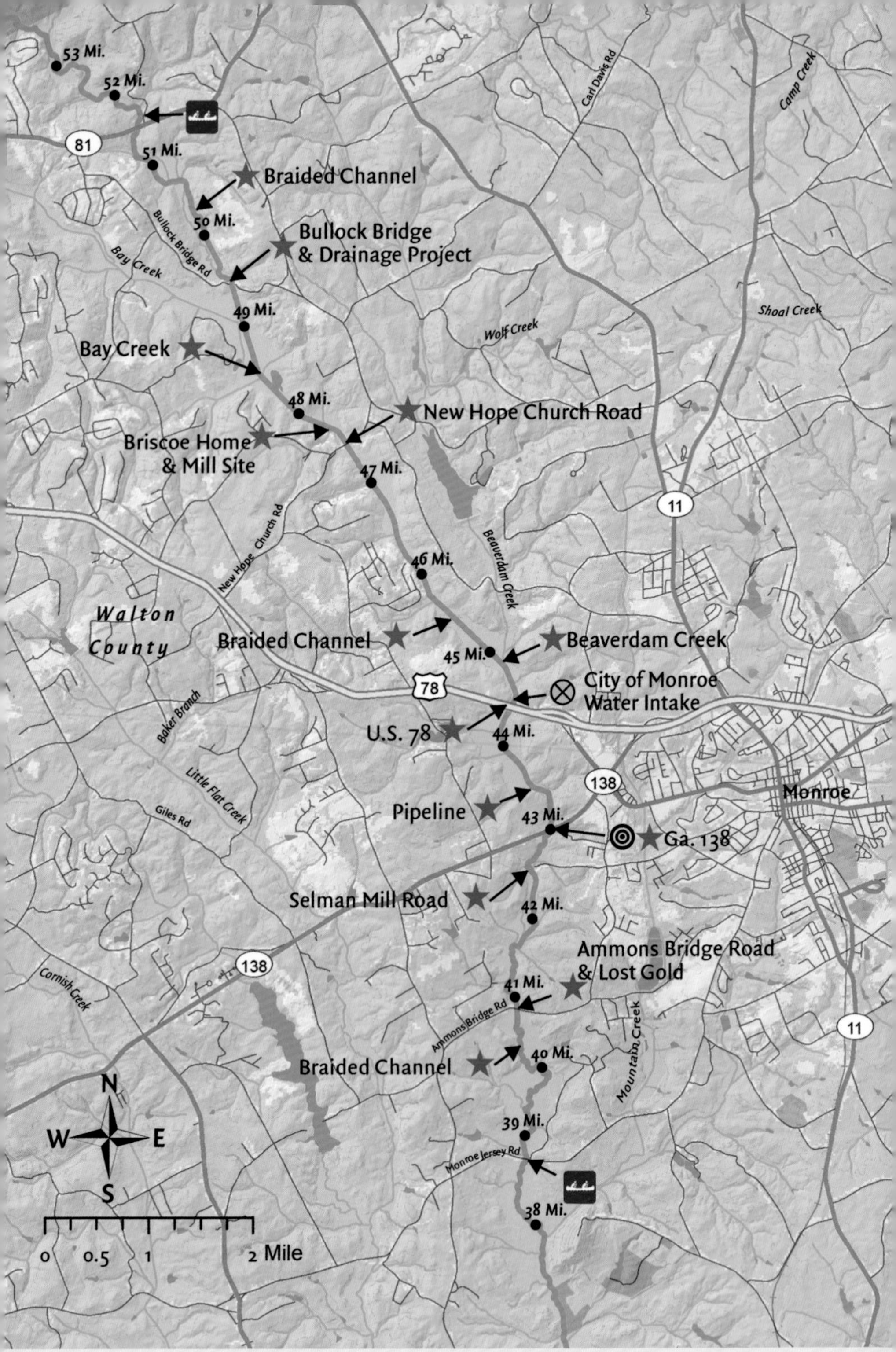

53 Mi.
52 Mi.
81
51 Mi.
Braided Channel
50 Mi.
Bullock Bridge Rd
Bullock Bridge
& Drainage Project
Bay Creek
49 Mi.
Bay Creek
Wolf Creek
Shoal Creek
Camp Creek
Carl Davis Rd
48 Mi.
New Hope Church Road
Briscoe Home
& Mill Site
47 Mi.
11
New Hope Church Rd
Beaverdam Creek
46 Mi.
Walton
County
Braided Channel
Beaverdam Creek
45 Mi.
78
City of Monroe
Water Intake
Baker Branch
U.S. 78
44 Mi.
138
Little Flat Creek
Monroe
Pipeline
Giles Rd
43 Mi.
Ga. 138
Selman Mill Road
42 Mi.
Ammons Bridge Road
& Lost Gold
138
Cornish Creek
41 Mi.
Ammons Bridge Rd
11
Braided Channel
40 Mi.
Mountain Creek
N
W
E
S
39 Mi.
Monroe Jersey Rd
38 Mi.
0
0.5
1
2 Mile

Monroe

Length 12 miles (Ga. 81 to Monroe Jersey Road)

Class I

Time 4–7 hours

Minimum Level Flows of at least 50 cfs at the New Hope Road gauge provide enough water to float this section, but not without numerous portages over deadfalls and strainers. This section is best paddled in the winter and early spring during flows of at least 100 cfs at the New Hope Road gauge. During flows above 300 cfs, the river begins spreading into the extensive floodplain swamps surrounding this section, making off-channel exploration possible.

River Gauge The nearest river gauge is located at New Hope Road upstream of this section: https://waterdata.usgs.gov/ga/nwis/uv/?site_no=02208150&PARAmeter_cd=00065,00060,00062,00010.

Launch Site There is neither parking nor a developed launch site at Ga. 81, but it is possible to access the river via the right-of-way at the bridge. River users must seek permission from property owners before accessing the river from private property.

DIRECTIONS From the intersection of Ga. 20 and Ga. 81 in Loganville, travel east on Ga. 81 for 5.6 miles to the bridge.

Take Out Site There is neither parking nor a developed launch site at Monroe Jersey Road, but it is possible to access the river via the right-of-way at the bridge. The best access is on river left beneath the bridge.

DIRECTIONS From Ga. 81 at the Alcovy River, travel east on Ga. 81 0.7 mile. Turn right on Double Springs Road and proceed 6.4 miles. Turn right on Bold Springs Road and travel 1.0 mile. Turn right on Ga. 11 and proceed 3.3 miles through Monroe to Alcovy Street. Turn right and travel 4.4 miles on Alcovy Street and Monroe Jersey Road to the bridge.

Alternative Take Out Sites Bridges at New Hope Church Road, U.S. 78, Ga. 138, and Ammons Bridge Road create trips of 4, 7, 8, and 10 miles respectively. There is neither parking nor a developed access point at any of these bridge crossings.

Access must be along the rights-of-way. River users must seek permission from property owners before accessing the river from private property.

Description Excursions on this section of river, which bisects Walton County, should be considered carefully. Frequent blowdowns and cross-river strainers on this narrow river can turn a short trip into a long, arduous journey involving multiple portages. Additionally, in numerous sections the river separates into multiple braided channels, some not much wider than a canoe, where the difficulties of cross-river strainers are pronounced. Between Ammons Bridge Road and Monroe

Jersey Road are places without a discernible channel. For these reasons, this section of river is lightly traveled. Though it runs through growing Walton County, its wide floodplain lends it a remote and isolated feel. Long stretches of the first five miles of this section run unnaturally straight—the result of dredging and drainage work conducted on the mainstem of the river in the early 1900s. Those seeking to explore this section should look to the high water in the winter and early spring months, when many strainers are submerged and opportunities to explore off the river's main channel increase.

Points of Interest

MILE 50.4 (33.872593, −83.815355) Braided Channel. Here the river splits as it spreads out in the low, flat floodplain. Follow the flowing water; the channels ultimately reconnect.

MILE 49.4 (33.861242, −83.807524) Bullock Bridge & Drainage Project. Beginning in 1928, a 177-foot pony truss bridge carried traffic over the river here. For most of the next 5 miles, the Alcovy runs unnaturally straight. That is because the channel is completely unnatural—the work of channelization and dredging projects undertaken in the early 1900s in an effort to drain and cultivate bottomlands. The Georgia General Assembly adopted its first drainage laws in 1911, in answer to calls from promoters who bemoaned the swampy lands along the state's streams as "worthless" except for growing "mosquitoes, scrubby willows, bulrushes . . . and frogs." In fact, much of this swampy land owed its condition, in part, to nearly a century of poor soil management on the state's sprawling plantations. Tilled soil, especially in the hilly Piedmont, quickly eroded, flowed downhill, and filled streams with silt, thus reducing their carrying capacity. Even when moderate rains came, the rivers overflowed their banks, spilling into bottomlands. The solution, in 1911, was to straighten and deepen the channels mechanically, and soon dredges were found across the state, digging up riverbeds and straightening bends. Work began on the Alcovy and numerous tributaries in 1916 with the goal of engineering some 21 miles of the Alcovy River, Bay Creek, and Beaverdam Creek and "drying up" some 2,000 acres of land. A report in a 1917 issue of the *Jackson Argus* newspaper described the work: "The dredge boat is 18 feet wide and 80 feet long. It has a fifty horsepower boiler and engine on it . . . The big steam shovel can lift and throw out one and a half cubic yards of dirt with each movement . . . They also have a 'house boat' 14 × 60 feet that is carried along with the dredge boat . . . with bunks for the men to sleep and . . . a complete commissary and kitchen." The correspondent went on to extol the benefits of the project: "Within three years these reclaimed bottoms will stop all importations of corn into Walton County." Farmers along the streams chipped in some $25,000 to pay for the work. Within a year of completion of the channelization, the *Atlanta Journal* reported a jump in property values along the channelized river and creeks. While the farmers of Walton County

NEAR BULLOCK BRIDGE, WALTON COUNTY

might have grown more corn, the river and streams suffered. We now know that the channelization and dredging of rivers and the draining of wetlands results in loss of aquatic biodiversity and declines in water quality. As it turns out, a river's sinuous nature and the woody debris that collects in its bends is critical for its health.

MILE 48.5 (33.848528, −83.802072) Bay Creek. At the junction of Bay Creek and the Alcovy on May 20, 1917, in the midst of work to channelize the river, fire destroyed the $15,000 dredge boat of Carr & Moore, the North Carolina–based company contracted to complete the project. The tragedy was noted in the *Jackson Herald*: "The work of drainage of this one of Walton's most important streams will be held up for a few days. However it is the purpose of the drainage people to reconstruct and begin work at the earliest possible date."

MILE 47.7 (33.842005, −83.790659) Briscoe Home & Mill Site. Just up the small creek on river right is this historic home and mill site, one of more than 25 sites on the National Register of Historic Places in Walton County. The mill and farmhouse, dating to the late 1890s, were the home of Phillip and Frances Brown Briscoe, whose son, Phillip Darling Briscoe, became the first mayor of the tiny town of Between in 1908, when it was incorporated. While the mill no longer stands—a modern house was built on the mill's foundation, overlooking the shoal-filled stream—the two-story farmhouse remains. Like a growing number of locations in Georgia, it was used as a backdrop for a movie: scenes in the 2009 movie *Get Low*, starring Bill Murray and Robert Duvall, were shot at the house.

MILE 47.5 (33.839776, −83.787617) New Hope Church Road. Upon its completion in 2012, the bridge spanning the river here was named in honor of Besse Brown Cooper when the Walton County resident turned 116 years old. At the time of her death, on December 4, 2012, she was recognized as the oldest person in the world by Guinness World Records. Upon her death, only seven other people had been documented as having lived longer than her 116 years and 100 days. Originally from Tennessee, she moved to Walton County during World War I because wages for schoolteachers were better in Georgia than they were in Tennessee. A suffragette during her early adulthood, she was active in recruiting other women to register to vote. She and her husband settled nearby in the Between community, and she lived independently until she was 105. She said that her secret to longevity was to mind her own business and not eat junk food. Grover Cleveland was the president when she was born; Barack Obama was the president when she died.

MILE 45.5 (33.816863, −83.767339) Braided Channel. Just downstream of the cleared pasture, riverside deck, and homesite here, the wide river channel returns to its braided and fickle ways. There are multiple narrow, strainer-choked channels from which to choose. Numerous strainers and cross-river deadfalls continue to the U.S. 78 bridge.

MILE 44.8 (33.810421, −83.760312) Beaverdam Creek. Although it is difficult to discern, thanks to the river's multiple channels, the confluence of this creek marks the southern boundary of the Alcovy drainage project. Downstream the river returns to its winding—and natural—ways.

BRAIDED CHANNEL, WALTON COUNTY

MILE 44.5 (33.805163, −83.758559) City of Monroe Water Intake. On river left here is the water intake for the city of Monroe. The city of more than 13,000 people depends on the Alcovy and the John T. Briscoe Reservoir, formed by a dam on Beaverdam Creek, for its primary water supply. Water is pumped from this location nearly 3 miles to the city's 10 million-gallons-a-day treatment plant, located near downtown, which in turn feeds a network of 241 miles of distribution lines and more than 8,000 customers.

MILE 44.4 (33.804759, −83.758878) U.S. 78. The twin bridges here, the first dating to 1950 and the second to 1986, are the latest in a long line of bridges built here since the mid-1800s, when at least six bridges spanned the Alcovy in Walton County. In January 1886, this bridge provided egress from Monroe to Atlanta for perhaps the most unusual foot traffic to cross any river in Georgia: a 6,000-pound elephant named Empress and a pair of camels. In December 1885, while the Giles Circus was visiting Monroe, the outfit declared bankruptcy, stranding the circus animals and performers in town and leaving local law enforcement with the responsibility of caring for the animals until an auction could be held to satisfy creditors. After the auction, the purchaser of the elephant and camels wanted them taken to Atlanta, where they could be boarded on a train. This required the three animals and their handler to travel more than 40 miles. After crossing the bridge, the procession soon ran into severe cold weather, which forced the quartet to seek shelter at a blacksmith's shop in Loganville, where the forge—and many blankets—kept the elephant warm. After a journey of at least five days, Empress and her entourage arrived in Atlanta, where she convalesced for a month. On her departure, a representative of the Sells Brothers Circus told the *Atlanta Constitution* that Empress was in first-class shape despite her arduous journey from Monroe: "She is fat as a mole and looks as healthy as it is possible for her to be. From the size of her feed bill I see no reason to complain that her appetite has not been good."

MILE 43.4 (33.793483, −83.752467) Pipeline.

MILE 43 (33.788193, −83.751639) Ga. 138. Beneath the bridge here is a small rocky shoal.

MILE 42.5 (33.782330, −83.754408) Selman Mill Road. This bridge on private land is still used. The now-closed public road that once led across it bears the name of key figure in Walton County history. George Selman, who was born in 1825, the son of a Revolutionary War veteran, would become known as the "founder of Monroe's industrial progress" during the post–Civil War era. Among the business ventures he initiated were the Monroe Oil and Fertilizer Company, the Bank of Monroe, and Monroe Cotton Mills. His circa-1830s home, which he married into, still stands near downtown Monroe, about 2 miles due east of this spot. In the 1870s, Selman acquired thousands of acres to the west of the home, encompassing the Alcovy, where he operated an extensive plantation. The half mile of river downstream of the bridge is relatively free of strainers and blowdowns, a notable absence in the run of the river between Ga. 81 and Monroe Jersey Road.

SELMAN MILL ROAD BRIDGE, WALTON COUNTY

MILE 40.8 (33.763784, −83.756330) Ammons Bridge Road & Lost Gold. During the Civil War, as Union cavalry raided local communities during the siege of Atlanta and later as Sherman's army marched to the Georgia coast, foraging off the produce of the state's farms and liberally requisitioning everything, including silk dresses, silverware, tobacco, and horses, local residents often attempted to hide their livestock and other valuables in the swamps along the Alcovy. A report in an 1885 edition of the *Sandersville (Ga.) Herald* attests to this: "Two men in Walton County the other day, while cutting down a tree near the Alcovy River, discovered one thousand dollars in gold, which had been plugged up in the hollow of a tree. It is thought the gold was put there during the war by someone, who possibly forgot the hiding place." The section between Ammons Bridge Road and Monroe Jersey Road downstream is an obstacle course of strainers, deadfalls, and narrow braided channels.

MILE 40.4 (33.754183, −83.751257) Braided Channel. On river left here are several dilapidated outbuildings. They mark the beginning of a full mile of extensively braided channels—some no wider than a canoe—to Monroe Jersey Road. At points there is no discernible channel. Exiting a boat and dragging it through the swampy and densely forested floodplain may be required. It is this wild, inaccessible, and inhospitable landscape that in the early 1900s likely attracted those engaged in the production of illicit refreshments. A 1912 edition of the *Walton News* relays the story of federal and local law enforcement busting a "moonshine establishment" along the Alcovy River in this vicinity. During the bust, the authorities captured some 400 gallons of beer and confiscated the

BRAIDED CHANNEL NEAR AMMONS BRIDGE ROAD, WALTON COUNTY

still. The paper reported that the still was taken to Monroe, cut into pieces, and sold for scrap metal. The Georgia General Assembly enacted a statewide prohibition on alcoholic beverages in 1908, and Georgia remained dry until 1935. Fast-forward some 85 years: Georgia is in the midst of a craft-beer-making renaissance, with more than 50 local breweries in operation. In 2019, two local breweries announced plans to begin production in nearby Monroe.

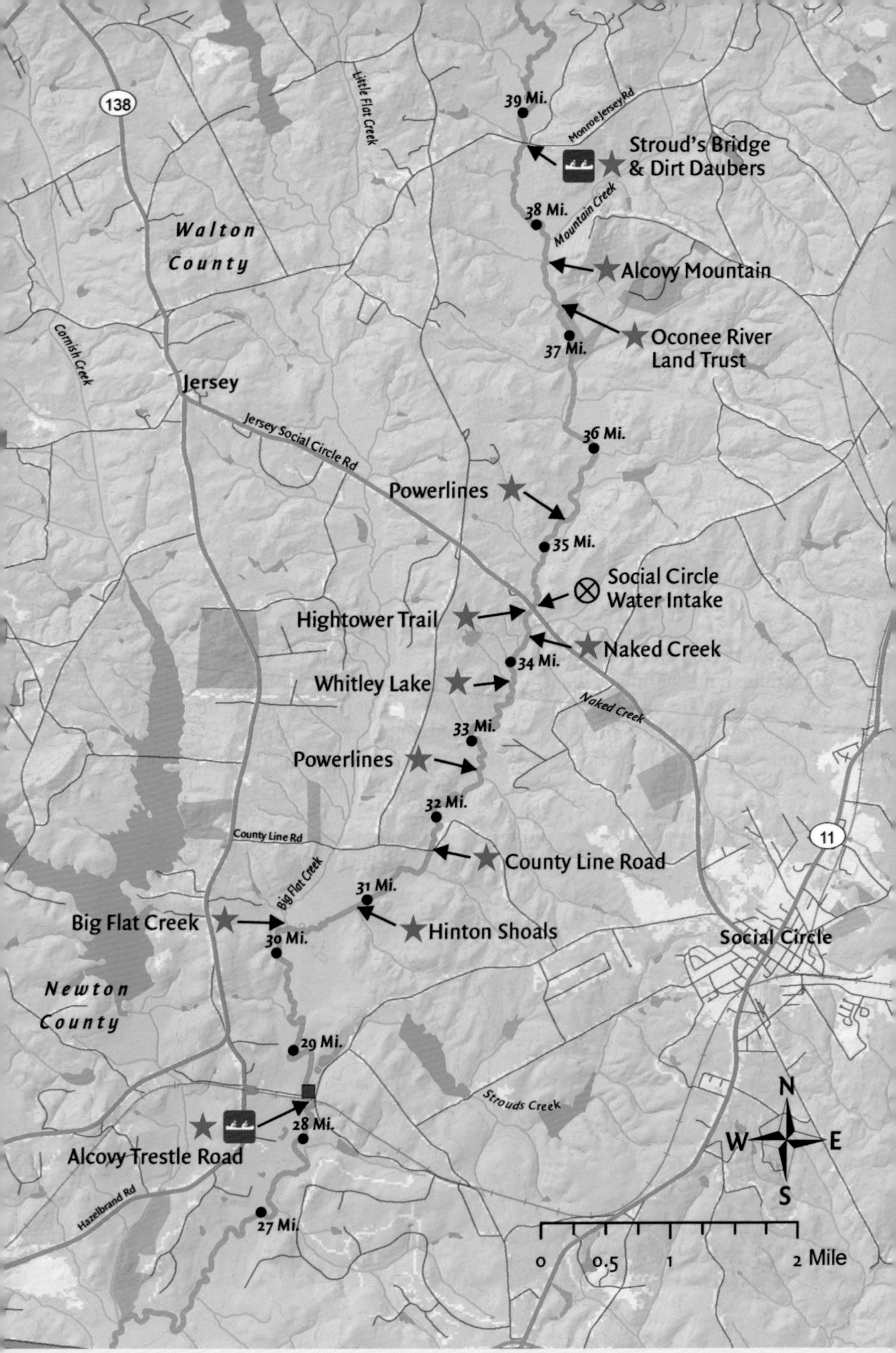
138
Little Flat Creek
39 Mi.
Monroe Jersey Rd
Stroud's Bridge
& Dirt Daubers
Mountain Creek
38 Mi.
Walton
County
Alcovy Mountain
Oconee River
Land Trust
37 Mi.
Cornish Creek
Jersey
Jersey Social Circle Rd
36 Mi.
Powerlines
35 Mi.
Social Circle
Water Intake
Hightower Trail
Naked Creek
34 Mi.
Whitley Lake
Naked Creek
33 Mi.
Powerlines
32 Mi.
11
County Line Rd
County Line Road
Big Flat Creek
31 Mi.
Big Flat Creek
Hinton Shoals
30 Mi.
Social Circle
Newton
County
29 Mi.
Strouds Creek
N
W
E
S
28 Mi.
Alcovy Trestle Road
Hazelbrand Rd
27 Mi.
0
0.5
1
2 Mile

Alcovy Trestle

Length 10 miles (Monroe Jersey Road to Alcovy Trestle Road)

Class I

Time 4–6 hours

Minimum Level Flows of at least 300 cfs at the Alcovy Trestle Road gauge provide enough water to float this section, but not without numerous portages over deadfalls and strainers. This section is best paddled in the winter and early spring, during higher flows of at least 400 cfs at the Alcovy Trestle Road gauge.

River Gauge The nearest river gauge is located at Alcovy Trestle Road, the take out site for this section: https://waterdata.usgs.gov/ga/nwis/uv/?site_no=02208450&agency_cd=USGS.

Launch Site There is neither parking nor a developed launch site at Monroe Jersey Road, but it is possible to access the river via the right-of-way at the bridge. The best access in on the east and upstream side of the bridge.

DIRECTIONS From the intersection of Ga. 11 (South Broad St.) in Monroe, travel southwest on Alcovy Street (it becomes Monroe Jersey Road) 4.5 miles to the bridge.

Take Out Site There is neither parking nor a developed launch site at Alcovy Trestle Road, but it is possible to access the river via the right-of-way between the road and the railroad trestle. The best access is on river right beneath the bridge.

DIRECTIONS From the Monroe Jersey Road bridge, travel west on Monroe Jersey Road 3.8 miles through Jersey. Bear left on Jersey Social Circle Road and proceed 0.1 mile. Turn right on Alcovy Station Road and travel 5.0 miles. Turn left on Alcovy Trestle Road and proceed 0.9 mile to the bridge and railroad trestle.

Alternative Take Out Sites Take out sites at Jersey Social Circle Road and County Line Road create trips of 5 and 8 miles, respectively. There is neither parking nor a developed access point at any of these bridge crossings. Access must be along the rights-of-way. River users must seek permission from property owners before accessing the river from private property.

Description Despite picking up the flow of several creeks, the Alcovy keeps up its inhospitable ways in this stretch. It remains narrow, choked with blowdowns and cross-river strainers, and prone to disperse into myriad braided channels. These elements can turn a short trip into a long, arduous journey involving multiple portages. But thanks to its wide floodplain, the river maintains a wild and remote feel. At multiple locations, the mainstem separates into braided channels, which increases the navigational challenges. The river flows through areas that have witnessed much history, including passing Hightower Trail, an ancient path that marked a river ford, and ending at the Alcovy Trestle Road bridge and adjacent railroad trestle, the site of much drama and notoriety since the Civil War.

Points of Interest

MILE 38.8 (33.743488, −83.754128) Stroud's Bridge & Dirt Daubers. Late 19th-century maps note this river crossing by this name. It is believed that James Stroud operated a gristmill on nearby Stroud's Creek, which empties into the Alcovy at the end of this river section near the Alcovy Trestle. Stroud was also a founding member of the nearby Harris Springs Church in Social Circle. On the underside of this bridge is a colony of dirt dauber nests. These skinny dirt tubes, which resemble the pipes of a pipe organ, were made by the appropriately named organ pipe dirt (or mud) daubers (*Trypoxylon politum*). These solitary wasps locate their nests on flat vertical surfaces sheltered from the rain and near their favored building material—moist, clayey dirt, which the Alcovy supplies in abundance. Each pipe may contain six or more egg chambers stocked with several paralyzed spiders. When the eggs hatch, the larvae consume the stashed spiders before forming a cocoon. When metamorphosis is complete, the adult dauber chews its way through the mud casing and emerges to find a mate and start the life cycle again.

MILE 37.7 (33.730325, −83.750095) Alcovy Mountain. Forming a strong contrast to the swampy bottomlands through which the Alcovy passes, this mountain on river left rises 300 feet above the river to a height of 1,072 feet, making it the highest point in Walton County. The forested peak is topped by a ridge of rock outcroppings and, of course, a cell tower.

PORTAGE, WALTON COUNTY

MILE 37.4 (33.724747, −83.748895) Oconee River Land Trust. On river left here are signs indicating that this property is protected under a conservation easement by this Athens-based land trust. The 195 acres were preserved between 2003 and 2011 by the property owner, Walter Wellman, and are now used for passive recreation. Conservation easements have become increasingly popular tools for landowners to permanently protect property in its natural or historic condition while also receiving tax benefits, including federal and state tax credits and deductions as well as reductions in local property taxes. While the property owner maintains possession of the property, land trusts, like the Oconee River Land Trust, hold the easement and are responsible for enforcing its conditions. Between 1993 and 2019, the Oconee River Land Trust protected more than 41,000 acres through 194 conservation easements.

MILE 35.4 (33.702368, −83.746620) Powerlines.

MILE 34.5 (33.693199, −83.751049) Social Circle Water Intake. On river left here, just upstream of the Jersey Social Circle Road bridge, is the water intake and drinking-water treatment plant for the city of Social Circle, located four miles to the southeast. The city can produce up to 1 million gallons a day from this site for the community of more than 4,000.

MILE 34.4 (33.692804, −83.751143) Hightower Trail. Jersey Social Circle Road follows the same path as this historic Native American path, which stretched from High Shoals on the Apalachee River northwest to the Chattahoochee River near present-day Roswell and then farther to the Etowah River. The trail, which historically marked the boundary between the Cherokee and Creek tribes, was a major thoroughfare for the first settlers of North Georgia. It was among the first Alcovy fords to be bridged when, in 1823, Thomas Autry constructed a span here. On November 17, 1864, a portion of the Union Army under the command of General William T. Sherman camped along the banks of the river here. The next morning, they crossed the river and marched into Social Circle—a town that had already been ransacked and burned by Union Cavalry raiders in July. With no supply lines from the north to bring in food for his army of 62,000 as it marched through Georgia, Sherman instructed his troops to "forage liberally on the country." In Social Circle, the soldiers confiscated, among other things, sweet potatoes, corn syrup, and hogs and captured $3,000 in gold. Five miles to the south at the Burge Plantation, the army left an indelible impression on Dolly Sumner Lunt Burge, who recorded her experience in *A Woman's Wartime Journal*, published in 1918. A widow trying to manage her large farm in the midst of chaos, she wrote: "Like demons they rush in! My yards are full. To my smoke-house, my dairy, pantry, kitchen, and cellar, like famished wolves they come, breaking locks and whatever is in their way. The thousand pounds of meat in my smoke-house is gone in a twinkling, my flour, my meat, my lard, butter, eggs, pickles of various kinds . . . wine, jars, and jugs are all gone. My eighteen fat turkeys, my hens, chickens, and fowls, my young pigs, are shot down in my yard and hunted as if they were rebels themselves. Utterly powerless I ran out and appealed to the guard. 'I cannot help you, Madam; it is orders.' . . . I saw nothing before me but starvation."

MILE 34.3 (33.689759, –83.751969) Naked Creek. Entering on river left here is this small, short, and peculiarly named tributary, which originates 2 miles to the southeast in Social Circle along the divide between the Ocmulgee and Oconee river basins. The historian John Goff, who chronicled Georgia place-names, asserts that the name is likely an example of "po' mouthing," which was common among the early settlers of Georgia. The hardships endured by these pioneers, Goff contends, led them to name geographic features to reflect their struggles. Some other examples include Needy Creek and Trouble Creek. But since early settlers likely bathed and swam in these waters—probably in the nude—the reference to "naked" could be imbued with as much pleasure as pain. Either way, the name's origins remain something of a mystery, as does the name of the town where it originates. Legend holds that the name was born when the first settlers gathered in a circle to pass a jug of spirits and socialize. If that story is true, this jovial gathering might have well led to the first incident of skinny-dipping in the small creek.

MILE 33.8 (33.684748, –83.753727) Whitley Lake. On river right, this small tributary delivers the outfall from Whitley Dam, a circa-1950 dam that forms a 7-acre private lake, one of 31 ponds and lakes in Walton County. Across the state are more than 5,000 such dams, with an average age of 55 years. Thus, Whitley Lake is typical of many of the state's man-made reservoirs. It was built long before the passage of the Clean Water Act in 1972, which requires that those seeking to build dams restore or improve the health of other streams or wetlands before damming a free-flowing stream. Dams have multiple negative impacts on streams, including the disruption and fragmentation of habitat for aquatic fauna like fish and mussels and the alteration of water temperatures and the movement of nutrients through a river system. The result is a decline in stream health and a loss of aquatic biodiversity.

MILE 32.6 (33.673893, –83.757400) Powerlines.

MILE 31.7 (33.666628, –83.763978) County Line Road. The bridge here is known as the T. C. Dally Memorial Bridge, a name that pays homage to Thomas Carroll Dally, a longtime farmer in the Jersey community and a Walton County commissioner for more than two decades. Dally passed away in 1968, but the span was known as Dally's bridge long before his death. The Dally family's roots in Jersey date to the first decades of the 1800s. In the 1960s, Willow Springs Church in Social Circle held baptisms in the river here.

MILE 30.9 (33.660145, –83.773531) Hinton Shoals. Here the river again assumes a straight line. Like portions of the river upstream, Hinton Shoals, was the target of drainage projects in the 1930s. This particular project was funded under the Depression-era Emergency Relief Administration and its affiliates for the purpose of draining lands and preventing malaria. In 1933, the *Atlanta Constitution* reported that more than $8,000 had been allotted for drainage and malaria

WETLANDS AT BIG FLAT CREEK, NEWTON COUNTY

work, and in January 1934 the *Constitution* reported that $17,976 in relief funds was being used for malaria control at Hennen [*sic*] Shoals on the Alcovy. On river left, near the end of this run of straight river, is a dammed tributary and an irrigation pump and pipe.

MILE 30.2 (33.657641, −83.782639) Big Flat Creek. On river right, this tributary meets the Alcovy in a remarkable fashion, creating an extensive swamp-like wetland that in high water provides access to acres of paddling. Beyond the confluence, in high water, the river spreads into multiple channels fronted on the west by a high ridge topped with houses in the Alcovy Forest subdivision. Big Flat Creek runs some 20 miles, draining portions of western Walton County. Near the creek's headwaters, the city of Loganville discharges treated wastewater into this creek. In 2019, the city of some 12,000, with 53 miles of sewer lines, discharged more than 1 million gallons a day to the creek.

MILE 28.4 (33.639495, −83.778460) Alcovy Trestle Road. A bridge has spanned the river here since before the Civil War, but through the years, it has seen it share of trouble. In 1864 during the siege of Atlanta, Union cavalry burned the bridge (along with the adjacent railroad bridge) in an attempt to cut supply lines to the entrenched Confederate troops in Atlanta. Some 60 years later, during Prohibition, the bridge was burned again, this time by moonshiners. Discovered with illicit whiskey east of here by Newton County law enforcement, the moonshiners fled west toward Covington and across the bridge. In covering their escape, they set it ablaze. Though Prohibition ended as a part of federal law in 1933, Georgia remained dry until 1935.

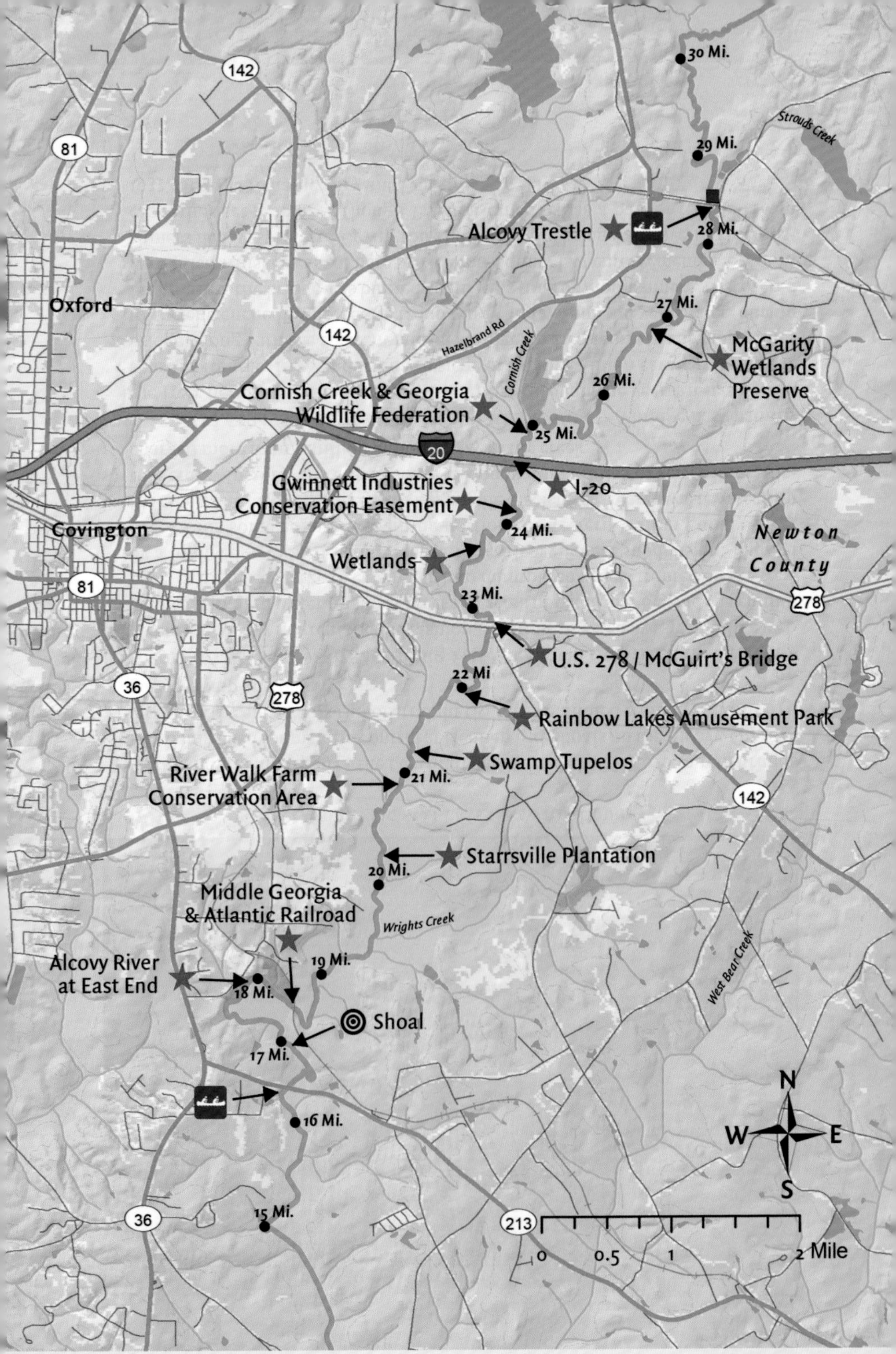
30 Mi.
142
81
Strouds Creek
29 Mi.
Alcovy Trestle
28 Mi.
Oxford
27 Mi.
142
Hazelbrand Rd
Cornish Creek
McGarity
Wetlands
Preserve
26 Mi.
Cornish Creek & Georgia
Wildlife Federation
25 Mi.
20
Gwinnett Industries
Conservation Easement
I-20
24 Mi.
Covington
Newton
County
Wetlands
81
23 Mi.
278
U.S. 278 / McGuirt's Bridge
22 Mi
36
278
Rainbow Lakes Amusement Park
Swamp Tupelos
River Walk Farm
Conservation Area
21 Mi.
142
Starrsville Plantation
20 Mi.
Middle Georgia
& Atlantic Railroad
Wrights Creek
West Bear Creek
Alcovy River
at East End
19 Mi.
18 Mi.
Shoal
17 Mi.
N
16 Mi.
W
E
S
15 Mi.
36
213
0
0.5
1
2 Mile

Covington

Length 12 miles (Alcovy Trestle Road to CR 213)

Class I

Time 4–6 hours

Minimum Level Flows of at least 100 cfs at the Alcovy Trestle Road bridge provide enough water to float this section, but not without numerous portages over deadfalls and strainers. This section is best paddled in the winter and early spring, during higher flows.

River Gauge The nearest river gauge is located at Alcovy Trestle Road, the launch site for this section: https://waterdata.usgs.gov/ga/nwis/uv/?site_no=02208450&agency_cd=USGS.

Launch Site There is not a developed launch site nor parking at Alcovy Trestle Road, but the river can be accessed on the west side of the river via the right-of-way between the road and the railroad trestle.

DIRECTIONS From exit 93 on I-20 (Ga. 142 Covington/Oxford), travel north on Ga. 142 for 0.3 mile. Turn right on Hazelbrand Road and proceed 2.9 miles to Alcovy Trestle Road. Turn right and proceed 0.4 mile to bridge. Parking is along the right-of-way on the south side of the road.

Take Out Site There is no developed public access at this location, but a usable take out is on river right beneath and downstream of the CR 213 bridge. Cars can be parked along the right-of-way on the west side of the river and the downstream side of the bridge.

DIRECTIONS From Alcovy Trestle Road bridge, go west on Alcovy Trestle Road 0.4 miles to Hazelbrand Road. Turn left and proceed 2.9 miles. Turn left on Ga. 142 and proceed 3.8 miles. Turn left on Ga. 36 and proceed 1.8 miles. Turn left on CR 213 and travel 0.6 mile. Park along the right-of-way on the west, downstream of the bridge.

Alternative Take Out Sites Taking out at U.S. 278 creates a 6-mile journey. There is neither a developed take out site nor parking at this location. Permission must be sought to access the river from private property. Scout take outs before your journey to ensure suitable access and parking.

DIRECTIONS From the Alcovy Trestle Road bridge, go west on Alcovy Trestle Road 0.4 miles to Hazelbrand Road. Turn left and proceed 2.9 miles. Turn left on Ga. 142 and proceed 1.4 miles. Turn left on U.S. 278 and travel 1.5 miles to the bridge over the river.

Description Narrow, often braided with multiple channels, and filled with a lumberyard's worth of deadfall and strainers, this section is recommended only for the adventurous. Those choosing the adventure should expect multiple portages around strainers each mile. High flows in winter and spring will limit the number of portages and can give access to some of the river's numerous bottomland swamps. The run is highlighted by a pure stand of swamp tupelos at the confluence of Cornish Creek, along with hundreds of acres of land protected through conservation easements in Newton County. And thanks to these wildlands, the section maintains a decidedly wilderness vibe despite its location in the heart of suburban Atlanta.

Points of Interest

MILE 28.4 (33.639373, −83.778520) Alcovy Trestle. Perhaps no other place on the river is as steeped in history and lore as this location, where Alcovy Trestle Road and the CSX railroad bridge span the river. The original Georgia Railroad bridge here was completed around 1845, and the community of Alcovy Station just west of the river soon sprouted. On July 22, 1864, Union cavalry under the command of Brigadier General Kenner Garrard descended on the covered railroad bridge and Colley's wagon bridge, capturing several passenger and baggage cars left on the west side of the trestle. After allowing passengers to remove their luggage, the raiding troopers set fire to cars as well as the bridges. Garrard's raiders cut critical communications and supply lines to the besieged city of Atlanta and rained terror on the people of nearby Covington. Remains of former stone abutments still stand beneath the current trestle.

ALCOVY TRESTLE, NEWTON COUNTY

Incidents of a less serious nature have also occurred here. In November 1935, newspapers across the state told the story of a young boy who jumped from the high trestle into the river twice and lived to tell about it: "The bridge is estimated to be 100 feet high by citizens in this section," reported the *Butler Herald*. "The boy told witnesses who reached the scene shortly after his second jump that 'Jesus told him to leap into the river and wash his sins away.'" And thanks to Covington's emergence as the "Hollywood of the South" in the late 1970s, this site was featured in the iconic TV series *The Dukes of Hazzard*. In 1979, filming took place on a Pratt truss metal bridge with wood decking that spanned the river. That bridge was replaced in 1985.

MILE 26.9 (33.625736, −83.787219) McGarity Wetlands Preserve. On river left here and descending along the east bank for nearly 1.5 miles to I-20 is this 136-acre site, which has been used by the University of Georgia's Odum School of Ecology since 1996 as an outdoor laboratory for wetlands research. It was acquired through a donation from developers who were required by the Clean Water Act to restore or preserve wetlands as compensation for destroying wetlands elsewhere. Eugene Odum, for whom the school is named, is considered the "father of modern ecology." Odum, in his 1953 textbook, *Fundamentals of Ecology*, set forth the idea of studying ecosystems by examining the interconnectivity of nature and mankind's impact on those systems. Odum had a personal connection with this area. His grandfather, William Pleasant Odum, moved to nearby Oxford in 1897 to enroll his children at Emory College at Oxford. That education apparently paid off for his progeny. William's son Howard Odum gained national prominence as a sociologist while working at UGA and at the University of North Carolina at Chapel Hill. In 1913, his wife gave birth to Eugene, who followed in his father's footsteps to academic fame.

MILE 24.9 (33.613562, −83.803154) Cornish Creek & Georgia Wildlife Federation. At the spot where Cornish Creek meets the Alcovy is what is considered the northernmost stand of pure swamp tupelos in Georgia. The low-lying forest becomes inundated during high water (6–7 feet or more at the Alcovy Trestle Rd. gauge) and can be accessed from the main channel. The property is appropriately owned by the Georgia Wildlife Federation (GWF), which led the fight to stop the dredging and channelization of the Alcovy in the late 1960s and early 1970s. While the early drainage projects on the Alcovy and other Georgia rivers were funded primarily by private landowners, by the mid-20th century the federal government, through the U.S. Soil Conservation Service (SCS), had taken ownership of the effort to "improve" the nation's rivers. The devastating effects of channelization did not go unnoticed by sportsmen who hunted ducks and cast for fish in these rivers. Studies showed that channelized streams saw a more than 90 percent drop in the abundance of game fish, so in the late 1960s, when the SCS proposed channelizing 80 miles of the Alcovy and its tributaries and draining some 4,000 acres of wetlands, the GWF and other organizations in Georgia's nascent environmental movement mobilized.

The Alcovy was not alone in being targeted for destruction. At the time, 164 similar projects were planned for Georgia's rivers and streams, and it seemed inevitable that all would be completed. No other federal agency oversaw the appropriateness of the projects, and so through the Department of Agriculture, drainage projects became self-perpetuating. Landowners were promised "improved" agricultural land at no cost, local governments welcomed the infusion of federal money, and congressional representatives relished bringing home the pork. And while ecologists recognized the damage done by these projects, few

CORNISH CREEK, NEWTON COUNTY

scientific studies looked at the their true costs. The scope of the boondoggle was mind-boggling: while the federal government was paying farmers not to produce crops, the Department of Agriculture was simultaneously spending millions to channelize streams and drain wetlands in order to put *more* land into farm production. Often the projects cost more per acre than the value of the land that would be put in production. As pork-barrel projects go, the Alcovy project was the whole pig.

Soon, the Alcovy became a national lightning rod in the effort to put an end to the destructive federal program. Articles on the controversy appeared in *Outdoor Life*, *Field and Stream*, and *Reader's Digest*; Georgia's Game and Fish Commission asked the feds to delay funding for the project; Governor Lester Maddox gave his blessing to Alcovy advocates seeking to lobby the state's congressional delegation; and Congressman Ben Blackburn, who represented the area, introduced legislation to provide more federal and state oversight of SCS projects. The Alcovy project ultimately died in the early 1970s when further studies deemed it "no longer economically feasible." Soon the SCS was out of the channelization business nationwide. In a pointed letter to the SCS, the Department of the Interior wrote: "If the emphasis on channelization continues, the result will be the ultimate destruction or serious degradation of irreplaceable and valuable public resources, including fish and wildlife." Much of the attention brought to bear on the Alcovy was the result of the work of the Georgia State University ecologist Charlie Wharton, author of *The Natural Environments of Georgia*. His 1970 research paper "The Ecology of Bottomland Hardwood Swamps of the Southeast" quantified the economic value of these wetlands, which at the time were considered "wasted land," and helped lead to a change in federal wetlands policy. With the passage of the Clean Water Act in 1972, channelization of streams essentially became prohibited. The federal law now requires that any entity wishing to alter streams or wetlands must minimize those impacts and restore damaged streams or wetlands elsewhere. Today, this stand of swamp tupelos serves as a living reminder of the fight to save the Alcovy.

The GWF's 115-acre Alcovy Conservation Center houses the organization's offices and conference space as well as extensive trails leading through the Alcovy's and Cornish Creek's woodlands and wetlands. The trails are open to the public during business hours; call 770-787-7887.

MILE 24.5 (33.610988, −83.806997) I-20. Running 202 miles across Georgia's midriff from the Alabama state line near Tallapoosa to the South Carolina state line at Augusta, this interstate highway was built between 1960 and 1977. Since then, the Georgia General Assembly has been bestowing special names on sections of the highway. This particular stretch of the road was designated the Purple Heart Highway to honor military veterans who died or were injured in combat since World War I. That conflict saw passage of the Selective Service Act. President Woodrow Wilson, realizing he could not muster a large enough army solely through volunteers, approved the draft. In Georgia, this was not particularly popular, partly because of Georgians' long-standing animosity to federal controls, but more pointedly because the draft threatened to remove black laborers from farms and disrupt the South's entrenched caste system. Many white landowners failed to deliver draft notices to their sharecroppers; others used their influence to keep rural draft boards from conscripting "their" laborers. One planter complained to the feds: "Why didn't this board get my consent before they could reclassify my negroes?" The end result was that many blacks were arrested for failing to register. In an ironic twist of patronage, Thomas Watson, a lawyer, former congressman, influential political operative, opponent of U.S. involvement in the war, and self-avowed white supremacist, defended in court two black men who had failed to register for the draft. Interest in the trial was so intense that it was held in an outdoor venue in Augusta to accommodate the crowds. Of the 2.8 million men who served overseas in World War I, some 350,000 were African Americans.

MILE 24.2 (33.605423, −83.803976) Gwinnett Industries Conservation Easement. The 115 acres on river right, stretching downstream about 0.7 mile, are permanently protected by a conservation easement owned by the Georgia Wildlife Federation. Gwinnett Industries agreed to preserve the land in 2000. In fact, virtually all the land bordering the river's western bank from this site downstream for some 3 miles is protected. Newton County owns an additional 300 acres adjacent to this property. The county acquired the land as part of its efforts to mitigate expected impacts of the county's proposed Bear Creek Reservoir. This property and others acquired in 1990s laid the groundwork for a recreational trail following the river corridor, though the trail has yet to be completed.

MILE 23.7 (33.601682, −83.808748) Wetlands. On river right, look for signs of beavers and otters. In fact, the nearly 2 miles of river sandwiched between I-20 on the north and busy U.S. 278 on the south is teeming with wildlife, thanks, in part, to the extensive wetlands dominating the landscape, which host an important array of animals.

Nationally, wetlands provide habitat for about 50 percent of the fish, more than 30 percent of the birds, and nearly 20 percent of mammals protected under the federal Endangered Species Act. Though these wetlands are not known to hold any federally protected animal species, among the other mammals found within the Alcovy's swampy environs are mink, muskrat, swamp rabbits, deer, squirrels, and raccoons.

MILE 22.7 (33.593017, −83.807570) U.S. 278 / McGuirt's Bridge. In 2019, the Georgia Department of Transportation completed construction of the twin bridges here, which carry U.S. 278. The project replaced a mid-1950s bridge. The remains of an even earlier version of the bridge can be seen just downstream. In the late 19th century, the span over the Alcovy River was known as McGuirt's Bridge.

MILE 22.1 (33.585548, −83.810670) Rainbow Lakes Amusement Park. Due east of here is the former site of Rainbow Lakes Amusement Park, a popular gathering spot for Newton County youth in the mid-20th century. During its existence, the park featured an outdoor bowling alley and a dance pavilion along the river. Reportedly, the park also catered to the community's baser desires, including illicit drink and gambling. In the 1960s, the park was reconstituted as an experiential education center for troubled youth. Today, the Rainbow Lakes property is a private K–12 Christian school—Covington Academy.

TUPELO TREES, NEWTON COUNTY

MILE 21.2 (33.579048, −83.818157) Swamp Tupelos. Along this sandbar is a picturesque stand of swamp, or water, tupelos (*Nyssa aquatica*). Their swollen bases and thinner upper trunks make them conspicuous. Leaves are oblong with a pointed end. In the spring, greenish-white flowers appear, followed by oblong green drupes that turn dark purple with pale dots in the fall. The fruits are intensely sour. While *Nyssa aquatica* is found in appropriate wetlands habitat as far north as Illinois—and on other Georgia rivers in the Piedmont—their abundance on the Alcovy is unusual. They can be found not only in low, moist, braided wetlands like this one, but also clinging to the banks along the river's numerous shoals downstream.

MILE 20.9 (33.575441, −83.818906) River Walk Farm Conservation Area. On river right here, stretching downstream for the next 2 miles, is this 217-acre tract of land owned by River Walk Farm LP, for which the Georgia Wildlife Federation holds a conservation easement. Georgia's conservation easement program allows property owners to permanently protect land by forfeiting their development rights and other uses of the property in exchange for both state and federal income tax benefits. Easements also usually reduce property taxes and can reduce estate taxes. These easements are typically held by a state or local government or nonprofit organization, which is responsible for monitoring and enforcing the terms of the easement. River Walk Farm is a large subdivision stretching along the same length of the river.

MILE 20.2 (33.567698, −83.819241) Starrsville Plantation. On river left here are signs for this shooting preserve, which spreads over 775 acres and occupies the next 1.5 miles of riverfront. The property is part of the Starrsville Historic District, included on the National Register of Historic Places. With its roots in the 1820s, the community took its name from the Starr family, specifically, Silas H. Starr Sr., born in 1782 in Maryland. Silas moved with his family as a boy to Georgia; he later became one of the first settlers of the area, establishing a store that became the Starrsville post office 1.6 miles east of the Alcovy along present-day CR 213. His son, Silas H. Starr Jr., was noted in the Southern Historical Associa-

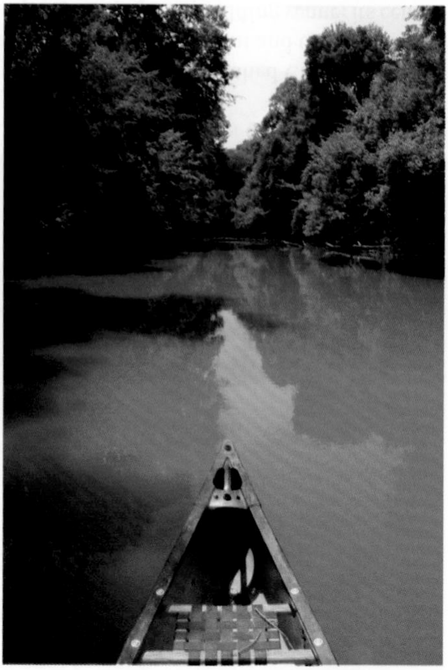

NEAR STARRSVILLE PLANTATION, NEWTON COUNTY

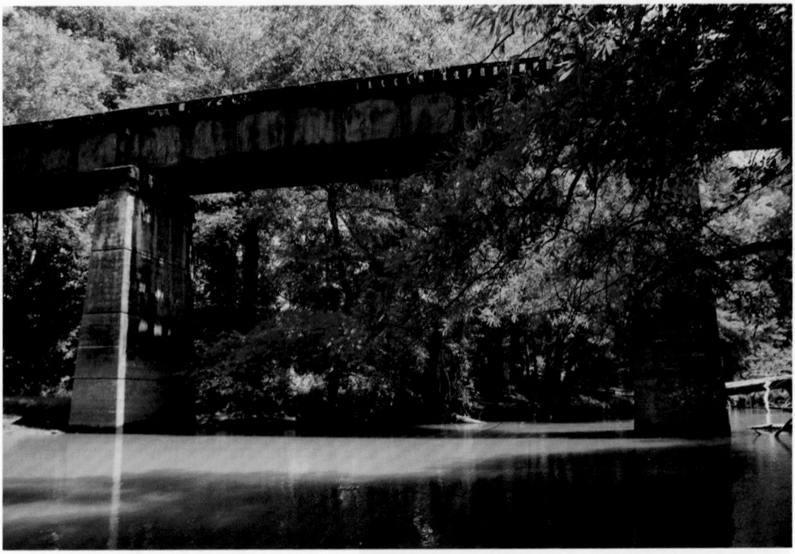

MIDDLE GEORGIA AND ATLANTIC RAILWAY, NEWTON COUNTY

tion's 1895 publication *Memoirs of Georgia*, as a distinguished Confederate veteran, prosperous general mercantile man, and "prominent and useful citizen." Today, the Starrsville Plantation property is a popular wedding venue; its centerpiece is a circa-1890s Victorian farmhouse that replaced the original 1820s-era home, which was destroyed by fire.

MILE 18.5 (33.551096, −83.832658) Middle Georgia & Atlantic Railroad. A railroad bridge has spanned the river here since 1894, when this line, running 64 miles from Milledgeville to Covington, was completed. This portion of the rail was in use until 2009; now portions of the line in Newton County are being converted into the Cricket Frog Trail, a multiuse recreational trail that will run nearly 15 miles from Covington to Newborn. The trail borrows its name from the native frog found in abundance along the Alcovy and the extensive wetlands bordering it. Cricket frogs are tiny ground dwellers not more than 1.5 inches in length. What they lack it size they make up for in leaping ability. The tiny frogs can jump more than three feet in one bound—the equivalent of a 6-foot-tall human leaping 200 feet. Leaping is their primary defense against predators. You are more likely to hear them than see them. Their call resembles the sound of steel marbles clicking together.

MILE 17.9 (33.554084, −83.837754) Alcovy River at East End. On river right here is yet another property owned by the Georgia Wildlife Federation, which manages the 17-acre parcel for conservation and educational purposes. An earlier attempt to maintain a canoe/kayak launch at this site failed, since the run from Ga. 278 to CR 213 is filled with deadfalls and strainers, making this an especially

SHOAL AT EAST END, NEWTON COUNTY

difficult section of river to run. Opposite this property, Newton County owns some 120 acres encompassing this large bend and extending up the river to the Middle Georgia & Atlantic Railway bridge.

MILE 16.9 (33.546645, −83.832622) Shoal. From this small shoal to Factory Shoals, some 8 miles downstream, shoals and rock outcroppings become numerous. While the Alcovy's descent through the Piedmont is less precipitous than that of its sibling streams, the Yellow and the South, some researchers theorize that many of the Alcovy's original shoals have been buried by tons of sediment washing into the river from the mid-1800s into the 20th century, when large portions of the uplands were cleared for row crops. This massive movement of soil, they argue, was responsible for creating the river's braided channels and extensive bottomland swamps.

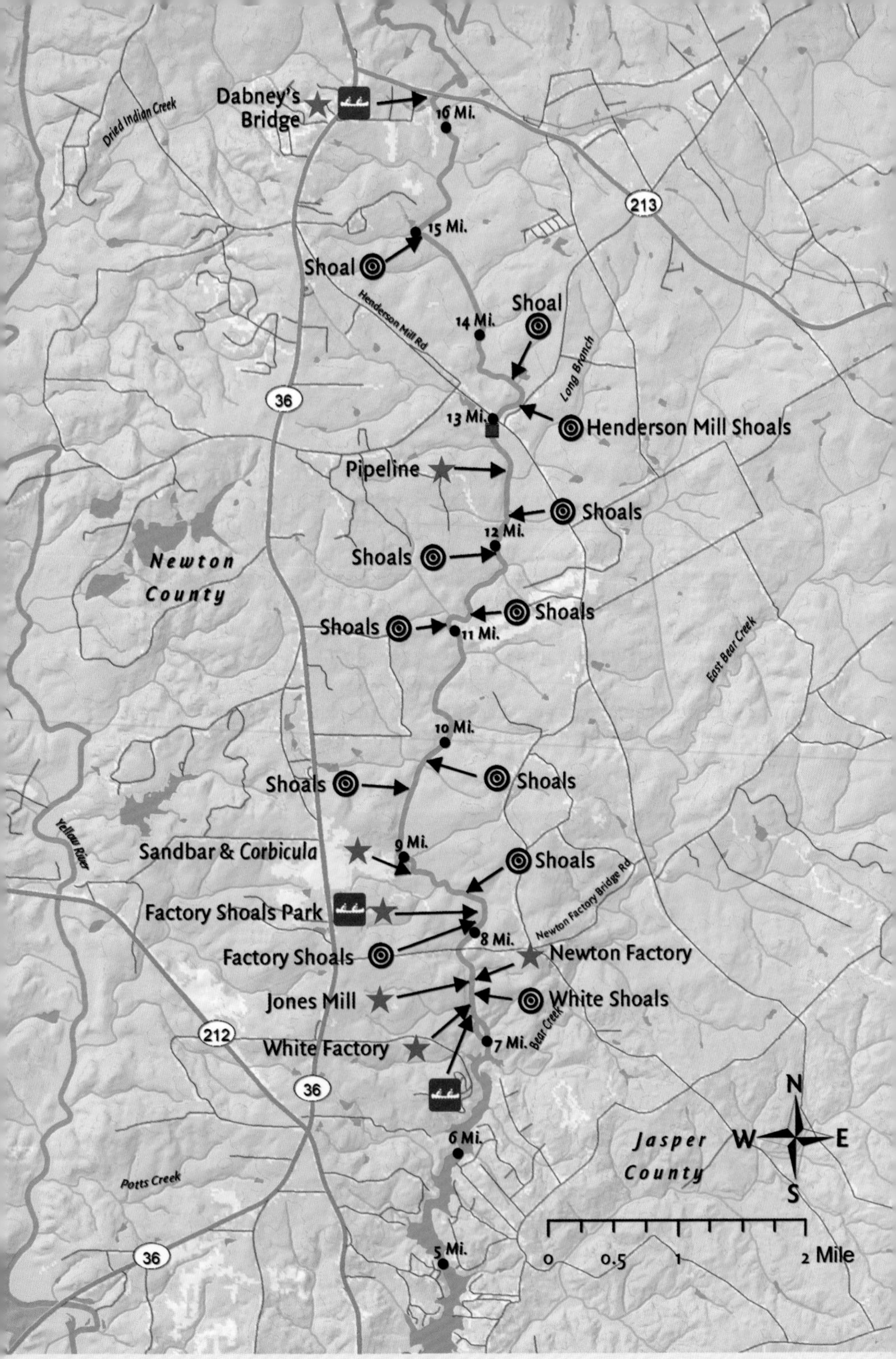

Dabney's Bridge
Dried Indian Creek
16 Mi.
213
15 Mi.
Shoal
Henderson Mill Rd
14 Mi.
Shoal
Long Branch
36
13 Mi.
Henderson Mill Shoals
Pipeline
Shoals
12 Mi.
Shoals
Newton County
Shoals
Shoals
11 Mi.
East Bear Creek
10 Mi.
Shoals
Shoals
Yellow River
Sandbar & Corbicula
9 Mi.
Shoals
Newton Factory Bridge Rd
Factory Shoals Park
8 Mi.
Factory Shoals
Newton Factory
Jones Mill
White Shoals
212
White Factory
7 Mi.
Bear Creek
36
N
W
E
S
Jasper County
6 Mi.
Potts Creek
0
0.5
1
2 Mile
36
5 Mi.

Factory Shoals

Length 9 miles (CR 213 to Factory Shoals Park)

Class I–IV

Time 4–6 hours

Minimum Level Flows of at least 200 cfs at the Henderson Mill Road gauge should provide enough water to float this section, though flows of 400 cfs are optimal for running the extensive rapids at Factory Shoals. At flows above 400 cfs, the rapids at Factory Shoals become increasingly difficult.

River Gauge The nearest river gauge is located at Henderson Mill Road, in the middle of this section: https://waterdata.usgs.gov/ga/nwis/uv/?site_no=02209000&PARAmeter_cd=00065,00060,00062,00010.

Launch Site There is neither a developed launch site nor parking at CR 213, but a usable launch can be found on the west and downstream side of the bridge.

DIRECTIONS From the intersection of Ga. 142 (Martin Luther King Jr. Ave.) and U.S. 278 east of Covington, travel south on Martin Luther King Jr. Avenue 2.5 miles. Turn left on Ga. 36 and proceed 1.8 miles. Turn left on Ga. 213 and proceed 0.6 mile to river. Parking in along the right-of-way on the west side of the river.

Take Out Site The take out site is a sandbar at the base of White Shoals within Newton County's Factory Shoals Park. Parking is available in the picnic area 300 feet from the river up a rugged footpath.

DIRECTIONS From CR 213, go west 0.6 mile to Ga. 36. Turn left and proceed 6.9 miles. Turn left on Newton Factory Bridge Road and travel 0.8 mile to the entrance to the park on the right. Turn right and proceed 0.4 mile. Turn right onto a one-way road to the picnic area and proceed 0.1 mile to the parking area on the side of the road at the picnic tables. A trail leads downhill through the picnic tables to the river.

Alternative Take Out Sites To create a 3-mile journey, take out at Henderson Mill Road. To avoid the Class II–IV rapids at Factory and White Shoals, take out at the Factory Shoals Park upper launch site. To run the Class II rapids above the Newton Factory Road Bridge and avoid the Class III rapids below the bridge, take out at the bridge.

DIRECTIONS TO THE FACTORY SHOALS PARK UPPER LAUNCH SITE From CR 213, go west 0.6 mile to Ga. 36. Turn left and proceed 6.9 miles. Turn left on Newton Factory Bridge Road and travel 0.6 mile to the entrance to the park. Turn left and follow the road 0.6 mile to the launch site. To park on the right-of-way at Newton Factory Bridge Road, do not turn into the park. Continue straight on Newton Factory Bridge Road and park along the right-of-way. There is limited parking at this location.

Description Leaving behind the swampy bottomlands upstream, the Alcovy below CR 213 begins behaving more like a typical Piedmont stream. It has better-defined banks, fewer cross-river strainers, and numerous shoals, which are spaced

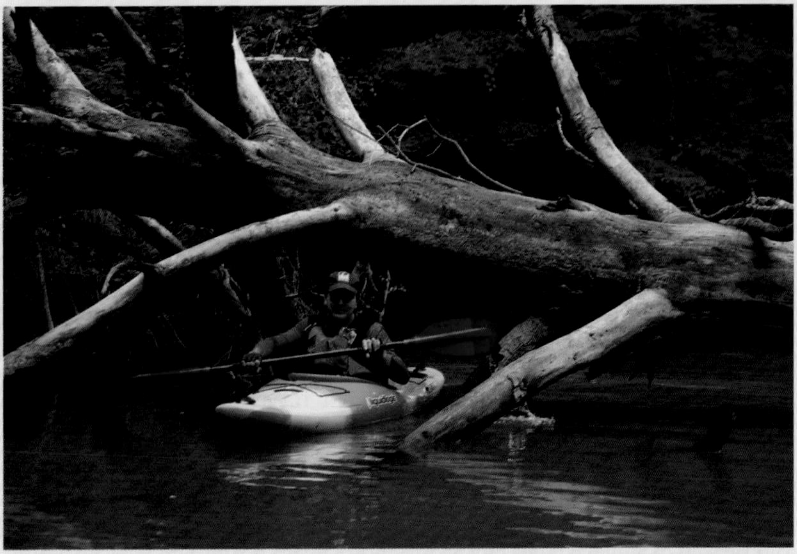

STRAINER, NEWTON COUNTY

out between long stretches of flatwater. Upstream of Factory Shoals, no obstacles exceed Class I in difficulty, but the final 0.8 mile through Newton County's Factory Shoals Park is almost continuous whitewater, with Class II–III rapids culminating in a 9-foot fall that pushes to Class IV in difficulty as the river rises. Factory and White Shoals should be attempted only by those with adequate whitewater paddling skills and should be scouted first. This section is among the most scenic of all Piedmont river runs in Georgia. The area is rich in history; the ruins of Newton Factory are still visible along the banks of the river.

Points of Interest

MILE 16.3 (33.542149, −83.833369) Dabney's Bridge. The ruins of pilings that supported a previous bridge are visible just downstream of the CR 213 bridge. In the early 1900s, this location was known as Dabney's Bridge.

MILE 14.9 (33.527001, −83.834712) Shoal.

MILE 13.5 (33.511204, −83.822460) Shoal.

MILE 13.2 (33.508718, −83.822108) Henderson Mill Shoals. Over the next 800 feet, the river descends over these shoals, which in the 19th century gave rise to the establishment of a gristmill that still stands on river left near the base of the shoals. When the mill was operating, these shoals would have been at the bottom of the millpond. An 1880 U.S. Army Corps of Engineers survey of the river notes a 180-foot-long, 5-foot high dam here that backed up the river some 4

HENDERSON MILL SHOALS, NEWTON COUNTY

miles. Isaac Henderson, who operated the mill during the mid-1800s, is noted as one of the earliest and most prosperous settlers in the area. Census records from 1850 show that he owned 47 slaves, farmed 2,100 acres, and produced 65 bales of cotton annually. He died in December 1864 in the midst of the Civil War, just months after Union cavalry barreled through his property in late July. The horse soldiers commanded by General George Stoneman were conducting a daring raid behind enemy lines to destroy railroads supplying Confederate troops in the besieged city of Atlanta. En route to their objective, they stopped long enough to demolish the bridge spanning the river here (remnants of a former bridge can be seen in the river just downstream of the current bridge), and they reportedly set fire to, but failed to destroy, the mill. Isaac's son, General Robert J. Henderson, who was off fighting at the time, came home following the Confederacy's surrender and operated the mill through the late 1800s. The mill continued to grind out flour and cornmeal until 1960. In the late 1960s, the mill was used as a restaurant and then became a private residence, which it remains today. Notable among those who have resided at the mill is Ray Bryan, who purchased the property in 1976 and lived there for nearly 20 years. The white-haired, white-bearded Bryan was among the Atlanta area's most famous mall Santa Clauses, taking down children's Christmas wish lists at Phipps Plaza in Buckhead for 23 years. At the height of Bryan's fame, Governor Joe Frank Harris named him Georgia's "official" Santa Claus. The large mill building rises three stories along the riverbank. It remains unclear how much of the original mill survived the Civil War, but current county records indicate that the existing structure was built in 1875.

MILE 12.5 (33.501409, –83.822541) Pipeline.

MILE 12.2 (33.496367, –83.822701) Shoals.

MILE 11.9 (33.493009, –83.823892) Shoals.

MILE 11.2 (33.485552, –83.828479) Shoals.

MILE 11.1 (33.484428, –83.829676) Shoals. These shoals are the most sizable ones located upstream of Factory Shoals. In contrast to its sister rivers—the South and the Yellow—the Alcovy, because of its less precipitous route through the Piedmont, did not spawn numerous milling operations. Late 19th-century river surveys describe the river as "sluggish" and "not favorable for power, being flat and with no falls." Those same surveys estimated that 2,052 horsepower would be available if all the Alcovy's falls and shoals were harnessed, and nearly all of that potential was contained in Factory and White Shoals. The engineers estimated the Yellow as capable of producing 6,690 horsepower, and the South was rated at 4,910 horsepower.

MILE 9.8 (33.469698, –83.833124) Shoals.

MILE 9.6 (33.467003, –83.834374) Shoals.

MILE 8.9 (33.458680, –83.833902) Sandbar & *Corbicula*. On river right here is a sizable sandbar that is often littered with the shells of this invasive mollusk species. In fact, it is hard not to stumble across Asian clams (*Corbicula fluminea*) on most stretches of the Alcovy. They litter the river bottom. A freshwater clam native to China, Korea, and Russia, this invader was first collected in the United States in the Columbia River in Washington in 1938. Since then, it has inexplicably spread across the country and can now be found in 38 states. Fish and birds are not considered likely culprits in the spread of this mussel, leaving humans as the only vector. The U.S. Fish and Wildlife Service surmises that accidental introductions through bait buckets and imported aquaculture species have been the primary causes of the mussels' dramatic spread through the country's rivers. *Corbicula* have been the bane of power plants and water-treatment facilities because the juveniles can get pumped into pipes, where they grow and eventually cause blockages. Because the clams are hermaphrodites, capable of self-fertilization, they are prolific reproducers. A single clam can release up to 70,000 juveniles each year. As populations of native mussels have declined, *Corbicula* have filled a void in the aquatic food chain, providing meals for fish and crayfish and mammals like muskrats, otters, and raccoons. Georgia is home to 98 species of freshwater mussels.

MILE 8.4 (33.456364, –83.829128) Shoals.

MILE 8.2 (33.455293, –83.825661) Factory Shoals Park. On river right is a small boat launch, a picnic area, and a restroom facility that is part of this Newton County park, which encompasses more than 400 acres of land on both sides of the river from this point to the base of White Shoals. Use this take out to avoid the Class II–III rapids downstream. The park features a campground, picnic areas, pavilions, restrooms, and walking trails along the river and among the ruins of the Newton and White factories, 19th-century industrial sites. The

DOG AND CAIRN AT FACTORY SHOALS, NEWTON COUNTY

county charges an entry fee of $2 per vehicle and $15 per night for campsites; call 678-699-2809.

MILE 8.1 (33.452506, −83.824628) Factory Shoals. From this spot, the river begins a more than 80-foot drop in elevation over the next mile. Above Newton Factory Bridge Road, the river drops over three Class II ledges. Routes will vary with the river's water level, with high water opening up more options. Below the Newton Factory Bridge Road bridge, an island splits the river, providing multiple routes, depending on water levels. The gradient increases, producing Class II–III rapids over the 800 feet immediately below the bridge. After descending the last of Factory Shoals, the river settles into a calm pool before descending through White Shoals.

MILE 7.5 (33.445996, −83.825453) Newton Factory. On river left here are some of the remains of this industrial site, which began harnessing the power of the Alcovy in the 1840s to mill cotton. The Newton Factory was later joined by the White Factory, across the river, sometime in the 1850s or 1860s. Census records from 1860 indicate a thriving community around the mills; 600 people lived in the post office district, including 64 who listed their occupations as factory workers. The dam here, as described in an 1885 Department of the Interior report, was 200 feet long and 6 feet tall and fed a 25-foot-long race that powered a cotton mill, sawmill, and gristmill. During the Civil War, a Union cavalry raid aimed at cutting railroad supply lines to the besieged city of Atlanta targeted the industrial facilities here. On July 28, 1864, a brigade of General George Stoneman's raiders descended on the White Factory and destroyed it. The Newton Factory, according to later Georgia Geological Survey records, met the same fate. As a result, the population of the Newton Factory post office district declined to 160 in 1870. Nevertheless, it appears that manufacturing continued at the site, since "Newton Factory Yarns" were advertised for sale in 1868 in the *Atlanta Constitution*.

MILE 7.4 (33.444505, −83.825955) Jones Mill. Located on river right, this mill is believed to have been the first industrial operation at these shoals. Remains of the mill's foundations and raceway can be seen along the wooded riverbank. Harrison Jones established a gristmill here in the early 1830s. By 1840, it was one of 12 gristmills operating in Newton County. Gristmills played a critical role in the early settlement of Georgia by providing a means for frontier families to transform their crops into usable and marketable commodities—flour and cornmeal. So important were gristmills that Georgia's earliest laws incentivized the construction of mills by providing land grants of up to 100 acres to prospective mill operators, and later the General Assembly granted operators the power of eminent domain, allowing them to take land needed for what many considered a "public utility." But as other operations—including sawmills and cotton mills—began harnessing the state's rivers and as more people settled along them, that law became controversial. In 1871, the Georgia Supreme Court ruled that individual millers did not have the right to use eminent domain. River surveys indicate that Jones Mill operated at least into the 1890s.

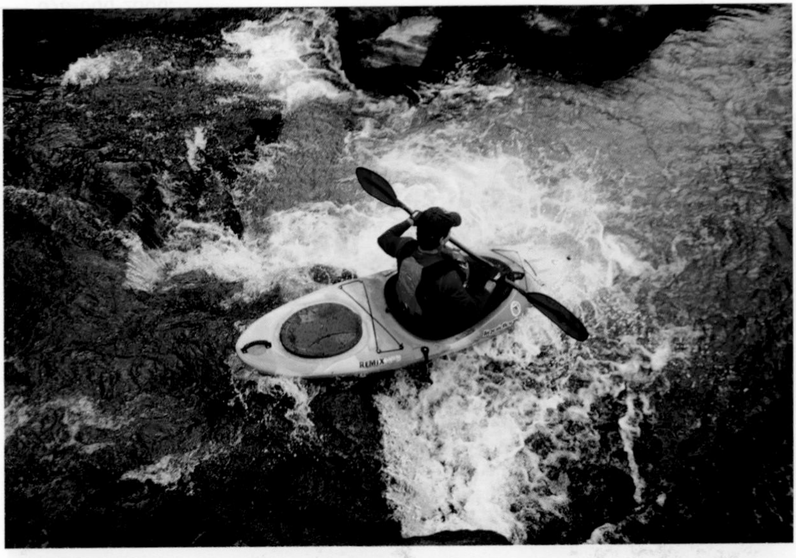

WHITE SHOALS, NEWTON COUNTY

MILE 7.4 (33.446017, −83.825773)

White Shoals. Here the river continues its precipitous descent over White Shoals. The next 900 feet are an almost continuous whitewater run with several Class II–III obstacles, culminating in 9-foot-high falls. Scouting, which is recommended, is made possible by trails on either side of the river and by multiple islands and rock outcroppings in the river.

WHITE SHOALS, NEWTON COUNTY

MILE 7.3 (33.443732, −83.825686)

White Factory. The ruins of this cotton mill can be seen in the woods along river right. Built sometime between 1850 and the early 1860s by Hugh White, this industrial complex was short lived. As noted above, Union cavalrymen reportedly destroyed the factory on July 28, 1864. Though it is likely that operations at the site were revived for a short time after the war, industrial activity at the Alcovy's falls had ceased by the 1890s. A river survey from that era reported: "Many years ago a large cotton factory stood on this site, but it was burned and never rebuilt." That is not to say that the Newton Factory area did not still support a small community. *Atlanta Constitution* reports from the late 19th century provide an interesting window into life along the Alcovy. In September 1874, the *Constitution* reported receiving "the finest specimen of okra we have seen this year"—a pod from W. D. Grant of Newton Factory, measuring 12 inches in length. In 1883, the *Constitution* reported two unusual deaths in Newton Factory: in June, a Mrs. Horton was "killed by lightning . . . while gathering flowers in the garden"; in November, the *Constitution* reported the death of a "colored man at Newton Factory who was stabbed in the bowels by his wife with a pair of scissors." The woman was not arrested, because the fatal wound was inflicted while "her husband was beating her over the head with a chair at the time."

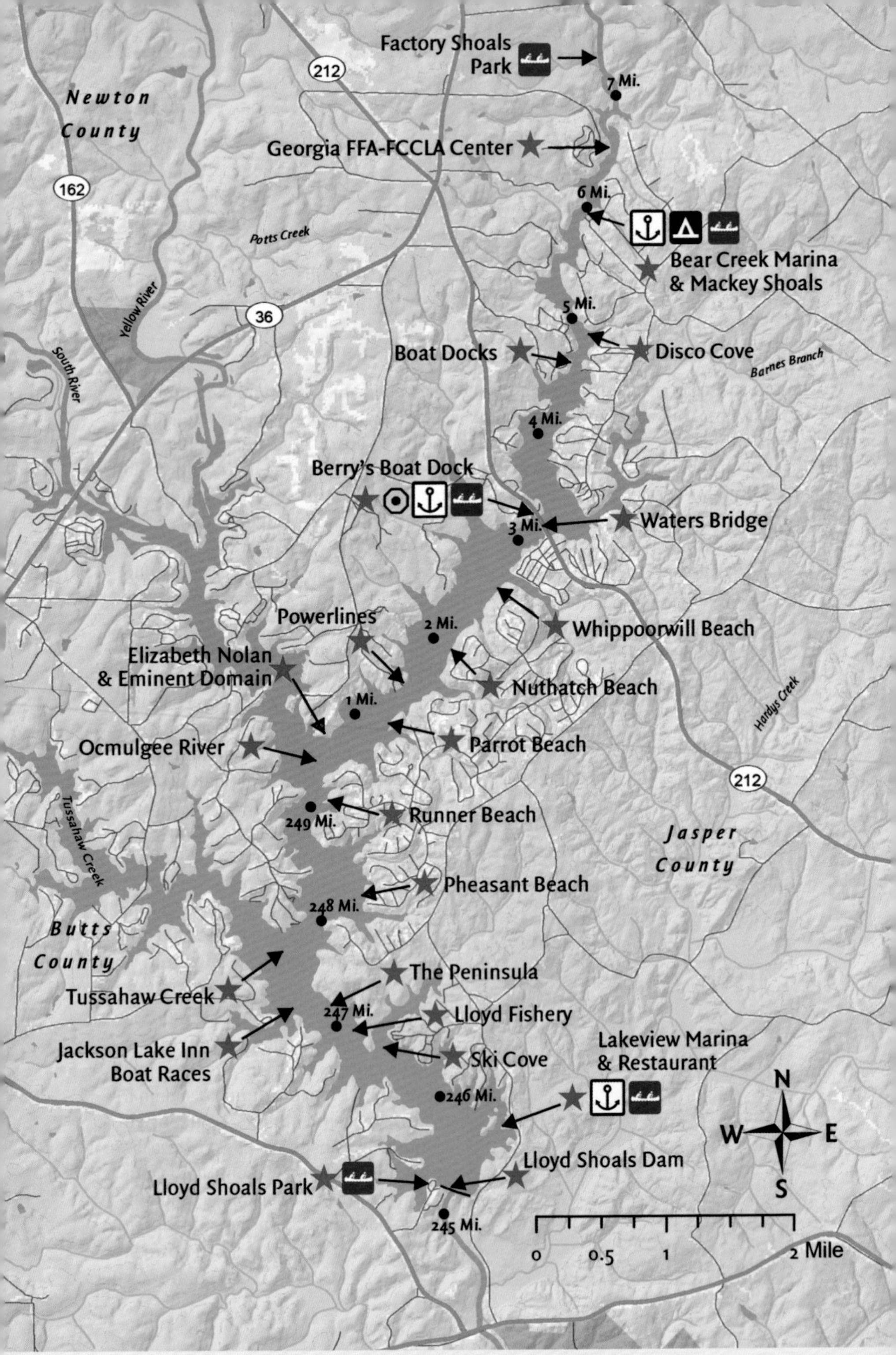
Factory Shoals Park
7 Mi.
Newton County
Georgia FFA-FCCLA Center
162
212
6 Mi.
Potts Creek
Bear Creek Marina & Mackey Shoals
Yellow River
36
5 Mi.
South River
Boat Docks
Disco Cove
Barnes Branch
4 Mi.
Berry's Boat Dock
Waters Bridge
3 Mi.
Powerlines
2 Mi.
Whippoorwill Beach
Elizabeth Nolan & Eminent Domain
Nuthatch Beach
1 Mi.
Hardys Creek
Ocmulgee River
Parrot Beach
212
Tussahaw Creek
249 Mi.
Runner Beach
Jasper County
Pheasant Beach
248 Mi.
Butts County
The Peninsula
Tussahaw Creek
247 Mi.
Lloyd Fishery
Jackson Lake Inn Boat Races
Ski Cove
Lakeview Marina & Restaurant
246 Mi.
N
W
E
S
Lloyd Shoals Dam
Lloyd Shoals Park
245 Mi.
0
0.5
1
2 Mile

Jackson Lake

Length 10 miles (Factory Shoals Park to Lloyd Shoals Dam)

Class I

Time 4–7 hours

Minimum Level Navigable year-round.

River Gauge The nearest river gauge is located at Henderson Mill Road, upstream of this section: https://waterdata.usgs.gov/ga/nwis/uv/?site_no=02209000&PARAmeter_cd=00065,00060,00062,00010. Information on lake levels can be found at the Georgia Power Company's website: https://www.georgiapower.com/community/environment/lakes-rivers/lake-levels.html.

Launch Site The launch site is a sandbar at the base of White Shoals within the Newton Factory Recreation Park. Parking is along a road in the picnic area. A rugged footpath leads from the picnic area to the launch site.

DIRECTIONS From the intersection of Ga. 36 and Newton Factory Road, travel 0.8 mile east on Newton Factory Road to the entrance to the park on the right. Turn right and proceed 0.4 mile. Turn right onto a one-way road to the picnic area and proceed 0.1 mile to the parking area on the side of the road at the picnic tables. The trail to the river can be seen on the right side of the road.

Take Out Site The take out site is a Georgia Power Company recreation area on the west side of Lloyd Shoals Dam that features a boat ramp, parking, a picnic area, pavilions, restrooms, and a beach.

DIRECTIONS From Factory Shoals Recreation Park, return to Newton Factory Road. Turn left and proceed 0.8 mile. Turn left on Ga. 36 and proceed 1.3 miles to a roundabout. Continue through the roundabout to Ga. 212, heading toward Monticello. Continue on Ga. 212 for 4.1 miles. Turn right on Jackson Lake Road and travel 6.5 miles. Turn right on Ga. 16 and proceed 0.2 mile. Turn right on Stark Road and travel 1.0 mile. Turn right on Dam Road and travel 0.3 mile. Where the road forks, bear right on Power Plant Road, proceeding 0.2 mile to the parking area at the boat ramp.

Alternative Take Out Sites Multiple boat ramps and private marinas along the shores of Jackson Lake provide opportunities for boat trips of varying lengths.

Outfitters Jackson Lake Rentals, owned by Barry Dendy, provides pontoon boat rentals and ski tube rentals with pickup at Berry's Boat Dock.

Jackson Lake Rentals, 770-713-7069, www.jacksonlakerentals.com

Description Constructed between 1908 and 1911, Lloyd Shoals Dam backs up the water of the Alcovy, Yellow, and South Rivers, along with Tussahaw Creek, to form the 4,750-acre Jackson Lake reservoir, which has 135 miles of shoreline. The Georgia Power Company manages the dam and reservoir. One of the oldest large reservoirs in Georgia, it is dotted with lakefront homes and has limited public access points. Several private marinas offer amenities along the lakeshore, as does a Georgia Power Company–maintained park adjacent to the dam. Though long sullied by pollution from Metro Atlanta's failing sewer systems and by non-point-source pollution—including loads of plastic and other trash—this resilient little lake remains a mecca for anglers, boaters, skiers, and more. In recent years, investments in wastewater management in the metro region have improved the health of the lake, and efforts to stem the tide of plastics and other trash flowing into the reservoir have gained momentum with the placement of litter traps on key tributaries.

Points of Interest

MILE 6.5 (33.433941, −83.823738) Georgia FFA-FCCLA Center. On the right shore is this 500-acre facility operated by the National FFA Organization (Future Farmers of America) and the Family, Career, and Community Leaders of America (formerly Future Homemakers of America). The center is a year-round educational camp facility promoting career development and leadership in youth. Among its offerings are wildlife and horse camps, parent-child adventure camps, and ropes-course programs. The facility has meeting rooms that can accommodate up to 1,200 people, along with lodging and dining services available for use by outside organizations. The center has its roots in the 1930s when FFA chapters in Georgia envisioned a camp where rural boys could gather during the summer for recreation. The first buildings on the site were constructed in 1938. FFA members collected rocks from the Alcovy River and Jackson Lake to build the

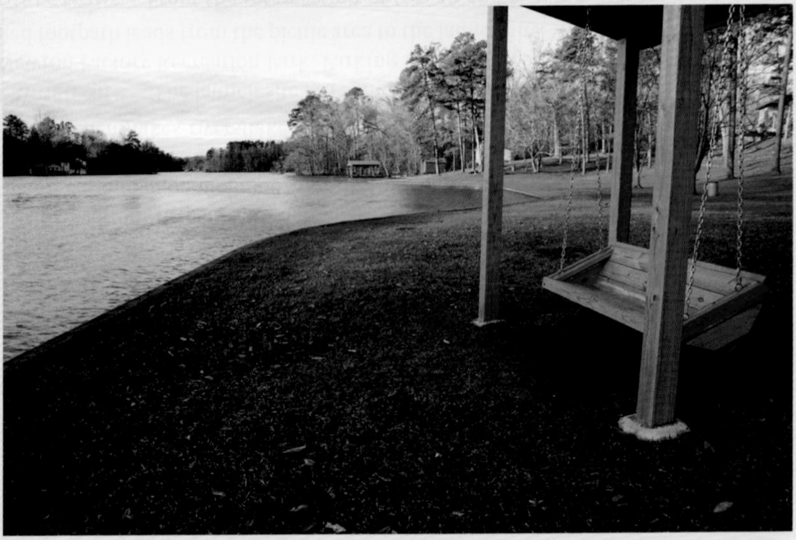

GEORGIA FFA-FCCLA CENTER, NEWTON COUNTY

fireplace in the camp's dining hall, and since then FFA and FCCLA members have played a role in raising money for the camp facilities. In the 1970s, candy sales help fund the construction of an Olympic-size swimming pool, and when the Olympics came to Atlanta in 1996, the center realized a windfall by hosting some 3,200 Germans for most of the summer. Today, the center serves more than 30,000 campers annually. The FFA was founded in 1929 to promote agricultural education and careers in agriculture. Today, only Texas and California have larger statewide memberships (43,000) than Georgia. The FCCLA became an entity in 1999 when the Future Homemakers of America changed its name to reflect the changing times. Formed in 1945 to teach teenage girls how to keep house, the organization has evolved into one focusing on a variety of issues, including teen pregnancy, nutrition, parenting, and career exploration.

MILE 6.0 (33.427127, −83.826644) Bear Creek Marina & Mackey Shoals. Located on the east shore of the lake, this marina offers a boat ramp, a dock, boat gas, an RV campground, boat storage, and a restaurant and bar; call 770-787-9621. Open April through October, the restaurant and bar become a popular local music venue, featuring live music throughout the summer season. Near this site, before the impoundment of the river at Lloyd Shoals Dam, were Mackey Shoals, the last of the river's shoals before it met the Ocmulgee. The shoals dropped 8 feet over 2 miles of river.

MILE 4.9 (33.413582, −83.826564) Disco Cove. On the east shore of the lake, a narrow cove extending from the Alcovy's main channel is locally known for its disco balls. When one lakefront property owner installed a reflective disco ball in a boathouse, neighbors soon followed suit, leading to this enclave of homes becoming known as Disco Cove.

MILE 4.7 (33.410584, −83.827756) Boat Docks. At this narrow passage of the Alcovy, boat docks extend from either side of the lake. Jackson Lake is home to more than 1,700 structures. With 135 miles of shoreline, that translates into about 13 docks for every mile of shoreline—a dock every 400 feet. As one of the oldest large reservoirs in Georgia—completed in 1911—and with no protected public land along its shores, it possesses perhaps the state's most developed shoreline.

MILE 3.2 (33.392934, −83.831546) Waters Bridge. Bridges that spanned the Alcovy and, later, Jackson Lake here played an interesting role in the sometimes brutal and embarrassing history of the South from the Civil War to the early 20th century. In July 1864, a detachment of General George Stoneman's cavalry crossed the bridge here and then burned it during a daring Union cavalry raid aimed at cutting the Macon railroad, which was supplying the Confederate troops defending Atlanta. Stoneman's cavalry was to connect with a cavalry led by General Edward McCook, converging from the west, but the destruction of this bridge left Stoneman's men on the east side of the Ocmulgee with no easy way to cross the river and rendezvous with McCook's troops. The raid ended in disaster for the Union forces. Of the more than 5,000 men who accompanied Stoneman and McCook on the raid, nearly half became casualties (killed, wounded, or missing).

Some 60 years later—in 1921—the lingering legacy of slavery played out on the first bridge to span Jackson Lake here. (The bridge pilings are still visible adjacent to the current bridge.) While slavery ended with the Civil War, debt slavery, or peonage, extended well into the 20th century. Plantation owners would routinely pay the fines of black prisoners in order to release them from jail, with the understanding that the prisoners would work for their patrons until their debt was paid. More often than not, there was no end to this work. Such was the case on the plantation of John Williams in Jasper County. When federal authorities began investigating peonage at his plantation, he systematically killed 11 of his workers in an attempt to cover up the practice. Two of his victims—men known only as Little Bit and Red—were chained, weighted, and thrown from Waters Bridge to drown in the recently impounded Jackson Lake. Williams was ultimately convicted of the murders, along with his black overseer, Clyde Manning, who carried out most of the killings and served as the primary witness against Williams. Manning contended that he killed the men on behalf of Williams because the boss had threatened his life: "It's your neck or theirs, Clyde, whichever you think the most of." Manning was sentenced to life and died several years later while working on a chain gang. Williams was killed in prison while attempting to prevent other inmates from escaping. Though both federal and state laws prohibited peonage, the practice persisted in the South more than 80 years after the end of slavery.

MILE 3.2 (33.394092, −83.833153) Berry's Boat Dock. In the cove on the north side of Waters Bridge is this marina, which offers boat storage, restrooms, and a boat launch. Launch fees apply; call 770-787-6179.

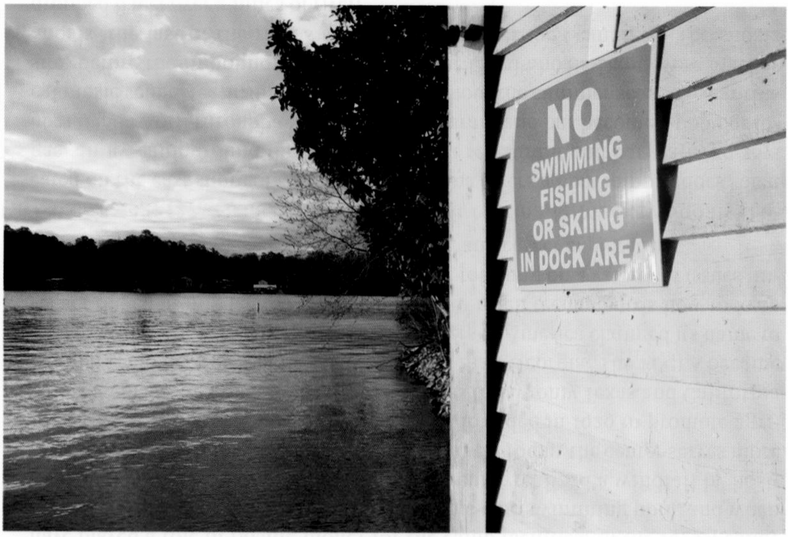

BERRY'S BOAT DOCK, NEWTON COUNTY

MILE 2.6 (33.385979, −83.837319) Whippoorwill Beach. On the east shore of the lake is this beach, which is part of the larger Turtle Cove development, a sprawling golf-tennis-swim-lake neighborhood that encompasses more than 3 miles of lakefront from Will White Neck, the cove located immediately upriver from this beach, to the mouth of Tussahaw Creek on the main body of the lake. Turtle Cove's beaches, boat ramps, and docks are reserved for homeowners. Whippoorwill is the northernmost of five Turtle Cove beaches, which include Nuthatch, Parrot, Runner, and Pheasant beaches.

MILE 2.0 (33.379167, −83.844014) Nuthatch Beach.

MILE 1.4 (33.374783, −83.848756) Powerlines. Powerlines coming from the powerhouse at Lloyd Shoals Dam span the lake here. More than 17,000 miles of powerlines cross the state—that is about the same number of miles in the state and interstate highway systems in Georgia, but considerably shorter than Georgia's systems of rivers and streams, which total about 70,000 miles!

MILE 1.2 (33.371107, −83.851184) Parrot Beach.

MILE 0.0 (33.348690, −83.863861) Elizabeth Nolan & Eminent Domain. Tucked into the peninsula of land bordered by the Yellow, Alcovy, and Ocmulgee Rivers was 142 acres owned by Elizabeth Nolan, who, like many in the area in 1909, didn't take kindly to the Central Georgia Power Company taking her land for a reservoir and hydropower plant. In an effort to keep her land, she filed suit against the company, challenging its authority under state law to condemn her property through eminent domain. Nolan faced a dilemma that has haunted riparian landowners since Georgia's beginnings. For years, the Georgia General Assembly accepted the practice of allowing individuals or companies to take private property for what was considered the "public good." In Georgia's earliest days, operators of gristmills were given this broad power. With the dawn of electricity, power companies soon enjoyed this same right, thanks to an 1897 act aimed at electrifying the state. Power companies could take land, but the company was required to provide just compensation. Though Nolan did lose her property, she was awarded $7,950 for it.

MILE 249.7 (33.366824, −83.860862) Ocmulgee River. Here, the Alcovy mixes with the Ocmulgee, which is formed 2 miles upstream by the confluence of the South and Yellow Rivers. Three miles downstream, Lloyd Shoals Dam blocks the Ocmulgee to create Jackson Lake. While at the time of its construction, in 1911, Jackson was the largest reservoir in Georgia (4,750 acres) and remained so until the 1950s, today it pales in comparison to such major impoundments as Lake Lanier on the Chattahoochee. At 38,000 acres, Lanier is the largest lake contained wholly in Georgia, but a comparison of Jackson and Lanier reveals some interesting statistics. Jackson and Lanier drain similarly sized land areas—1,420 square miles for Jackson and 1,040 square miles for Lanier. Consequently, flows into Jackson are virtually identical to those coming into Lanier from the Chattahoochee and other streams. But Lanier, unlike Jackson, is a flood control reservoir and stores 2.5 million acre-feet of water. Jackson holds just 29,000 acre-feet. So while Jackson's drainage basin is slightly larger, it has only about 1 percent of the storage capacity of Lanier. The upshot is that water flows through the lake quickly and lake levels fluctuate little on this "run of the river"–style reservoir.

MILE 249.1 (33.362815, −83.860172) Runner Beach.

MILE 248.2 (33.352345, −83.854086) Pheasant Beach.

MILE 247.7 (33.346363, −83.864412) Tussahaw Creek. Some 7 miles up this arm of Jackson Lake is Henry County's Tussahaw Creek Reservoir. Built by the Henry County Water and Sewerage Authority between 2003 and 2007, the dam and reservoir store some 9 billion gallons of water. It was constructed over the objections of multiple complainants. Neighboring Butts County filed lawsuits to prevent the condemnation of 952 acres in Butts County needed for the reservoir, arguing that the taking of land would benefit only Henry County residents. Additionally, the Georgia River Network (GRN) and Altamaha Riverkeeper (ARK) appealed the federal environmental permits issued for the project, contending that the water-supply project might be unnecessary and should not be built until regional water-supply plans had been finalized. Ultimately, Butts and Henry Counties settled their dispute by agreeing on a plan to share water from the reservoir, and a federal judge ruled against GRN and ARK's petition. At the heart of the controversy was how to best meet the water needs of Metro Atlanta's growing population—by building new and expensive water infrastructure or by leaning on more cost-effective conservation measures. Between 1990 and 2010, Henry County's population grew from about 58,000 to 205,000, sending Henry County water planners scrambling to secure new supplies. The authority dismissed Jackson Lake as a water source because of its poor water quality and opted instead for the $60 million reservoir project. Since the completion of the Tussahaw Creek Reservoir, Metro Atlanta communities have implemented more aggressive water-efficiency measures, which have leveled water demand despite population increases. As a result, plans to build many water-supply reservoirs in neighboring counties have been postponed or abandoned. Reasor's Landing, a marina, is located 3 miles upstream on the Tussahaw Creek arm of the lake. The marina offers a boat ramp, a dock, boat gas, boat parts and service, and a convenience store; call 770-504-1245.

MILE 247.3 (33.340115, −83.863146) Jackson Lake Inn Boat Races. During Jackson Lake's early days, powerboat racing was an attraction, and Carl Flock, owner of the Jackson Lake Inn, took advantage of the sport's popularity. Beginning in the late 1920s, he held regular races from his property, located on the west shore here. The races attracted crowds of up to 5,000 people, and Flock entertained them with more than just fast boats. His peninsula included a large concession stand and a dance pavilion, a 250-foot fishing pier, two large dining halls, a dozen cabins, and four bowling alleys. A 1941 racing event featured an appearance by Jack Jacks, a stuntman featured in the 1941 movie *Moon over Miami*, starring Don Ameche. The *Atlanta Constitution* reported that Jack would "leap an eight-foot barrier" on skis and "pilot his 'flying boat,' the 'Flat Foot Floogie,' over an eight-foot hurdle." By the early 1950s, however, the property had been sold and divided into lots for sale. At this approximate location before the construction of the dam was Dempsey's Ferry.

MILE 247.1 (33.340156, −83.858289) The Peninsula. On the east shore here is what was the last remaining large parcel of undeveloped land on Jackson Lake. In 2019, investors began subdividing and selling lots. Before World War II, little development occurred along the lake, but with the spread of paved roads, Jackson Lake became a popular weekend getaway for Atlantans, who began building camps and fishing cabins. The lakefront population has remained mostly part-time residents, but as the Atlanta suburbs have pushed outward, the number of year-round residents has increased. With the development of the Peninsula, local Realtors estimated that more than 50 percent of Jackson Lake's homes were occupied by full-time residents. There is a bald eagle nest on the Peninsula.

MILE 246.9 (33.337710, −83.855063) Lloyd Fishery. Before the impoundment of Jackson Lake, the free-flowing Ocmulgee split into three channels here, coursing around Flat and Mountain Islands. It is believed that between Mountain Island and the east bank of the river was a fish weir, or trap—a rock dam used to capture fish. Native Americans built the V-shaped dams usually in shallow locations adjacent to shoals. The traps funneled fish to waiting baskets at the downstream end of the "V." Early settlers adopted this highly efficient fishing practice, maintaining the ancient rock dams or building their own. Bill Frazier, a historian of fish traps, used deed records to pinpoint this submerged archaeological site in the 1990s. An 1868 deed refers to "Loyd Fishery," and later deeds note the granting of "rights to fishing, fishery and fishing ground."

MILE 246.6 (33.335515, −83.851077) Ski Cove. Prized for its calm water, this half-mile-long cove extending to the east is considered a favorite spot for skiing by lake enthusiasts.

LAKEVIEW MARINA, JASPER COUNTY

MILE 245.7 (33.327861, –83.835290) Lakeview Marina & Restaurant. Located on the east shore of the lake, within view of the dam, this facility offers a boat ramp, a dock, boat gas, boat service, boat rentals, RV campsites, motel rooms, and a restaurant; call 770-775-1111 or (restaurant) 770-775-3892.

MILE 245.3 (33.321492, –83.842384) Lloyd Shoals Dam. Constructed from 1908 to 1911, this hydropower project was colossal for its day. It was the highest dam in the Southeast at the time, stretching 100 feet above the riverbed, and was the largest reservoir created in Georgia until after the 1940s. At its base, the dam is 95 feet wide, narrowing to 11 feet wide at its apex. It takes its name from the shoals on which it was built, described in late 19th-century river surveys as having a fall of 39 feet over a distance of 2 miles, the "principal part of which occur[s] . . . in a distance of 2,000 feet." The project required the business acumen of W. J. Massee, president of the Central Georgia Power Company, who lured northern investors to fund the project. In March 1909, Massee hosted more than 100 investors at the dam site for a barbecue featuring 14 smoked pigs as well as goats and sheep. The affair was reported in great detail by the *Butts County Progress*: "Northern capitalists do not sit down to a barbecue like that every day . . . and some of them doubted if their digestive apparatus was equal to the task . . . "Take down the address of my wife and you can put my body in a plain box," said one of the northern party who was doubtful of the outcome after he had partaken of the repast for some time and was being urged with true Georgia hospitality to eat more." With money secured through barbecue diplomacy, the project rose from the riverbed, built by a crew of up to 500 workers.

LLOYD SHOALS DAM, BUTTS COUNTY

When completed, the massive engineering feat had some unintended consequences. Since the dam backed stagnant water into Jasper, Butts, and Newton Counties, an outbreak of malaria soon ensued. Farmers abandoned their homes and crops and fled to safer environs, since many fell ill and several died in the years immediately following the creation of the reservoir. In September 1911, residents of the area were so stricken that they appealed to Governor Hoke Smith. The governor visited the affected area and shot off a letter to the Central Georgia Power Company, urging it to address the mosquito infestation. This it did in the style of the early 20th century—crews spread kerosene oil over the surface of the lake. The "mosquito control squad" continued its work well into the 1930s. By March 1914, 205 citizens in Butts, Jasper, and Newton Counties had filed lawsuits against the power company because of the mosquitoes and nuisance conditions. Newton County sought to have the lake declared a public nuisance and drained. The Georgia Supreme Court, however, ultimately sided with the power company.

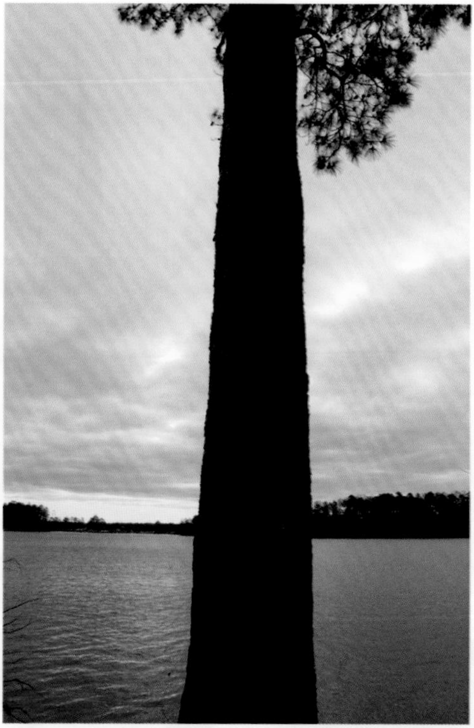
PINE AT SUNRISE, BUTTS COUNTY

MILE 245.3 (33.321203, −83.845104) Lloyd Shoals Park. The only public boat ramp and recreation area on Jackson Lake, this facility features a boat ramp, a dock, restrooms, a picnic pavilion, and a swimming area; the amenities are wheelchair accessible.

ROCK OUTCROPPING, WILCOX COUNTY

OCMULGEE RIVER

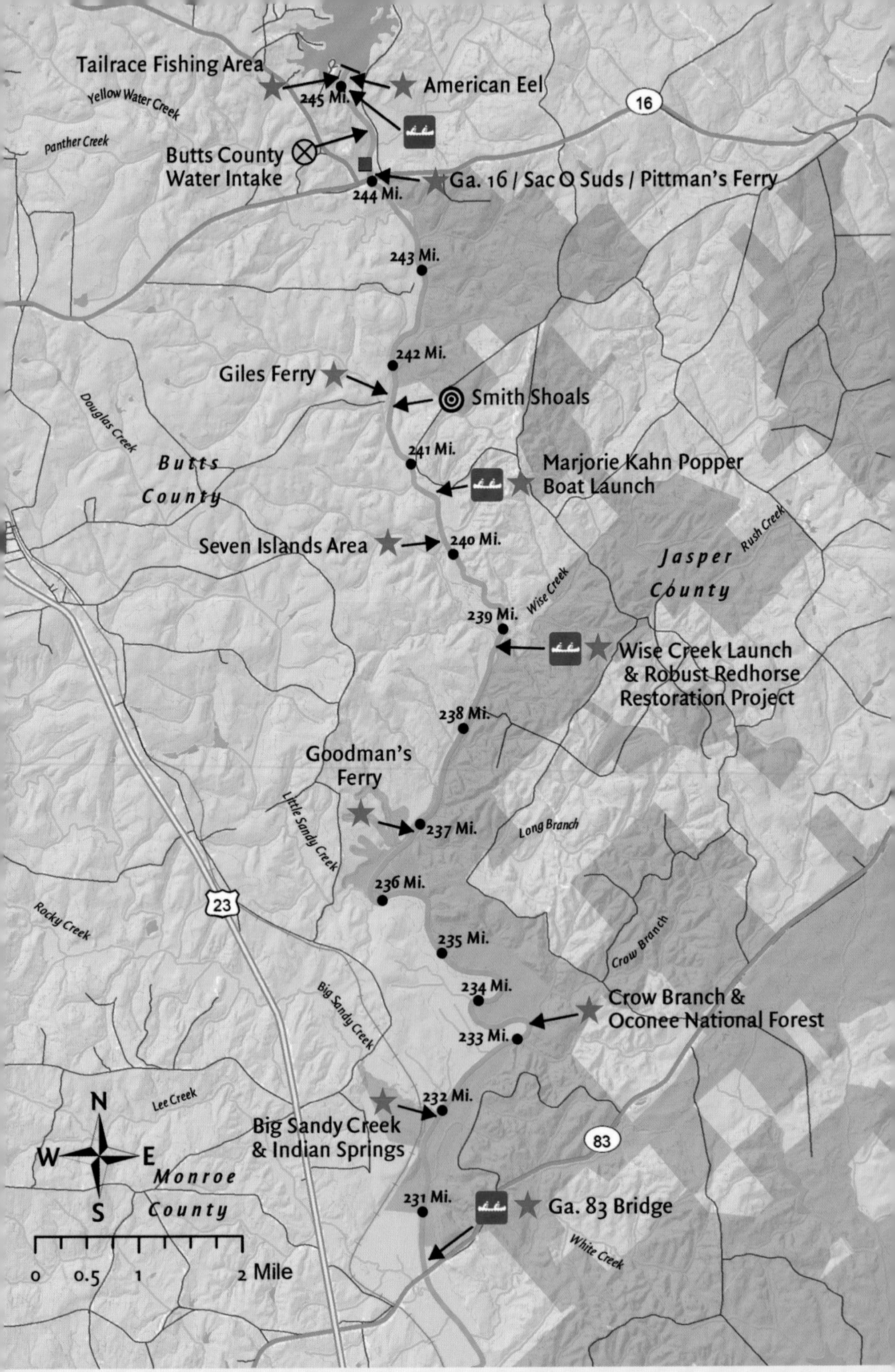

Tailrace Fishing Area
American Eel
Yellow Water Creek
245 Mi.
16
Panther Creek
Butts County
Water Intake
Ga. 16 / Sac O Suds / Pittman's Ferry
244 Mi.
243 Mi.
242 Mi.
Giles Ferry
Smith Shoals
Douglas Creek
241 Mi.
Butts
County
Marjorie Kahn Popper
Boat Launch
Rush Creek
Seven Islands Area
240 Mi.
Jasper
County
Wise Creek
239 Mi.
Wise Creek Launch
& Robust Redhorse
Restoration Project
238 Mi.
Goodman's
Ferry
Little Sandy Creek
237 Mi.
Long Branch
236 Mi.
23
Rocky Creek
235 Mi.
Crow Branch
234 Mi.
Big Sandy Creek
Crow Branch &
Oconee National Forest
233 Mi.
Lee Creek
232 Mi.
Big Sandy Creek
& Indian Springs
83
N
W
E
S
Monroe
County
231 Mi.
Ga. 83 Bridge
White Creek
0
0.5
1
2 Mile

Lamar Mill

Length 13 miles (Lloyd Shoals Dam to Ga. 83)

Class I–III

Time 5–8 hours

Minimum Level Flows of 400 cfs at the Ga. 16 gauge near Jackson are sufficient for floating this section of the river. Paddlers venturing on the river during flows below 400 cfs can expect frequent encounters with shoals. As flows rise above 1,000 cfs, the Class III Lamar Mill rapid becomes challenging.

River Gauge The nearest river gauge is located at Ga. 16 just downstream of the launch site for this section. Before launching on this section, check this river gauge, since releases from Lloyd Shoals Dam can cause river levels to rise by up to a foot: https://waterdata.usgs.gov/ga/nwis/uv/?site_no=02210500&PARAmeter_cd=00065,00060,00062,00010.

Launch Site The launch site is located at the Georgia Power Company's Ocmulgee River Public Access area on the east side of the river 0.4 mile downstream of Lloyd Shoals Dam with a parking area and a boat ramp.

DIRECTIONS From the intersection of East 3rd Street (Ga. 16) and U.S. 23 in Jackson, travel east on Ga. 16 for 7.3 miles. Cross the river and turn left on Jackson Lake Road (CR 364) and proceed 0.9 mile to the entrance to the access area on the left.

Take Out Site The take out site is a Georgia Department of Natural Resources boat ramp with parking on river left adjacent to the Ga. 83 bridge.

DIRECTIONS From the Georgia Power Company's Ocmulgee River Public Access area, return to Jackson Lake Road. Turn right and proceed 0.9 mile. Turn right on Ga. 16 and proceed 3.9 miles. Turn left on Higgins Road and travel 1.9 miles. Turn left on U.S. 23 and proceed 9.0 miles. Turn left on Ga. 83 and proceed 1.2 miles to the entrance to the boat ramp on the right.

Alternative Take Out Sites The Marjorie Kahn Popper Boat Launch, in the Oconee National Forest, creates a 4-mile trip, and the Wise Creek Canoe Launch can be used to create a 6-mile trip. The former avoids the Class II–III shoals at Lamar Mill shoals; the latter takes in those shoals, but avoids an 8-mile stretch of mostly flatwater at the end of this section.

DIRECTIONS To reach the Marjorie Kahn Popper Boat Launch from the Georgia Power Company's Ocmulgee River Public Access area, return to Jackson Lake Road. Turn right and proceed 0.9 mile. Turn left on Ga. 16 and proceed 1.7 miles. Turn right on Concord Church Road and proceed 1.5 miles. At the fork in the road, bear to the right and continue on Smith Mill Road for 2.6 miles to the parking area for the boat launch on the right. To reach the Wise Creek Canoe Launch, continue on Smith Mill Road 1.0 mile. At the fork, bear left, staying on Smith Mill Road for 2.0 miles.

At the next fork, bear to the right and continue for 0.9 mile. Turn right on Forest Service Road 1098 and continue 1.1 miles to the parking area at the boat launch.

Outfitters Ocmulgee Outdoor Expeditions provides canoe and kayak rentals and shuttle service.

Ocmulgee Outdoor Expeditions, 478-733-3386, www.ocmulgeeoutdoorexpeditions.com

Ocmulgee Adventures provides kayak and tube rentals and shuttle service.

Ocmulgee Adventures, 54 Hwy. 16 West, Monticello, 31064, 770-504-9272

Description This 14-mile run through Butts and Jasper Counties is arguably the most scenic 14 miles of the Ocmulgee, featuring several shoal and island complexes and miles of protected river front in the Oconee National Forest. Class I–III shoals make the upper 6 miles of the run popular with whitewater enthusiasts. History buffs will also get their fix, especially at the Seven Islands area. The islands were a traditional crossing place for Native Americans. Later, the botanist William Bartram passed through the area, and during the Civil War, Union soldiers marching a path of terror and destruction from Atlanta to Savannah crossed the river here. The stone ruins of the 19th-century cotton mill that those soldiers destroyed remain along the river's shore. As time travel goes, it is a beautiful setting.

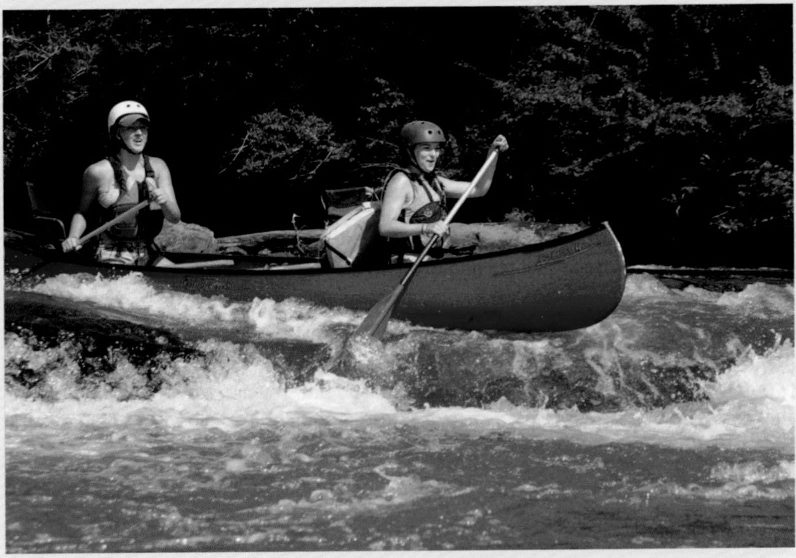

LAMAR MILL SHOALS, JASPER COUNTY

Points of Interest

MILE 245.2 (33.320564, −83.841958) American Eel. One of the most unusual-looking fish in the Ocmulgee also has one of the most unusual life cycles. Its upstream range on the Ocmulgee is here at the base of Lloyd Shoals Dam. The American eel, a long slender fish with dorsal and pelvic fins running the length of its body, lives its adult life in Atlantic Coast rivers, but ventures far out to the Sargasso Sea to spawn. The young eels drift on ocean currents back to coastal waters and then venture back up rivers to mature. They once ranged far into the Ocmulgee river system, but Lloyd Shoals Dam keeps them from their historic up-stream habitats. Fish surveys have found eels between Lloyd Shoals Dam and the Juliette Dam some 18 miles downstream, indicating that the eels can ascend the lowhead dam at Juliette—an amazing feat for any fish, especially one as willowy as the eel. During the 2019 relicensing process for Lloyd Shoals Dam, federal agencies required the Georgia Power Company to conduct an eel study to determine the abundance of eels in this section of river and to evaluate the potential for passage of American eels through this 1911 dam.

MILE 245.1 (33.319220, −83.842816) Tailrace Fishing Area. This fishing area, with a pier extending over the river's edge, is accessed via Dam Road and Power Plant Road on the west side of the river.

MILE 244.4 (33.312505, −83.837607) Butts County Water Intake. The water-intake facility on river right belongs to the Butts County Water and Sewer Authority, which pumps water from the Ocmulgee and the Towaliga Rivers to provide about 800 million gallons of water annually to the citizens of Butts County. This intake is permitted to remove 10 million gallons daily from the river and marks the first drinking-water intake on the mainstem of the South River or the Ocmulgee River downstream of Metro Atlanta.

MILE 244.1 (33.306289, −83.836847) Ga. 16 / Sac O Suds / Pittman's Ferry. Just upstream of where Ga. 16 now spans the river, travelers in the 1800s crossed by using Cargile's Ferry. In 1847, Joseph Pittman married into the Cargile family, and by the late 1800s, the ferry had taken the Pittman name. In 1923, the ferry was the site of a horrific murder. Charles A. Pittman, the ferryman, who also operated a nearby store, was robbed and murdered on the night of July 20, 1923. A group of men from neighboring Jasper County rowed a boat across the river and summoned the 68-year-old shopkeeper to his store. There they struck him with an axe and stabbed him with a knife before carrying his body to the ferry and throwing it in the river. Evans McDowell and Flem Linch were later convicted of the murder, and hanged. The ferry operated until 1935, when a bridge was built to carry Ga. 16. The Cargile-Pittman home, which dates to 1826, still stands along Stark Road just east of the river, and it is still owned by Pittman descendants. On the Jasper County side of the river is Sac O Suds, a convenience store made famous in the 1992 movie *My Cousin Vinny*, which pivots on the murder of a shopkeeper. The movie, which earned Marisa Tomei an Oscar for best support-

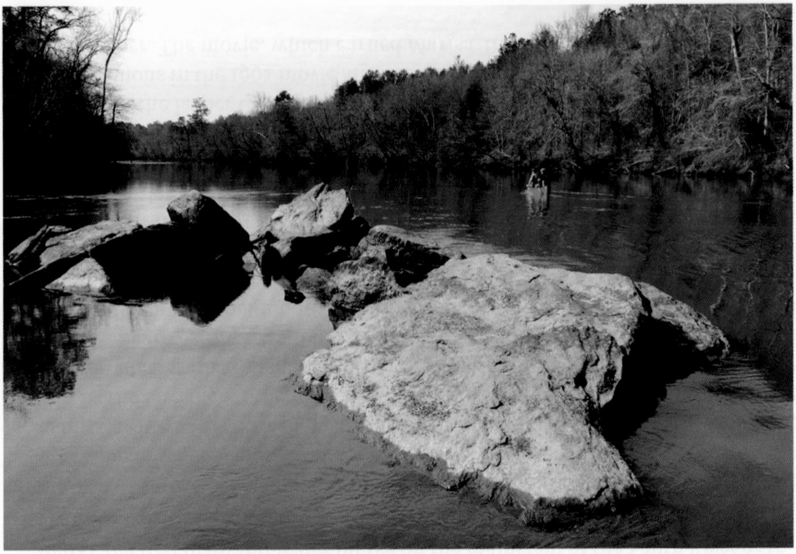

NEAR GILES FERRY, BUTTS COUNTY

ing actress, was shot at numerous locations in Jasper County, including Sac O Suds and the Jasper County courthouse.

MILE 241.8 (33.276994, −83.832615) Giles Ferry. Cuts in the bank here mark the site of this historic ferry, which was authorized by the Georgia General Assembly in 1821. Joel Wise, the son of a Revolutionary War soldier, Joseph Wise, established the ferry. It continued operating well into the 20th century under the name Giles Ferry. Besides offering passage between Jasper and Butts Counties, it served as a gathering place for the community. A May 1913 edition of the *Butts County Progress* noted an "enjoyable fish fry" at the landing: "The boys of the settlement came together and had the finest fish fry you ever saw. We not only had fish in profusion, but a pot of soup that nothing would tempt us to leave, not even the nectar that Jupiter sipped."

MILE 241.7 (33.275537, −83.832954) Smith Shoals. On river left here, a narrow arm of the river begins wrapping around a large island. In the main channel over the next mile, the river descends a series of shoals and ledges known as Roach's or Smith Shoals. Beginning in the 19th century, a gristmill and woolen mill harnessed the power of the river here. The mill operated into the early 20th century. Local boosters had at one point hoped that this area (and the greater falls downstream at Lamar Mill) could be transformed into an industrial complex, but rail transportation was the missing link. The *Jackson Argus* editorialized in its issue of March 27, 1897: "on the Ocmulgee river is water power sufficient to employ two million dollars of capital and thousands of operatives." Lamenting the destruction of Ocmulgee Mills by Union troops more than 30 years earlier, the paper continued: "Since then these magnificent waterfalls have stood almost idle for want of transportation facilities. Had the southern railway followed the course of the river when it was built there is no telling what manufacturing interest would have been put in operation near this . . . All efforts to build up manufactories at the river have been unsuccessful on account of the distance from railway."

MILE 240.6 (33.264147, −83.824888) Marjorie Kahn Popper Boat Launch. This Georgia Department of Natural Resources canoe and kayak launch features ample parking and a 250-foot boat slide that allows users to slide their boats on an elevated chute from the parking area to the river. The launch bears the name of the woman who provided the land for the facility.

MILE 240.1 (33.257663, −83.823868) Seven Islands Area. Here the river splits around a series of islands, the largest of which is known as Forty Acre Island, and descends to the Lamar Mill rapid, a Class II–III obstacle. In high water (flows above 2,000 cfs), it is possible to take the narrow channel to the left of the first island, but this route is recommended only for experienced whitewater boaters. Most choose the main channel, which flows first to the far right around a small island and over a small ledge before reaching a length of flatwater above Lamar Mill. At the head of the Lamar Mill rapid, staying left and then working back to the center of the river provides the more gradual Class II descent. More experienced boaters can go river right, where there are two Class III falls. The far-right channel around the small island on river right should be avoided.

This beautiful and seemingly wild setting belies the years of human occupation here. The site is mentioned in the journals of 17th-century fur traders, and William Bartram visited (and described) the area during his wanderings in the 1770s. In 1843, the Georgia General Assembly incorporated the Planters Manufacturing Company, a wool and cotton mill, here. By 1849, the mill was employing 75 workers and producing 800 yards of cloth daily, but six years later the business went belly up and was sold on the courthouse steps to investors, who put $42,000 into improving the facilities and changed the name to Ocmulgee Mills. It was this mill that was destroyed during the Civil War. In November 1864, Sherman's army torched it during its March to the Sea. Wrote the Union soldier Thomas Christie: "We came in sight of the Ocmulgee; a fine river; crossed on a pontoon bridge laid above the dam at the Mills. The Ocmulgee Mills were two splendid buildings, which the Rebels has used night and day for the manufacture of cloth for the army: they were destroyed as soon as the army got over the bridge." Ocmulgee Mills never recovered, but by 1885, a sawmill and a gristmill were harnessing the river, and in 1907 a U.S. Geological Survey described Lamar Mill as a "large merchant mill for grinding corn and wheat." In the 1930s, the federal government proposed building a $1.8 million hydropower dam here. Thankfully, that project, along with a proposal for damming the river at Dames Ferry downstream, never took off. The stone remains of the old mill (now on private property) can be seen along the banks on river right. Taking the far-right channel at the base of the rapid provides an excellent view of these ruins.

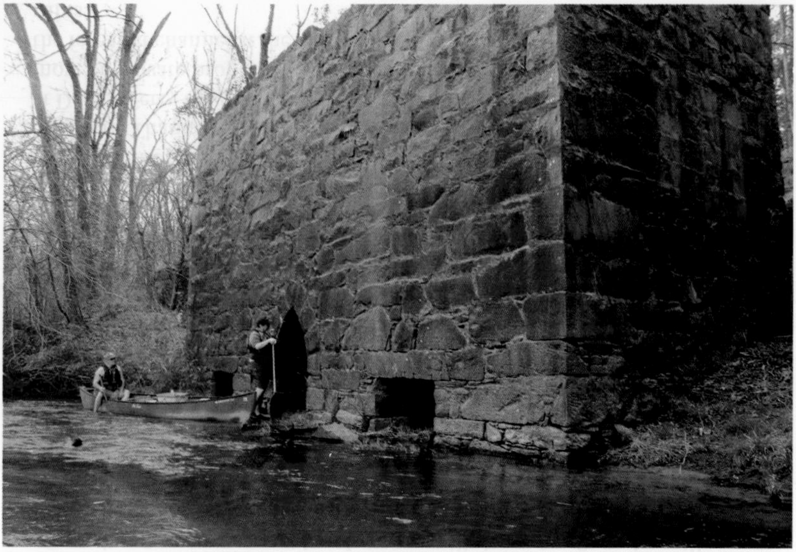

MILL RUINS, BUTTS COUNTY

MILE 238.9 (33.243585, –83.814594) Wise Creek Launch & Robust Redhorse Restoration Project. On river left here, beyond the shoal at the head of Nelson Island, is the mouth of Wise Creek and a boat launch within the Oconee National Forest. In 2018, the launch was closed because of unsafe conditions created when a stream-bank stabilization project built of numerous large timbers failed and spilled into the river, exposing the sharp metal spikes used to secure the timbers to one another. The launch was reopened in 2019. The stabilization project, completed in 2000 through the efforts of the U.S. Forest Service, the Georgia Department of Natural Resources (DNR), the Georgia Power Company, and the Georgia River Network, was intended to prevent further erosion of the riverbank here and to improve the habitat of the robust redhorse, a fish thought extinct until it was rediscovered in 1991 in the Oconee River. The redhorse is often referred to as a "mystery fish" because so little is known about this member of the sucker family. The DNR has begun a captive-breeding program and has released approximately 6,500 redhorses into the Ocmulgee. The Robust Redhorse Conservation Committee is studying the fish in hope of restoring it to the Ocmulgee and other Georgia rivers. As the name implies, it is a large fish (an average length of 25 inches) highlighted by a rose-colored tail fin. It feeds largely on *Corbicula* (small invasive Asian clams) and prefers to spawn in shallow water over gravel deposits. The fish might have remained unknown to scientists if not for federal environmental regulations; it was rediscovered when the DNR collected fish during an environmental assessment associated with the relicensing of Georgia Power's Sinclair Dam on the Oconee River. The failure of the stabilization project was a hard lesson in the difficulty of controlling wild rivers. Inevitably, it seems, the river wins.

MILE 236.9 (33.219062, −83.827009) Goodman's Ferry. A 1907 Geological Survey of Georgia publication notes this location and five other ferries operating between Jasper and Butts Counties in the 15 miles of the Ocmulgee downstream of present-day Lloyd Shoals Dam. The concentration of ferries in this run of the river speaks to the importance of the area as a transportation route during the precolonial era. The Upper Creek Trading Path crossed the Ocmulgee at Seven Islands, and it became a well-traveled route by early explorers and settlers. By the 1820s, the Georgia General Assembly had recognized eight ferries across the Ocmulgee in Jasper County.

MILE 233.2 (33.193177, −83.807682) Crow Branch & Oconee National Forest. On river left is this stream, which flows entirely within the 30,000-plus acres of the Oconee National Forest in Jasper County. The national forest flanks the east bank of the river for some 13 miles from the Ga. 36 bridge upstream to Ga. 83 downstream. In total, the Oconee National Forest encompasses more than 115,000 acres. It is estimated that only 7 percent of the trees in this forest are more than 120 years old—evidence of our past and current dependence on these forests. The forest is also home to the federally protected red-cockaded woodpecker, a species that requires old-growth pines for its survival. Ward's Ferry operated near the mouth of Crow Branch during the 1800s and early 1900s.

MILE 231.9 (33.180454, −83.822382) Big Sandy Creek & Indian Springs. About 7 miles upstream on this creek is Indian Springs State Park. Indian Springs, sulfur springs giving rise to Big Sandy Creek, were used for centuries by Native Americans and revered for their healing powers. In 1823, the Creek Indian chief William McIntosh established a hotel there, and it was at this location that McIntosh and others signed the Treaty of Indian Springs, ceding Creek lands in Georgia to the U.S. government. Three months later, McIntosh was murdered by fellow tribesmen who felt betrayed by their leader. The springs and McIntosh's hotel, which still stands, remained a popular resort well into the 20th century and are now part of the state park. During the resort's heyday, several hotels, some with 700 rooms, catered to thousands of annual visitors.

MILE 230.4 (33.159318, −83.823815) Ga. 83 Bridge. One of the older bridges spanning the Ocmulgee, the Ga. 83 bridge was completed in 1958 and was the first bridge to span the river here. Bridges Ferry operated at this location before then. The site is slated to receive a new bridge in 2021. The boat ramp is on river left, just upstream of the bridge.

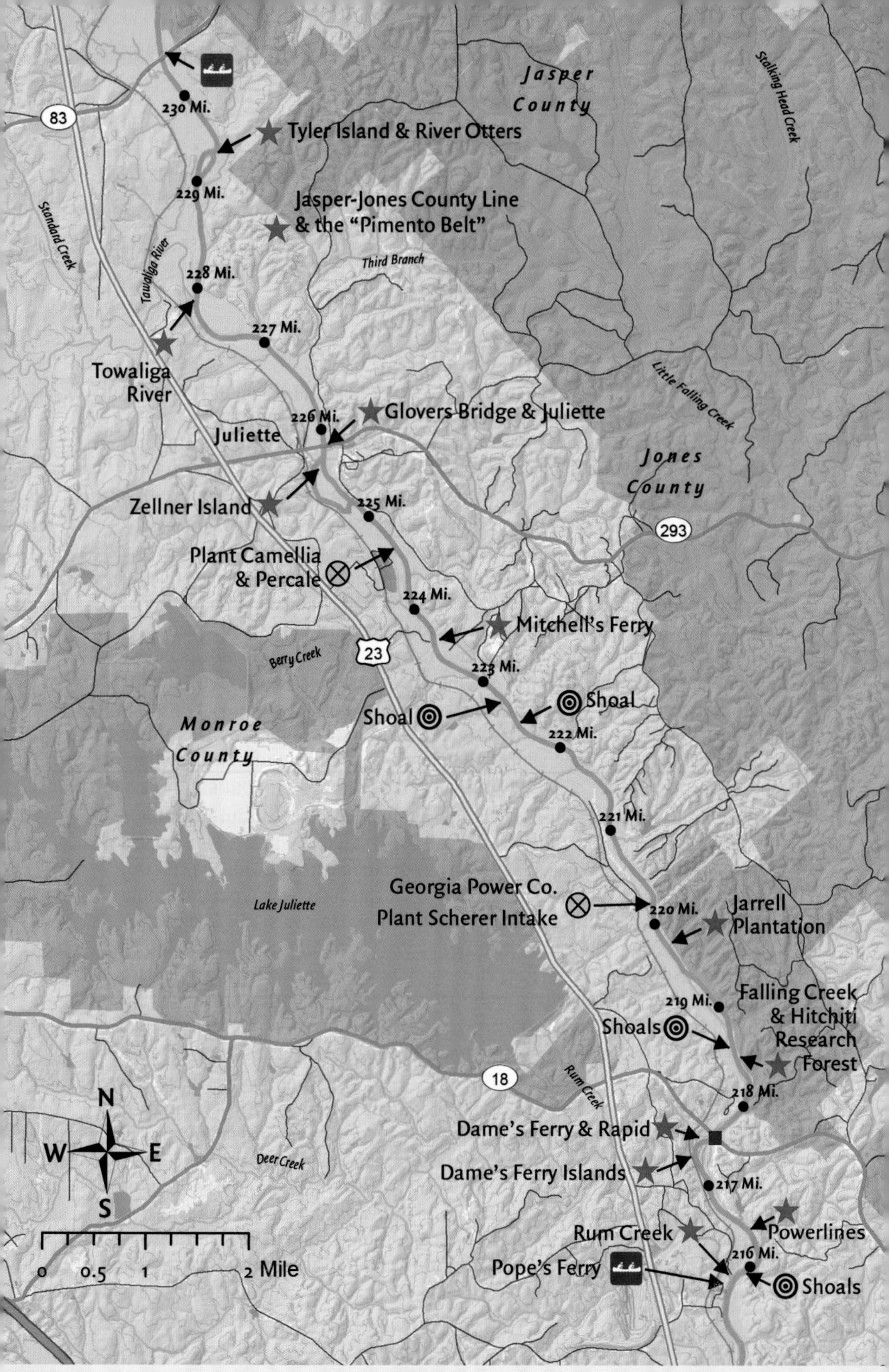

Jasper County
Stalking Head Creek
83
230 Mi.
Tyler Island & River Otters
229 Mi.
Jasper-Jones County Line & the "Pimento Belt"
Standard Creek
Towaliga River
Third Branch
228 Mi.
227 Mi.
Towaliga River
Little Falling Creek
226 Mi.
Glovers Bridge & Juliette
Juliette
Jones County
Zellner Island
225 Mi.
293
Plant Camellia & Percale
224 Mi.
Mitchell's Ferry
Berry Creek
23
223 Mi.
Shoal
Shoal
222 Mi.
Monroe County
221 Mi.
Georgia Power Co. Plant Scherer Intake
220 Mi.
Jarrell Plantation
Lake Juliette
219 Mi.
Falling Creek & Hitchiti Research Forest
Shoals
18
Rum Creek
218 Mi.
N
W
E
S
Dame's Ferry & Rapid
Deer Creek
Dame's Ferry Islands
217 Mi.
Powerlines
Rum Creek
216 Mi.
0 0.5 1 2 Mile
Pope's Ferry
Shoals

Dame's Ferry

Length 14 miles (Ga. 83 to Pope's Ferry)

Class I–II

Time 6–8 hours

Minimum Level Flows of 400 cfs at the Ga. 18 gauge at Dame's Ferry are sufficient for floating this section of the river.

River Gauge The nearest river gauge is located at Ga. 18 / Dame's Ferry in the middle of this section: https://waterdata.usgs.gov/ga/nwis/uv/?site_no=02212735&PARAmeter_cd=00065,00060,00062,00010.

Launch Site The launch site is a Georgia Department of Natural Resources boat ramp with parking at Ga. 83 located on the east and upstream side of the bridge.

DIRECTIONS From the intersection of U.S. 23 and Ga. 83 northeast of Forsyth, go east on Ga. 83 for 1.0 mile to the river and continue past bridge 0.3 mile to the entrance to the boat ramp on the right.

Take Out Site The Pope's Ferry take out site is on river right with a boat ramp and a parking area. A Georgia Department of Natural Resources boat ramp, it is maintained by Monroe County.

DIRECTIONS From the entrance to the boat ramp at Ga. 83, go west on Ga. 83 for 1.3 miles to U.S. 23. Turn left and proceed 12.9 miles. Turn left on Pope's Ferry Road and proceed 0.2 mile and then bear right on Popes Ferry Lane for 0.4 mile to the boat ramp.

Alternative Take Out Sites A 4.5-mile trip can be made by using the boat ramp at Juliette Road.

DIRECTIONS From the entrance to the boat ramp at Ga. 83, go west on Ga. 83 for 1.3 miles to U.S. 23. Turn left and proceed 3.6 miles. Turn left on Juliette Road and proceed 0.9 mile to the entrance to the boat ramp on the right.

Outfitters Ocmulgee Outdoor Expeditions provides canoe and kayak rentals and shuttle service.

Ocmulgee Outdoor Expeditions, 478-733-3386,
www.ocmulgeeoutdoorexpeditions.com

Ocmulgee Adventures provides kayak and tube rentals and shuttle service.

Ocmulgee Adventures, 54 Hwy. 16 West, Monticello, 31064, 770-504-9272

Description A tale of two rivers in 14 miles of the same river, this run has two distinct characters. The first 4 miles is slow-moving water piled up behind Juliette Dam; the final 10 miles return to the river's free-flowing Piedmont ways, with intermittent shoals breaking up long stretches of flatwater. Juliette Dam, made somewhat famous in the 1991 movie *Fried Green Tomatoes*, marks the community of Juliette, and a side trip to "town" will be rewarded with a plate of the namesake southern delicacy at the local café. Further downstream, portions of the Piedmont National Wildlife Refuge and the shoals at Dames Ferry highlight the journey. Portages around Juliette Dam can be lengthy and arduous, making these 14 miles a good candidate for being split into two trips.

Points of Interest

MILE 229.4 (33.146819, −83.814667) **Tyler Island & River Otters.** River otters have been spotted at this island in the past. A typical otter will range over 50 miles of its home river during the year. They are most active from late evening through early morning. Otters eat mostly fish, but also dine on crayfish, mussels, and amphibians, growing to a weight of up to 25 pounds. Of course, they are known for their playfulness. If you could swim 7 miles an hour and run up to 18 miles an hour, perhaps you would be playful too.

MILE 228.2 (33.132097, −83.816122) **Jasper-Jones County Line & the "Pimento Belt."** On river left here is the county line separating Jasper and Jones Counties. Beginning in the 1910s, a little-known piece of Georgia's agricultural history played out in what can best be described as Georgia's Pimento Belt. Beginning in 1913, a Spaulding County farmer named S. D. Riegel and his sons began experimenting with growing a Spanish variety of pimentos. The vegetable had become a popular canned item in U.S. grocery stores, and a cream cheese–pimento combo was growing in popularity in northern markets. The Riegels ultimately perfected a hybrid that performed well in Georgia and also developed an efficient system for roasting and canning the peppers. With that, production spread from Griffin into neighboring counties and became concentrated in a belt running from Meriwether County in the west to Jasper County in the east. Jackson, in Butts County, had its own cannery. From the 1930s into the 1960s, Georgia was the country's leading producer of pimentos, with thousands of acres planted. Southern housewives soon produced their own version of pimento cheese by combining the peppers with cheddar cheese and mayonnaise. That version became an iconic food of the South. In 2017, pimientos were not planted in enough abundance to warrant inclusion in Georgia's farm gate report.

MILE 227.9 (33.126894, −83.817203) **Towaliga River.** Pronounced "Tow-aleega" or "Tye-lye'gee," this river begins in Henry County and flows through Spalding, Butts, and Monroe Counties. Historians disagree on the meaning of the Native American name. Some say it means "sumac place," but others suggest the name comes from the Muskogean word "Towelaggie," which means "roasted scalps" or "scalp place," the river being a spot where Native American war parties paused to dry scalps. Scalping has both Old World and New World origins. The practice of taking a scalp as proof of an enemy's demise was adopted by some American colonists. In fact, colonial governments soon began offering bounties for Native American scalps. The largest-known Native American villages in the area were located at the confluence of the Towaliga and the Ocmulgee.

MILE 225.8 (33.107907, −83.795057) Glovers Bridge & Juliette. The low-slung bridge here dates to 1971, but bridges have spanned the river here since 1907. That was the year when Juliette Milling and the Glover Manufacturing Company built Glovers Bridge upstream of the current span, charging a toll of 10 cents for each automobile or wagon that crossed. Just downstream of the bridge is the lowhead Juliette Dam, which drops some 20 feet to the river below, creating a serious navigational hazard during high flows. During the 19th century and into the early 20th, the dam diverted water to power a gristmill (in Juliette) and the Glover Cotton Mills (across the river in East Juliette). The Juliette Mill, still standing on river right adjacent to the dam, operated until 1957; when constructed, in 1927, it was said to be the world's largest water-powered gristmill. The East Tennessee, Virginia and Georgia Railroad, which passed through Juliette, also fueled the local economy, but with the closing of the mill, Juliette became something of a ghost town through the latter half of the 20th century. Today, it is best known as the setting for the 1991 movie *Fried Green Tomatoes*, starring Kathy Bates and Jessica Tandy, and indeed, the movie is largely responsible for the revival of the small town. When film crews arrived on location in 1990, the building that now houses the Whistle Stop Café sat vacant. It was refurbished for filming, and facades were added to the few existing structures to simulate a small town at the turn of the century. With the success of the movie, Juliette's fortunes have turned, and now several businesses cater to tourists who come from around the world to see Juliette and eat fried green tomatoes at the Whistle Stop Café.

JULIETTE MILL AND DAM, MONROE COUNTY

The dam that originally gave rise to Juliette is still capable of generating electricity, but in 2014 the Eastern Hydroelectric Corporation lost its license to operate when it failed to install fish ladders that would allow migratory American shad to reach spawning grounds farther upstream. In 2018, the company unsuccessfully appealed that decision. Now the future of the dam and the powerhouse is uncertain. The Juliette Dam is the first obstacle that migrating fish encounter when ascending the Altamaha and the Ocmulgee from the Atlantic Ocean. Shad, a critically important fish in colonial America, are still sought after by commercial and recreational anglers. They also play an important role in the aquatic food chain, providing meals for sport fish such as bass and crappie. Local boosters consider the dam an iconic part of the landscape and critical to the historic character of Juliette and the tourism economy that the community relies on. Advocates for free-flowing rivers argue that removing the dam would restore long stretches of the historic river channel, including Glover Shoals, on which the dam now sits, and improve habitat for migratory fish, mussels, and other aquatic wildlife. Removal of the dam would also eliminate an arduous portage. There is no easy route around the dam, though the east side provides the most direct route.

MILE 225.6 (33.104249, −83.795833) Zellner Island. Located immediately below Juliette Dam, this 35-acre island bears the name of a prominent early family in Monroe County. Andrew Zellner crossed the Ocmulgee and settled in the area in 1824, rearing eight children and surviving until 1892, his 94th year. His son, B. H. Zellner, represented Monroe County in the Georgia General Assembly and served as a county commissioner from 1876 to 1883. A planter and miller, he was, according to the Southern Historical Association, one of the largest landowners in Monroe County. In most cases, the Ocmulgee's islands are, in fact, private property, usually owned by riparian landowners on one side of the river or the other.

SHOALS AT JULIETTE, MONROE COUNTY

MILE 224.7 (33.094519, –83.783005) Plant Camellia & Percale. The water-intake structure on river right here is a relic from Georgia's rich textile history. It pumped water to Plant Camellia, one of 14 textile mills operated by the Macon-based Bibb Manufacturing during the late 1960s. Bibb built the plant in the woods along the river and bestowed on the unincorporated area the name Percale—to promote the kind of cotton sheets manufactured there. Among other things, workers made bedsheets emblazoned with National Football League team logos. The name, suggested by Bibb's marketing manager, was chosen over other nominees—including Romeo, proposed because of the area's proximity to Juliette. Originating in 1876, Bibb Manufacturing grew into one of the state's largest employers through the mid-20th century, but after about 1950, U.S. textile plants struggled to compete with lower-cost overseas facilities. As a result, textile employment in Georgia dropped 50 percent between the 1950s and 2000. Bibb Manufacturing went through bankruptcy reorganization in 1996 and was purchased by the Dan River Corporation in 1998. In 2006, the Development Authority of Monroe County purchased Plant Camellia, and the property is now home to Gro-Green, a company that manufactures and distributes erosion-control products aimed at protecting streams and rivers from sediment-laden stormwater runoff (the leading cause of water pollution in Georgia). Monroe County still owns the riverfront here and may in the future use the water intake for a public water supply. The county has historically purchased water from neighboring Macon-Bibb and Butts Counties, which both withdraw water from the Ocmulgee.

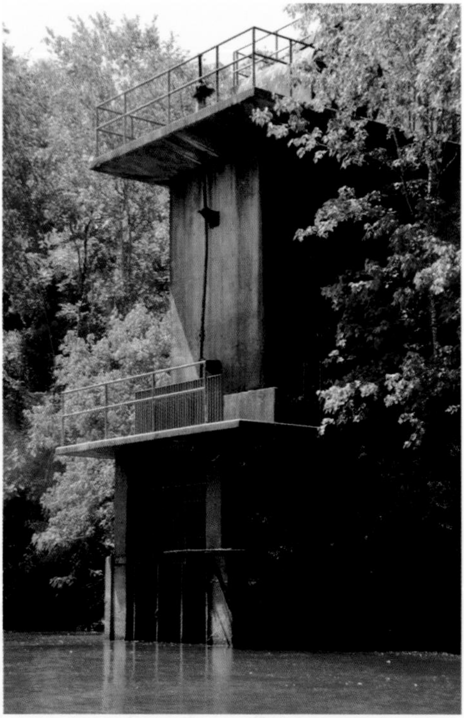

PLANT CAMELLIA WATER INTAKE, MONROE COUNTY

MILE 223.6 (33.082267, –83.775944) Mitchell's Ferry. This ferry, dating to the 1800s, operated into the early 1900s.

MILE 222.8 (33.074305, –83.763905) Shoal.

MILE 222.5 (33.070998, –83.761230) Shoal.

MILE 220.2 (33.047577, −83.738445) **Georgia Power Co. Plant Scherer Intake.** Here the Georgia Power Company withdraws water from the Ocmulgee River and pumps it to Lake Juliette, a reservoir formed by a dam on Rum Creek, built to serve Plant Scherer, one of the largest coal-fired power plants in the country. Scherer burns about 11 million tons of coal each year, turning water into steam to turn electric turbines. Water from the Ocmulgee is essential to this effort. Its primary job is to cool the steam and turn it back into water in order to repeat the electricity-generating process. Each of the plant's 540-foot-tall cooling towers can circulate 268,000 gallons of water a minute, losing about 8,000 gallons through evaporation. The plumes of white clouds that can be seen emanating from these towers are vapor that once ran as water in the Ocmulgee River and Rum Creek. The importance of water to our state's supply of electricity cannot be understated. It is why Georgia Power is the largest user of water in the state, and why aggressive energy-efficiency and conservation measures, coupled with renewable energy sources like wind and solar, can help reduce water-withdrawal pressure on rivers.

A troublesome by-product of the electricity generation at Scherer is coal ash, the toxic-laden residue left from burning coal. New federal regulations on the disposal of coal ash prompted by catastrophes in Tennessee and North Carolina, where coal ash polluted miles of rivers, led Georgia Power in 2016 to announce that it would close its coal ash ponds and begin dry storage of the ash in lined landfills. Those plans included leaving the 553-acre unlined ash pond at Scherer in place and using what the company called "advanced engineering methods" to cover and contain any contaminants. But Georgia Power's tests of its ponds at Scherer showed that groundwater had already been tainted with coal ash toxins. Altamaha Riverkeeper and other groups have urged the company to excavate the ash on-site and move it to a safer disposal site. That would entail a massive project; there are some 15.4 million tons of coal ash stored at Scherer.

MILE 219.8 (33.042421, −83.735900) **Jarrell Plantation.** On river left here is more than 200 acres of state-owned land that is part of the Jarrell Plantation State Historic Site. The site preserves the farm of John Fritz Jarrell, who settled the land in 1847. At the dawn of the Civil War, the Jarrell family farmed with 42 slaves. During the war, as Union soldiers marched from Atlanta to Savannah in November 1864, they burned outbuildings on the farm, stole the family's livestock, and freed the slaves. After the war, with the labor of tenant farmers rather than slaves, the Jarrells rebuilt and expanded the farm. By the late 19th century, under the direction of John's son, Dick Jarrell, the farming operation included a sawmill, cotton gin, gristmill, shingle mill, planer, sugar cane press, and syrup evaporator. Many of the farm's historic buildings remain today, along with the original Jarrell family home, which dates to the 1840s. In 1974, the Jarrell family donated the buildings to establish this historic site.

MILE 218.6 (33.027962, −83.724083) **Shoals.**

MILE 218.5 (33.026679, −83.723426) Falling Creek & Hitchiti Research Forest. This picturesque creek drains much of the Oconee National Forest northeast of the Ocmulgee. The Hitchiti Research Forest is a portion of the Oconee National Forest that is managed to improve habitat for the federally protected red-cockaded woodpecker—so named because of the red spot that crowns its black head. Like most of us, the red-cockaded is particular about where it raises its young, preferring to build its nesting cavities in aging pines infected with a wood-eating fungus. Few southern pines get this fungus before they reach 80–90 years old. As old-growth pines in Georgia were systematically harvested in the late 1800s and early 1900s, populations of the red-cockaded woodpecker declined precipitously. The bird was among the first animals placed on the endangered species list, in 1970. Since then, habitat management like that undertaken in the Hitchiti forest has helped steadily expand the species' numbers. In 1993, there were 4,400 known locations where the birds survived; now that number has grown to 7,800 locations. Falling Creek is also home to the Altamaha shiner, a state-protected species of minnow found only in the Piedmont region of the Oconee and Ocmulgee Rivers. Like the woodpecker, it depends on specific habitat to survive: free-flowing, sediment-free streams with rocky to sandy substrates.

MILE 217.3 (33.016012, −83.728221) Dame's Ferry & Rapid. This is the site of one of the earliest river ferries in Middle Georgia. Zachariah Booth first operated the ferry here, beginning around 1810. After John Dame married Booth's daughters (one in 1811 and another in 1815), the Dame family took control of the ferry, operating it until 1872. That year, the Hodge family purchased the ferry; they oper-

DAMES FERRY RAPID, MONROE COUNTY

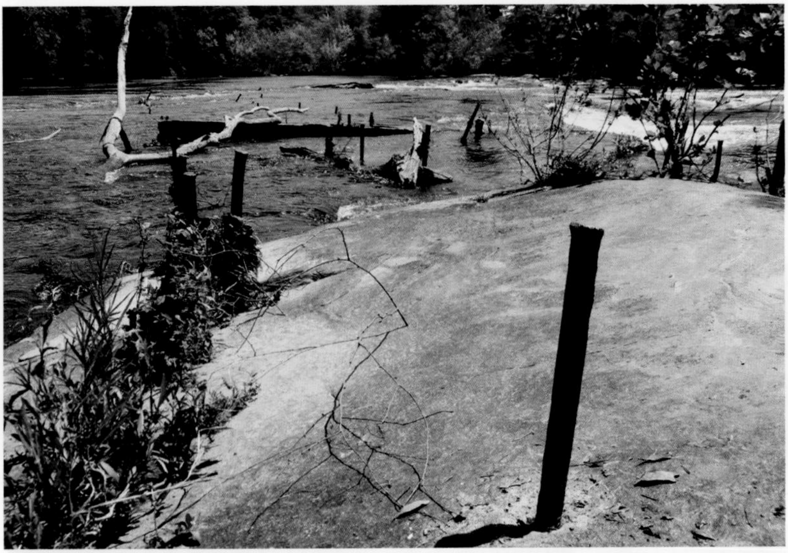

DAM RUINS AT DAMES FERRY, MONROE COUNTY

ated it until 1962, when the construction of a bridge made it obsolete. The ferryboat was then moved to the Flint River in Macon County, where it gained fame as the last operating ferry in Georgia. During the ferry's earliest days, it served as an important connection to Creek Indian lands west of the Ocmulgee. Under Hodge's ownership, the shoals below the ferry were harnessed to power a sawmill, planning mill, gristmill, and cotton gin. Rebar extending above the river's surface at the head of the shoals marks the site of Hodge's milldam, and in low water, parts of the dam's wooden structure can still be seen. In honor of the family that stewarded this property for nearly a century and donated it to the state for the bridge, the Georgia General Assembly in 1963 named the new span the S.A. Hodge, Senior, Bridge. The best route through this Class II shoal is over a pair of precipitous ledges on river right (to the left of the westernmost island), commonly called "The Steps." At higher water levels, it is possible to navigate the more gradually descending shoals on river left.

MILE 217.2 (33.012323, −83.729016) Dame's Ferry Islands. Through the years, Dame's Ferry and the islands below it have been this site of much mischief, mayhem, intrigue, and tragedy. Among the news items recorded with a Dame's Ferry dateline: In 1893, a dispute between an African American ferryman named Bob Carson and a local farmer, W. H. Green, resulted in an exchange of gunfire and the death of Carson. In 1897, Mack Howard was shot and killed during a poker game near Dame's Ferry. In 1918, R. W. Barron, the son-in-law of the ferry owner, S. A. Hodge, perished when his boat capsized during high water while en route to visit family for Christmas. In 1925, a train derailment and wreck at Dame's

Ferry (the railroad runs parallel to the river) killed one man and injured several others. In September 1927, a 24-year-old African American man was arrested for raping a white woman in a Dame's Ferry pea patch. In less than a month, he was put on trial, sentenced to death, and executed in the state's electric chair. That same year, suspects in a Macon murder made a hiding place of Dame's Ferry. In 1955, a man who fell asleep between the railroad tracks at Dame's Ferry miraculously survived being passed over by a 113-car-long train. And in 1964, two anglers drowned when their boat was washed over the rapids.

But undoubtedly, the most intriguing tale from Dame's Ferry was the capture of the convicted murderer Tom Allen on these islands in 1896. Allen was convicted in 1894 of shooting and killing a man in a Macon bar and was scheduled to be executed in the winter of 1895. But he slipped out of jail and remained a fugitive for more than a year. On the night of April 20, 1896, having tracked Allen to these islands, Bibb County sheriff Sam Westcott and a posse of nine men, under the cover of darkness and with their movements further concealed by the roar of the nearby shoals, waded from the west bank of the river to the islands. The details of the capture were recorded in riveting detail across two columns in the *Atlanta Constitution*: "At the command of Sheriff Westcott, the deputies and himself ran rapidly into the open space with leveled Winchesters. Westcott cried out to Allen and his men: 'The first man who moves will be riddled with bullets.' The surprise and demoralization of Allen and his companions were complete." Allen reportedly told authorities after his capture that he had suffered greatly while a fugitive and was glad that the "agony of suspense" was over. Allen's escape ultimately saved his life. After his recapture, multiple appeals reduced his sentence to life in prison.

MILE 216.3 (33.001309, −83.719344) Powerlines.

MILE 215.9 (32.998774, −83.721451) Shoals.

MILE 215.8 (32.997559, −83.723576) Rum Creek. Originating north of Forsyth, this tributary flows about 20 miles through Monroe County, and is dammed to form Lake Juliette, some 4 miles upstream. According to Ken Krakow in his book *Georgia Place-Names*, the "Rum" in the name of this creek comes from the rum produced by a sugarcane mill once located a few miles upstream.

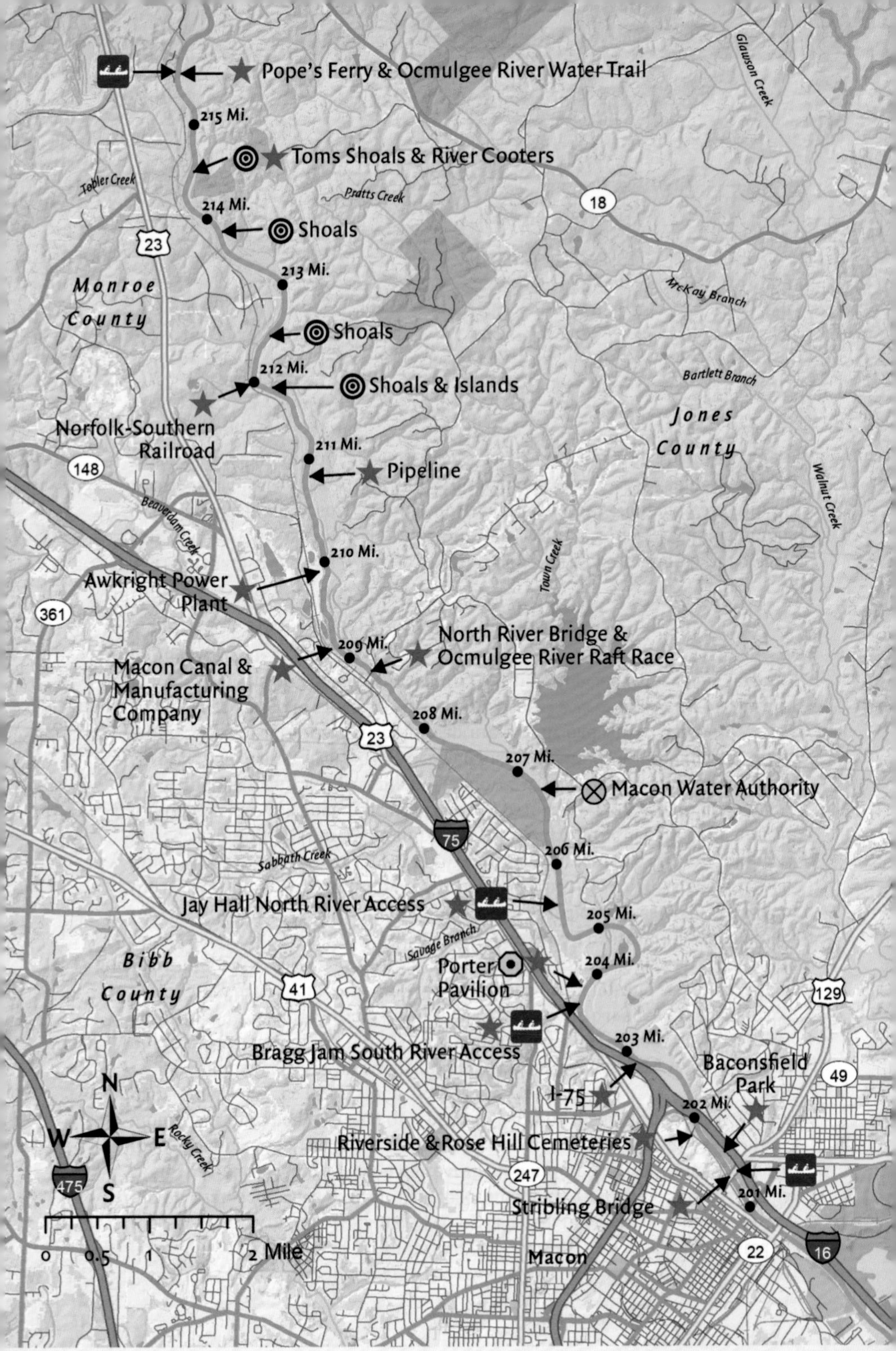

Pope's Ferry & Ocmulgee River Water Trail
215 Mi.
Toms Shoals & River Cooters
Tobler Creek
Pratts Creek
18
214 Mi.
Shoals
23
213 Mi.
Monroe
County
McKay Branch
Shoals
212 Mi.
Shoals & Islands
Bartlett Branch
Norfolk-Southern
Railroad
Jones
County
211 Mi.
148
Pipeline
Walnut Creek
Beaverdam Creek
210 Mi.
Town Creek
Awkright Power
Plant
361
North River Bridge &
Ocmulgee River Raft Race
209 Mi.
Macon Canal &
Manufacturing
Company
208 Mi.
23
207 Mi.
Macon Water Authority
75
206 Mi.
Sabbath Creek
Jay Hall North River Access
205 Mi.
Savage Branch
Porter
Pavilion
204 Mi.
Bibb
County
41
129
Bragg Jam South River Access
203 Mi.
Baconsfield
Park
49
I-75
N
202 Mi.
W
E
Riverside & Rose Hill Cemeteries
Rocky Creek
475
S
247
Stribling Bridge
201 Mi.
0
0.5
1
2 Mile
Macon
22
16
Glawson Creek

Amerson

Length 14 miles (Pope's Ferry to Spring Street)

Class I

Time 6–8 hours

Minimum Level Flows of 400 cfs at the Ga. 18 gauge at Dame's Ferry are sufficient to float this section.

River Gauge The nearest river gauge is located at Ga. 18 / Dame's Ferry upstream of this section: https://waterdata.usgs.gov/ga/nwis/uv/?site_no=02212735&PARAmeter_cd=00065,00060,00062,00010.

Launch Site The launch site is a Georgia Department of Natural Resources boat ramp and parking area maintained by Monroe County and located on the west side of the river.

DIRECTIONS From I-75 at exit 171 (U.S. 23 / Riverside Drive), travel north on U.S. 23 for 5.2 miles. Turn right on Pope's Ferry Road and proceed 0.3 mile. Turn right on Pope's Ferry Lane and proceed 0.4 mile to the boat ramp.

Take Out Site The take out site is a boat ramp on river left at Spring Street in Macon adjacent to a parking area for the Ocmulgee Heritage Trail, a riverside recreational path.

DIRECTIONS From the Pope's Ferry boat ramp, return to U.S. 23. Turn left and proceed 5.2 miles to the I-75 interchange. Take the I-75 south ramp and proceed 5.4 miles. Take I-16 east 1.1 miles to exit 1A (U.S. 23 / Spring St.). At the light, turn right and then immediately left into the Ocmulgee Heritage Trail's Spring Street Landing area.

Alternative Take Out Sites By using the take out sites in Amerson River Park, it is possible to create 10-mile and 12-mile trips. Additionally, the 2-mile run between Amerson River Park's two access points is a popular tube float.

DIRECTIONS From the Pope's Ferry boat ramp, return to U.S. 23. Turn left and proceed 9.4 miles. Turn left on Pierce Avenue, pass underneath I-75, and then turn immediately right on North Pierce Avenue, continuing 0.3 mile to the entrance to Amerson River Park. To access the park's north launch (farthest upstream), turn left after the entrance and proceed 0.7 mile to the launch. To access the south launch, continue straight at the entrance through the roundabout for 0.4 mile to the parking area.

Outfitters Ocmulgee Outdoor Expeditions provides canoe and kayak rentals and shuttle service.

Ocmulgee Outdoor Expeditions, 478-733-3386,
www.ocmulgeeoutdoorexpeditions.com

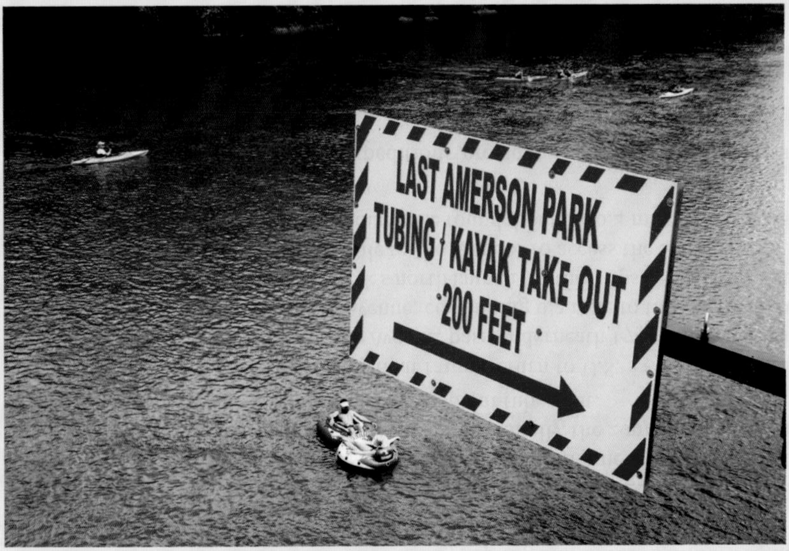

TUBES AND KAYAKS AT AMERSON PARK, BIBB COUNTY

$10 Tubing, located in Amerson River Park, provides tube rentals for the 2-mile run in the park.

$10 Tubing, 2552 North Pierce Ave., Macon, 31204,
844-386-8823, www.rivertubing.com

Description This 14-mile run takes in the Ocmulgee's final miles in Georgia's Piedmont as it spills over the fall line into the Coastal Plain. The first 6 miles include frequent shoals, but shortly after passing beneath the River North Boulevard bridge, the rocks and shoals recede, giving way to the sandy bottoms that predominate from here to the Altamaha. The river passes around Amerson River Park, a 180-acre Macon-Bibb County facility that is one of the crown jewels of the area's Ocmulgee Heritage Trail, a multipurpose recreational trail running from Amerson River Park along the river through Macon. The river, which winds into the heart of Macon, is also rich in history.

Points of Interest

MILE 215.6 (32.993767, −83.724671) Pope's Ferry & Ocmulgee River Water Trail. Beginning in the 1810s, Cullen Pope operated a ferry at this site, providing an important link to Creek Indian lands west of the Ocmulgee. By 1834, the Georgia General Assembly had officially recognized Pope's Ferry and established the rates that Pope could collect: "For a loaded wagon and team fifty cents; for a four wheel carriage and two horses fifty cents; for a gig and horse twenty five cents; for a Jersey wagon and horse thirty seven and a half cents; for a cart and oxen twenty five cents; for a man and horse twelve and a half cents; for each foot passenger six and one fourth cents; for each head of neat cattle three cents; for each head of hogs, goats and sheep two cents; and for a led or loose horse six and one fourth cents." Today, it costs nothing to launch a boat from here. The site is a key link in the Ocmulgee River Water Trail (ORWT), an ongoing effort to create a boating trail stretching some 250 miles from Lloyd Shoals Dam to the Altamaha River. The ORWT Partnership now consists of representatives from multiple counties, all working to improve access to the river and promote recreational uses of it.

MILE 214.6 (32.980019, −83.722225) Toms Shoals & River Cooters. These shoals mark the location of a historic Native American ford on a trail known as Toms Path. At these shallow shoals, you might encounter Georgia's most common river turtles (and perhaps the most ubiquitous of all the river's creatures). River cooters are readily recognized by the yellow to cream markings on their shells, heads, and necks and a somewhat serrated shell edge in the rear. They can reach lengths of almost 17 inches and are commonly seen basking themselves in the sun on the tops of rocks and riverside strainers. They dine on aquatic vegetation, and their appetite is such that in some places they have been used to control invasive water hyacinth. Despite their apparent abundance, these and other Georgia turtles face threats, primarily overharvesting for export to Asian countries where the appetite for turtles, served in soups and stews, is immense. As stocks of wild turtles have declined in Asia, those countries have turned to the

NEAR TOM SHOALS, MONROE COUNTY

United States, and particularly to the Southeast, for new supplies. In 2018, the Center for Biological Diversity reported that more than 17 million wild-caught turtles were exported from the United States between 2011 and 2016. Georgia's Department of Natural Resources implemented regulations intended to prevent the overharvesting of river cooters and other species in 2012. The word "cooter" was introduced to the American South by slaves. In Africa, "kuta" is the word for turtle in some languages.

MILE 213.8 (32.972432, −83.717126) Shoals.

MILE 212.5 (32.958223, −83.708630) Shoals.

MILE 212.0 (32.951846, −83.710851) Norfolk-Southern Railroad. At this sharp bend to the east is one of the many spots where this railroad can be seen on river right. It parallels the river for more than 30 miles from Macon north to Jackson. This line was originally constructed in 1882 as part of the East Tennessee and Georgia Railroad, a 158-mile route connecting Macon to Atlanta, Rome, and points north. In 1886, the 88-mile ride from Macon to Atlanta took four hours. The first railroad in these parts ran farther west, on a 26-mile route from Macon to Forsyth. It opened on December 10, 1838, and the first locomotive to run on the tracks was appropriately named the *Ocmulgee*. To get the locomotive to the tracks, it was first unloaded from a seagoing vessel at the port in Darien on the Altamaha River, transferred to a river steamer, and then shipped up the Altamaha and Ocmulgee Rivers to Macon. As railways became more ubiquitous and proved more dependable for shipping goods than steamboats plying unpredictable rivers, the locomotive ultimately hastened the end of steamboat navigation on the Ocmulgee.

MILE 211.8 (32.951315, −83.708352) Shoals & Islands.

ROCK ISLAND, MONROE COUNTY

MILE 210.8 (32.939069, −83.701656) Pipeline. This pipeline, along with the compressor station located just west of the river, is part of Kinder Morgan's 6,900-mile Southern Natural Gas pipeline system, which stretches from Louisiana in the west to South Carolina in the east and from Florida in the south to Tennessee in the north. The proliferation of new pipelines and the expansion of existing ones during the first two decades of the 21st century are indicative of the country's changing energy portfolio. In 1911, when Lloyd Shoals Dam upstream was completed, the United States derived the vast majority of its energy supplies from hydropower. As the demand for electricity increased and the population expanded, coal became the predominant energy source during the second half of the 20th century. Today, natural gas is fast outpacing coal as the fuel of choice, and hydropower accounts for less than 3 percent of the country's energy supply. The one constant, however, has been water. Whether at a dam or at a coal- or gas-powered plant, water is integral to the process.

MILE 209.9 (32.926969, −83.697990) Arkwright Power Plant. On river right is the site of the Georgia Power Company's decommissioned Arkwright Power Plant. The plant closed in 2002 after 60 years of burning coal to produce electricity. It was named for the first president of the Georgia Power Company, Preston Arkwright, who in 1906 bought the Atlanta Crackers baseball team and located the team's playing field along one of Atlanta's streetcar lines in an effort to boost ridership—a ploy that would, not coincidentally, increase demand for the company's electricity, too. Arkwright was such a booster of the company that contemporaries sometimes described him as an "electricity evangelist," and upon

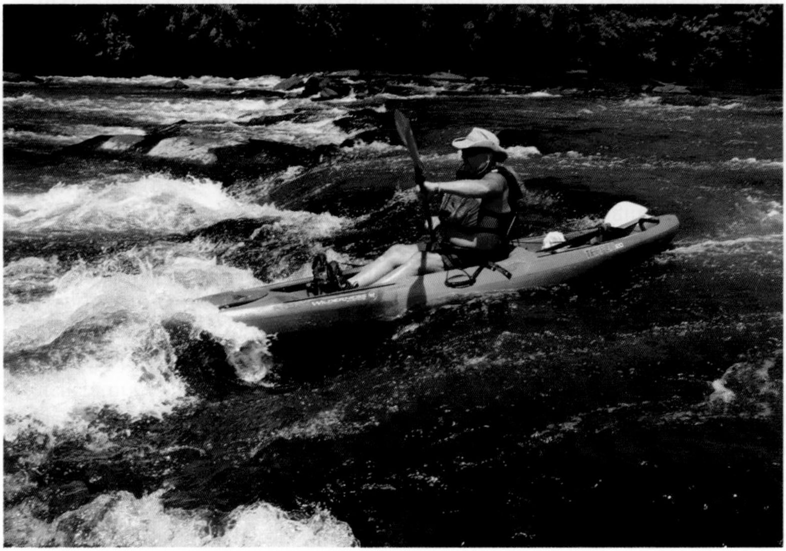

SHOALS AT ARKWRIGHT, BIBB COUNTY

his death in 1946, Atlanta mayor William Hartsfield described Arkwright as "by common consent, our No. 1 citizen." The Arkwright Power Plant came online between 1941 and 1943, at a time when electricity demand for defense purposes were ramped up during World War II and when drought conditions limited the output of the company's numerous hydropower dams. When completed, Arkwright was the largest power plant in Georgia, producing 3,000 megawatts a day. The Ocmulgee played a critical role by providing cooling water for the steam generators. When Georgia Power shuttered the plant in 2002, the company had no solar or wind power in its portfolio. Less than 20 years later, Georgia's total solar capacity had grown to nearly 2,000 megawatts, and less than 30 percent of Georgia Power's generation is derived from coal combustion.

On river left, opposite the plant site, the river splits around an island. In higher water, it is possible to explore the narrow channel on the far left, which flows over a suspected rock weir, or fish trap, of unknown origins.

MILE 209.2 (32.916060, −83.695806) Macon Canal & Manufacturing Company. In 1871, local investors formed this company around the grand vision of building a canal from a point on the river near the mouth of Beaverdam Creek (on river right) to Macon. Proponents of the plan envisioned a canal carrying water to the center of the city and generating power to run mills and factories along its banks. The idea for this 10-mile canal persisted into the late 1800s. A headline in the *Atlanta Constitution* on August 16, 1890, proclaimed: "Outlook for the Macon Canal Company Very Bright." Optimism ran high: "The company has been informed by a number of manufacturing enterprises that they will use the canal power of electricity, instead of steam. It is proposed to generate electricity for all kinds of manufactories, printing presses, illuminating uses, etc. . . . Macon justly regards the canal project as the largest and most valuable scheme ever suggested or contemplated in this city." Ultimately, the engineering realities likely dissuaded the investors. Construction would have required the excavation of a ridge north of the city. If that wasn't enough, a cemetery also lay in the path of the proposed canal route.

MILE 208.7 (32.913041, −83.690076) River North Bridge & Ocmulgee River Raft Race. Imitating the success of the famed Ramblin' Raft Race on the Chattahoochee River in Atlanta, Macon, from 1978 to 1981, hosted its own "Woodstock on Water." The race began at this bridge and wound 6 miles to Spring Street. At its peak, the event brought more than 3,000 people to the river on some 1,000 boats and rafts, most of the homemade variety. Among the more memorable vessels were a floating Volkswagen Beetle and an inflatable raft in the shape of Air Force One. Proceeds from the event were used for beautification projects in Macon.

MILE 206.7 (32.897638, −83.661731) Macon Water Authority. The water-intake structure on river left provides Macon's water supply. Water is pumped from here to Javors Lucas Lake and the authority's Amerson Water Treatment Plant. The man-made reservoir and treatment facility came online in 2000, a direct consequence of Tropical Storm Alberto, which stalled over Central Georgia in early

July 1994. The storm forever altered Macon. Massive flooding submerged Macon's Riverside Water Treatment Plant, destroyed over half of the buildings on the site, and wrecked a pumping station that was under construction. Around 50,000 people were left without water for three weeks. Federal disaster-aid funds led to the construction of these new facilities. Water is drawn from the Ocmulgee during periods of high flows (up to 65 million gallons a day) and stored in the 650-acre, 6.5 billion-gallon reservoir, where it is then pumped to Macon. The facility is an example of a new breed of water-supply projects called "off-stream" reservoirs because a tributary rather than the mainstem of a river is dammed. These projects allow water suppliers to vary the amount of water they withdraw from the river, providing greater protection of river flows. But they also require the damming and destruction of smaller streams and cost millions to build. The Amerson plant's price tag was some $125 million.

MACON WATER AUTHORITY INTAKE, JONES COUNTY

MILE 205.6 (32.881671, −83.657810) Jay Hall North River Access. This launch on river right marks the upper end of Macon-Bibb County's Amerson River Park. When the park opened, in 2015, the ramp became a popular launch site for 2-mile tube trips to the park's lower launch. Over the next 2 miles, travelers can see the infrastructure of this park, including a pair of riverfront pavilions.

MILE 203.8 (32.870923, −83.653203) Porter Pavilion. This pavilion, sitting high above the river, is now an event space within Amerson River Park. Previously, it was the intake structure for Macon's Riverside Water Treatment Plant, which was destroyed by flooding from Tropical Storm Alberto. Believe it or not, the towering structure was underwater during the storm and its aftermath. At the height of the flood, the city was completely cut off by floodwaters, which blocked all roads in and out of the city. When the water receded, the 100-year-old water treatment facility lay in ruins, and the Macon Water Authority soon embarked on building a new facility (the Amerson Water Treatment Plant and Lake Javors Lucas upstream). That left some 160 acres of unused, blighted property. Between 2000 and 2015, Macon-Bibb County began investing in projects to develop the old waterworks site into a community amenity. A $6 million grant from the U.S. Department of Transportation aided in the construction of Porter Pavilion, boat launches, and other amenities, and in 2015 the park celebrated its grand "re-opening." Now, some 450,000 people visit the park annually, many to float the 2 miles of river that stretch around the peninsula of land that makes up the park. The park is named for Frank C. Amerson, who served on the Macon Water Authority board for 36 years and died in 2012. The park is a crown jewel in the Ocmulgee Heritage Trail, which will ultimately connect the park to downtown Macon and the Ocmulgee National Monument. The park features picnic areas and pavilions, a playground, a tubing vendor, and restrooms. Amerson River Park, 478-803-0484, https://amerson.maconbibb.us.

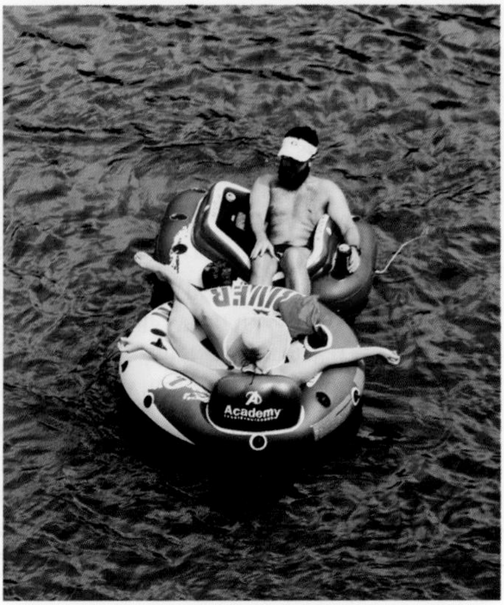

TUBING AT AMERSON PARK, BIBB COUNTY

MILE 203.7 (32.868981, –83.654206) Bragg Jam South River Access. Amerson River Park's lower river access was funded by Bragg Jam, a Macon music festival originally organized to celebrate the lives of musicians Brax and Tate Bragg. The brothers died tragically in a car accident in 1999. In the event's first 20 years, it generated more than $200,000 for local community causes.

MILE 202.8 (32.861185, –83.644206) I-75. On river right here, the river lies within earshot of the roar of this interstate highway. I-75 runs from Hialeah, Florida (below Miami), to Sault Ste. Marie, Michigan, at the Canadian border—a distance of 1,786 miles. The highway through Georgia was completed in 1977.

MILE 201.8 (32.851380, –83.633860) Riverside & Rose Hill Cemeteries. On river right here overlooking the Ocmulgee are two of Macon's most famed burial places. Rose Hill, dating to 1840, and Riverside, established in 1887, are the final resting place of some 600 Confederate and Union soldiers and tens of thousands of others, including some of Macon's most notable residents. Topping the list are three members of the Allman Brothers Band: brothers Duane and Greg Allman and bandmate Berry Oakley. Among others interred here are Hazel Jane Raines, the first woman in Georgia to earn a commercial pilot's license; John Fletcher Hanson, recognized as the father of the Georgia Institute of Technology; and John Birch, a U.S. military intelligence officer killed by Chinese communists in 1945 whose name was taken by the anticommunist organization the

John Birch Society. Friends of John Birch said that he likely would not have approved of the use of his name for the organization.

MILE 201.6 (32.848412, −83.629906) Baconsfield Park. On river left here beyond the roar of I-16 is land that once held this "whites only" city park. Upon his death in 1914, U.S. senator Augustus Bacon of Macon left the land to the city as a park, on the stipulation that it would serve the "white women and children of the city of Macon." The 75-acre park opened in 1920 with playgrounds, ball fields, and beautifully landscaped walking paths. Later it housed a small zoo where Maconites marveled at peacocks, moose, and bobcats. In the 1960s, lawsuits were brought against the park's board of managers, demanding that it be integrated. The case ended at the U.S. Supreme Court, which ruled in favor of the plaintiffs, but rather than integrate the park, Bacon's heirs sued to get the land returned to the family. That case also wound up before the Supreme Court. This time the justices ruled in favor of Bacon's heirs. The court held that because the provision of Bacon's will designating the park for the use of whites only could not be legally enforced, the land should revert to Bacon's heirs. Activists during the early 1970s tried in vain to acquire the property from Bacon's heirs and save the park. The land has since succumbed to residential and commercial development. The Supreme Court justices who sealed Baconsfield's fate did so with regret. Justice Hugo Black, writing for the majority, stated: "When a city park is destroyed because the Constitution requires that it be integrated, there is reason for everyone to be disheartened."

MILE 201.4 (32.845954, −83.628164) Stribling Bridge. Macon's Spring Street Bridge is named in honor of a famous professional boxer who hailed from Macon. William Lawrence "Young" Stribling Jr. fought 286 bouts and lost only 12. He recorded 127 career knockouts, and was knocked out only once—a technical knockout in the 15th round of a world-championship fight with the German Max Schmeling in 1931. He came from a colorful family in Bainbridge and spent his early childhood as part of a family vaudeville act that included a "boxing match" between four-year-old William and his two-year-old brother, "Baby." The family's act took them to 38 countries before they settled down in Macon. At the age of 15, Stribling became a professional boxer, and during the 1920s he toured the country in a bus, taking on any local champions that would step in the ring. After serving in the U.S. Army Reserve Air Corps and earning his pilot's license, Stribling began flying his own plane to matches around the South. He died in October 1933 at the age of 29 from injuries sustained in a wreck while riding his motorcycle to the Macon hospital, where his wife had just given birth to their third child. Thousands filed by his casket as it lay in state at the city auditorium before the popular boxer was interred at Riverside Cemetery, overlooking the Ocmulgee. In 1965, Stribling was inducted into the Georgia Sports Hall of Fame, located in Macon. Interestingly, 38 years after Stribling's demise—also during October—Macon lost another pop icon in the same manner when the musician Duane Allman died in a motorcycle wreck in the city. In November of the following year, Allman's bandmate the bassist Berry Oakley also died in a wreck while riding his motorcycle in Macon.

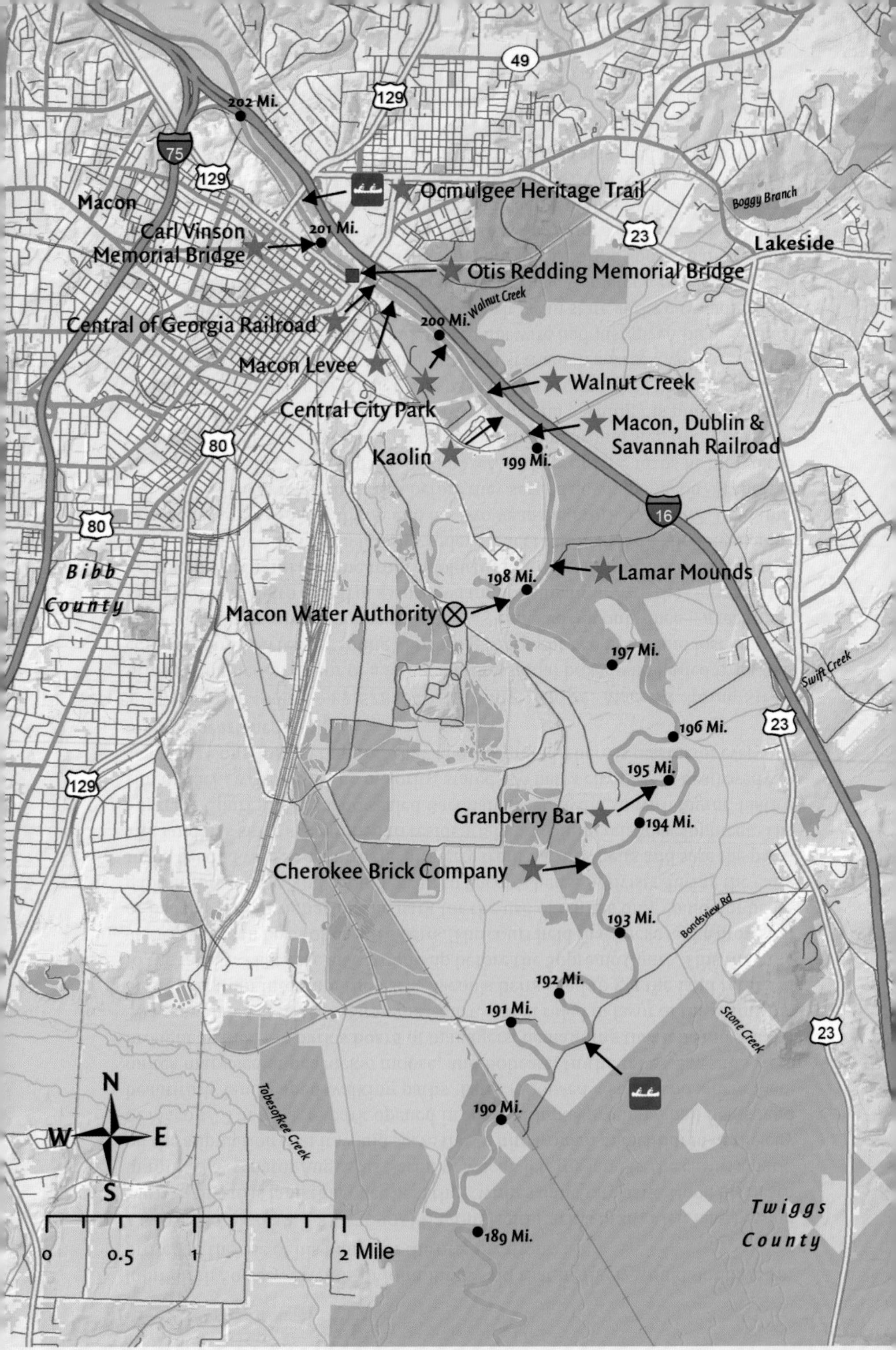
49
129
202 Mi.
75
129
Macon
Ocmulgee Heritage Trail
Boggy Branch
Carl Vinson
Memorial Bridge
201 Mi.
23
Lakeside
Otis Redding Memorial Bridge
Walnut Creek
Central of Georgia Railroad
200 Mi.
Macon Levee
Walnut Creek
Central City Park
Macon, Dublin &
Savannah Railroad
80
Kaolin
199 Mi.
16
80
Bibb
County
198 Mi.
Lamar Mounds
Macon Water Authority
197 Mi.
Swift Creek
196 Mi.
23
195 Mi.
129
Granberry Bar
194 Mi.
Cherokee Brick Company
193 Mi.
Bondsview Rd
192 Mi.
191 Mi.
Stone Creek
23
N
190 Mi.
W
E
Tobesofkee Creek
S
Twiggs
County
189 Mi.
0
0.5
1
2 Mile

Macon

Length 10 miles (Spring Street to Bondsview Road)
Class I
Time 4–6 hours
Minimum Level Navigable year-round.

River Gauge The nearest river gauge is at the Martin Luther King Jr. Boulevard bridge downstream of the launch site for this section: https://waterdata.usgs.gov/ga/nwis/uv/?site_no=02213000&PARAmeter_cd=00065,00060,00062,00010.

Launch Site The launch site is a boat ramp at Spring Street in Macon adjacent to the parking area for the Ocmulgee Heritage Trail.

DIRECTIONS From I-16 at exit 1A southbound (U.S. 23 / Spring St.), turn right and then immediately left into the Ocmulgee Heritage Trail's Spring Street parking area.

Take Out Site The take out site is an unimproved boat launch on river left at Bondsview Road. There is no parking area at this location, but it is possible to park along the right-of-way.

DIRECTIONS From the Ocmulgee Heritage Trail parking area, return to Spring Street. Turn right and then immediately right again onto the entrance ramp to I-16. Proceed on I-16 for 4.5 miles to exit 6 (U.S. 23 / Ocmulgee East Blvd.) Turn right at the exit and proceed 1.2 miles. Turn right on Level Acres Drive and proceed 0.1 mile. Turn right on Bondsview Road and proceed 2.0 miles to river.

Outfitters Ocmulgee Outdoor Expeditions provides canoe and kayak rentals and shuttle service.

Ocmulgee Outdoor Expeditions, 478-733-3386,
www.ocmulgeeoutdoorexpeditions.com

Description What starts as a distinctly urban paddle after a few short miles enters a vast and secluded section of river flanked by large tracts of undeveloped private property and the 7,764-acre Bond Swamp National Wildlife Refuge. Bridges dominate the first mile; but by mile 10, a black bear in the bottomland forest is a more likely sighting. The Ocmulgee's floodplain is the one place in the state other than the North Georgia mountains and the Okefenokee Swamp where you might encounter these apex predators. The river leaves behind the shoals of the Piedmont and assumes the sinuous winding path of a Coastal Plain river. Sharp oxbows and sandbars become numerous.

Points of Interest

MILE 201.3 (32.845292, −83.627406) Ocmulgee Heritage Trail. The Spring Street boat landing is adjacent to this recreational trail, which is part of a system of trails envisioned to connect multiple cultural and recreational areas in the Macon area. It is the brainchild of NewTown Macon, a nonprofit organization founded in 1996 with funding from the Peyton Anderson Foundation (which provided funding for the publication of this book). In addition to leveraging private money to develop the Ocmulgee Heritage Trail, NewTown Macon funds economic development projects within the city. During its first 20 years of operation, the organization helped bring in investments totaling some $350 million to improve downtown. The Ocmulgee Heritage Trail will ultimately encompass more than 15 miles of recreational trails along the river.

MILE 201.0 (32.841659, −83.624947) Carl Vinson Memorial Bridge. This bridge—along with many other things—bears the name of one of the longest-serving members of Congress in U.S. history. Vinson was first elected to Congress in 1914 and was reelected 26 times before retiring in 1965. His 50 years of service in Congress is surpassed by only six other legislators. Though he hailed from a landlocked district, he became closely associated with the U.S. Navy. Considered the "Father of the Two-Ocean Navy," he served as chair of the House's Naval Affairs Committee and later the Armed Services Committee. He was so influential in funding defense projects that he came to be known as the "Admiral." When rumors flew that President Eisenhower would appoint him secretary of defense, he told reporters he would decline such an appointment: "I'd rather run the Pentagon from here," he said. His hometown was Milledgeville, but he attended Mercer University's law school in Macon. Among the other things named in his honor: an aircraft carrier, the University of Georgia's Institute of Government, and a road in Warner Robins.

MILE 200.7 (32.838729, −83.620438) Otis Redding Memorial Bridge. On river right in the Charles H. Jones Gateway Park is a statue of the "King of Soul," whose name also was bestowed upon the Martin Luther King Jr. Boulevard bridge over the river here. Born in Dawson, Redding moved to Macon with his family when he was a toddler, and once there he sowed his musical roots by singing in the Vineville Baptist Church and performing in local talent shows. In fact, he won one Macon talent show so many times that organizers eventually prohibited him from competing. In 1962, he made his first recordings, at Stax Records in Memphis, and by 1967 he had run off a string of hit singles. He is best known for "Sittin' on the Dock of the Bay," a song he wrote and recorded shortly before his death in a small-plane crash in 1967. Though his statue overlooks the Ocmulgee, the song was inspired by a stay on a houseboat in Sausalito, California. His family operates the Macon-based Otis Redding Foundation. A recreational trail leading from this park crosses the bridge and resumes paralleling the river downstream to Walnut Creek and then into the Ocmulgee Mounds National Historical Park.

CENTRAL OF GEORGIA RAILROAD, BIBB COUNTY

MILE 200.5 (32.837795, −83.618733) Central of Georgia Railroad. A railroad has spanned the river here since 1851, when the Central of Georgia completed its connection from Savannah to Macon. At the time, it was said to be the longest railroad in the world (190 miles) under a single owner (the Central Railroad and Canal Company). In those early years, it carried much of the cotton that had previously been shipped downriver, marking the beginning of the end of commercial navigation on the river. In the early 1840s, steamboats were commonly seen on the river in Macon, but within ten years the fortunes of the steamboats had declined considerably. As recounted in Carlton A. Morrison's *Running the River*, an edition of the *Macon Messenger* reported on the rare arrival of a steamboat in 1856: "Now, scarcely one, two or three boats are seen in the course of the year . . . Other improvements of the age [railroad] have become too fast for them and Young America cannot stand the sinuosities of a river where a railroad track is to be found in its vicinity."

MILE 200.4 (32.836537, −83.616553) Macon Levee. On river right here, stretching from the Otis Redding Memorial Bridge more than 5 miles downstream, is this concrete and earthen dike intended to protect Macon from flooding. Dating to the 1950s, the levee has been the subject of much concern and controversy since the historic flood of 1994 overtopped and broke through it. Studies have indicated that that catastrophic flood was intensified by the levee and the raised bed of I-16, which parallels the river on its east side. These earthen berms flanking the river constricted the river's flow, keeping it from dispersing into the river's natural floodplain and pushing it into other low-lying areas. This problem had been foreseen by Colonel Dan Kingman with the U.S. Army Corps of Engineers in a report to Congress in 1911: "It may be and undoubtedly will be asked that levees be built in certain localities for certain special purposes or to protect certain interests, but as soon as this is begun it is sure to lead to extensions and as one bank of the river is leveed the property owners on the other side will be forced to rear banks for their own protection. The levee system on the Mississippi River began on a small scale and for special localities and increased until it became a great work beyond the resources of the riparian states. I would therefore advise that the United States should have nothing to do with the construction of levees along this river system, and if ever the State of Georgia undertakes to build a system of levees or to permit them to be built, that the United States withdraw from all effort to improve navigation on the river." Kingman's advice was, of course, ignored, and 100 years later the levee system is still a thorn in the side of local leaders. The Corps of Engineers, which inspects the levee annually, has called it minimally acceptable and weakened with age, but funds to repair and strengthen it are limited. (Macon-Bibb County has responsibility for its maintenance.) The levee protects from flooding the city's Central City Park, the Macon-Bibb sewage treatment plant, a local landfill, and several industrial facilities.

MILE 199.9 (32.832341, −83.610328) Central City Park. Located behind the levee here, Central City Park, developed in 1871, famously hosted the Georgia State Fair from 1886 through 1960. It is also home to Luther Williams Field, a baseball park dating to 1929 that has been the home of numerous minor-league teams. Among the baseball greats who played on the field are the Hall of Famers Tony Perez and Chipper Jones as well as Pete Rose. Most recently, the Macon Bacon, a collegiate summer team, played on the historic field. Macon—with its phonetically unique name, commonly pronounced "Make-in"—has had some fun with sports teams' names. In addition to the Bacon, among the other jerseys donned in town have been the Macon Music (baseball) and Macon Whoopee (hockey).

MILE 199.5 (32.827886, −83.605200) Walnut Creek. This creek on river left drains the Ocmulgee Mounds National Historical Park. The park is home to archeological sites that trace human occupation of the land to some 17,000 years ago. The most notable of the park's features are five mounds and an earth lodge believed to have been constructed during the early Mississippian Period, AD 800–1100. The earth lodge's walls and ceiling were rebuilt in the 1930s by workers with the Civilian Conservation Corps and the Works Progress Administration, but the dirt floor of the lodge is original. The circular lodge seated 50 people around a large fire pit, but the most intriguing element of the lodge was a massive and mysterious clay image of a bird within a seating platform in the dirt floor—a feature that is still visible. Archaeologists are uncertain of the bird's meaning, but believe the lodge was used as a community meeting place, the equivalent of today's city council chambers. Twice a year, in February and October, sunlight hits the entrance at just the right angle to illuminate the fire pit and the bird effigy, leading some archeologists to believe that the lodge also served as a calendar

NEAR WALNUT CREEK, BIBB COUNTY

marking the times for seasonal rituals or ceremonies. The archeological dig in the 1930s—undertaken by some 800 workers—is still considered the largest dig ever conducted in the United States. It uncovered 2.5 million artifacts and helped piece together the time line of human occupation of the site. In 2019, Congress renamed the Ocmulgee National Monument the Ocmulgee Mounds National Historical Park and provided funds to expand the park from 700 to 2,800 acres.

MILE 199.3 (32.825571, −83.603706) Kaolin. Embedded in the bank on river right here is this gray-white clay, which has made Middle Georgia famous. The state's kaolin belt runs along the fall line from Columbus to Macon to Augusta—the area where millions of years ago sediment from upstream mountains was deposited along the coastline by ancient rivers. These vast deposits have made Georgia the nation's leading producer of "china clay," which, in addition to being used to produce porcelain, finds its way into all manner of consumer products, including paper, plastics, paint, inks, wire insulation, and even auto body parts. Sandersville, located about 50 miles east of this site, proudly proclaims itself the Kaolin Capital of the World. At one time, Georgia's kaolin industry mined more than 8 million metric tons annually, but in 2015 production had declined to about 5,000 tons. The clay makes fun body paint, for those so inclined, and in Middle Georgia it is commonly eaten. Advocates of eating the clay claim that it can soothe digestive problems (it was once the main ingredient in Kaopectate), but if consumed in large amounts, it can lead to blockages of the digestive system.

MILE 199.1 (32.823976, −83.600530) Macon, Dublin & Savannah Railroad. Chartered in 1885, this railroad was not completed until 1902. At that time, it posed a competitive threat to the Central of Georgia Railroad, which crossed the river just upstream. Not surprisingly, the Central of Georgia took action to maintain its freight monopoly to the coast, filing a lawsuit preventing the city of Macon from giving land to the upstart competitor for a depot. Today, both lines still operate—the Central of Georgia as part of the Norfolk Southern system, and the Macon, Dublin & Savannah (now known as the Georgia Central) as part of the Genesee & Wyoming system. Of particular note, the center pier of this bridge is circular, indicating that it was originally constructed as a swing bridge to allow for the passage of river steamers. During low water, a line of wooden posts can be seen just downstream of the bridge. These are the remains of extensive training walls built by the U.S. Army Corps of Engineers in the early 1900s to constrict the river's flow and deepen the channel for steamboats. Between 1878 and 1910, the corps constructed more than a half mile of training walls and spur dams and some 2 miles of bank revetments in the Altamaha, Ocmulgee, and Oconee Rivers—many of those structures were in these reaches just downstream of Macon.

MILE 198.2 (32.811694, −83.598150) Lamar Mounds. About 1,500 feet due east of this location is what is known as the Lamar Mounds, two Native American mounds that have been dated to about 1350. Though part of the Ocmulgee Mounds National Historical Park, the site can be visited only on ranger-guided tours or by special permit. The more significant mound is constructed in a spiral pattern with a ramp to the summit that circles the mound four times counterclockwise. It is the only mound of its kind in the country. The inhabitants of this site were likely decimated by disease when they encountered Hernando de Soto and his men in 1540. Survivors eventually banded together with others to form the Creek Nation.

MILE 197.9 (32.808170, −83.602279) Macon Water Authority. On river right here is the discharge from the Lower Poplar Street Water Reclamation Facility. Originally built in 1959, this plant is on the receiving end of 1,000 miles of sanitary sewer lines that service Macon-Bibb County. Like most sewage treatment facilities, it is located downstream of the city's water intake (9 miles upstream) and the customers served by the sewer system. The location is less about aesthetics and more about engineering. Sewage is most economically conveyed via gravity, and so sewage treatment facilities are usually sited downslope from the communities they serve. Nevertheless, Macon's sewer system relies on more than 50 pump stations to "lift" the sewage over elevated areas, where gravity won't do the trick. About 18 millions gallons of treated effluent is discharged here daily.

MILE 195.1 (32.791410, −83.583750) Granberry Bar. At low water, the remains of wood pilings can be seen extending above the waterline. The pilings were part the U.S. Army Corps of Engineers' early 20th-century work to remedy this shallow spot on the river, which was noted in an 1889 survey of the river. The pilings run diagonally from river left upstream toward river right, and were intended

GRANBERRY BAR, BIBB COUNTY

to constrict the river's flow and provide a deeper channel for steamboats. In the late 1800s and early 1900s, extensive work was performed on the 5 miles of the river just below Macon. In 1904 alone, the corps drove 170 posts into the riverbed in order to construct some 400 feet of training dikes in this reach of river. The spaces between the posts were then filled with 4,000 cubic yards of brush and 370 cubic yards of stone. The work was forever frustrating and futile, but it never prevented the corps from soliciting additional funds for the project. A 1903 report noted: "Owing to freshets, unforeseen changes in the channel, and damages to the dikes and dams and regulating constructions, it will be necessary to provide further funds to complete the improvement as originally planned, which improvement should be continued until the benefits desired are realized." That year, the corps asked for an additional $75,000 for the Ocmulgee project—the equivalent of nearly $2 million today.

MILE 193.6 (32.783462, −83.592084) Cherokee Brick Company. On river right here is several thousand acres of land where mining for clay has taken place continuously for more than a century. The Cherokee Brick Company harvests clay from this floodplain and turns it into bricks used in projects all over the Southeast. The result of the mining is acre upon acre of wetlands, created as water fills the mining pits. The company's kilns are located nearly 3 miles east of this point because of the river's penchant for overflowing its banks. A flood in 1902 destroyed two kilns and prompted the company's owners to relocate to higher ground. The property is now part of a 4,000-acre historic district recognized on the National Register of Historic Places.

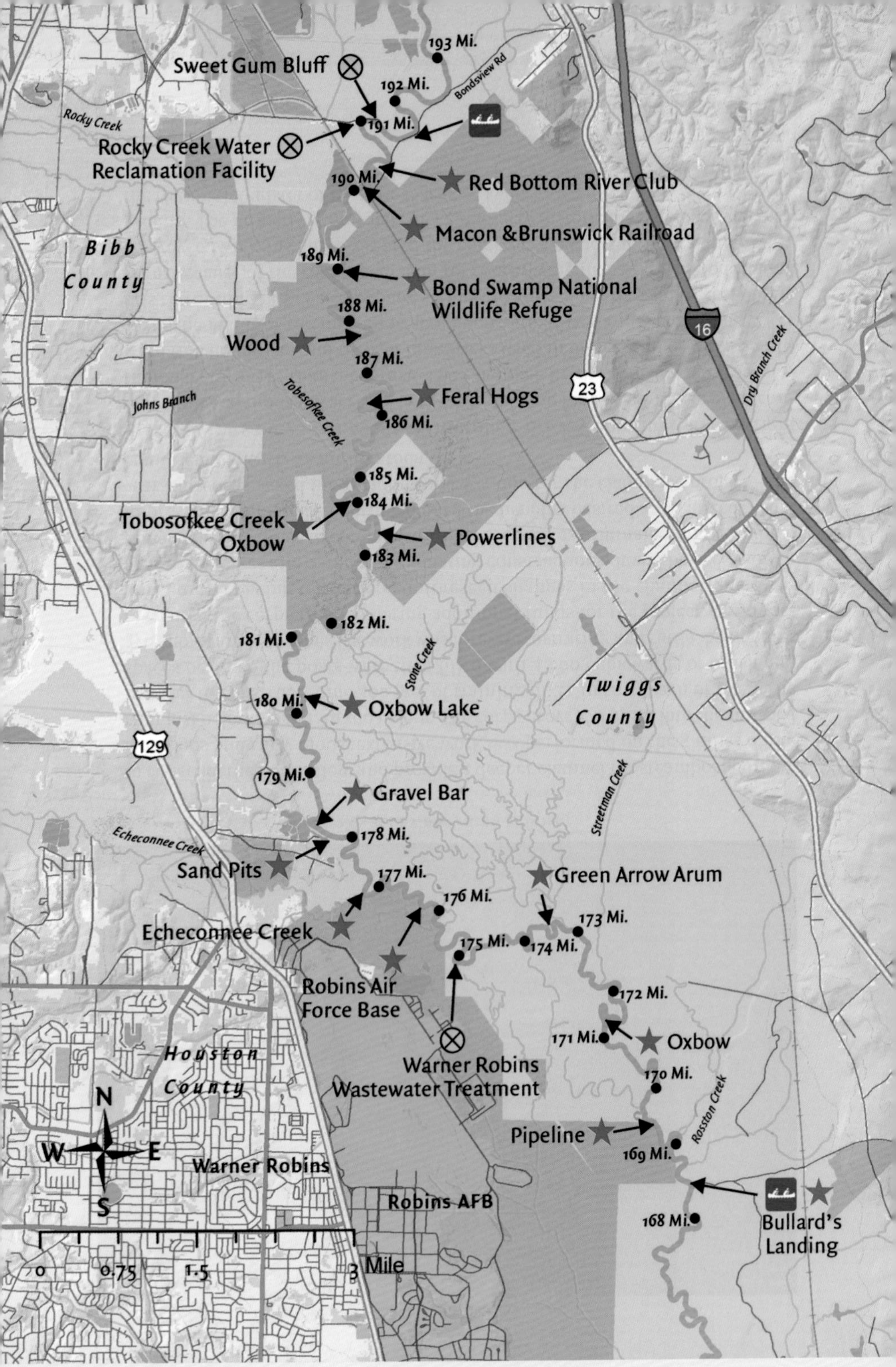
193 Mi.
Sweet Gum Bluff
192 Mi.
Bondsview Rd
Rocky Creek
191 Mi.
Rocky Creek Water
Reclamation Facility
190 Mi.
Red Bottom River Club
Macon & Brunswick Railroad
Bibb
County
189 Mi.
Bond Swamp National
Wildlife Refuge
188 Mi.
16
Wood
187 Mi.
Dry Branch Creek
23
Feral Hogs
Johns Branch
Tobesofkee Creek
186 Mi.
185 Mi.
184 Mi.
Tobosofkee Creek
Oxbow
Powerlines
183 Mi.
182 Mi.
181 Mi.
Stone Creek
Twiggs
County
180 Mi.
Oxbow Lake
129
179 Mi.
Gravel Bar
Streetman Creek
Echeconnee Creek
178 Mi.
Sand Pits
177 Mi.
Green Arrow Arum
176 Mi.
173 Mi.
Echeconnee Creek
175 Mi.
174 Mi.
Robins Air
Force Base
172 Mi.
171 Mi.
Oxbow
Houston
County
Warner Robins
Wastewater Treatment
170 Mi.
N
Rosston Creek
W
E
S
Pipeline
169 Mi.
Warner Robins
Robins AFB
168 Mi.
Bullard's
Landing
0
0.75
1.5
3 Mile

Bond Swamp

Length 22 miles (Bondsview Road to Bullard's Landing)
Class I
Time 7–11 hours
Minimum Level Navigable year-round.

River Gauge The nearest river gauge is located at the Martin Luther King Jr. Boulevard bridge, upstream of the launch site for this section: https://waterdata.usgs.gov/ga/nwis/uv/?site_no=02213000&PARAmeter_cd=00065,00060,00062,00010.

Launch Site The launch site is an unimproved boat launch along Bondsview Road; parking is limited.

DIRECTIONS From I-16 at exit 6 (U.S. 23 / Ocmulgee East Blvd.), go south on U.S. 23 for 1.2 miles. Turn right on Level Acres Drive and proceed 0.1 mile. Turn right on Bondsview Road and proceed 1.9 miles to the river.

Take Out Site Bullard's Landing is located on river left with a boat ramp and parking.

DIRECTIONS From the Bondsview Road launch, return to U.S. 23. Turn right and proceed 11.6 miles. Turn right on Bullard Road and proceed 1.0 mile to New Bullard Road. Cross New Bullard Road and continue straight on the dirt road 1.8 miles to the boat ramp.

Outfitters Ocmulgee Outdoor Expeditions provides canoe and kayak rentals and shuttle service.

Ocmulgee Outdoor Expeditions, 478-733-3386,
www.ocmulgeeoutdoorexpeditions.com.

Description This 22-mile run, flanked largely by federal land in the Bond Swamp National Wildlife Refuge and large private timber holdings, is among the most remote sections of the Ocmulgee. From Bondsview Road to Bullard Landing, the river contains an almost continuous series of oxbows, rounds, bights, sandbars, and cut banks as it weaves through a vast floodplain that in places stretches some 3 miles in width. Strainers, including occasional cross-river deadfalls, are not uncommon, forcing portages. The landscape is wild. Black bears roam the bottomlands, but you are more likely to see (or hear) wild hogs rooting and squealing in the woods. The river skirts Robins Air Force Base, and the sounds of the base, including aircraft landing and taking off, sometimes interrupt the relative quiet of the river swamp.

Points of Interest

MILE 191.2 (32.768217, −83.598304) **Sweet Gum Bluff.** This bluff, noted on 1889 river survey maps, is now occupied by the water intake for Graphic Packaging International, a paper-manufacturing facility that has operated at this site since 1948. The plant can pump up to 18 million gallons a day from the river, using it to convert local pines—and local kaolin—into coated paperboard used for packaging consumer products. The papermaking process is a water-intensive one in which steam and chemicals are used to break down wood chips into a soft cellulose pulp. The pulp is then essentially dehydrated to create the paper.

MILE 190.9 (32.767969, −83.601484) **Rocky Creek Water Reclamation Facility.** On river right here is this Macon Water Authority discharge point, which sends about 18 million gallons of treated wastewater into the Ocmulgee daily. The Rocky Creek facility dates to the early 1970s; it was built as a joint treatment facility with the Macon Kraft Company, the forerunner of Graphic Packaging International. About half of Rocky Creek's effluent originates with the paper manufacturer. This discharge is another example of how the Clean Water Act has helped restore the nation's waterways. Shortly after the plant opened in 1948, a series of fish kills—and complaints from downstream neighbors—prompted headlines such as this one in the *Atlanta Constitution*: "Mills Hard on Finny Ones: Pay Rolls Vs. Fish Up For Georgia Debate." State leaders came to the defense of the pulp mill—and the jobs and tax revenue it created. Said the director of the

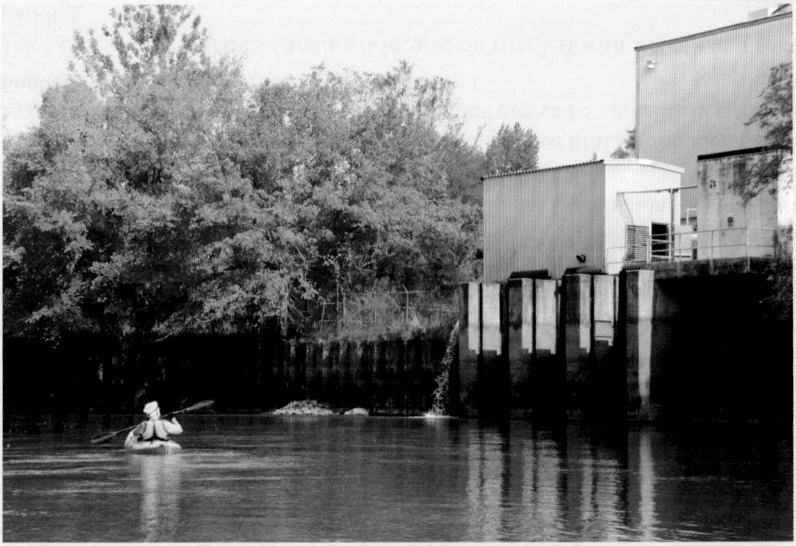

SWEET GUM BLUFF, BIBB COUNTY

state's Agricultural and Industrial Development Board: "It's very important not to scare the pants off the entire paper industry." Despite the reluctance of some state leaders to hold the mill accountable, the outcry led to an investigation by the state attorney general and ultimately to an agreement that the mill would cease "excessive dumping" of waste into the river. But it took more than 20 years before federal legislation addressed the problems of industrial and municipal waste discharged into the nation's rivers. Today, state permits regulate the volume and the contents of effluent discharged into the state's waterways.

MILE 190.5 (32.762989, −83.598057) Red Bottom River Club. The private boat ramp on river left is used by this small neighborhood of riverfront cabins and mobile homes. The community is virtually surrounded by the 7,700-acre Bond Swamp National Wildlife Refuge, which flanks both banks of the river for most of the next 8 miles downstream.

MILE 190.1 (32.759745, −83.600523) Macon & Brunswick Railroad. A bridge has spanned the river here since around 1863, when some 50 miles of this line from Macon to Brunswick was completed. That track was built using slave labor. Construction began anew in 1869 when Georgia leased nearly 400 state prisoners (mostly former slaves) to the company building the track. This convict-leasing system proved so advantageous to the state that by 1876 the Georgia legislature had adopted laws allowing the leasing of prisoners to private companies for periods of up to 20 years. For the state and the companies leasing the prisoners, the system was quite profitable. For the prisoners, the system was as brutal and unjust as slavery. Prisoners were routinely overworked, underfed, whipped, and even killed, yet despite these injustices, the convict-leasing system persisted until 1907. The center pier of this bridge includes the mechanism for a pivoting drawbridge that was put in place to accommodate river navigation sometime in the late 19th or early 20th century.

MILE 189.1 (32.748416, −83.603789) Bond Swamp National Wildlife Refuge. Beginning at this location, the refuge occupies both banks of the river for the next 4 miles. Spanning more than 7,700 acres of mostly bottomland swamp and forest, the refuge was established in 1989. It has been preserved thanks, in part, to the generosity of Mary Johnston Ray, who in 1979 bequeathed some 5,000 acres of what would become the refuge to Mercer University in Macon to support the institution's medical school. She chose the medical school for the gift because her only son had an intellectual disability and she believed that modern medicine could improve the condition of people like her son. In turn, Mercer sold the property to the Nature Conservancy for $2.5 million, and that organization held the land until Congress appropriated funds for the U.S. Fish and Wildlife Service to purchase it. In 1989, it was home to one of eight known active bald eagle nests in the state. Today, there are more than 200 documented nesting sites. Protection of habitat and the banning of the toxin DDT have played critical roles in the rebound of bald eagle populations.

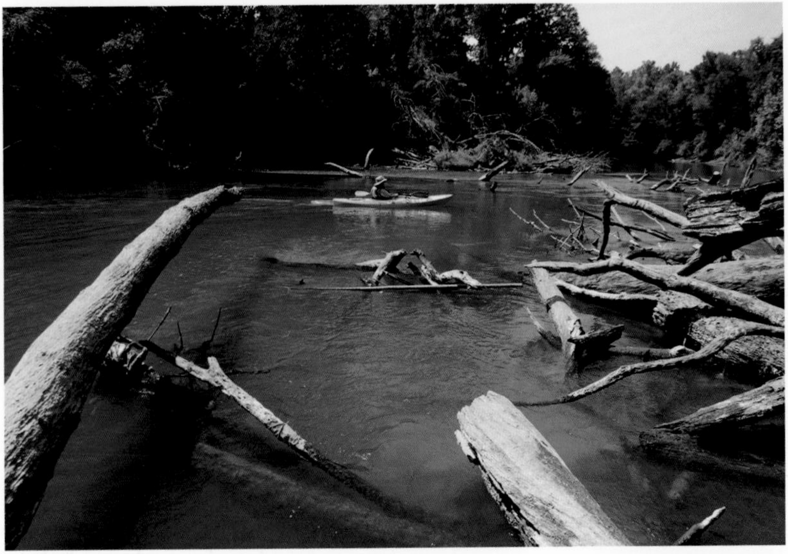

WOOD, BIBB COUNTY

MILE 187.7 (32.739398, −83.599891) Wood. Over the next several miles, the river winds to and fro between cut banks and sandbars, constantly eroding banks and felling riverside trees. In low water especially, strainers and deadfalls can partially or completely block the river. Though fallen timber complicates navigation, it supports the aquatic food chain, providing habitat for myriad organisms, including fish and the aquatic insects on which fish feed. The wood is nothing new. When the U.S. Army Corps of Engineers surveyed the river in 1888, it found 400 trees, snags, and logs needing to be removed between Macon and Hawkinsville, a distance of about 70 miles.

MILE 186.3 (32.729822, −83.600229) Feral Hogs. A legacy that dates back to the 1500s, when Hernando de Soto roamed these parts with his army and a contingent of pigs, feral hogs are today among the most common mammalian wildlife you might encounter along the Ocmulgee. While de Soto's men introduced hogs to North America, subsequent generations of free-range farmers added to the wild population. The introduction of Eurasian wild boars in the late 1800s for hunting purposes further contributed to feral hog populations. In Georgia, they are considered a nuisance species because of the damage they do to cropland and native wildlife—especially ground-nesting birds such as wild turkey and bobwhite quail. (Hogs have an affinity for their eggs.) Typical feral hogs weigh 100–150 pounds, and can tip the scales at more than 300, though news reports of hunters taking hogs over 800 pounds surface regularly. Because hogs have no sweat glands, they like to cool off in wallows, which can often be found on the back sides of sandbars. Thus, spotting them along the river is fairly common. More likely, however, they can be heard squealing in the forests—a sound that can be otherworldly.

MILE 184.2 (32.718068, −83.600606) Tobosofkee Creek Oxbow. As late as 2007, the river once looped for nearly 0.75 mile to the north and west here, but since then the Ocmulgee has cut through the land mass that once created this oxbow. Now the former river is an oxbow lake that is fed on the far west by Tobosofkee Creek, a tributary that winds some 60 miles through Lamar, Monroe, and Bibb Counties to this location. The meaning of the creek's Native American name, like many of the indigenous names associated with Georgia water bodies, is the subject of debate. Sofkee, however, is the name of a corn gruel—similar to grits—that was a favored food of Native Americans.

MILE 183.4 (32.712892, −83.596801) Powerlines.

MILE 180.3 (32.690685, −83.608584) Oxbow Lake. Hidden behind the phalanx of trees on river left is a small oxbow lake created in the late 20th century. Like other Coastal Plain rivers, the Ocmulgee is constantly cutting new paths through the floodplain.

MILE 178.4 (32.673182, −83.605914) Gravel Bar. At low water levels, this bend holds an extensive gravel bar.

MILE 178.2 (32.671687, −83.603143) Sand Pits. On river right here is an abandoned structure that marks the site of historic sand and dirt mines that have operated since the mid-20th century.

MILE 177.2 (32.664215, −83.597783) Echeconnee Creek. Pronounced "Itch-e-cone-e," this tributary forms the boundary between Bibb and Houston (pronounced How-stun) Counties. Local youth have referred to it as "Itchy Creek." The name is a Creek Indian word meaning "deer trap creek," from "echo," "deer" and "conna," "trap." The story goes that Native Americans attacked deer that came to drink at this creek; the steep banks made it difficult for the deer to escape. Those old enough and sober enough to remember the Atlanta Pop Festival, which was held just upstream along this creek near Byron, may recall an incident that occurred at the festival on July 4, 1970, in which revelers participated in a "mass skinny-dip" in the creek. As reported the *Atlanta Constitution*: "As many as 400 were splashing in the creek at one point and about 50 of them were nude. Numerous teenage girls walked bare-breasted through the area." The segregationist governor Lester Maddox, for one, was offended, calling the rock music festival "a tragedy in our state" and telling reporters, "You would expect something like this going on in the jungle but not in America." The outspoken and controversial governor was out of the state that weekend, attending the New England Rally for God, Family and Country in Boston.

MILE 176.3 (32.662554, −83.587954) Robins Air Force Base. For the next 6 river miles, the Ocmulgee essentially parallels the runways at this U.S. Air Force complex, which sprawls over some 7,000 acres, including some 2,200 acres of wetlands, mostly located between the river and the main part of the base. The base performs maintenance on a host of aircraft, including transport planes such as the C-5 Galaxy and C-130 Hercules, as well as F-15 Eagle fighter jets. Don't be surprised if you hear the roar of aircraft, since the runway—the largest in the state of Georgia—is less than a mile from this spot. At the right time of day (6:30 a.m. and 5 p.m.), you may also hear reveille and retreat played over the base's loudspeakers—the sound tends to carry across the Ocmulgee's flat floodplain forest. Construction of the base began in August 1941, and was ramped up significantly with the country's entry into World War II in December of that year. Originally known as the Georgia Air Depot, it was named in honor of Brigadier General Augustine Warner Robins, who is recognized as the father of modern air force logistics.

MILE 174.9 (32.655024, −83.582343) Warner Robins Wastewater Treatment. The two pipes here issue forth effluent from the Robins Air Force Base sewage treatment facility. The facility is permitted to discharge up to 69 million gallons a day into the river and nearby Horse Creek. The base is considered the state's largest industrial complex, with some 23,000 military and civilian workers. Just downstream of this discharge is the city of Warner Robins's wastewater discharge, which sends up to 3 million gallons of treated sewage to the river daily. Before the establishment of the air force base, in the early 1940s, Warner Robins was known as Wellston, a community of some 50 people. Today, the city is home to more than 60,000.

MILE 173.4 (32.658555, −83.566536) Green Arrow Arum. At this location (and many others on the river), you may find this aquatic plant (*Peltandra virginica*), which has tall stems supporting large arrowhead-shaped leaves. During the

GREEN ARROW ARUM, HOUSTON COUNTY

summer, conspicuous blooms form beneath the sheltering leaves. The bloom is a yellow spadix surrounded by a green, white, and yellow sheath, or spathe 6–12 inches long. The blackish berries that follow are a favorite food of ducks.

MILE 171.4 (32.648394, −83.557966) Oxbow. Based on maps dating from the late 20th century, this oxbow on river right was cut off from the river's main channel sometime after the mid-1980s.

MILE 169.5 (32.633641, −83.548973) Pipeline.

MILE 168.5 (32.625738, −83.542891) Bullard's Landing. Originally a steamboat landing dating to the mid-1800s, this site bears the name of Daniel Bullard (1805–1894), who was, according to newspaper accounts of the time, one of the wealthiest men in the area. For a time in the late 1800s, Bullard's Landing was the de facto head of navigation on the Ocmulgee, since low railroad bridges between the landing and Macon blocked steamboats bound upstream. As drawbridges replaced these bridges in the late 1800s, Maconites' hopes of establishing commercial navigation to the Georgia coast were once again buoyed. But the river was forever tempering their enthusiasm. In 1904, Macon business interests arranged a steamboat excursion to Hawkinsville, whose residents had planned a banquet to celebrate the towns' common interest in developing the Ocmulgee. The Macon river boosters boarded a southbound steamer in town early in the morning and hoped to reach Hawkinsville before scheduled activities that evening, but by 3 p.m. they had gotten only as far as Bullard's Landing. With 40 river miles still to go, they departed the water and headed for the railroad, picking up the train at Bullard's Station, a mile to the east. As reported in the *Hawkinsville Dispatch and News* on February 19, 1904, although the banquet was a success, the demonstration of the river's navigability was less so. Among the speakers at the dinner was a representative from the Southern Railway, who was quick to note that the railroad took the Macon dignitaries on the final leg of their journey. He said the railway supported river navigation, quipping, "Had it not been for navigation, the Southern would now have $20 less fare in its coffers." This section of river also proved difficult to navigate for the timber rafts that frequented it during this era. In May 1899, a timber raft belonging to the Standard Lumber Company capsized here, causing one raft hand to drown. A solitary gnarled oak festooned with Spanish moss now marks this historic landing, which has a concrete boat ramp and an unpaved parking area.

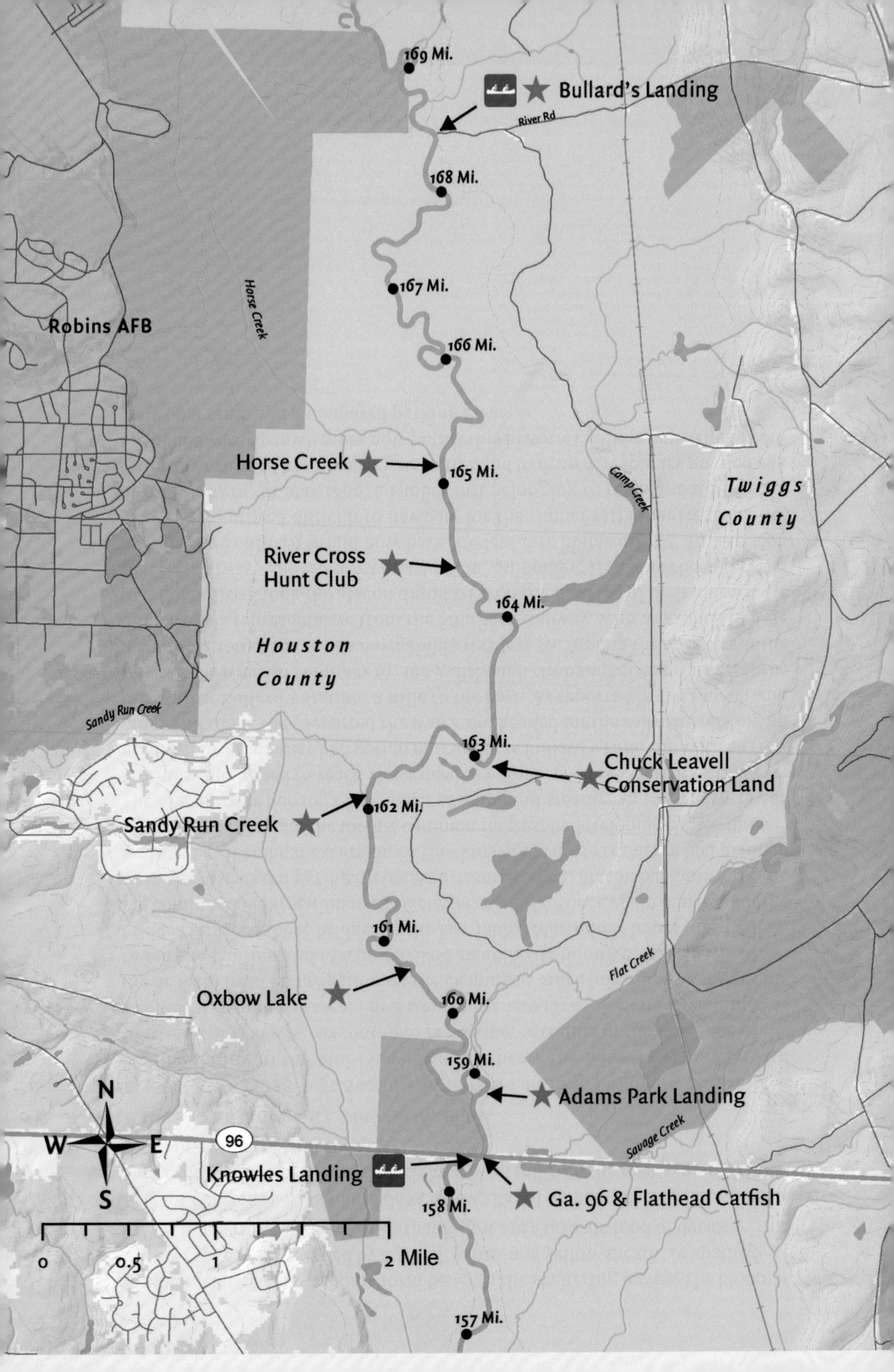
169 Mi.
Bullard's Landing
River Rd
168 Mi.
167 Mi.
Horse Creek
Robins AFB
166 Mi.
Horse Creek
165 Mi.
Camp Creek
Twiggs
County
River Cross
Hunt Club
164 Mi.
Houston
County
Sandy Run Creek
163 Mi.
Chuck Leavell
Conservation Land
162 Mi.
Sandy Run Creek
161 Mi.
Flat Creek
Oxbow Lake
160 Mi.
159 Mi.
Adams Park Landing
N
W
E
S
96
Savage Creek
Knowles Landing
Ga. 96 & Flathead Catfish
158 Mi.
0
0.5
1
2 Mile
157 Mi.

Warner Robins

Length 10 miles (Bullard's Landing to Ga. 96)

Class I

Time 4–6 hours

Minimum Level Navigable year-round.

River Gauge The nearest river gauge is located at the Martin Luther King Jr. Boulevard bridge upstream of the launch site for this section: https://waterdata.usgs.gov/ga/nwis/uv/?site_no=02213000&PARAmeter_cd=00065,00060,00062,00010.

Launch Site The launch site is at Bullard's Landing, located at the end of Bullard Road, with a boat ramp and parking.

DIRECTIONS From I-16 at exit 18 (Bullard Rd. / Jeffersonville), go south on Bullard Road 3.7 miles to U.S. 23. At the intersection, continue straight on Bullard Road 2.7 miles to the parking area and boat ramp.

Take Out Site The take out site is on river right just downstream of the Ga. 96 bridge, with a boat ramp and parking.

DIRECTIONS From Bullard's Landing, return to U.S. 23. Turn right and proceed 7.0 miles. Turn right on Ga. 96 and proceed 5.8 miles to the entrance to the boat ramp, on the left.

Outfitters Ocmulgee Outdoor Expeditions provides canoe and kayak rentals and shuttle service.

Ocmulgee Outdoor Expeditions, 478-733-3386,
www.ocmulgeeoutdoorexpeditions.com.

Description This wild and remote 10-mile stretch continues the river's meandering ways. Though it includes more straightaways than the previous 20 miles, oxbows and cut-offs remain common as the river bounces between cut banks and point sandbars. Strainers and deadfalls that block the entire river occur occasionally. Much of the land surrounding the river is preserved as timber, hunting, and conservation property, including some owned by one of the state's most famous conservationists, Chuck Leavell, keyboardist for both the Allman Brothers Band and the Rolling Stones.

Points of Interest

MILE 168.4 (32.625738, −83.542891) Bullard's Landing. Daniel Bullard (1805–1894) was among Twiggs County's most prominent residents. His name is attached to this historic steamboat landing as well as Bullard's Station, a depot on the Macon and Brunswick Railroad (later the Southern Railway), where Bull-

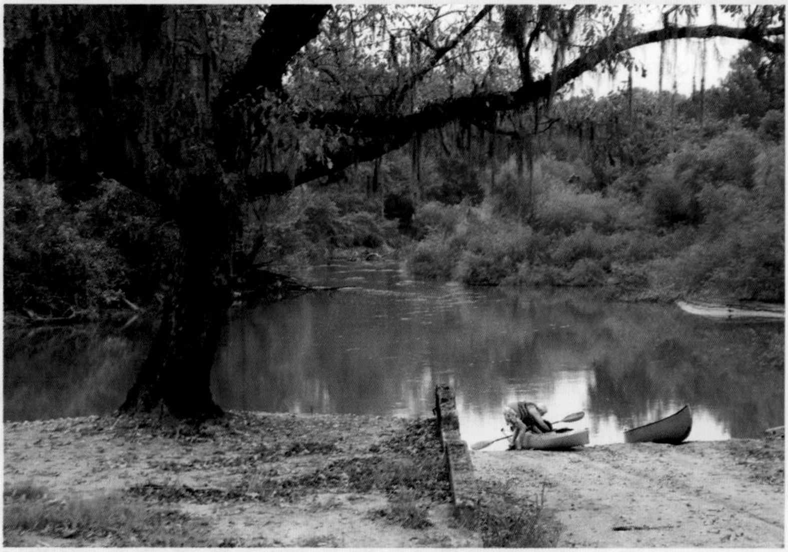

BULLARD'S LANDING, TWIGGS COUNTY

ard served as the railroad agent for many years. Eulogized in the *Macon Telegraph* as an "honest, quiet, industrious and kind-hearted, God-fearing man" who was "universally liked and respected in the community," he must have been terribly embarrassed when in 1888 his son and grandson were arrested for robbing the ticket office at their family's namesake train depot.

MILE 165.2 (32.598736, −83.541589) Horse Creek. This tributary, which drains much of Robins Air Force Base, has been the source of much controversy regarding a class of chemicals known as polyfluoroalkyl substances, or PFAS. Used in fire-fighting foams and in household products such as nonstick pans and stain-resistant carpets, PFAS do not break down naturally in the environment, and as a result they enter the food chain, bioaccumulating in animals and people. In use since the 1950s, they have been linked to kidney and testicular cancer and a host of other health problems. At Robins, the primary source of PFAS is fire-fighting foam. In 2007, the release of 20,000 gallons of it caused a fish kill in Echeconnee Creek. Horse Creek, flowing past the base's firefighting training areas, where the foam is used regularly, has been found to contain PFAS. Beginning in 2016, the air force tested streams and groundwater around the base, finding contamination in 62 of 77 groundwater samples as well as in some surface-water samples. Though the potential health risks of PFAS have been documented for decades, the U.S. Environmental Protection Agency, as of 2019, has yet to begin regulating the chemicals, providing only guidelines for recommended safe levels in drinking water.

In high water, the creek can be navigated upstream of its mouth for a distance.

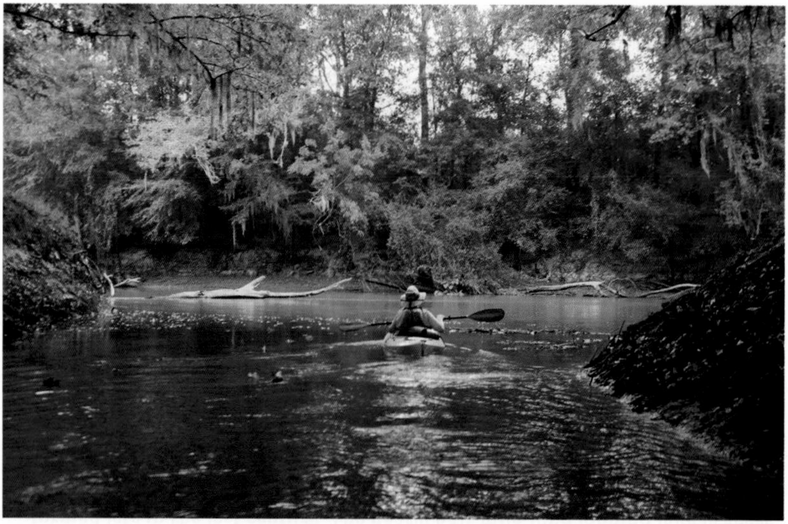

HORSE CREEK, HOUSTON COUNTY

MILE 164.4 (32.590212, −83.539446) River Cross Hunt Club. Riverfront signs here mark this 1,800-acre tract as a hunting preserve.

MILE 163.2 (32.574512, −83.536486) Chuck Leavell Conservation Land. On river left here is several hundred acres of land owned by the famed keyboardist Chuck Leavell and his wife, Rose Lane White, a Twiggs County native, as part of their Charlane Plantation holdings. While Leavell is best known as a keyboardist (first with the Allman Brothers Band and later with the Rolling Stones), he has also made a name for himself in the conservation movement, penning several books on forestry and sustainability; establishing the Mother Nature Network, an environmental news website; and managing (along with Rose Lane and their family) Charlane Plantation, a tree farm and hunting preserve. Leavell, a native of Alabama, came to know Middle Georgia through Rose Lane. The two met in the early 1970s when she worked as a secretary at Macon's Capricorn Records, and they eventually settled on her ancestral land in Twiggs County. The Leavells have preserved numerous properties in conservation easements, working with organizations such as the Ocmulgee Land Trust. Since 2004, the Macon-based trust has preserved some 10,000 acres of land along the Ocmulgee, mostly in Macon-Bibb and Twiggs Counties.

MILE 162.1 (32.571822, −83.548344) Sandy Run Creek. About 3 miles upstream on this tributary is the city of Warner Robins's Sandy Run Wastewater Treatment Plant, capable of processing 12 million gallons of sewage daily. In 1859, the Georgia General Assembly authorized Carlton Wellborn and Barnett Holliman to establish a ferry across the river here. The ferry is noted on late 19th-century river surveys, suggesting that it operated through the turn of the century. It may

PORTAGE, HOUSTON COUNTY

well have been the river access point for L. L. Watson of Wellborn's Mill (now Warner Robins), who was noted in the *Hawkinsville Dispatch* of June 1, 1876, for a haul of 13 catfish that weighed in at 132 pounds. The largest was a 25-pounder. According to the *Dispatch*: "He sold the fish in Perry yesterday at five cents a pound, which was the cheapest meat in the market."

MILE 160.6 (32.557877, −83.543897) Oxbow Lake. On river right is an oxbow lake formed late in the last century. The nearly half-mile-long looping lake is accessible in high water.

MILE 158.8 (32.548023, −83.537323) Adams Park Landing. Up until the late 1800s, an oxbow looping to the northeast brought the Ocmulgee to this landing. Today, that oxbow has been cut off, leaving behind the landing and the unique history of Adams Park. When passenger service opened on the Macon and Brunswick Railroad in 1870, Adams Park became a popular excursion destination for Macon residents, who attended picnics, barbecues, and dances there. By the late 1880s, the community was a noted producer of watermelons; the Phillips Melon Company grew 800 acres of the vines, producing thousands of melons that were shipped on the railroad.

In 1891, Benjamin W. Hitchcock, a successful New York music publisher and dabbler in real estate, hatched a plan to create a "Georgia Colony," a progressive new city in the South's agricultural belt. Supported by the likes of the popular Georgia governor John B. Gordon, he placed ads in the *Atlanta Constitution*, offering free tickets to a barbecue, concert, and land auction at the site of his proposed city. Hitchcock told Atlanta reporters: "I think we will have a big town at Adams Park. I have already sold several hundred lots to New Yorkers and I know everybody who goes down to Adams Park will be greatly pleased." Atlantans gobbled up the tickets, and on the appointed day, a trainload of prospective Adams Park residents headed south, though many had no intention of attending the auction in the rural hinterlands. Much to Hitchcock's dismay, when they reached Macon, a large contingent exited the train to enjoy the city's charms and take in a baseball game between Atlanta and Macon teams. Nevertheless, the festivities in Adams Park soon commenced; 73 lots were sold, putting $767 in Hitchcock's pockets. When the train returned to Macon and Atlanta, Hitchcock ordered the conductor to chug by the Macon depot, leaving his freeloading passengers stranded. Among those freeloaders were several members of the *Atlanta Constitution* staff, a predicament that caused the next day's paper to be published late. Despite the initial enthusiasm, including a reported crowd of 2,500 people at one of his early auctions, Hitchcock's Georgia Colony never got off the ground. Though it was settled by numerous immigrants from Europe and New England in the mid-1890s, by 1897 the New England Mortgage and Security Company of Boston was offering the 16,000 acres at Adams Park to state leaders for $5 an acre as the potential site of a state penitentiary.

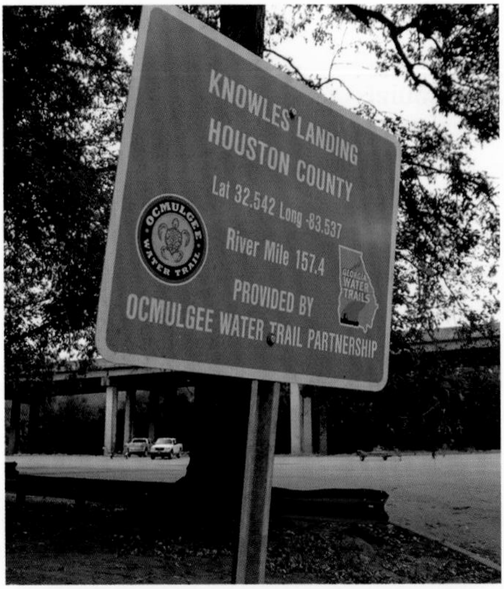

KNOWLES LANDING AT GA. 96, HOUSTON COUNTY

MILE 158.4 (32.542648, −83.536441) Ga. 96 & Flathead Catfish. In 2009, Tom Head of Warner Robins pulled in a 103-pound flathead catfish from a trotline set just upstream of this bridge. As of 2019, it remained among the largest flathead catfish ever landed in Georgia. The fish was near 16 inches wide at its head. Though mammoth, it did not best the state record of 83 pounds because it was not caught on a rod and reel. Flatheads are nonnative species that were introduced into the Altamaha and other coastal Georgia river systems in the 1970s. Since that time, flathead populations have soared while populations of bullhead catfish and redbreast sunfish have declined. Scientists who study the rivers' freshwater mussels hypothesize that flathead catfish have also caused declines in mussel populations by reducing the availability of fish to host larval mussels during critical stages of the mussels' life cycle. Between 2007 and 2018, in an effort to control flathead populations, the Georgia Department of Natural Resources removed more than 79,000 from the Satilla River.

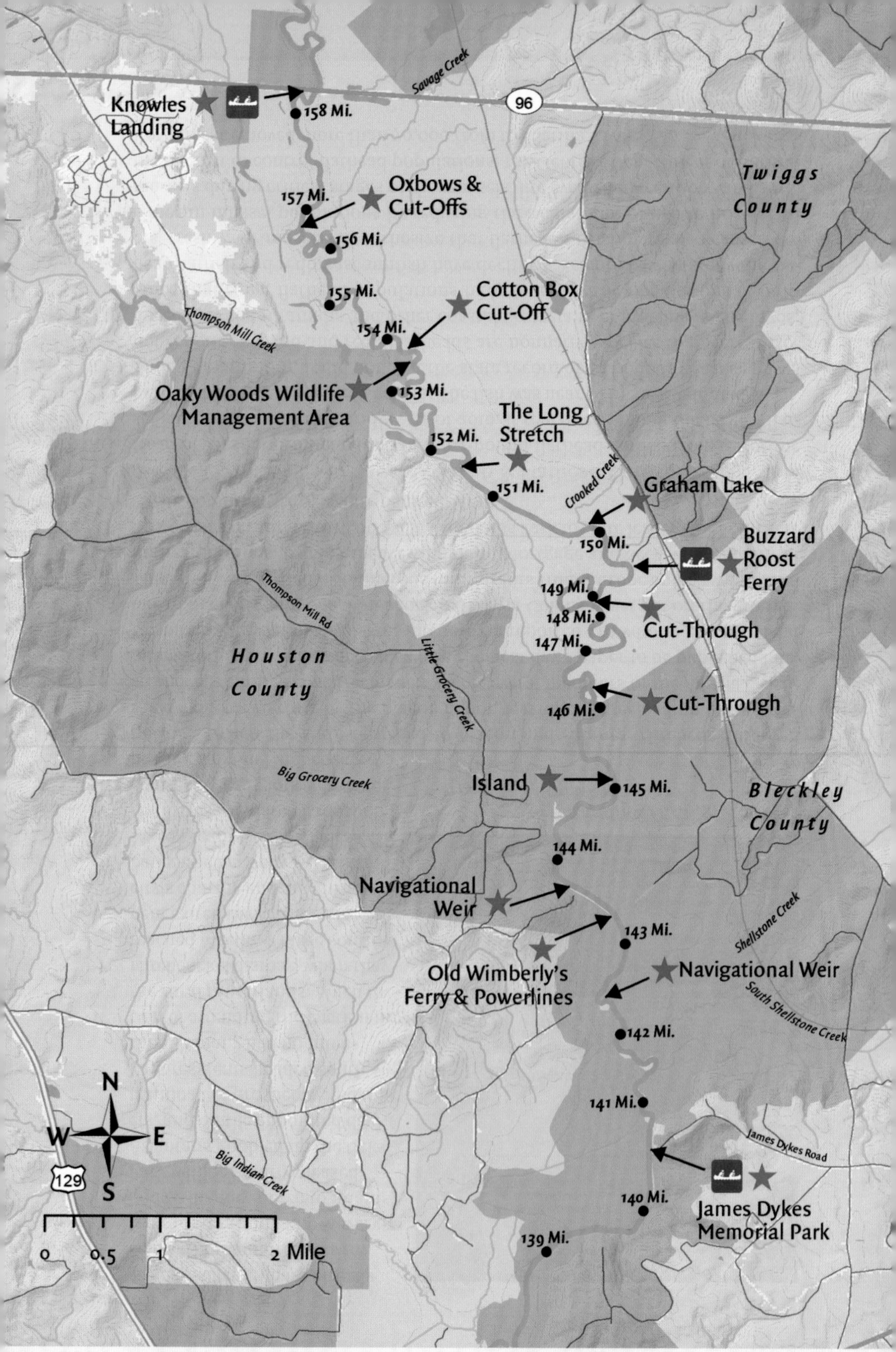
Knowles Landing
158 Mi.
96
Savage Creek
Twiggs County
Oxbows & Cut-Offs
157 Mi.
156 Mi.
155 Mi.
Cotton Box Cut-Off
154 Mi.
Thompson Mill Creek
Oaky Woods Wildlife Management Area
153 Mi.
The Long Stretch
152 Mi.
151 Mi.
Crooked Creek
Graham Lake
150 Mi.
Buzzard Roost Ferry
149 Mi.
148 Mi.
Cut-Through
147 Mi.
Thompson Mill Rd
Houston County
Little Grocery Creek
146 Mi.
Cut-Through
Big Grocery Creek
Island
145 Mi.
Bleckley County
144 Mi.
Navigational Weir
143 Mi.
Shellstone Creek
Old Wimberly's Ferry & Powerlines
Navigational Weir
South Shellstone Creek
142 Mi.
141 Mi.
N
W
E
S
James Dykes Road
129
Big Indian Creek
140 Mi.
James Dykes Memorial Park
139 Mi.
0
0.5
1
2 Mile

Oaky Woods

Length 17 miles (Ga. 96 to James Dykes Memorial Park)
Class I
Time 7–9 hours
Minimum Level Navigable year-round.

River Gauge The nearest river gauge is located at the Martin Luther King Jr. Boulevard bridge upstream of the launch site for this section: https://waterdata.usgs.gov/ga/nwis/uv/?site_no=02213000&PARAmeter_cd=00065,00060,00062,00010.

Launch Site Knowles Landing is located on the west and downstream side of Ga. 96, with a boat ramp and parking.

DIRECTIONS From the intersection of U.S. 129 and Ga. 96 south of Warner Robins, take Ga. 96 east 3.6 miles to the entrance to the boat ramp, on the right, on the west side of the river.

Take Out Site The James Dykes Memorial Park take out site is on river left, with a boat ramp, parking area, and picnic pavilion.

DIRECTIONS From the entrance to the boat ramp, turn right on Ga. 96 and proceed 5.8 miles to U.S. 23. Turn right and proceed 1.2 miles. Turn right onto Albert Jenkins Road and proceed 5.1 miles. Turn left on Magnolia Road and travel 3.6 miles. Turn right on James Dykes Road and proceed 2.0 miles to the boat ramp and parking area.

Alternative Take Out Site Westlake Landing creates an 8-mile run from Ga. 96. This is an unimproved landing with a parking area.

DIRECTIONS From the entrance to the boat ramp, turn right on Ga. 96 and proceed 5.8 miles to U.S. 23. Turn right and proceed 1.2 miles. Turn right onto Albert Jenkins Road and proceed 2.4 miles. Turn right on East Westlake Road and travel 1.9 miles to Westlake Road. Turn right and then immediately left across the railroad tracks and proceed 0.3 mile to the river.

Outfitters Ocmulgee Outdoor Expeditions provides canoe and kayak rentals and shuttle service.

Ocmulgee Outdoor Expeditions, 478-733-3386,
www.ocmulgeeoutdoorexpeditions.com.

Description This 17-mile run of mostly torturous oxbows, cut-throughs, cut banks, and point sandbars is interrupted occasionally by long straightaways, where the river seems to have settled on a course. Sloughs and oxbow lakes, especially during high water, provide off-the-main-channel diversions, and at low water the extensive 100-plus-year-old work of the U.S. Army Corps of Engineers can be seen in numerous rock weirs and islands. Much of this section is bordered by the Oaky Woods Wildlife Management Area, a 12,750-acre state-owned property.

Points of Interest

MILE 158.3 (32.542176, −83.537124) Knowles Landing. This Ocmulgee River Water Trail site, with a boat ramp and a parking area, bears the name of the longtime Bonaire resident John Knowles. A World War II veteran and recipient of two Purple Hearts, Knowles was also an avid Ocmulgee River angler. On his 95th birthday, in 2018, he received 4,457 greeting cards from across the country. He died in April 2019. Houston County named the landing in his honor in 1995.

MILE 156.8 (32.526075, −83.538352) Oxbows & Cut-Offs. Here, the river splits, with a cut-off on river left and a looping oxbow on river right. This spot begins a mile of river that includes five oxbows and three cut-offs. In low water, expect many strainers, including some cross-river obstacles that must be portaged. Savage Creek, which drains parts of Twiggs County, joins the Ocmulgee on river left among these many oxbows. The creek's name is said to memorialize the murder of white settlers along the tributary by members of the Creek Nation during the early years of Georgia history. Between 1770 and 1783, Georgia colonists reported 204 raids on white settlements by Native Americans, which resulted in the deaths of 103 colonists and 27 Native Americans.

MILE 153.6 (32.510577, −83.522251) Cotton Box Cut-Off. Noted on an 1890 U.S. Army Corps of Engineers survey of the river, this cut-off eliminated an oxbow that looped to the northeast. In the ensuing 120-plus years, the river has changed course again, essentially reclaiming the form of the original oxbow. "Cotton Box" is of note because the name likely reflects the wreckage of a cotton box that surveyors found at this location. Cotton boxes were among the first commercial vessels floated on the Ocmulgee. An 1886 U.S. Treasury Department report described the boxes: "Cotton from the interior was shipped by means of boxes varying from 22 to 24 feet wide by 60 to 80 feet long, made of heavy pine timber with square sides and ends, with the bottom sloped up at each end. They were steered by a long heavy oar or sweep, worked from a platform at each end, with several able-bodied men at each sweep to keep the craft from running ashore in the short bends in the crooked streams as they floated down-stream to market. These boxes carried from 400 to 600 bales of cotton each, and on reaching destination they were sold for building material or fire-wood, and the men generally walked back home." When steamboats began plying the Ocmulgee, these boxes were employed as barges that were sometimes pushed or pulled by the boats.

MILE 153.5 (32.510351, −83.520401) Oaky Woods Wildlife Management Area. Here on river right is the northern boundary of this state wildlife management area (WMA), which protects some 12,000 acres of land bordering the Ocmulgee's western flank for most of the next 16 miles. It was created in 2010 when the state purchased, for $29 million, some 10,000 acres of land from politically connected developers with ties to then-governor Sonny Perdue. The state could have purchased the land in 2004, but the governor, who had just purchased 101 adjacent acres, declined, saying the state couldn't afford it. Meanwhile, the owners proposed building a 30,000-home residential development on the property. These

THE LONG STRETCH, TWIGGS COUNTY

land dealings prompted ethics complaints from Democrats and spawned a Save Oaky Woods movement, which advocated for conservation of the property. After years of public pressure from hunters, anglers, and conservationists, the state purchased the land in the final days of Perdue's tenure in office. The WMA now safeguards important habitat for black bears, the federally protected fringed campion (a wildflower), and several state champion trees. It is a popular destination for hunters and anglers.

MILE 151.5 (32.497561, −83.514888) The Long Stretch. Among the Ocmulgee's many hairpin oxbow turns, the one that precedes this aptly named straightaway is perhaps the most picturesque. A narrow spit of land extends some 400 feet to the northwest, separating the upstream and downstream sections of the oxbow and providing a stunning panoramic view from the outside of the sharp bend. It helps that the downstream portion begins a long—and rare—mile-long straightaway noted on historic maps as "The Long Stretch."

MILE 150.1 (32.490252, −83.494422) Graham Lake. This half-mile-long slough on river left is fed by Crooked Creek and offers off-the-main-channel exploration even during periods of low water.

MILE 149.5 (32.485650, −83.488229) Buzzard Roost Ferry. On river left here is Westlake Landing, which has a rough boat ramp and parking. It marks the location of this historic ferry, which dates to the mid-1800s. At the close of the Civil War, in May 1865, Union soldiers from the 72nd Indiana Volunteer Infantry were stationed here for nearly two weeks. The stories documented by Benjamin F. McGee in *The History of the 72nd Indiana Volunteer Infantry of the Mounted Lightning Brigade* paint a vivid picture of the time and place. Their job was to ensure than any

Confederate soldier passing across the ferry possessed proper parole papers and had put down his rifle. During their stay, the Hoosiers hunted squirrels along the riverside, discovered official state papers of Tennessee that had been hidden in large trunks nearby, and witnessed firsthand the brutality of slavery when a young slave woman came to the ferry, asking the Union soldiers for protection. Soon, the slave's master appeared, demanding her return. The Union commander acquiesced, but several soldiers surreptitiously tracked the pair: "The boys knew the plantation where she belonged . . . and started toward the swamp as if going after squirrels. When out of sight, they quickened their pace and soon came in sight of the negro quarters and when within a quarter of a mile of the place heard the cries of the poor unfortunate girl as the bloody lash was plied to her naked back . . . The three boys in blue rushed in, and in language more forcible than elegant ordered hostilities to cease; the bloody victim was released and the overseer ordered to strip to the belt . . . No mercy was shown and the heartless brute who a few minutes before gloated over the misery and suffering of his victim was made to feel the potency of his own treatment . . . The girl was also released from these devils and given freedom." As the soldiers neared the end of their duty at the ferry, captured riverboats brought them relief: "Today we . . . heard one of those boats whistle and the sound came rolling up through the swamp like a harbinger of peace and good will. In about an hour the 'Governor Troup' came slowly winding up through the trees and landed below our ferry. She was loaded with commissary stores. You may never, never know how we laughed to see a cracker box once more. It had been nearly two months since we had seen one, and with hearts overflowing with gratitude we felt like showering unnumbered blessings upon the head of the man who invented hard tack. It took the boat eight days to make the trip from Savannah and some of our boys who were on the boat as guards had a fine time shooting alligators as they came up. A shot from an ordinary rifle has but little effect on their tough old hides, but our Spencers went to the spot every time. The men had a very large one, eight feet long, on board, which they had just killed."

MILE 149.0 (32.481193, −83.493906) Cut-Through. In 2019, the river was just feet away from cutting through the narrow spit here and creating a nearly mile-long oxbow lake to the west. Circa-1890 river maps show that this oxbow was protected by a spit of land several hundred yards wide, illustrating the slow, persistent nature of Georgia's Coastal Plain rivers.

MILE 146.4 (32.470470, −83.494022) Cut-Through. Here the river splits: the western branch flows around a small oxbow to the west, and the eastern branch flows more directly south, cutting through the tongue of this oxbow.

MILE 145.1 (32.459064, −83.489834) Island. On river right just upstream of this island is the northern boundary of the 15,000-acre Ocmulgee Wildlife Management Area. The WMA flanks the eastern bank of the river for the next 14 miles.

MILE 143.6 (32.446329, −83.495654) Navigational Weir. Here the river splits around a narrow island of rocks almost 500 feet long, which was created during the late 19th and early 20th centuries when the U.S. Army Corps of Engineers attempted to make the Ocmulgee navigable between Hawkinsville and Macon. A corps survey conducted in 1909 suggested that to make the Altamaha River sys-

NAVIGATIONAL WEIR, BLECKLEY COUNTY

tem viable for steamboats, 25.3 miles of earth and 5.4 miles of rock would need to be removed from the river bottom. Once removed, it was often stacked in training dikes or islands like this one to constrict the water flow and deepen the channel.

MILE 143.3 (32.442937, −83.489368) Old Wimberly's Ferry & Powerlines. Near here was the site of this ferry, which dates to the early 1800s. Ezekiel Wimberly was a pioneer settler of Twiggs County, moving to the area in 1809. He commanded the Twiggs Militia, and in that capacity he erected three forts along the Ocmulgee. He fought in the War of 1812, served Twiggs County as both a state representative and a senator, and attained the rank of general in the Georgia Militia before his death in 1843. More than a century later, in 1956, the Georgia General Assembly named the recently built Ga. 96 bridge over Savage Creek in his honor.

MILE 142.4 (32.432009, −83.489346) Navigational Weir. On river left here is a rock weir that was used to constrict and deepen the river channel for steamboats. By 1903, the federal government had invested nearly $400,000 in improving the Ocmulgee since 1876—the equivalent of more than $11 million today. Lumber was the primary product flowing down this avenue of commerce: in 1902, some 34 million board feet, valued at $443,820, was rafted to Darien, though steamboats carried nearly 9,000 tons of freight that year, valued at $625,590. Cotton, fertilizer, lumber, bricks, rosin, turpentine, iron, and steel were among the products most commonly shipped via steamboat.

MILE 140.7 (32.414513, −83.483318) James Dykes Memorial Park. This Bleckley County–maintained park includes a boat ramp, parking area, and covered picnic pavilion located on the flank of Stephens Bluff. James Dykes served two terms as mayor of Cochran and served multiple terms as a state representative and senator between 1945 and 1962. Mentioned as a possible gubernatorial candidate in 1966, he took his own life at age 50 in December 1966.

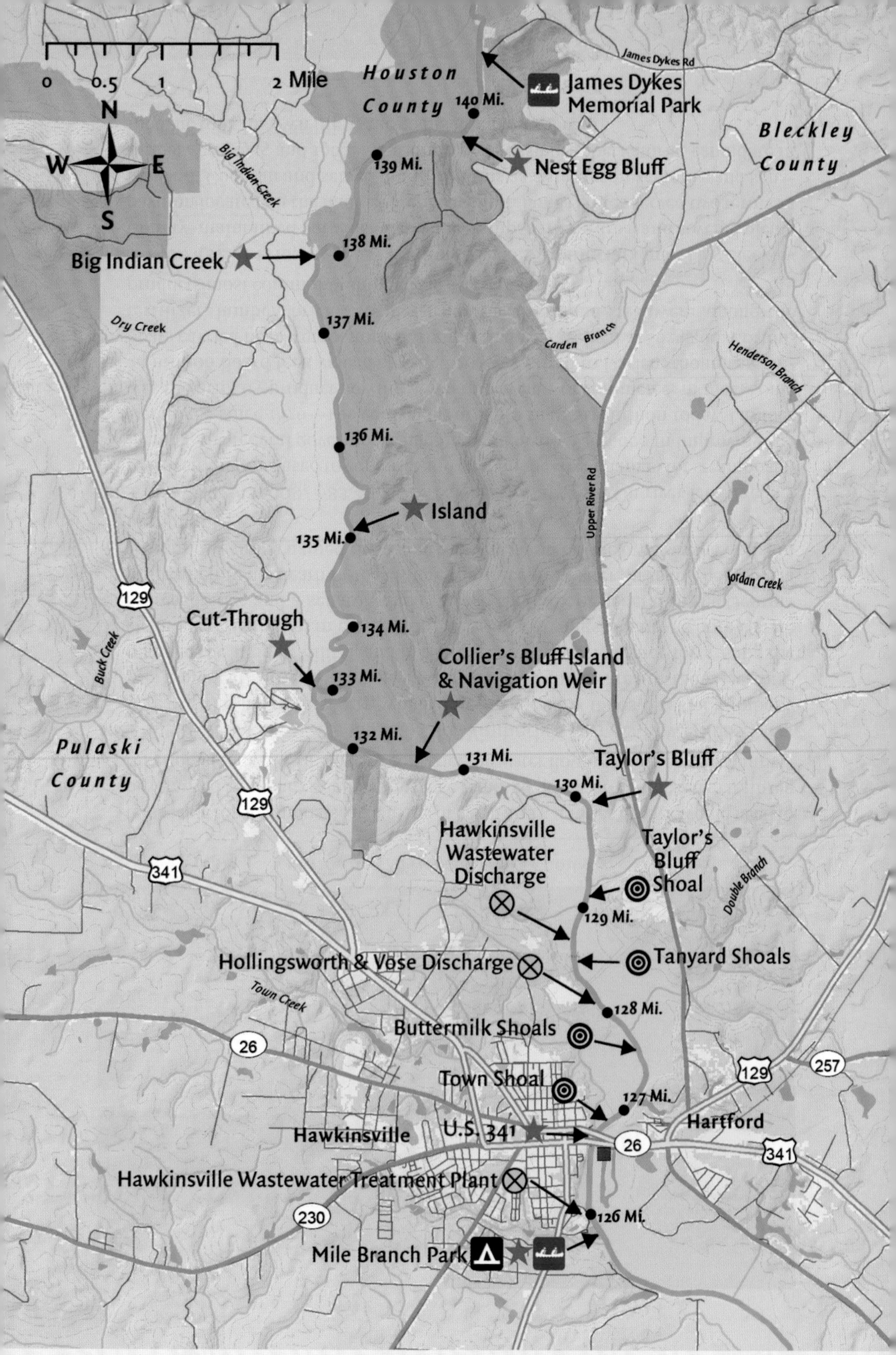

0
0.5
1
2 Mile
N
W
E
S
Houston County
James Dykes Rd
James Dykes Memorial Park
140 Mi.
Bleckley County
139 Mi.
Nest Egg Bluff
Big Indian Creek
138 Mi.
Big Indian Creek
Dry Creek
137 Mi.
Carden Branch
Henderson Branch
136 Mi.
Upper River Rd
Island
135 Mi.
Jordan Creek
129
Cut-Through
134 Mi.
Buck Creek
Collier's Bluff Island & Navigation Weir
133 Mi.
Pulaski County
132 Mi.
131 Mi.
Taylor's Bluff
130 Mi.
129
Hawkinsville Wastewater Discharge
Taylor's Bluff Shoal
Double Branch
341
129 Mi.
Hollingsworth & Vose Discharge
Tanyard Shoals
Town Creek
128 Mi.
Buttermilk Shoals
26
129
257
Town Shoal
127 Mi.
Hawkinsville
U.S. 341
Hartford
26
341
Hawkinsville Wastewater Treatment Plant
230
126 Mi.
Mile Branch Park

Hawkinsville

Length 15 miles (James Dykes Memorial Park to Mile Branch Park in Hawkinsville)
Class I
Time 6–8 hours
Minimum Level Navigable year-round.

River Gauge The nearest river gauge is located at the U.S. 341 bridge in Hawkinsville, just upstream of the take out site for this section: https://waterdata.usgs.gov/ga/nwis/uv?site_no=02215000.

Launch Site The launch site is at James Dykes Memorial Park, with a boat ramp, parking area, and picnic pavilion.

DIRECTIONS From the intersection of Ga. 96 and U.S. 23 north of Cochran, travel south on U.S. 23 for 1.2 miles. Turn right on to Albert Jenkins Road and proceed 5.1 miles. Turn left on Magnolia Road and travel 3.6 miles. Turn right on James Dykes Road and proceed 2.0 miles to the boat ramp and parking area.

Take Out Site The Mile Branch Park take out site is on river right and features a boat ramp, parking area, picnic pavilions, restrooms, walking trails, and camping areas. Restrooms remain closed except for special events, but can be opened if a camping request is made with the Pulaski County Commissioners office, 478-783-4154.

DIRECTIONS From James Dykes Memorial Park, return to Magnolia Road. Turn right and travel 3.0 miles. At that point, Magnolia Road becomes Upper River Road. Continue on Upper River Road 6.0 miles. Turn right on Alternate U.S. 129, proceed 0.2 mile, and then bear right onto U.S. 341 toward Hawkinsville. Continue 1.0 mile and turn left on Jackson Street. Travel 0.9 mile. Turn left on County Road and proceed 0.2 mile to the park entrance, on the right.

Alternative Take Out Site Uchee Shoals Boat Landing in Hawkinsville is located about a mile upstream of Mile Branch Park, just upstream of the U.S. 341 bridge in Hawkinsville, and features a boat ramp and parking area.

DIRECTIONS From James Dykes Memorial Park, return to Magnolia Road. Turn right and travel 3.0 miles. At that point, Magnolia Road becomes Upper River Road. Continue on Upper River Road 6.0 miles. Turn right on Alternate U.S. 129, proceed 0.2 mile, and then bear right onto U.S. 341 toward Hawkinsville. Continue 0.8 mile and turn right on 1st Street. The entrance to the park is on the right.

Outfitters Ocmulgee Outdoor Expeditions provides canoe and kayak rentals and shuttle service.

Ocmulgee Outdoor Expeditions, 478-733-3386,
www.ocmulgeeoutdoorexpeditions.com

Three Rivers Outdoors provides canoe and kayak rentals and shuttle service.
612 McNatt Falls Road, Uvalda, 30473,
912-594-8379, www.explorethreerivers.com

Description Beyond James Dykes Memorial Park, the character of the river changes significantly. Mostly gone are the winding oxbows found upstream, which are replaced by long straightaways that in places butt against impressive high bluffs. The river widens, and strainers and deadfalls become rare. At low water especially, the work of the U.S. Army Corps of Engineers in the late 19th and early 20th centuries to make the river navigable for steamboats manifests itself in rock wing dams and islands. As the river approaches Hawkinsville, it passes over numerous small shoals associated with this work, making this journey something like a passage through more than 100 years of river navigation history.

Points of Interest

MILE 139.8 (32.404211, −83.485684) **Nest Egg Bluff.** This picturesque bluff rises more than 100 feet from the riverbank. At its base is a good example of the rock wing dams that the U.S. Army Corps of Engineers built to deepen the river channel for steamboat navigation in the late 1800s. In fact, in 1856 this was the site of a steamboat disaster involving the *Charles Hartridge*, which is described in Carlton Morrison's *Running the River*. The *Georgia Messenger* newspaper provided an account: "[The steamboat] was proceeding down river when she struck a snag, which rendered it necessary to run her on a sandbar. This being done, the boilers exploded, destroying much of the upper portion of the boat, which immediately took fire and was totally destroyed with the cargo, consisting of about 500 bales of cotton."

MILE 137.7 (32.389024, −83.506762) **Big Indian Creek.** The name of this blackwater stream is reportedly a nod to Tustanagee Thlucco, a chief of the Creek Nation who was known as "Big Warrior" because of his imposing size. An advocate of "civilizing" the Creek Nation and adopting the culture of the budding American nation, he was a key player in Creek-American relations during the early 1800s. After signing the Treaty of Fort Jackson, in which the Creek Nation was forced to give up some 22 million acres of land, Tustanagee opposed all future land concessions. In 1825, he led a delegation of Creeks to Washington, D.C., to oppose the Treaty of Indian Springs, and he died while there. That treaty ceded all Creek lands in Georgia, plus 3 million acres in Alabama, to the United States.

MILE 135.1 (32.355808, −83.500598) **Island.**

MILE 133.2 (32.336546, −83.505390) **Cut-Through.** On river left here is a large sandbar that marks the beginning of a cut-through that eliminates a half-mile-long oxbow to the east. The sandbar was the former river bottom. Portions of the oxbow are yet accessible in high water. Maps indicate that this oxbow existed as part of the river's main channel from the late 19th century until the late 20th. The cut-through may have been formed during the 1994 flooding caused by

NEST EGG BLUFF, BLECKLEY COUNTY

Tropical Storm Alberto, since that event reconfigured many locations along the river's course.

MILE 131.4 (32.327250, −83.490703) Collier's Bluff Island & Navigational Weir. A U.S. Army Corps of Engineers map from 1890 shows two islands at this location and describes "a ledge projecting into the channel" that should be removed and "placed in training dikes." By 1904, the corps had reported this work completed. Today, only one island remains, connected to the north bank of the river via a rock training dike. The intent was to force the river's flow to the south bank and increase the channel depth. The 4 miles of river between here and Hawkinsville were particularly problematic for the corps, since four other shoals required extensive excavation of rocks.

MILE 129.8 (32.323208, −83.464511) Taylor's Bluff. This bluff, rising more than 100 feet from the riverbed and topped by several houses, reveals the river's ancient history. For most of the last 200 million years, what is now South Georgia was periodically a vast sea, and as a result, it is possible to find fossils in many bluff exposures. Fossil hunters have found at Taylor's Bluff sand dollar fossils that date back 34 million years.

MILE 129.1 (32.311803, −83.464619) Taylor's Bluff Shoal. Here at low water a rock weir is visible extending from the river's eastern bank to a narrow rock island. From the tail of the island, a rock training dike extends more than 500 feet downriver, creating a 90-foot-wide channel on river right. A U.S. Army Corps of Engineers report to Congress from the early 1900s indicates that this and other work on Tanyard, Buttermilk, and Town Shoals, located just downstream, had been completed by 1904.

MILE 128.7 (32.306380, –83.466620) Hawkinsville Wastewater Discharge. On river right here is the discharge from Hawkinsville's North Water Pollution Control Plant, one of two small facilities operated by the city. Like all municipal and industrial wastewater-treatment facilities, it is regulated by Georgia's Environmental Protection Division, which prescribes how much effluent can be released and the quantity of pollutants that can be discharged. This facility is permitted to discharge up to 1 million gallons daily.

MILE 128.5 (32.304119, –83.465934) Tanyard Shoals. Maps from around 1890 show a narrow rock shoal extending nearly the width of the river here. What exists today is something entirely different. At low water, a rock weir can be seen extending from the river's western bank to the head of a narrow rock island that then extends nearly 400 feet downstream. At the tail of the island, an additional rock weir extends from the eastern bank downriver, pushing the river's flow to the west bank. The channel created is about 80 feet wide. Imagine navigating a 40-foot-wide, 130-foot-long steamboat through this passage. To give a sense of the work undertaken to tame the river for navigation: according to a 1911 report to Congress, the U.S. Army Corps of Engineers employed a steam-powered pile driver, a dredge boat, and a snag boat, along with 8 barges, to accomplish its work on the Altamaha River system.

MILE 128.1 (32.298189, –83.461452) Hollingsworth & Vose Discharge. On river right, spilling from a pipe and over cypress knees, is the discharge from this industrial facility, which manufactures paper used to produce air, water, and oil filters for use in automobiles, trucks, buildings, industrial processes, and a host of other applications. A state permit allows the company to discharge up to 1.2 million gallons of treated wastewater here daily.

MILE 127.5 (32.293293, –83.455919) Buttermilk Shoals. Like Tanyard Shoals, Buttermilk was heavily reengineered in the late 1800s and early 1900s by the U.S. Army Corps of Engineers. Today, a rock weir extending from the western bank directs the river's main flow to far river left through a 90-foot-wide channel between the man-made island and the river's eastern bank. Despite these improvements, steamboat navigation above Hawkinsville never really took hold. The obstacles between Hawkinsville and Macon were simply insurmountable. By 1911, even Macon's boosters of river navigation had all but thrown in the towel.

MILE 126.8 (32.284599, –83.460706) Town Shoal. A rock weir on river left here marks the location of this historic shoal, blasted and reconfigured by the U.S. Army Corps of Engineers in the late 1800s and early 1900s. The Uchee Shoals Boat Landing is located on river right just downstream of this shoal and upstream of the U.S. 341 bridge. For about 100 years from 1891, upstream of this shoal, was a bridge carrying the Wrightsville and Tennille Railroad over the Ocmulgee. That road survived until 1941; the bridge was dismantled in the 1990s.

MILE 126.7 (32.283152, –83.462626) U.S. 341. A bridge has spanned the river here since 1880, when a wooden structure was built—the first bridge across the Ocmulgee south of Macon. Shortly thereafter, that structure was replaced by steel stringers that included a draw mechanism to allow for the passage of steamboats. In 1921, Pulaski County replaced that span with a $250,000, 1,900-foot-long bridge with a center-pivot draw system. On the day of its dedication, a crowd of 10,000 gathered to eat barbecue and hear speeches from dignitaries, including Governor Thomas Hardwick. That bridge was replaced in 1959 with twin bridges; the present spans were constructed in 2017 and 2018.

BROWN WATERSNAKE, PULASKI COUNTY

Had you been at this site in July 1876, you would have caught the launching of a small paddlewheel steamboat named the *Susie*. The *Hawkinsville Dispatch* had the story: "The 'Susie' was brought down on a wagon, and was greeted with cheers and loud huzas from the admiring spectators. The launching of a well-equipped side-wheel boat being a thing of rare or seldom occurrence in Hawkinsville." The owners intended to run the vessel only for pleasure excursions. In addition, commercial ships docked at this location throughout the 19th and early 20th centuries, and river navigation played a vital role in Hawkinsville's economy. Because of the vagaries of steamboat travel upstream, Hawkinsville became the de facto head of navigation, and as a result it became an important shipping point. Today, with a population of 5,000, it is known as the "Harness Horse Capital of Georgia," since it is the winter training headquarters for many harness racers and holds an annual harness racing festival each April. The town, founded in 1830, derives its name from Benjamin Hawkins, the U.S. agent to the Indians south of the Ohio River from 1796 until 1816. Hawkins established his Indian agency on the Flint River northwest of here and was widely admired by early Georgians for his efforts to "civilize" Native Americans and assimilate them into the white man's culture.

MILE 126.0 (32.273171, −83.462757) Hawkinsville Wastewater Treatment Plant. On river right here is this discharge from the larger of Hawkinsville's two sewage treatment plants. The city can discharge up to 1.3 million gallons daily here.

MILE 125.8 (32.270763, −83.461065) Mile Branch Park. One of the premiere boat landings along the Ocmulgee and the Ocmulgee River Water Trail, this well-appointed park features a boat ramp, a parking area, picnic shelters, overnight camping with restroom and shower facilities, and a lengthy nature trail. Those seeking overnight camping with access to restrooms should contact the Pulaski County Commissioners office, 478-783-2811.

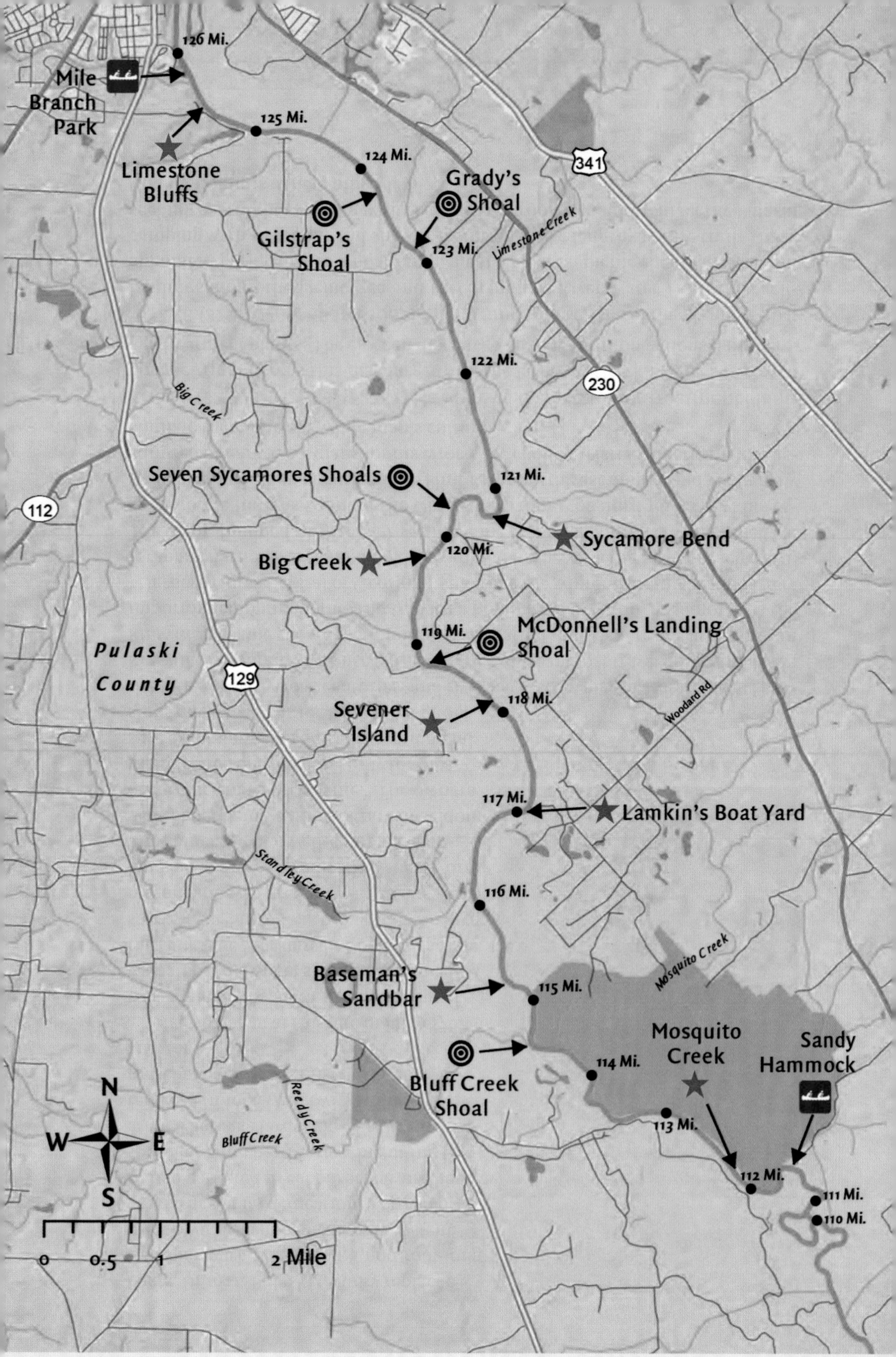

126 Mi.
Mile Branch Park
125 Mi.
Limestone Bluffs
124 Mi.
Grady's Shoal
341
Gilstrap's Shoal
123 Mi.
Limestone Creek
122 Mi.
230
Big Creek
Seven Sycamores Shoals
121 Mi.
112
Sycamore Bend
120 Mi.
Big Creek
119 Mi.
McDonnell's Landing Shoal
Pulaski County
129
118 Mi.
Sevener Island
Woodard Rd
117 Mi.
Lamkin's Boat Yard
Standley Creek
116 Mi.
Mosquito Creek
Baseman's Sandbar
115 Mi.
Mosquito Creek
Sandy Hammock
114 Mi.
Bluff Creek Shoal
Reedy Creek
Bluff Creek
113 Mi.
N
W
E
S
112 Mi.
111 Mi.
110 Mi.
0
0.5
1
2 Mile

Pulaski

Length 14 miles (Mile Branch Park in Hawkinsville to Sandy Hammock Landing)
Class I
Time 5–8 hours
Minimum Level Navigable year-round.

River Gauge The nearest river gauge is located at the U.S. 341 bridge in Hawkinsville, just upstream of the launch site for this section: https://waterdata.usgs.gov/ga/nwis/uv?site_no=02215000.

Launch Site The launch site is located at Mile Branch Park in Hawkinsville which features a boat ramp, a parking area, picnic pavilions, restrooms, walking trails, and camping. Restrooms remain closed except for special events, but can be opened if a camping request is made with the Pulaski County Commissioners office, 478-783-4154.

DIRECTIONS From the intersection of Broad Street (U.S. 341) and Jackson Street (U.S. 129) in Hawkinsville, travel south on Jackson Street 0.9 mile. Turn left on County Road and proceed 0.2 mile to the park entrance, on the right.

Take Out Site The Sandy Hammock take out site is on river left, with a boat ramp and parking.

DIRECTIONS From Mile Branch Park, return to Jackson Street. Turn right and proceed 0.9 mile. Turn right on Broad Street (U.S. 341) and proceed 0.9 mile. Turn right on Ga. 230 and travel 11.0 miles. Turn right on Sand Hammock Road (dirt) and proceed 1.6 miles to the parking area and boat ramp.

Outfitters Three Rivers Outdoors provides canoe and kayak rentals and shuttle service.

Three Rivers Outdoors, 612 McNatt Falls Road, Uvalda, 30473,
912-594-8379, www.explorethreerivers.com

Description If any portion of Georgia's Coastal Plain rivers can be described as "rocky," this section is it. At low water, the river reveals numerous shoals: Grady's, Gilstrap's, Seven Sycamores, and more—virtually all of them reengineered in the late 19th and early 20th centuries to make way for steamboats. During the late 1800s, this 14-mile run of river included no less than nine steamboat landings. At high water, only the swiftness of the water flow at these shoal-filled sites will provide evidence of what is hidden beneath the surface. Just below Hawkinsville, the river shows off limestone bluffs, and for most of the stretch the banks are well defined, with few oxbows. As a result, sandbars are less abundant than they are upstream, but still present.

Points of Interest

MILE 125.5 (32.266803, −83.458725) Limestone Bluffs. Rising above the water on river right are these impressive bluffs. Believed to be Marianna limestone (formed 23 million to 66 million years ago), it harbors fossilized sea creatures from that time period, when this portion of Georgia was a vast sea.

MILE 123.7 (32.256888, −83.432509) Gilstrap's Shoal. This shoal was described by J. L. Van Ornum, during his 1888 survey of the river for the U.S. Army Corps of Engineers, as a "ledge projecting from right side of river two thirds across." He notes as well a "good channel on left side." That description still holds today, the rock ledge being visible during low water. Idolet Gilstrap was a Revolutionary War veteran, and his descendants won land in Pulaski County during lotteries held in the early 1800s. In 1818, Idolet's son, Jeremiah, upon his death in Pulaski County, bequeathed his property to his wife. But as directed in his will, in the event that she remarried, she was to receive only $75, two cows and calves, and "one good feathered bed and furniture," with the remaining property to be split between his children.

MILE 123.2 (32.250139, −83.427088) Grady's Shoal. This shoal, with a conspicuous V shape, could well have been created by Native Americans or early settlers as a fish trap. An 1888 survey of the river describes this shoal as an "artificial barrier of stone," suggesting that the surveyor, J. L. Van Ornum, believed this to be a man-made structure. Native Americans and early settlers used V-shaped

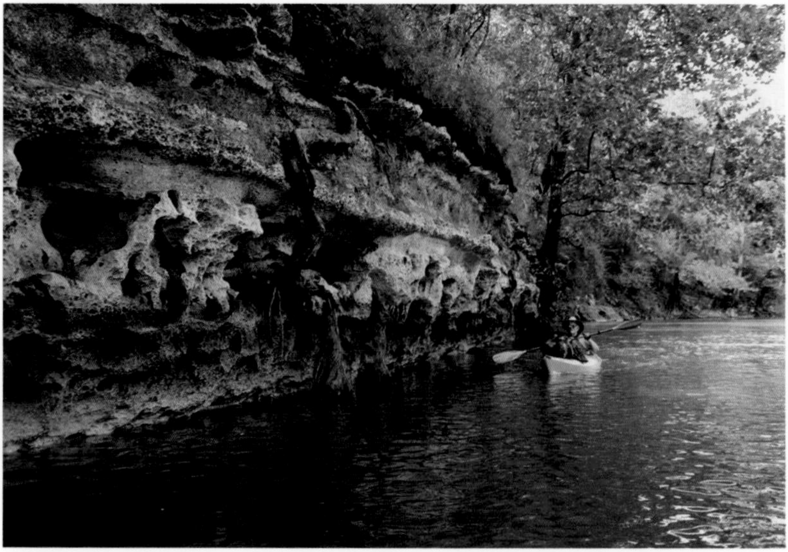

LIMESTONE BLUFFS, PULASKI COUNTY

rock dams to corral fish into a basket at the point of the "V." At this site, the point would have been on far river right. Fish traps and the passage of fish up and down rivers were of extreme importance to early Georgians, since the river's fish provided sustenance. During the first century of the state's existence, dozens of laws passed by the General Assembly addressed fish traps and fish passage. In conflict were the rivers' competing uses: industry, in the form of mills and milldams; and the river's natural fisheries. In 1821, the fisheries—and no doubt the spawning runs of American shad—took precedence as lawmakers passed legislation making it unlawful for "any person to place any obstruction to the passage of fish in the Ocmulgee and its principal branches." As millers began harnessing the river, and as the importance of milled flour and corn in frontier settlements grew, state leaders made exceptions, passing a law requiring at least 30 feet of the Ocmulgee channel be "kept open for the free passage of fish." As the state's growing population led to overharvesting of the river's fish, the General Assembly began placing limits on how fish could be caught, adopting in 1897 a law making it illegal in Bibb County to catch fish by any method other than hook and line. Just downstream of this shoal on river right was Harrell Cedar Landing, a circa-1900 boat landing.

MILE 120.7 (32.218266, −83.414517) Sycamore Bend. Here is a rare oxbow on this section of river; in low water, a large point sandbar appears on river right. During the Ocmulgee's steamboat era, spanning the late 19th and early 20th centuries, you would have found Limestone Creek Landing on river left in this bend.

MILE 120.3 (32.218675, −83.420505) Seven Sycamores Shoal. This shoal, noted on the U.S. Army Corps of Engineers 1888 survey as requiring the removal of 50 cubic yards of rock to create a passage for steamboats, was a jumping-off spot for a group of pleasure boaters who embarked on the steamer *Cumberland* in Hawkinsville during October 1880. The voyage, recounted in the *Hawkinsville Dispatch* on October 7 of that year, illustrated the vagaries of steamboat travel on the Ocmulgee. The *Cumberland* steamed off from Hawkinsville at a brisk pace, but soon stopped to unclog soot-filled flues, causing a lengthy delay. By late afternoon, the boat had travelled just 6 miles, to this location, and the group of joyriders opted to be dropped off onshore and to find their way back to Hawkinsville on the land. The newspaper correspondent described the ensuing adventure: "We landed in one of the densest canebrakes on the river. Through this canebrake we travelled three miles . . . In going through we scared many bears from their dens, but didn't see any. After being an hour in the swamp, we came to an opening, found a house, hired two wagons . . . and came to town never to forget our trip on the *Cumberland*."

MILE 119.7 (32.212951, −83.424348) Big Creek. This tributary provides off-the-main channel exploration, especially in high water.

MILE 118.7 (32.199495, −83.423147) McDonnell's Landing Shoal. Like Grady's Shoal upstream, this shoal is aligned in a distinctive V shape that points downstream, in a design similar to that of known fish weirs on other rivers. The shoal is not noted in U.S. Army Corps of Engineers surveys from the late 1800s. During

MCDONNELL'S LANDING SHOAL, PULASKI COUNTY

that same time period, McDonnell's Landing was located at this bend, and about 2,000 feet upstream was Kennedy's Wood Landing.

MILE 118.2 (32.195541, −83.4137320) Sevener Island. Just downstream of this island and on river left is a large agricultural water-withdrawal system. It is one of eight sites on the river in Pulaski County where farmers hold permits to withdraw water. The importance of Georgia's surface water and groundwater to the state's agricultural community can hardly be overstated. The state has issued more than 24,000 water-withdrawal permits for farms, including more than 400 in Pulaski County.

MILE 117.1 (32.182086, −83.408874) Lamkin's Boat Yard. At this bend are rock shoals, a high cut bank, and a private boat ramp. This site has likely been used as a boat landing since the mid-1850s. According to a family history, John Lewis Lamkin came to this part of the state in 1817, riding a horse while his family "accompanied him in a handsome old-fashioned carriage."

MILE 115.3 (32.160760, −83.410745) Baseman's Sandbar. Though the river changes its course often in the Coastal Plain, some things remain the same. On river left here is a large sandbar that was also noted on a circa-1890 river survey.

MILE 114.6 (32.153438, −83.4073980) Bluff Creek Shoal. Here near the mouth of Bluff Creek, on river right, is a rock shoal. Bluff Creek Landing was a noted steamboat landing at this location in the late 1800s.

MILE 112.2 (32.138716, −83.376653) Mosquito Creek. Some would argue that this could be the name of any creek in Georgia, since the biting pests are ubiquitous. Though small in size, this insect has had an oversized influence on Georgia's (and the world's) history. In 1806, outbreaks of malaria, a disease spread by mosquitoes, at the (then) state capital of Louisville were one of the factors prompting legislators to move the capital to Milledgeville. In the early 1900s, public-work projects to reduce mosquito populations resulted in the elimination of thousands of acres of the state's wetlands. Over time, this destruction of the state's natural "kidneys," which collect and filter water, has contributed to poor water quality in the state's rivers and streams. In the 1940s, as soldiers preparing to fight in World War II came from across the country to train in Georgia's many military bases, the federal government established in Atlanta the Malaria Control in War Areas (MCWA) program. Its purpose was to prevent soldiers training in mosquito-filled Georgia from contracting malaria and to prevent returning soldiers from bringing the disease back into the United States. The MCWA grew into the U.S. Centers for Disease Control and Prevention, one of the largest employers in Metro Atlanta. For this, we can thank the mosquito.

CYPRESS NEAR SANDY HAMMOCK, PULASKI COUNTY

MILE 111.5 (32.139754, −83.367831) Sandy Hammock. This launch site, which has a boat ramp and a parking area, was once known as Wild Boar Landing.

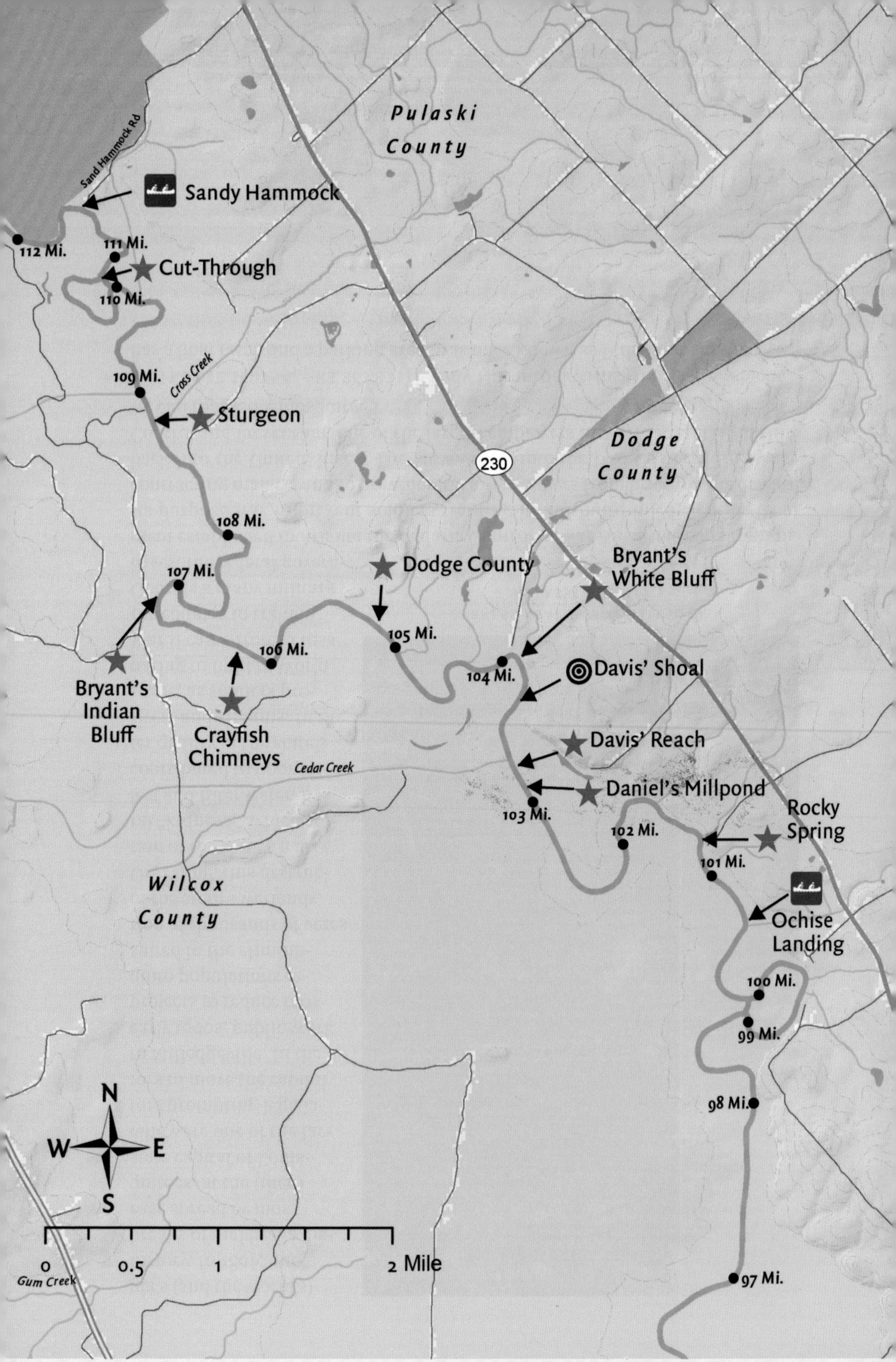

Pulaski County
Sand Hammock Rd
Sandy Hammock
112 Mi.
111 Mi.
Cut-Through
110 Mi.
109 Mi.
Cross Creek
Sturgeon
230
Dodge County
108 Mi.
Dodge County
107 Mi.
Bryant's White Bluff
105 Mi.
106 Mi.
104 Mi.
Davis' Shoal
Bryant's Indian Bluff
Crayfish Chimneys
Davis' Reach
Cedar Creek
Daniel's Millpond
103 Mi.
Rocky Spring
102 Mi.
101 Mi.
Wilcox County
Ochise Landing
100 Mi.
99 Mi.
N
W
E
S
98 Mi.
0
0.5
1
2 Mile
Gum Creek
97 Mi.

Wilcox

Length 10 miles (Sandy Hammock Landing to Ochise Landing)

Class I

Time 4–6 hours

Minimum Level Navigable year-round.

River Gauge The nearest river gauge is located at the U.S. 341 bridge in Hawkinsville, upstream of the launch site for this section: https://waterdata.usgs.gov/ga/nwis/uv?site_no=02215000.

Launch Site Sandy Hammock Landing is located at the end of Sand Hammock Road, with a boat ramp and parking.

DIRECTIONS From the intersection of U.S. 341 and Ga. 230 (Lower River Rd.) in Hartford, travel south on Lower River Road 11.0 miles. Turn right on Sand Hammock Road (dirt) and proceed 1.6 miles to the parking area and boat ramp.

Take Out Site The Ochise Landing take out site is on river left, with a boat ramp and parking.

DIRECTIONS From Sandy Hammock, return to Ga. 230 (Lower River Rd.). Turn right and proceed 5.9 miles. Turn right on the unmarked dirt road and proceed 0.5 mile to the boat ramp and parking area.

Outfitters Three Rivers Outdoors provides canoe and kayak rentals and shuttle service.

Three Rivers Outdoors, 612 McNatt Falls Road, Uvalda, 30473, 912-594-8379, www.explorethreerivers.com

Description This 10-mile run packs a lot into a short distance: oxbows and cut-throughs, impressive bluffs, sandbars, shoals, 100-year-old navigational structures, a blue hole spring, towering cypress, and abundant wildlife. Long straightaways mixed with bouts of winding oxbows make for a varied and interesting journey. The river remains wide, with few strainers or deadfalls to impede navigation.

Points of Interest

MILE 110.7 (32.133632, −83.365719) Cut-Through. Here the river cuts through the neck of a kidney-shaped oxbow that loops to the southwest. This cut-through has been forming for more than 100 years. Maps from around 1900 indicate a small cut-through beginning to form at this site. The oxbow lake created by the cut is nearly a mile long and accessible at both ends. In the late 1800s, the steamer *Comet* sank here, and in 1893 its remains were removed by the U.S. Army Corps of Engineers.

MILE 108.8 (32.122339, –83.360194) Sturgeon. These prehistoric fish, which look like living dinosaurs, have been spotted in this run of river. Both the Atlantic and shortnose sturgeon are native to the Altamaha River system. Migratory fish, they spend the fall and winter mostly in estuaries along the Georgia coast, but in the spring they move up the state's coastal rivers to spawn. They remain in the rivers through the summer. Sturgeon are among the state's largest freshwater fish. Atlantic sturgeon can reach lengths of more than eight feet and weigh up to 200 pounds; shortnose sturgeon are slightly smaller. Prized for their caviar, they were extensively harvested in the 19th and 20th centuries, leading to declining populations. Shortnose sturgeon were among the original animals protected under the Endangered Species Act in 1973; Atlantic sturgeon soon joined them. Overharvesting and dams that block their migratory routes are thought to be the primary threats to their survival. Among their most mysterious habits is that they make giant leaps out of the water. Scientists do not agree on the reasons for this behavior. They could be gulping or expelling air, catching airborne prey, shedding eggs during spawning, or communicating with other sturgeon to direct them to cool-water refuges in the hot summer. What is certain is their leaps can be spectacular—and sometimes dangerous. Motorboat-sturgeon collisions have resulted in serious injury and even fatalities in neighboring Florida. The long, slender, scale-less fish have rows of bony scutes running down their backs and sides, and they sport a shovel-like nose, with the mouth hidden on the fish's underside.

SANDBAR AND WILLOW, PULASKI COUNTY

MILE 106.8 (32.107836, −83.359499) Bryant's Indian Bluff. On river right here, a private boat ramp marks the beginning of this bluff, which is noted on 19th-century maps of the Ocmulgee. Indian Bluff Shoals is located around the sharp bend. In 1893, the steamer *Swan*, a 360-ton, 103-foot-long, 29-foot-wide vessel that drew just 18 inches, sank in this tight oxbow, despite being one of the shallowest-draft boats plying the Ocmulgee at the time. The U.S. Army Corps of Engineers removed the wreck that same year.

MILE 106.3 (32.103806, −83.351229) Crayfish Chimneys. On river right here (and at many other places along the Ocmulgee in the Coastal Plain) may be seen these curious structures made by burrowing crayfish. Usually 4–6 inches high, these lumpy chimneys of sand and clay look like the turret of a sand castle that a child might construct at the beach. Burrowing crayfish, as the name suggests, burrow tunnels into the ground to reach the water table. Some species spend their entire lives in these burrows, emerging only to forage for food or to mate. Other crayfish live most of their lives in open water, but may retreat to burrows during times of drought, to avoid frost during the winter, or, in the case of females, to lay and brood eggs. There are 72 known species of crayfish in Georgia, and the Ocmulgee River basin is home to 14 of them, 10 of which can be found in the Coastal Plain region. The most likely maker of these chimneys is the ornate crayfish (*Procambarus howellae*).

MILE 105.3 (32.106158, −83.337647) Dodge County. Here the river passes out of Pulaski County and into Dodge County, an area whose infamous, unscrupulous land dealings in the late 1800s came to be known as the Dodge County Land Wars. The "wars" were precipitated when northern speculators purchased vast swaths of land in this part of Middle Georgia during the 1830s and 1840s. The absentee owners were not aware that their land was being settled by hardy Georgians, and they didn't much care until the squatters began exploiting the longleaf pine and cypress forests in earnest after the Civil War. By that time, some 300,000 acres had passed through the hands of several northern capitalists before being bought by William P. Eastman and William Dodge, operating as the Georgia Land and Lumber Company. Soon, wholesale logging of the land between the Oconee and Ocmulgee Rivers was under way. But in the preceding years, locals had established homesteads on much of the land. In fact, Telfair County had sold many parcels to citizens in the 1840s when the first investors failed to pay their property taxes. Thus, the stage was set for conflict between hardscrabble farmers and wealthy northern capitalists. After years of legal disputes and court battles, the conflict boiled over in 1890 when a posse of men organized by the local sheriff murdered an agent for the lumber company. Despite court rulings in favor of the lumber company, many of the squatters refused to leave their land, and it wasn't until the 1920s that all the land disputes were settled. Dodge County and its seat of government, Eastman, bear the names of the primary investors in the lumber company. And though the northern entrepreneurs brought with them economic development of the likes never seen in these parts, Dodge and Eastman were generally despised by the people that lived in the jurisdictions named in their honor.

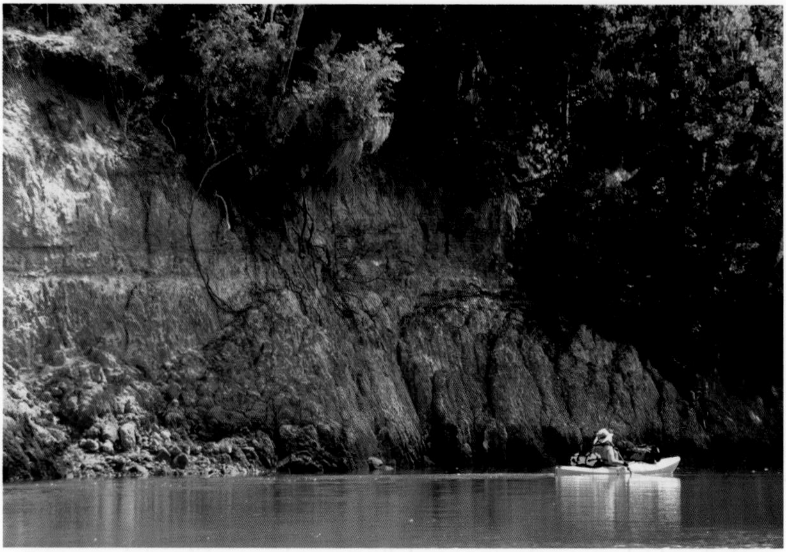

BLUFF, DODGE COUNTY

MILE 103.8 (32.103925, –83.323968) Bryant's White Bluff. The bluff on river left here served as a landing during the river's steamboat era (the late 19th and early 20th centuries). In 1904, it played a role in a legal dispute between I. M. Frank and the Southern Railway that was precipitated by the undependable nature of steamboat travel. Frank had contracted with the railroad to deliver goods from Savannah to this bluff. The goods were to travel by rail to the Ocmulgee Depot near Lumber City and then upriver by steamboat to the bluff. But when they arrived at the depot, it was discovered that the steamboat was not running. The railroad instead sent the goods via rail to Abbeville, but they never reached the bluff. Court records show that when the shipment was finally returned to Savannah "the goods were found to be badly damaged . . . from the fact that rats had burrowed into them and one of the rats had died and its dead body had been let in among the dry goods for several months." Frank won a ruling against the railway for failure to deliver the goods without rats.

MILE 103.6 (32.100385, –83.323609) Davis' Shoal. At low water, a series of rock reefs are visible here that 19th-century U.S. Army Corps of Engineers surveys describe as a pair of shoals extending from opposite banks that "should be straightened by the removal of . . . about 150 cubic yards of rock."

MILE 103.3 (32.094824, –83.323901) Davis' Reach. This mile-long straightaway is noted for a 1,950-foot-long navigational dike. All that remains of the century-old dike constructed by the U.S. Army Corps of Engineers is two parallel lines of weathered wooden posts running on a diagonal through the middle of the river—and at low water, across a lengthy sandbar. The posts were driven into the riverbed, and the space between them was filled with rock and brush in an effort

CYPRESS SHADE, WILCOX COUNTY

to constrict the river's flow and deepen the channel. In the late 1800s, just upriver of the training dike was Harrell's Ferry. Many Harrells in the area were associated with the Ocmulgee River. A notable example was John Harrell, a prominent planter of the China Hill area who died when the steamer *General Manning* exploded and sank on the river near Jacksonville in 1861.

MILE 103.1 (32.093393, −83.323020) Daniel's Millpond. Though not visible from the river, this historic millpond on private property sits about a quarter mile to the east of the river. During the 1800s and early 1900s, it was a popular recreation spot for Dodge County residents. *The History of Dodge County* noted its attractions: "[It is] one of the most beautiful picnic grounds in the State of Georgia, whose water is as clear as crystal, and making it possible for the 'picnickers' to enjoy boating, and while thus engaged watch the finny tribes sporting through its waters . . . It is only a mile from the Ocmulgee River, and the usual custom of the 'picnickers' is to stroll down to the river bank after dinner and engage in target shooting or boating on the beautiful stream."

MILE 101.3 (32.089365, −83.305382) Rocky Spring. Marked by rocky shoals and islands, on river left is the mouth of this picturesque blue hole spring, which sits on private property. More common along the Flint River, to the west, these blue hole springs are where the Floridan aquifer interfaces with surface water. Among the world's most productive aquifers, the Floridan is the primary drinking source for some 10 million people, mostly in Florida and South Georgia. It also produces these uncommonly beautiful springs. Across the 100,000 square miles of the Floridan aquifer, including all of Florida and portions of South Carolina, Georgia, and Alabama, the Floridan issues forth at 824 springs, 56 of which are found in Georgia. The springs produce water at a constant temperature of 68–70 degrees, making the outlet of this spring an ideal place to cool off on hot days.

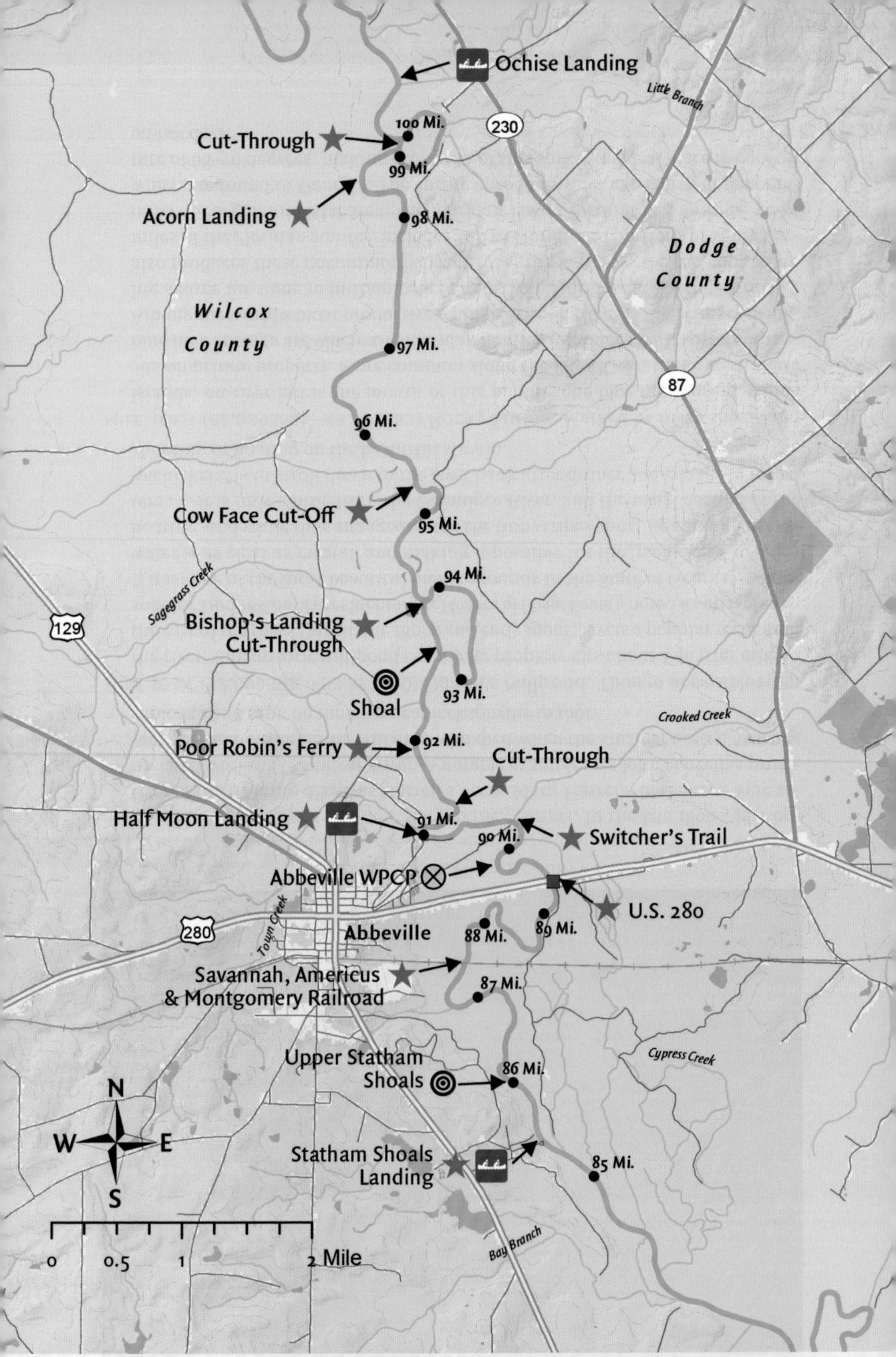

Ochise Landing
Little Branch
230
100 Mi.
Cut-Through
99 Mi.
Acorn Landing
98 Mi.
Dodge
County
Wilcox
County
97 Mi.
87
96 Mi.
Cow Face Cut-Off
95 Mi.
Sagegrass Creek
94 Mi.
129
Bishop's Landing
Cut-Through
93 Mi.
Shoal
Crooked Creek
Poor Robin's Ferry
92 Mi.
Cut-Through
Half Moon Landing
91 Mi.
90 Mi.
Switcher's Trail
Abbeville WPCP
U.S. 280
280
Town Creek
Abbeville
88 Mi.
89 Mi.
Savannah, Americus
& Montgomery Railroad
87 Mi.
Upper Statham
Shoals
86 Mi.
Cypress Creek
N
W
E
S
Statham Shoals
Landing
85 Mi.
Bay Branch
0
0.5
1
2 Mile

Abbeville

Length 15 miles (Ochise Landing to Statham Shoals Landing)
Class I
Time 7–9 hours
Minimum Level Navigable year-round.

River Gauge The nearest river gauge is located at the U.S.280 bridge in Abbeville, in the middle of this section: https://waterdata.usgs.gov/ga/nwis/uv?site_no=02215260.

Launch Site Ochise Landing is located 0.5 mile off Lower River Road in Dodge County, with a boat ramp and parking.

DIRECTIONS From the intersection of U.S. 280 and Ga. 87 (Abbeville Hwy.) east of Abbeville, travel north on Ga. 87 for 4.6 miles. Bear left on Ga. 230 (Lower River Rd.) and proceed 2.2 miles to the unmarked dirt road on the left. Turn left and proceed 0.5 mile to the boat ramp and parking area.

Take Out Site Statham Shoals Landing is located on river right, with a boat ramp and parking.

DIRECTIONS From Ochise Landing, return to Lower River Road. Turn right and proceed 2.2 miles. Merge onto Ga. 87 and proceed 4.6 miles to U.S. 280. Turn right and proceed 3.6 miles to Abbeville. Turn left on Broad Street (U.S. 129) and travel 2.2 miles. Turn left on Statham Shoals Road (dirt) and proceed 0.3 mile. Turn left on Denniston Lane and then take the next right onto an unmarked dirt road. Proceed 0.2 mile to the parking area and boat ramp.

Alternative Take Out Site Half Moon Landing in Abbeville creates an 8-mile journey. It features a boat ramp and paved parking area.

DIRECTIONS From Ochise Landing, return to Lower River Road. Turn right and proceed 2.2 miles. Merge on to Ga. 87 and proceed 4.6 miles to U.S. 280. Turn right and proceed 3.3 miles to Abbeville. Turn right on Half Moon Road and proceed 0.7 mile to the boat ramp and parking area.

Outfitters Three Rivers Outdoors provides canoe and kayak rentals and shuttle service.

Three Rivers Outdoors, 612 McNatt Falls Road, Uvalda, 30473,
912-594-8379, www.explorethreerivers.com

Description This 15-mile run through Dodge and Wilcox Counties serves up plenty to entice the curious. Off-the-main-channel sloughs and oxbows provide extensive opportunities for exploration during high water; at low water, a unique shoal with surprising whitewater is revealed just upstream of Abbeville. Though the river is mostly wild and remote, as it passes close to Abbeville, riverfront residen-

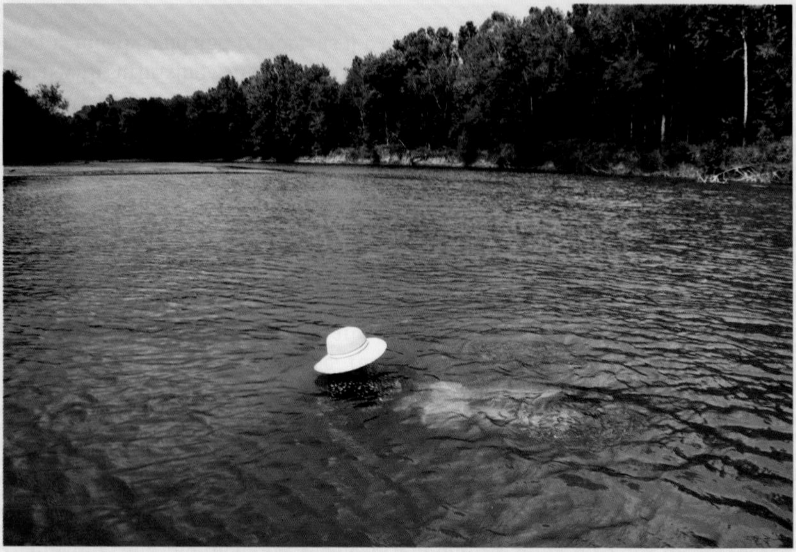

SWIMMING, DODGE COUNTY

tial development provides a change of scenery. Downstream of Abbeville, the river passes beneath a historic railroad drawbridge. At low-to-average water levels (usually found throughout the summer and fall), sandbars are abundant.

Points of Interest

MILE 100.1 (32.076114, –83.300293) Cut-Through. Here the river has cut through the narrow neck of land, creating a mile-long oxbow lake to the east that is accessible in high water. The Dodge County Public Boat Ramp is located on this slough, but the river's wandering ways isolated this ramp, rendering it inaccessible except in high water and necessitating the construction of Ochise Landing upstream. Along this oxbow lake is Phelps Bluff.

MILE 98.6 (32.072244, –83.305590) Acorn Landing. During the Ocmulgee's steamboat era, along this bluff on river right was this landing in Wilcox County. In 1892–1893, five steamers worked the Ocmulgee, hauling some 23,500 tons of freight valued at $935,250, mostly consisting of lumber, turpentine, and resin. Additionally, it was estimated that 91,000 tons of lumber were rafted down the Ocmulgee annually during this period. While cotton was still important to the area, the value of the products derived from the area's vast longleaf pinelands and shipped on the Ocmulgee was 14 times as large as the value of the cotton shipped on Ocmulgee steamers.

MILE 95.4 (32.039022, −83.297443) Cow Face Cut-Off. On river right here, hidden in the riverside forest is an extensive oxbow lake at what was known as Cow Face Bar in the late 1800s. The original channel of the river was bypassed around the turn of the century when the river began forming, in the lexicon of the day, a "suck," a place where the river's flow was being sucked away from its normal course. Ultimately, this cut-off (of the oxbow) or cut-through was formed, and it began stealing flow from the river's main path. In 1902, intent on making a channel for steamboats, the U.S. Army Corps of Engineers accelerated the natural process by manually widening the cut.

MILE 94.3 (32.026178, −83.296141) Bishop's Landing Cut-Through. Here the river splits, with the main flow going straight on a newer channel and cutting off the old channel on river left. On river right just beyond the entrance to the new channel is yet another secluded and beautiful oxbow lake that is accessible in most water levels. Abandoned by the new main channel are the sites of two 19th-century steamboat landings—Bishop's and Newsome's Plank. In low water, the upper end of the old channel is clogged, but in high water it can be accessed.

MILE 93.4 (32.021775, −83.294138) Shoal. This unexpected shoal, unlike other rock reefs in an area with no significant fall, has enough gradient to create some whitewater and small waves, especially at low water. The shoal is also prone to collecting wood and strainers and thus should be approached with caution. It can be heard well before it is seen, but a concrete bridge pier just upstream of the shoal is a good landmark. The pier is what remains of a temporary bridge built over this cut-through to enable the harvesting of timber on the 100-acre island sometime after 2015.

SHOAL AT BISHOP'S LANDING CUT-THROUGH, WILCOX COUNTY

MILE 91.9 (32.010694, –83.297028) **Poor Robin's Ferry.** On May 8, 1865, Confederate president Jefferson Davis, his family, and a small entourage crossed the Ocmulgee here on what was then known as Brown's Ferry. Davis, having been forced from the Confederacy's capital at Richmond a month earlier, hoped to make it to the West and rally the remains of the Confederate Army there. Meanwhile, the Union Army, believing that he was complicit in the assassination of President Lincoln, was in hot pursuit. Soldiers were especially interested in the $100,000 bounty for his capture. On the morning of May 10, Davis was captured about 26 miles southwest of Abbeville. The only casualties from the encounter were two Union soldiers who were shot and killed by friendly fire as the troops surrounded Davis's encampment. Even surrounded, Davis attempted to flee under the cover of his wife's overcoat, but was quickly apprehended. His capture in women's clothes was exploited with much hyperbole: northern newspapers depicted the incident with Jefferson in a wig and hoopskirt. The dramatic capture led to a popular song of the era, "Jeff in Petticoats," with the lyrics: "Just on the out-'skirts' of a wood his dainty shape was seen. / His boots stuck out, and now they'll hang old Jeff in Crinoline." Davis was never executed. He spent more than two years in jail and became a symbol of southern nationalism during Reconstruction. Davis and the legacy of the Confederacy still loom large here. In 1905, Jeff Davis County, several miles downstream, was named in his honor, and in 2015, on the 150th anniversary of his capture, locals organized the Chasing Jefferson Davis Marathon, a 26.2-mile run from Abbeville to the site of Davis's capture, now a 13-acre state historic site.

NEAR POOR ROBIN SPRING, WILCOX COUNTY

Poor Robin Spring, located just off river on private land here, was for decades a well-known local recreation site. In 1895, the *Macon Telegraph* described it thus: "[It is] one of the most remarkable springs in the country and is famed for its remarkable curative power. All manner of skin diseases and sores can be cured by drinking the water and bathing in it . . . It's depth at low water is about 15 feet and it is so clear that a grain of rice can be seen at its bottom." During the early 1900s, owners of the spring developed a large swimming pool fed by the spring, and it remained a popular gathering place, steadily pumping out more than a million gallons a day from the Floridan aquifer. In 2006, the 56-acre parcel, valued by the county at around $80,000, was sold to Premium Waters, Inc., a producer of bottled water based in Minneapolis, for $650,000, a sale price that attests to the enduring value of the spring. Premium Waters pumps up to 60,000 gallons a day from the spring and trucks it to a bottling plant in nearby Douglas; the company markets it under the Emerald Springs name. In addition to being the site of a ferry and a well-known spring, this location also served as a steamboat landing.

MILE 91.4 (32.004680, −83.291350) Cut-Through. The river's path here is relatively young. U.S. Geological Survey maps from the 1970s show a small oxbow here looping to the northeast. That loop is now an isolated oxbow lake.

MILE 91.0 (32.001096, −83.295599) Half Moon Landing. This landing on river right, surrounded by a residential area, provides a boat ramp and parking and serves as a popular access point in Wilcox County. In 1920, it was the site of a curious incident involving a state senator. The nearby *Montgomery Monitor* had the story: "State Senator Dr. J. D. Maynard one morning this week went to his nets in the mouth of a small stream [Town Creek] that runs into the Ocmulgee at Half Moon Landing . . ., dragged his nets to the top of the water and found that he had made a big haul. Four large shad, one carp, one of the largest warmouth bream seen in this section and a monster rattlesnake. The snake was five and a half feet long and . . . had 23 rattles." Downstream of Half Moon Landing are numerous residences, the owners of which have gone to great lengths to fortify the riverbanks and keep the dynamic Ocmulgee from carving a new path in this sharp bend. Bank armoring—the placing of riprap, concrete, and other hardened material—can prevent bank erosion at the location where it is placed, but traditionally leads to the accelerated erosion of unarmored banks nearby. As other landowners act to save their property, the armoring spreads.

MILE 90.3 (32.002681, −83.283151) Switcher's Trail. Noted in circa-1890s maps, this trail ultimately became the first bridge at Abbeville to span the Ocmulgee, connecting Dodge and Wilcox Counties with a wooden span. A contract to build a steel truss bridge with a 190-foot draw span for the passage of steamboats was issued to the Austin Brothers Bridge Company in Atlanta in 1918. Remains of this former span can be seen on river left.

MILE 89.8 (31.998304, −83.286397) Abbeville WPCP. On river right, Abbeville's Water Pollution Control Plant is permitted to discharge up to 280,000 gallons of treated sewage into the river daily. The city's sewer system services some 2,800 residents.

MILE 89.4 (31.996693, −83.279203) U.S. 280. The 1994 bridge that spans the river here carries U.S. 280 west for a mile and a half to Abbeville, the seat of government for Wilcox County. The city and county are known for two commodities that color the culture of the South: watermelons and wild hogs. Wilcox County sits astride the part of the state's watermelon belt located between the Ocmulgee and Flint Rivers; it is among the top producers in Georgia. Meanwhile, the bottomland forests and swamps along the Ocmulgee provide ideal habitat for feral hogs. Capitalizing on the area's large hog population, Abbeville hosts each May the Ocmulgee Wild Hog Festival. Among other things, the festival features a children's pig chase, during which youngsters try to capture a small hog, and a baying contest, in which dogs are judged on how well they can bay a wild hog. Dogs are traditionally used to hunt wild hogs. They find, chase, and then bay at the prey until the hunters arrive.

MILE 87.6 (31.987720, −83.289878) Savannah, Americus & Montgomery Railroad. The center-pivot drawbridge here dates to 1952. Though built long after the river's steamboat era, federal law at the time required draw spans on what was still considered a commercially significant river; thus, the rusting gears on the center pier remain as a testament to a bygone era. The first railroad bridge here was completed around 1888 by the Savannah, Americus and Montgomery Railroad (SAM), a railway that was spawned by investors in Americus who objected to the high shipping rates being charged by the Central of Georgia Railway, which enjoyed a transportation monopoly in the city. The dispute between Americus and the Central became so heated in the 1870s and 1880s that the Central removed the name "Americus" from its system maps, replacing it with "Way Station Number Nine." By 1886, the SAM extended from Americus to Abbeville, and around 1888 the SAM began operating steamboats on the Ocmulgee, using a landing just downstream of the bridge to transfer goods from trains to boats bound for the Georgia coast. During its first year of operation, SAM boats carried about $1.3 million in goods, including 70,000 barrels of rosin and turpentine, 15,000 bales of cotton, 10,000 sacks of oats, 5,000 barrels of flour, and 20,000 sacks of guano.

In addition to the SAM boat landing, a shingle mill operated by A. B. Russell was sited on river right, just downstream of the railroad. During this era, Abbeville was an important boat building center, and many of its steamers plied the Ocmulgee, including the *Satilla* (1892), *City of Americus* (1888), *Biscayne* (1888), *Toccoa* (1889), and *City of Hawkinsville* (1896). The steamer *Maggie Bell* sank at the SAM wharf, requiring removal by the U.S. Army Corps of Engineers in 1894. Today, Wilcox State Prison, housing some 1,800 inmates, sits about 2,000 feet west of the river.

MILE 86.0 (31.974695, −83.283364) Upper Statham Shoals. Described in an 1890 U.S. Army Corps of Engineers survey as "serious obstructions and dangerous at low stages of the river," these shoals were quickly dealt with by the corps. In 1894, the engineers reported to Congress that *U.S. Steam Hoister No. 1* was engaged in blasting a "channel through the rock shoals and removing bowlders [*sic*] obstructing the channel," as well as clearing a "channel 100-feet wide and more than 3 feet deep at Stadem's [*sic*] Shoals." The rocks piled on river right are likely some of those removed "bowlders."

NEAR STATHAM SHOALS, WILCOX COUNTY

MILE 85.5 (31.968476, −83.279553) Statham Shoals Landing. The site of this public boat ramp and unpaved parking area bears the name of one of Wilcox County's most celebrated residents of the 1800s. Nat Statham, born in 1795, lived to be 97, and thus he had the luxury of telling his stories to many. A member of the Georgia Militia, Statham rescued the wounded Mark Wilcox at the Battle of Breakfast Branch in 1818 on the west side of the Ocmulgee downstream of this location. After battling Native Americans, Statham stayed on in the area, and during his later years was visited frequently by newspaper reporters. In 1888, the *Macon Weekly Telegraph* reported on the 93-year-old and his role in piloting the first steamboat to reach Macon, the *North Carolina*, which arrived in town on January 15, 1829, to much fanfare. The *Telegraph* reported: "The joyful intelligence was proclaimed to our citizens by the loud roar of artillery." The journey from Darien took eight days, and the captain of the ship indicated it was made without difficulty. The ship's pilot (who actually steered the boat upriver), one Thomas Wilcox, told a different, harrowing story of the journey. The way was so risky that Wilcox ultimately left the boat. If Statham's account is to be believed, perhaps the 34-year-old took the pilot's post after Wilcox's departure. Statham was also featured in a brief item that appeared in the March 18, 1886, edition of the *Hawkinsville Dispatch*. It described him as a gallant Indian fighter who "has had three sets of natural teeth." The account seems far-fetched, but in fact there is a condition, hyperdontia, in which a person grows additional teeth.

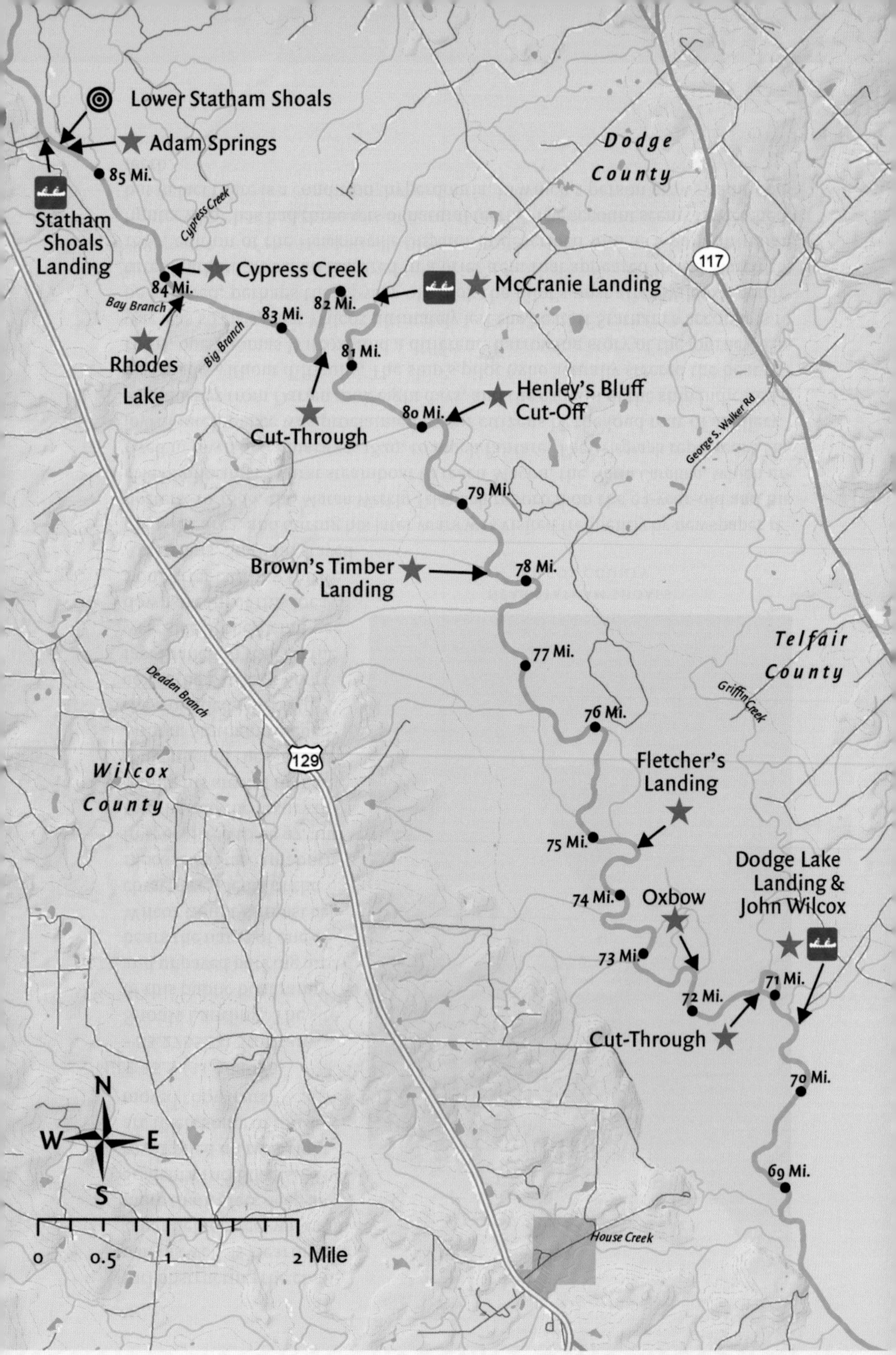

Lower Statham Shoals
Adam Springs
85 Mi.
Statham Shoals Landing
Cypress Creek
Cypress Creek
84 Mi.
Bay Branch
Rhodes Lake
Big Branch
83 Mi.
82 Mi.
McCranie Landing
81 Mi.
Cut-Through
80 Mi.
Henley's Bluff Cut-Off
Dodge County
117
George S. Walker Rd
79 Mi.
Brown's Timber Landing
78 Mi.
77 Mi.
Telfair County
Griffin Creek
Deaden Branch
76 Mi.
129
Wilcox County
Fletcher's Landing
75 Mi.
74 Mi.
Oxbow
Dodge Lake Landing & John Wilcox
73 Mi.
72 Mi.
71 Mi.
Cut-Through
70 Mi.
69 Mi.
N
W
E
S
0
0.5
1
2 Mile
House Creek

Dodge

Length 16 miles (Statham Shoals Landing to Dodge Lake Landing)
Class I
Time 7–9 hours
Minimum Level Navigable year-round.

River Gauge The nearest river gauge is located at the U.S. 280 bridge in Abbeville, upstream of this section: https://waterdata.usgs.gov/ga/nwis/uv?site_no=02215260.

Launch Site Statham Shoals Landing is located off Statham Shoals Road near Abbeville, with a boat ramp and parking.

DIRECTIONS From the intersection of U.S. 280 (Main St.) and U.S. 129 (Broad St.) in Abbeville, travel south 2.2. miles on U.S. 129. Turn left on to Statham Shoals Road (dirt) and proceed 0.3 mile. Turn left on Denniston Lane and then take the next right onto an unmarked dirt road. Proceed 0.2 mile to the parking area and boat ramp.

Take Out Site Dodge Lake Landing is located on an oxbow slough on river left and may not be accessible in low water. Flows of at least 2,000 cfs and levels of 3.5 feet or higher at the Abbeville gauge are recommended if the trip will end at this landing. The landing features a boat ramp and parking.

DIRECTIONS From Statham Shoals Landing, return to U.S. 129. Turn right and proceed 2.2 miles to Abbeville. Turn right on U.S. 280 (Main St.) and travel 6.2 miles to Rhine. Turn right on Reeves Street / 1st Street and immediately bear right on Reeves. Travel 0.6 mile, turn right on Ga. 117, and proceed 6.5 miles. Turn right on County Road 15 (Dodge Lake Rd.; dirt) and proceed 2.1 miles to the boat ramp and parking area.

Alternative Take Out Site McCranie Landing creates a 5-mile journey. It features a boat ramp and parking area.

DIRECTIONS From Statham Shoals Landing, return to U.S. 129. Turn right and proceed 2.2 miles to Abbeville. Turn right on U.S. 280 (Main St.) and travel 6.2 miles to Rhine. Turn right on Reeves Street / 1st Street and immediately bear right on Reeves. Travel 0.6 mile, turn right on Ga. 117, and proceed 0.3 mile. Turn right on Hopewell Church Road and proceed 3.2 miles to the boat ramp and parking area.

Outfitters Three Rivers Outdoors provides canoe and kayak rentals and shuttle service.

Three Rivers Outdoors, 612 McNatt Falls Road, Uvalda, 30473, 912-594-8379, www.explorethreerivers.com

Description The highlight of this 16-mile run is Adam Springs, a cold, clear blue hole spring located just downstream of the launch site at Statham Shoals. Beyond the shoals and spring at this location, the river leaves behind straightaways and more defined banks and again descends into a forested floodplain stretching 2 miles wide or more in places. Oxbows, cut-offs, and off-river sloughs are abundant, as are sandbars. Water levels can dramatically change the experience, since Dodge Lake Landing, located on an off-river slough, is accessible only during high water (above 3.5 feet at the Abbeville gauge).

Points of Interest

MILE 85.4 (31.967504, −83.277321) **Lower Statham Shoals.** Like the upper Statham Shoals, this obstruction was of much concern to the U.S. Army Corps of Engineers in the late 1800s. The corps' 1890 report to Congress estimated that it would need an appropriation of $6,000 to make this shoal navigable for steamboats. Only three other shoals on the river (Taylors Bluff, Tanyard, and Buttermilk, just upstream of Hawkinsville) required more money to "fix." The initial survey described lower Statham Shoals as a "troublesome and dangerous shoal extending across the river." The current shoal merely creates a few riffles in low water.

MILE 85.4 (31.967738, −83.276752) **Adam Springs.** On river left at the base of Statham Shoals, a clear cold stream flows into the river. The long spring run flows from upstream along the river's east bank from a beautiful pool of cold, emerald-to-turquoise water. The spring is located on private property.

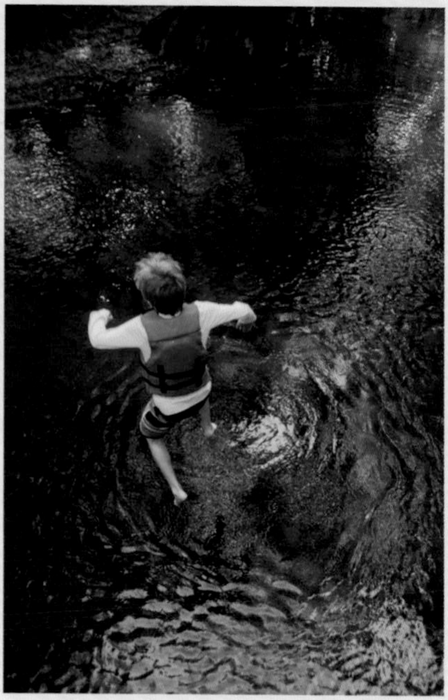

ADAM SPRINGS, DODGE COUNTY

MILE 84.1 (31.954892, −83.264002) **Cypress Creek.** This creek (mouth on river left) and its history are a testament to the role that the area's vast stands of longleaf pine played in the development of this part of the state. In 1851, the Georgia General Assembly granted John B. Coffee, A. McIntyre, and John McIntyre a fifteen-year concession to charge those who might float logs down the creek "not more than fifty cents a thousand for such timber or timbers." In exchange, the three men were responsible for keeping the stream open so that timber could be floated down the small creek. The final destination for all the Cypress Creek timber was Darien and the Georgia coast.

MILE 83.7 (31.951672, −83.260872) Rhodes Lake. On river right here are this slough and an unkempt boat ramp that marks Jordan's Bluff and Brown's Ferry, the site of much drama during the 1800s. In March 1818, 34 members of the Telfair County Militia crossed the river here from east to west to avenge the murder of a local resident named Joseph Burch by Creek Indians. In dispute was the land west of the Ocmulgee, which was then owned and occupied by the Creek Nation. The militia descended on a group of about 60 Creeks as they ate breakfast near a spring. During the ensuing brief battle, five members of the militia and four Creeks were killed. Among those wounded was Mark Wilcox, who was carried back to the river by Nat Statham. (See page 257 for more on Nat Statham.) The firefight became known as the Battle of Breakfast Branch. In the Treaty of Indian Springs (1821), the Creeks relinquished claims to land between the Ocmulgee and Flint Rivers. In the late 1800s, after more than 60 years of settlement, another conflict broke out over the use of land adjacent to the river. When Mack and Ross Wilson attempted to build a railroad to the bluff and a sawmill they operated there, George Reeves attempted to block the road's path. The confrontation led to a standoff on March 1, 1893, in which Reeves shot and wounded Ross. Mack Wilson then returned fire and killed Reeves.

MILE 82.5 (31.946773, −83.242373) Cut-Through. On river right, the Ocmulgee has begun to carve a new path and cut off the oxbow leading to McCranie Landing. In 2019, the cut-through channel narrowed to a strainer-filled passage, but in time the new path will likely widen and rob the oxbow of its flow.

MILE 81.6 (31.951540, −83.236232) McCranie Landing. In low water, this access point is marked by a large sandbar that limits access to the boat ramp. In the late 1800s, this bend and bluff were known as Widow Marks Boat Yard.

MILE 79.7 (31.938698, −83.225785) Henley's Bluff Cut-Off. On river left is an inlet to an oxbow that once curved beneath Henley's Bluff, to the east. Today the river makes a sharp turn to the south, creating a 0.7-mile-long oxbow lake at Henley's Bluff. Just beyond the tail of this oxbow on river right is the inlet to yet another oxbow lake that has been cut off by the river's new path. In the late 1800s, the river's twisting course here covered 1.6 miles; today the same passage is made in 0.6 mile, a testament to the ever-changing nature of Georgia's Coastal Plain rivers. In fact, in an 1890 report to Congress, F. C. Armstrong with the U.S. Army Corps of Engineers noted the early formation of these cut-offs at Henley's Bluff, and made the following recommendation: "The sloughs . . . being incipient cut-offs, should be closed" in order to maintain the river's existing channel.

MILE 78.4 (31.921992, −83.220674) Brown's Timber Landing. On river right is the former site of this landing, where, during the river's timber heyday (1870s–1920s), the region's longleaf pines were rolled into the river and formed into massive timber rafts that were then sent to Darien and the Georgia coast.

The timber rafts were typically about 40 feet wide and as much as 200 feet long; they were held together with binder logs running from port to starboard and secured to the floating timbers below with wooden pegs. The bows of the rafts were fashioned into a V-point, and the sterns were square. At both the bow and the stern were long sweeps, or oars, made from young saplings. These sweeps were secured to blocks on the rafts that served as fulcrums, allowing the raftsmen to use the sweeps to guide the raft around the river's many bends. In those days, the pilots of the rafts would call out instructions for the oarsmen: "Bow White" and "Bow Injun." The former was instruction to move the vessel to the east side of the river, that is, Georgia territory; the latter, to move the vessel west toward territory of the Creek. The commands were a holdover from the days of pole boating and timber rafting when the Ocmulgee served as the border between the two nations. Darien processed a peak of 116,000,000 board feet of lumber in 1900.

MILE 74.6 (31.892805, −83.199938) Fletcher's Landing. Though no sign of this landing exists today, this is yet another of the turn-of-the-century steamboat landings on the Ocmulgee that relied upon the U.S. Army Corps of Engineers to keep the river navigable. While much blasting of shoals and dredging of the river bottom was conducted, the most common maintenance was the removal of snags—trees that had washed off cut banks and into the river. This unending task required the help of steam-powered hoists or cranes. To understand the difficulty of this endeavor, consider this description by F. C. Armstrong, an assistant engineer, in an 1890 report to Congress: "Snags were removed entire; no cutting was done. Probably as large a one as has been handled was 110 feet long . . . and 4½ feet inner diameter, with earth hanging to roots. I estimate the weight of it as 30 tons."

MILE 72.3 (31.879281, −83.191721) Oxbow. On river left here is an outlet to an oxbow lake. The lake was formerly part of the river's main channel, a mile-long bend sweeping to the north. The river's backwater sloughs and oxbows are usually excellent spots to view alligators. Generally distrustful of humans, they will quickly retreat to cover beneath the water, so most sightings involve only glimpses of the shy creatures. Occasionally, you may hear them rather than see them. The bellow of a male alligator sounds a bit like a balky outboard motor sputtering to life. Scientists believe the males bellow to signal their size and ward off smaller gators seeking a mate. The practice, they believe, helps prevent physical confrontations between rival males.

MILE 71.0 (31.877246, −83.182290) Cut-Through. A relatively young cut-through, this passage cuts off a short oxbow to the northeast that is still accessible. Maps from the late 1970s show the river's main channel following the oxbow.

MILE 70.6 (31.873922, −83.178166) Dodge Lake Landing & John Wilcox. On river left here is a slough leading to this public boat ramp, located 0.2 mile off the main channel. The ramp is accessible only in high water (3.5 feet or higher at the Abbeville gauge). There is a private gravel ramp at the mouth of the slough.

MORNING, DODGE COUNTY

It should not be mistaken for the concrete public landing located on the slough itself. This site was among the first to be settled along the Ocmulgee, in the first decade of the 19th century. John Wilcox and his family established a boatyard here and played a role in the drama that precipitated the Battle of Breakfast Branch in 1818. That drama involved the shooting of John Burch and his son Littleton by Creek Indians as the Burches made camp on the west side of the Ocmulgee near Oscewichee Spring (then in Indian territory), about one mile west of this location. The Creeks descended on the father and son, shooting and killing the father and believing they had killed both. But Littleton, feigning death after being scalped, struggled back to the Ocmulgee, crossed the river, and found his way to the home of John Wilcox, where he relayed his harrowing story. Within days, Wilcox, his sons, and others of the Telfair County Militia gathered to cross the river and avenge John's death, only to be turned away by a superior force during the Battle of Breakfast Branch. According to a family history, Wilcox built and launched more than 40 pole boats from this spot, and was commissioned during the War of 1812 to transport supplies on the Ocmulgee for the army. In 1816, he was appointed by the Georgia General Assembly to a commission charged with opening the river to navigation. For this work, he came to be known as Captain Wilcox, and Wilcox County, created in 1857, was named in his honor.

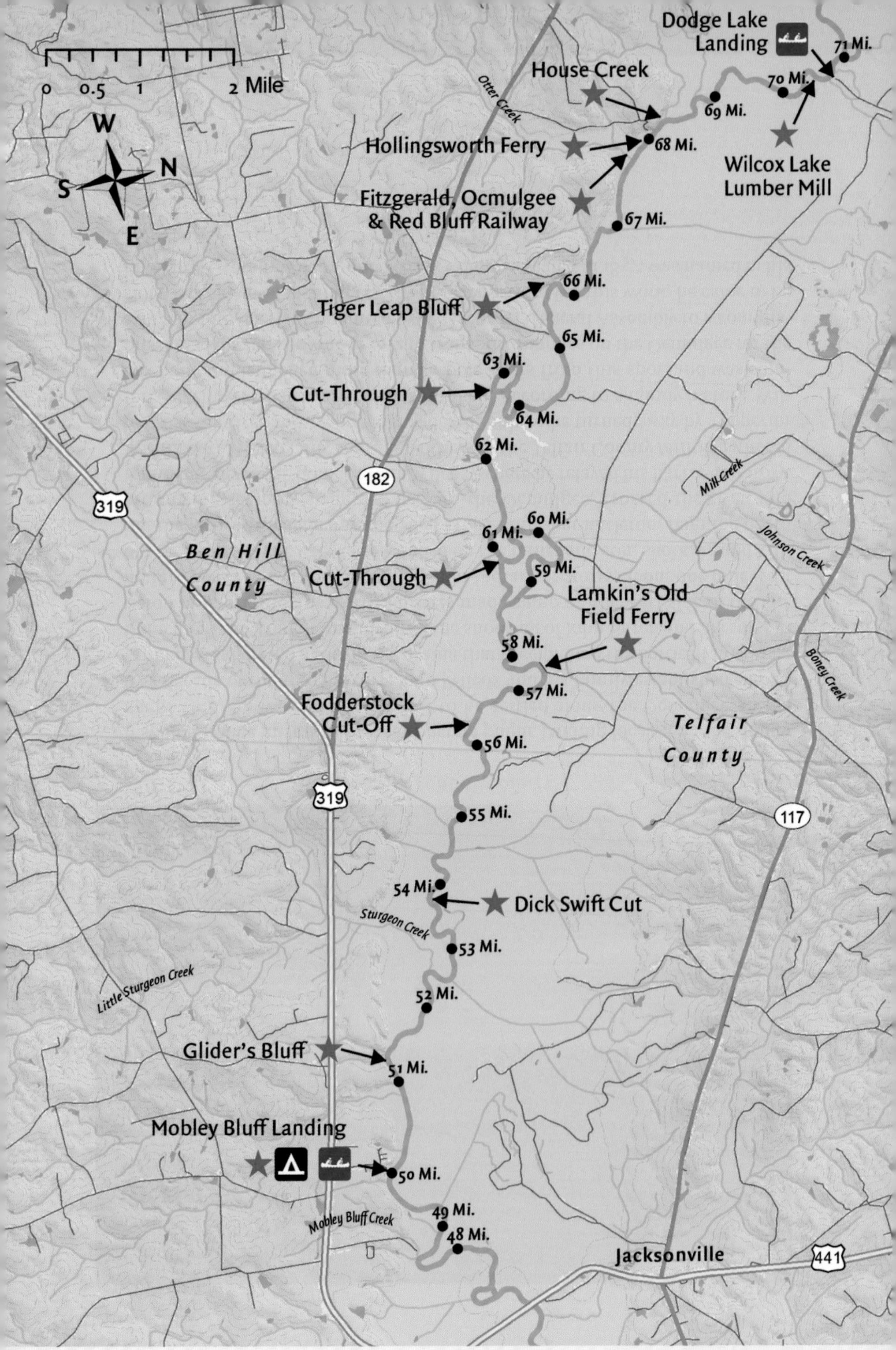
0 0.5 1 2 Mile
W
N
S
E
Dodge Lake Landing
71 Mi.
70 Mi.
69 Mi.
House Creek
Otter Creek
Hollingsworth Ferry
68 Mi.
Wilcox Lake Lumber Mill
Fitzgerald, Ocmulgee & Red Bluff Railway
67 Mi.
66 Mi.
Tiger Leap Bluff
65 Mi.
63 Mi.
Cut-Through
64 Mi.
62 Mi.
182
319
Mill Creek
60 Mi.
61 Mi.
Ben Hill County
Johnson Creek
Cut-Through
59 Mi.
Lamkin's Old Field Ferry
58 Mi.
Boney Creek
57 Mi.
Fodderstock Cut-Off
56 Mi.
Telfair County
319
55 Mi.
117
54 Mi.
Dick Swift Cut
Sturgeon Creek
53 Mi.
Little Sturgeon Creek
52 Mi.
Glider's Bluff
51 Mi.
Mobley Bluff Landing
50 Mi.
49 Mi.
Mobley Bluff Creek
48 Mi.
Jacksonville
441

Ben Hill

Length 20 miles (Dodge Lake Landing to Mobley Bluff Landing)
Class I
Time 9–12 hours
Minimum Level Navigable year-round.

River Gauge The nearest river gauge is located at the U.S. 280 bridge in Abbeville, upstream of this section: https://waterdata.usgs.gov/ga/nwis/uv?site_no=02215260.

Launch Site Dodge Lake Landing is located at the end of County Road 15 (Dodge Lake Rd.), with a boat ramp and parking. Located 0.1 mile from the main river channel, this site is not accessible in low water. Minimum flows of 2,000 cfs and a gauge height of at least 3.5 feet at the Abbeville gauge are needed to access this boat ramp.

DIRECTIONS From the intersection of Ga. 117 and U.S. 280 (2nd St.) in Rhine, go south on Central Street one block. Turn right on 1st Street and then immediately left onto Central Street (Ga. 117) and proceed 7.0 miles. Turn right on County Road 15 and travel 2.1 miles to the boat ramp, on the right.

Take Out Site Mobley Bluff Landing is located on river right. It features a boat ramp, parking area, picnic pavilion, and tent camping area in the midst of a residential area along the river. Restrooms may be out of order.

DIRECTIONS From Dodge Lake Landing, return to Ga. 117. Turn right and proceed 12.2 miles to Jacksonville. Turn right on U.S. 441 and proceed 2.5 miles. Turn right on U.S. 319 and proceed 2.9 miles. Turn right on Mobley Bluff Road and proceed 0.6 mile to the boat ramp.

Outfitters Three Rivers Outdoors provides canoe and kayak rentals and shuttle service.

Three Rivers Outdoors, 612 McNatt Falls Road, Uvalda, 30473,
912-594-8379, www.explorethreerivers.com

Description This 20-mile section marks the beginning of the Ocmulgee's "Big Bend," its shift from a southward path to an eastern one. It is perhaps the river's quintessential run through the Coastal Plain, featuring the three Bs: bluffs, bows (oxbows), and bars (sandbars). Beginning on an oxbow lake off the river's main channel, this section includes a host of additional oxbow lakes and backwater sloughs that provide endless hours of off-the-main-channel exploration during high water. With these features also come a host of alligators that—at the right time of year—seem to be found at the inlet to each of these sloughs. Picturesque bluffs and cut banks are frequent, along with the corresponding point sandbars on the opposite bank. With a wide floodplain, this section is remote. Human intrusions, in the form of fish camps and the occasional riverfront house or weekend cabin, are limited to the highest bluffs on the river's south bank in Ben Hill County.

Points of Interest

MILE 70.6 (31.873800, −83.178325) **Wilcox Lake Lumber Mill.** You would hardly know it now, but in the late 1800s the Telfair County side of the river here was a beehive of activity. This was the end of the line for the Normandale and Ocmulgee River Railroad, a logging railroad owned by William Dodge's Georgia Land and Lumber Company. The railroad ran from a sawmill here to Normandale, some 18 miles to the northeast, where the lumber company operated its largest mill as well as a turpentine still. That community once numbered more than 500 people, and the company built some 100 homes for mill workers. On this end of the railroad, sawn lumber and timber was loaded on steamboats or fashioned into rafts bound for the company's sawmills near Darien. The boom was relatively short-lived. In 1892, the mill at Normandale burned; it was never rebuilt. By 1906, most of the vast stands of pines in the area had been harvested, and mill operations moved on to other locales.

MILE 68.4 (31.847976, −83.177893) **House Creek.** A slough on river right marks the outlet of this tributary, which hugs Red Bluff and forms the county line between Wilcox and Ben Hill Counties. In the 19th century, the Bowen family dammed the creek about 2 miles upstream of the mouth and established a gristmill and a sawmill. Robert V. Bowen, a Confederate war veteran and undoubtedly an opportunistic and ambitious entrepreneur, made a name for himself in Reconstruction-era Georgia by astutely navigating the changing business and transportation landscape at the close of the 19th century. After establishing the mills on House Creek, he began purchasing land and harvesting timber. By 1883, the *Hawkinsville Dispatch* described him as the "largest taxpayer" in Wilcox County, with 20,000 acres of property. During that period, he moved to Hawkinsville and began investing in Ocmulgee River steamboats, purchasing the *Colville* and building the *Abba*, a vessel named after his youngest daughter. Perhaps recognizing the futility of river navigation, he then began investing in railroads, building a line between Abbeville and Waycross that would become the Seaboard Railroad. His influence must have been considerable, for in 1889 the General Assembly passed a law prohibiting hunting and fishing on his land in Wilcox County. He was elected to the statehouse in 1898 and served until 1904. Bowen's Mill, or at least its pond, survived into the 1940s and remained a popular local recreation area into the 1950s with a café, swimming pool, bowling alley, and, of course, fishing. Today, the Bowen's Mill property is a campground and convention site catering to Christian groups.

Also along House Creek is the Bowens Mill Fish Hatchery, a state facility that raises hybrid and striped bass for stocking in public reservoirs, as well as bluegill, shellcrackers, largemouth bass, and channel catfish. Some of the fish raised at the hatchery—striped bass, for instance—are raised there because the fish no longer reproduce naturally in our rivers, dams having blocked their historic migratory routes. An account from the *Hawkinsville Dispatch*, dated March 8, 1877, illustrates how dams affected the Ocmulgee's fishery: "The shad run up

HOLLINGSWORTH FERRY TRAINING DIKE, TELFAIR COUNTY

the Ocmulgee and when they reach the mouth of House Creek they ascend it as far as Bowen's Mills where there is a dam difficulty insurmountable." To catch the fish below the dam, anglers simply dipped nets into the water and fished out the obstructed shad. Shad, the salmon of the Atlantic Ocean, were a critical food source for early settlers, and their annual spring runs up coastal rivers were highly anticipated at the end of lean winters. As far back as the 1870s, attempts were made to stock shad in the Ocmulgee basin to improve the fishery. Today, dams upstream at Juliette and Jackson limit the shad's spawning habitat.

MILE 67.9 (31.844493, −83.174407) Hollingsworth Ferry. In mid-channel here is a narrow island with two lines of wooden posts extending upriver. The posts are visible in low water. This training dike, originally 1,350 feet long, was built by the U.S. Army Corps of Engineers in the late 1800s or early 1900s, and then frequently repaired by adding new stones and brush between the parallel posts. It served to narrow and deepen the river's channel. Also at this location during that era was Hollingsworth Ferry. In addition to moving travelers across the river, the ferry served as a boat landing. In 1902, steamboats ran from Brunswick to Hollingsworth Ferry three times a month.

MILE 67.7 (31.842454, −83.172582) Fitzgerald, Ocmulgee & Red Bluff Railway. In the early 1900s, this railroad ran from Fitzgerald, some 15 miles to the southwest, to a location near here known as Garbutt's Landing, where it connected with river steamers. The enterprise was designed to ship goods from the booming town of Fitzgerald, where the Garbutt family owned a cotton mill and other enterprises. At that time, Fitzgerald had been a town for less than a decade. Its rapid development was due to Philander Fitzgerald, an Indiana attorney and the publisher of the *American Tribune*, a widely circulated newspaper catering to Union Civil War veterans. In the late 1800s, as midwestern farmers struggled against extended drought conditions, Fitzgerald proposed establishing a veterans' colony in South Georgia. His idea was warmly received by Georgia governor William Northen, and soon Fitzgerald was advertising stock in the colony through his newspaper. As the money rolled in, Fitzgerald purchased some 50,000 acres in 1895, and shortly thereafter the veterans began pouring south. Within a two-month period in 1895, the population of the area that was to become the town of Fitzgerald jumped from 100 to 4,000. The idea of Yankee soldiers settling in the Deep South just miles from where Confederate president Jefferson Davis was captured, and within 60 miles of the infamous Andersonville Prison, certainly raised some eyebrows, but soon Fitzgerald became known for the harmony between men who just 30 years earlier had met on the battlefield. Veterans, both Confederate and Union, gathered regularly to trade war stories, and parades were held in which the veterans in blue and gray marched together. To this day, street names on the west side of Main Street bear the names of Confederate leaders, and those on the east side are named for Union leaders. The Lee-Grant Hotel was among the first large structures built in the fledgling city; Blue-Gray Park sits near the town center. By 1910, Fitzgerald boasted a population of nearly 6,000.

While his namesake city flourished, Philander Fitzgerald found himself embroiled in legal trouble associated with his veterans' colony ventures. In 1906, he was indicted for mail fraud, accused of taking some $35,000 from veterans who had invested in another proposed Georgia colony. He pleaded guilty to the charges and paid a fine of $1,500. Later, he was forced to pay $40,000 for fraud related to a failed colony in Texas. Fitzgerald's Blue-Gray Museum, housed in the town's historic railroad depot, celebrates the unique history of the town's founding.

MILE 65.6 (31.825690, −83.153395) Tiger Leap Bluff. On river right is this colorfully named bluff. It rises about 40 feet above the river. Tigers, by the way, can leap 20–30 feet horizontally.

MILE 63.5 (31.815760, −83.136693) Cut-Through. In high water, this narrow cut-through on river left may be passable. The cut-through bypasses a narrow oxbow that wraps beneath a picturesque bluff where, in the late 1800s, Storey's Landing was located.

MILE 60.8 (31.810207, −83.107615) Cut-Through. Here the river splits, carving a new path through a wood-choked channel to the right. In 2019, the river's former channel flowed to the left but was narrowing and filling at this inlet, which leads to a 2-plus-mile oxbow fronted by Yellow Bluff at its northernmost point. The outlet to the oxbow, a half mile downstream, remained fully open in 2019.

MILE 57.5 (31.813161, −83.088086) Lamkin's Old Field Ferry. Also known as Boney Ferry, this high bluff was home to a ferry, a boat landing, and a railroad during the late 19th century and early 20th. As late as 1911, only two highway bridges crossed the Ocmulgee between its mouth and Macon; Lamkin's was one of 16 ferries providing service across the river. With the completion of the highway bridge at Jacksonville in 1936, this ferry crossing waned in importance. The

Cullen Boney family came to this area along the river in the 1820s. Besides this historic ferry, nearby Boney Creek bears their name.

MILE 56.3 (31.800455, −83.080658) Fodderstock Cut-Off. On river right, some of the river's flow is directed to a narrow channel noted in the U.S. Army Corps of Engineers 1889 report to Congress as "the worst place on the river." An 1890 survey described a "bad cut-off, about 70 feet wide and 8 feet deep," that "diverts a considerable quantity of water." The recommended solution was to spend $750 in tax dollars to close the developing cut-through by piling debris at its inlet, thus maintaining the river in its original channel. Unlike many of the corps' other efforts to tame the Ocmulgee, this endeavor appears to have been successful. A comparison of maps from the corps' original survey and present-day maps shows that while the cut-off still exists, it remains just a small side channel, much as it did in 1890.

MILE 53.7 (31.788948, −83.052870) Dick Swift Cut. Though no evidence remains today, this run of river struck fear in the hearts of men plying the waters to Darien in the 1870s. From the U.S. Army Corps of Engineers 1880 report to Congress: "The current here is rapid and the channel filled with logs and stumps; it was a terror for boatmen and raftsmen." That year, the corps spent several weeks dredging logs and stumps from the river bottom here. One cypress stump they pulled measured nearly 12 feet in diameter.

MILE 51.3 (31.777915, −83.026589) Gilder's Bluff. This bluff on river right bears the name of one of the early settlers of Irwin County (now Ben Hill County). John S. Gilder served as sheriff of Irwin County (1822–1824), state representative (1823–1825), and state senator (1827).

MILE 50.0 (31.774849, −83.007629) Mobley Bluff Landing. On river right are this Georgia Department of Natural Resources boat ramp and Ben Hill County Park, which is surrounded by a small residential area. The park includes covered picnic pavilions as well as tent and RV campsites. Mobley Bluff bears the name of one of the first settlers to venture to the west bank of the Ocmulgee in the early 1800s—Ludd Mobley. Mobley sold land to Irwin County in 1832 for the site of the county courthouse and jail. He served as a state senator from the area throughout the 1820s and as sheriff in the early 1830s. The family remained tied to the river: one of Ludd's grandsons, Byrd Mobley, captained Ocmulgee River steamboats in the late 1800s, including the *Halycon* and the *Cumberland*. In 1996, the facilities at Mobley Bluff were dedicated in honor of Dewey and Buris McGlamry. Dewey served Ben Hill County in various capacities for more than 40 years. As roads superintendent, he was known for his thrift and gained fame for saving the county millions by always purchasing surplus equipment from the federal government. In addition to naming this park for him and his wife, the county named a road in his honor. He died in 1994.

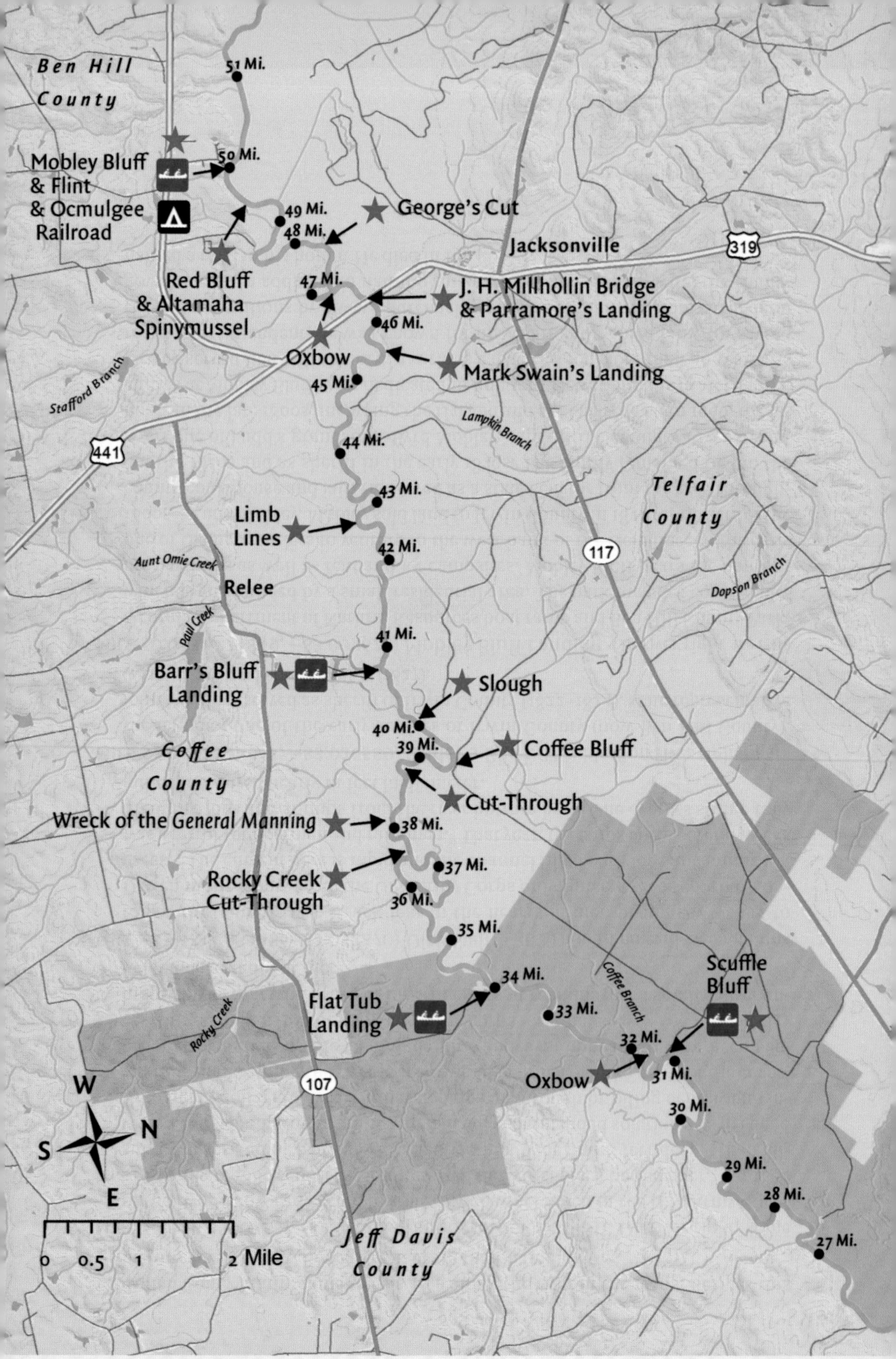

Ben Hill County
51 Mi.
50 Mi.
Mobley Bluff & Flint & Ocmulgee Railroad
49 Mi.
48 Mi.
George's Cut
Jacksonville
319
Red Bluff & Altamaha Spinymussel
47 Mi.
J. H. Millhollin Bridge & Parramore's Landing
46 Mi.
Oxbow
Mark Swain's Landing
45 Mi.
Stafford Branch
Lampkin Branch
441
44 Mi.
43 Mi.
Telfair County
Limb Lines
42 Mi.
117
Aunt Omie Creek
Relee
Dopson Branch
Paul Creek
41 Mi.
Barr's Bluff Landing
Slough
40 Mi.
39 Mi.
Coffee Bluff
Coffee County
Cut-Through
Wreck of the General Manning
38 Mi.
37 Mi.
Rocky Creek Cut-Through
36 Mi.
35 Mi.
Scuffle Bluff
34 Mi.
Coffee Branch
Flat Tub Landing
33 Mi.
Rocky Creek
32 Mi.
31 Mi.
Oxbow
107
30 Mi.
W
N
S
E
29 Mi.
28 Mi.
27 Mi.
0 0.5 1 2 Mile
Jeff Davis County

Jacksonville

Length 17 miles (Mobley Bluff Landing to Scuffle Bluff Landing)
Class I
Time 7–10 hours
Minimum Level Navigable year-round.

River Gauge The nearest river gauge is located at the U.S. 280 bridge in Abbeville, upstream of this section: https://waterdata.usgs.gov/ga/nwis/uv?site_no=02215260.

Launch Site Mobley Bluff Landing is located at the end of Mobley Bluff Road in a residential area along the river. The landing features a boat ramp, parking area, picnic pavilion, and RV and tent camping area. Restrooms may be closed or out of order.

DIRECTIONS From the intersection of Ga. 117 and U.S. 441 in Jacksonville, travel south on U.S. 441 for 2.5 miles. Turn right on U.S. 319 and proceed 2.9 miles. Turn right on Mobley Bluff Road and proceed 0.6 mile to the boat ramp.

Take Out Site Scuffle Bluff Landing is on river left with a boat ramp and parking. The landing is located within the Horse Creek Wildlife Management Area.

DIRECTIONS From Mobley Bluff Landing, return to U.S. 319. Turn left and proceed 2.9 miles. Turn left and proceed 2.5 miles to Ga. 117 in Jacksonville. Turn right and travel 6.9 miles. Turn right on Scuffle Bluff Road and proceed 0.3 mile. Bear slightly left and continue on the dirt road 2.1 miles to the entrance to the boat ramp, on the left.

Alternative Take Out Site Barr's Bluff Landing is located 0.4 mile up an off-river slough 9 miles from Mobley Bluff.

DIRECTIONS From Mobley Bluff Landing, return to U.S. 319. Turn left and proceed 2.9 miles. Turn right on U.S. 441 and proceed 1.4 miles. Turn left on Ga. 107 and proceed 2.6 miles. Turn left on County Road 173 (Barrow's Bluff Rd.) and proceed 1.0 mile to the boat ramp.

Outfitters Three Rivers Outdoors provides canoe and kayak rentals and shuttle service.

Three Rivers Outdoors, 612 McNatt Falls Road, Uvalda, 30473, 912-594-8379, www.explorethreerivers.com

Description For off-the-main-channel explorations, it is hard to beat this 17-mile run through the southern section of the Ocmulgee's Big Bend. After this, it turns northeast for its ultimate collision with the Oconee. No less than a dozen oxbow lakes and sloughs connect to the main channel in high water, providing access to enchanting swamp-like passages flanked by cypress, willow, and tupelo. Sandbars and cut-bank bluffs remain common; Coffee Bluff is a notable highlight. Regular cut-throughs, some filled with fallen trees, attest to the ever-changing nature of the river as it continuously cuts new paths through the floodplain forest. The final 3 miles of the run are flanked by the Horse Creek and Flat Tub Wildlife Management Areas.

Points of Interest

MILE 50.0 (31.775047, −83.007626) **Mobley Bluff & Flint & Ocmulgee Railroad.** In the 1830s and 1840s, during an era when steam-powered travel via boat and rail was seen as the key to economic progress, this bluff played a role in a grandiose plan to connect the Ocmulgee to the Flint River via a canal or railroad. In 1827, the Georgia General Assembly authorized the wealthy Sapelo Island planter Thomas Spalding to construct a railroad or canal between the two rivers and thereby create an inland "passage" from the Atlantic Ocean to the Gulf of Mexico. In 1835, Spalding purchased land at Mobley Bluff, and in 1840 he set his plan in motion. The construction project was unique in Georgia because it was not carried out by slaves. Though Spalding was a slave owner, he had misgivings about the institution. Furthermore, the engineer he hired, Abbott Brisbane, had his own elaborate plans. A recent convert to Roman Catholicism, Brisbane envisioned a utopian Catholic community in southwestern Georgia. To that end, he enticed recent Irish Catholic immigrants from New York to join him in this endeavor. Having secured the commitment from a large number of Irish immigrants, the group—accompanied by a Catholic priest—sailed to Darien and then up the Altamaha and Ocmulgee to Mobley's Bluff. Grading of the railroad began from the bluff and continued west on a direct route to Albany. Through 1842 and 1843, progress in grading the line moved steadily, and the workers named settlements along the road Loyola, St. Bernard, and St. Patrick. But by the summer of 1843, funds for the ambitious enterprise had dried

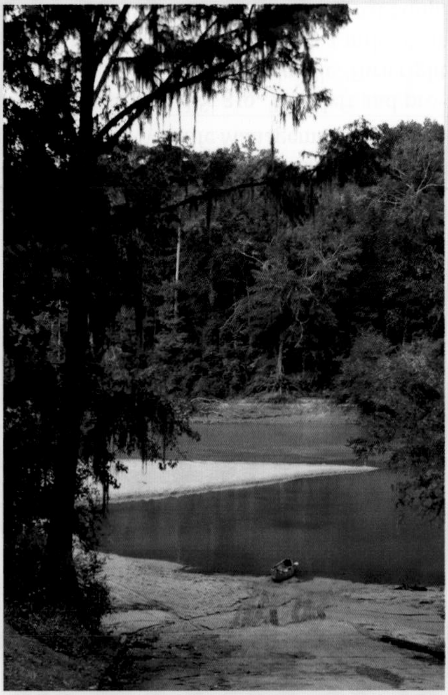

MOBLEY BLUFF LANDING, BEN HILL COUNTY

up. Unpaid and hungry, the workers revolted in September 1843 and cornered Brisbane in his cabin. According to one account, the workers "beat the plausible Brisbane with stones and cudgels." Nelson Tift and a militia from nearby Albany were summoned to rescue Brisbane, who, despite seeing the railroad fail, continued to work toward establishing a Catholic colony on the land between the Flint and the Ocmulgee. Indeed, many of the workers stayed on in the area, and during the rest of the 19th century, Catholic priests from Savannah regularly traveled upriver to hold Mass at Mobley's Bluff, Bowen's Mill, and Abbeville.

Spalding and Brisbane were slightly ahead of their time. Following the Civil War, several railroads (including the Savannah, Americus and Montgomery upstream near Abbeville) combined rail and steamboat travel to move goods to and from Georgia's western reaches to ports on the coast.

MILE 49.5 (31.776597, −83.000648) Red Bluff & Altamaha Spinymussel. On river right are a series of riverfront cabins and fish camps that mark the site of Red Bluff, a steamboat landing during the late 1800s and early 1900s. This bluff also marks the upper reaches of the known range of the Altamaha spinymussel (*Elliptio spinosa*), a federally protected freshwater mussel found only in the Altamaha River basin. The most notable features of these medium-size mussels (3–4 inches wide) are the spines or spikes (up to an inch long) that grow from the tops of their shells. This feature makes them look something like an alien spacecraft. In fact, they are becoming more and more alien even in their historic habitat. The mussel is no longer known to exist in either the Oconee or the Ohoopee River, and malacologists—scientists that study mussels—are finding fewer and fewer of them in the Ocmulgee and the Altamaha. For that reason, nearly 150 miles of the Altamaha and Ocmulgee have been classified as critical habitat for this rare creature. Filter feeders that are among the first to be affected by pollution, freshwater mussels are considered the most imperiled group of animals in the country. Dams and reservoirs have decimated their habitat and blocked the fish migrations upon which mussels depend. Mussels use fish to carry their fertilized eggs as they grow to adulthood, and many mussel species depend upon specific fish hosts. If the host fish is not available, the mussels are unable to reproduce. The host fish of the rare and elusive spinyshell (they typically bury themselves 2–4 inches deep in the sand) is unknown.

MILE 47.6 (31.787259, −82.990752) George's Cut. On river left is a slough that in the 1800s was the river's main channel. George's Cut broke through an oxbow point, thus isolating this slough. The "old river" is accessible, and within its swampy confines is a robust stand of spatterdock. With round, heart-shaped leaves that grow to 16 inches in diameter and float on the water's surface, and small round yellow flowers, this native perennial aquatic plant is a beauty, and a considerable benefit to wildlife. Its seeds are eaten by deer, muskrats, beavers, raccoons, and waterfowl.

MILE 46.7 (31.787213, −82.982518) Oxbow. On river right here is a relatively recently formed oxbow lake that is still accessible from its downstream outlet. In low water, the inlet, located just upstream, is blocked by a sandbar, but in high water it too may be accessible.

J. H. MILLHOLLIN BRIDGE, TELFAIR COUNTY

MILE 46.3 (31.791934, –82.979635) J. H. Millhollin Bridge & Parramore's Landing. The bridge carrying U.S. 441 between Jacksonville and Broxton was completed in 1987. Before its construction, the iconic J. H. Millhollin Bridge, dating to 1936, spanned the river here. Named for the Coffee County state senator who helped secure funding for it, when completed, in the midst of the Great Depression, it replaced what the *Atlanta Constitution* identified as one of the state's two remaining operational ferries. It was unique in that it consisted of two iron trusses—a camelback and a Warren, with the Warren truss pivoting on a center pier and serving as the draw portion of the span.

Just beyond the bridge on river left is a boat ramp. This ramp is privately owned, and the short road leading from the highway is gated. This is also likely near the site of Parramore's Landing, a river landing frequented by pole boaters in the first half of the 19th century. At this landing, John Parramore operated a tavern that was, as the author Fussell Chalker describes it in *Pioneer Days along the Ocmulgee*, the "scene of many incidents affording insight into the mode of river life common to the times." Chalker records that Gibson Clarke "was presented by the Telfair Grand Jury in 1814 for 'committing assault' upon James Rogers at the house of John Parramore 'by pointing a pistol at him.'" Also, James Pridgen and Stephen Vinton were presented to the grand jury in April 1818 for playing cards "at or near John Parramore's Landing on board a boat lying in the Ocmulgee River." In October of that year, John Sikes and Christopher Edwards "did fight at Parramore's Public House to the terror of the citizens."

MILE 45.6 (31.793100, −82.970579) Mark Swain's Landing. Though nothing remains to indicate its presence, in the 1800s this was the site of a steamboat landing. Mark was the son of Thomas Swain, who came to Telfair County around 1808. Thomas established a ferry across the river here and assisted in the construction of a road from here to Tallahassee, Florida, in 1822. It was likely across this ferry in 1859 that John F. McRae, a U.S. deputy marshal, brought 36 Africans who were among the human cargo of the sailing ship *Wanderer*, known as one of the very last ships to import enslaved Africans to the United States. The importation of slaves had been outlawed by Congress in 1807 and was later made punishable by death, but the illegal and lucrative trade continued almost until the Civil War. When word came of the *Wanderer*'s arrival at Jekyll Island, rumors of the illegal activity spread across Georgia. Meanwhile, friends of Charles Lamar, the well-connected Savannahian who orchestrated the voyage of the *Wanderer*, were scattering the illegal cargo across Georgia. McRae learned of a possible group moving through the area west toward Alabama, and on March 1, 1859, he intercepted Richardson Aiken and a caravan of both legal slaves and recently arrived Africans in nearby Worth County. McRae led the group back to Jacksonville, where he resided, and held the group in the county jail. The Africans languished in jail, since no instructions came from federal authorities regarding their fate. After Aiken was released, he returned to the jail, paid the county for the boarding of the Africans, and promptly continued west with his captives. Despite the release of the human evidence, McRae testified before a Savannah grand jury, and that testimony was enough to bring charges against Lamar. But as Lamar had counted on in case of such an eventuality, the Savannah trial jury refused to convict him. Newspapers reported at length on the saga of the *Wanderer*'s human cargo and Lamar's trial, adding fuel to the already-simmering fire brewing between the North and South over slavery and states' rights. The Civil War broke out the following year.

MILE 42.6 (31.784308, −82.941343) Limb Lines. Along this stretch of river and many other sections of the Ocmulgee—especially those runs near public boat ramps—you may encounter "limb lines." These baited setlines and hooks are tied to tree branches overhanging the river. The Georgia Department of Natural Resources encourages anglers to check these lines regularly and remove them at the end of the fishing day, but many anglers leave these lines in place for extended periods, creating navigational hazards for other boaters. Be mindful of these setlines and the hooks that may be submerged in the water.

MILE 40.8 (31.782989, −82.916225) Barr's Bluff Landing. A narrow slough on river right here leads 0.4 mile to this Ocmulgee River Water Trail boat ramp and parking area. Formerly known as Barrow's Bluff, this steamboat landing played an important role in the history of Coffee County. In 1854, lumber milled along the Ocmulgee was floated down to this bluff and then transported by oxcart 20 miles south to Douglas and used to build the county's first courthouse. Later, in 1903, the Wadley and Mt. Vernon Railroad completed a line from Douglas to Barrow's Bluff, thus creating a connection to the Atlantic coast via river steamers.

The Dorminy Price Lumber Company, having purchased several thousand acres of timberland in the area, began running lumber and naval stores to the bluff for transport down river. The *New York Lumber Trade Journal* noted on April 1, 1904: "The extension of the Wadley & Mount Vernon Road [i.e., railroad] is through some of the finest timber lands in Georgia." At that time, the main channel of the Ocmulgee looped to this landing, but this oxbow has since been cut off from the main channel. The narrow slough at the oxbow's outlet now provides the only access to this historic landing.

MILE 40.1 (31.787277, −82.905620) Slough. On river left here is an off-river slough worthy of exploration, especially in high water.

MILE 39.5 (31.791446, −82.896635) Coffee Bluff. This long, looping bluff is a classic example of a cut bank and adjoining point sandbar. It bears the name of General John E. Coffee, an early settler of Telfair County, Indian fighter, road builder, and politician. Coffee, who operated a plantation along the river here, may be best known for completing a 120-mile frontier road from Swain's Ferry, just upstream, to the Florida state line north of Tallahassee in 1823. Before his road-building duties, he was hired in 1808 to survey lands along the Ocmulgee in advance of state land lotteries. The Ocmulgee's high waters complicated the surveying (workers were forced to swim through flooded bottomlands during the operation), and as a result, his surveys failed to account for thousands of acres. In 1832, he was elected to Congress, and thanks to the slow transmission of news at the time, he was posthumously elected to a second term in 1836. He had died just eight days before the election. Coffee County, on the opposite bank of the river here, is named in his honor.

MILE 38.8 (31.783916, −82.898182) Cut-Through. On river left here is a newly developed cut-through. Choked with wood in 2019, it is likely to continue to widen and deepen as it captures more of the river's flow.

MILE 38.1 (31.780070, −82.889580) Wreck of the *General Manning*. In March 1860, the steamer *General Manning* was plying the river near here when its boilers exploded. The explosion and subsequent sinking of the boat led to the deaths of 14 people, including Joseph Williams, Jacob Parker, and John Harrell, prominent planters from the nearby China Hill community in Telfair County. In the late 1860s, Congress adopted new laws requiring inspections of steamboats in an effort to eliminate these types of incidents. The wreck occurred on an oxbow that came to be known as Steamboat Lake; the oxbow has long since been cut off from the main channel of the river.

MILE 37.5 (31.781613, −82.882755) Rocky Creek Cut-Through. Here the river splits: the main flow moves south, and the old channel diverts to the northeast. This cut-off eliminates a 1.6-mile-long oxbow. The inlet to the oxbow, on river left, is accessible in high water, but may become blocked in low water. The outlet, 0.4 mile downstream on the main channel, is accessible even in low water. The current through the new channel is swift, and the passage is filled with wood. Rocky Creek empties into the river in the middle of this cut-through. This creek is notable because some 4 miles upstream it flows through the Nature Conservancy's Broxton Rocks Preserve, a 1,650-acre natural area that features a waterfall on Rocky Creek, with accompanying cliffs, rock ledges, and cave-like crevices—a unique habitat in flat South Georgia. The oxbow slough that has been created is an excellent place to find waterbirds, including the black-crowned night heron. This stocky but striking gray heron sports a distinctive black cap and back. The birds tend to be more approachable than great blue herons or egrets.

MILE 34.0 (31.790274, −82.857045) Flat Tub Landing. A slough on river right here leads about 600 feet to this public boat ramp and unpaved parking area. In low water, access to this ramp may be limited. This ramp also marks the beginning of the Flat Tub and Horse Creek Wildlife Management Areas, which occupy both sides of the river for most of the next 8 miles. Archaeological surveys in the Flat Tub area, and throughout the Ocmulgee's Big Bend, point to continuous human occupation of this river valley for more than 10,000 years.

MILE 31.7 (31.812763, −82.841136) Oxbow. On river right here is a large sandbar that in low water blocks the inlet to a half-mile-long oxbow to the southeast. The outlet of the oxbow is open about 700 feet downstream on the main channel, providing access to this slowly forming oxbow lake.

MILE 31.0 (31.815760, −82.839113) Scuffle Bluff. This Georgia Department of Natural Resources and Ocmulgee River Water Trail boat ramp, on river left, was completed in 2016. It sits near the site of this unusually named 19th-century riverboat landing.

NEAR SCUFFLE BLUFF, TELFAIR COUNTY

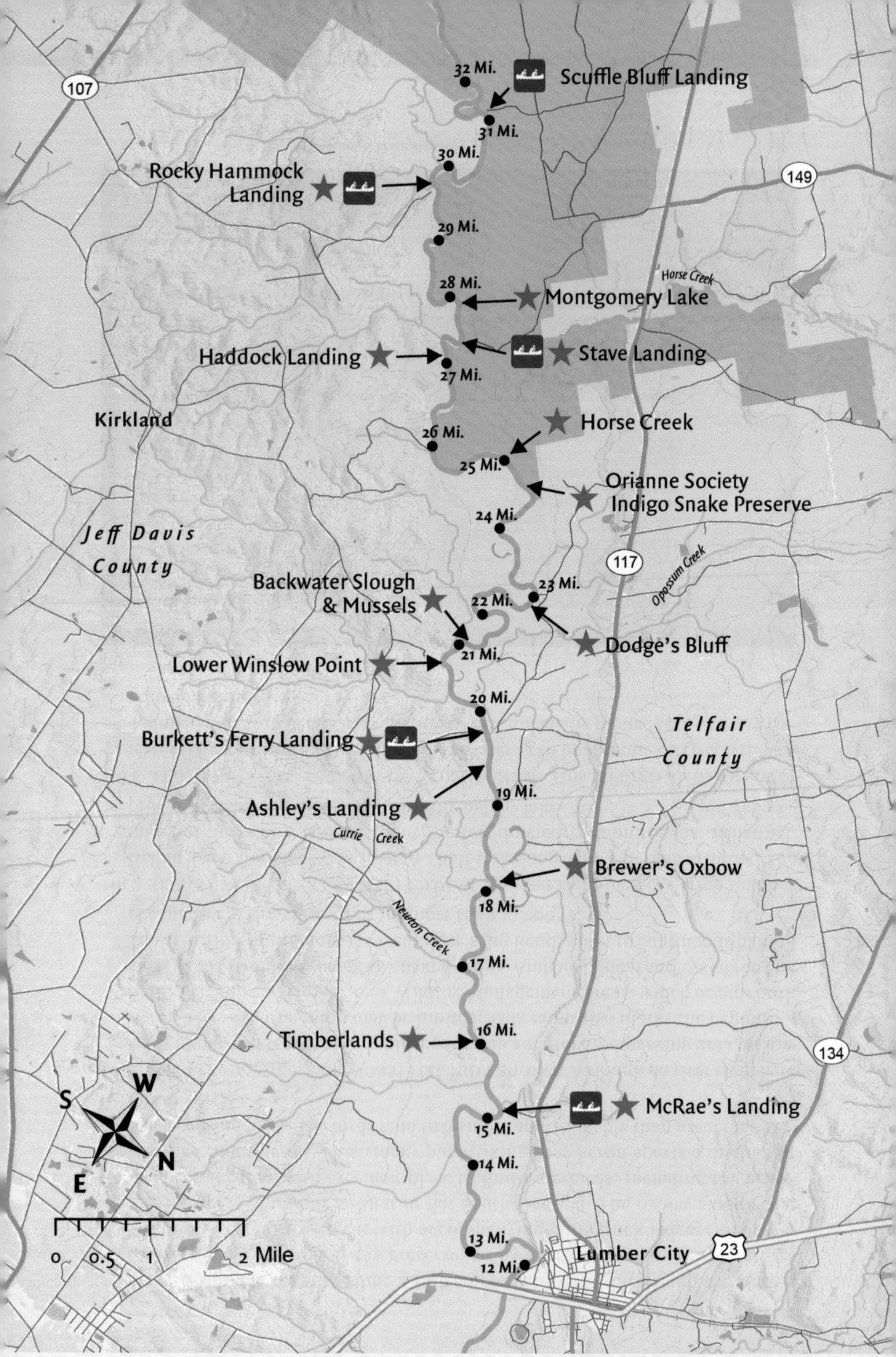

32 Mi.
Scuffle Bluff Landing
107
31 Mi.
30 Mi.
Rocky Hammock Landing
149
29 Mi.
Horse Creek
28 Mi.
Montgomery Lake
Haddock Landing
Stave Landing
27 Mi.
Kirkland
26 Mi.
Horse Creek
25 Mi.
Orianne Society Indigo Snake Preserve
24 Mi.
Jeff Davis County
117
Opossum Creek
23 Mi.
Backwater Slough & Mussels
22 Mi.
Dodge's Bluff
21 Mi.
Lower Winslow Point
20 Mi.
Telfair County
Burkett's Ferry Landing
19 Mi.
Ashley's Landing
Currie Creek
Brewer's Oxbow
18 Mi.
Newton Creek
17 Mi.
16 Mi.
Timberlands
134
McRae's Landing
15 Mi.
14 Mi.
S
W
N
E
13 Mi.
12 Mi.
Lumber City
23
0 0.5 1 2 Mile

Lumber City

Length 15 miles (Scuffle Bluff Landing to McRae's Landing)
Class I
Time 7–10 hours
Minimum Level Navigable year-round.

River Gauge The nearest river gauge is located at the U.S. 341 bridge in Lumber City, downstream of this section: https://waterdata.usgs.gov/ga/nwis/uv?site_no=02215500.

Launch Site Scuffle Bluff Landing is located 2.4 miles south of Ga. 117 on Scuffle Bluff Road, within the Horse Creek Wildlife Management Area. The landing features a boat ramp and parking.

DIRECTIONS From the intersection of Ga. 117 and U.S. 441 in Jacksonville, travel east on Ga. 117 for 6.9 miles. Turn right on Scuffle Bluff Road and proceed 0.3 mile. Bear slightly left and continue on the dirt road 2.1 miles to the entrance to the boat ramp, on the left.

Take Out Site McRae's Landing is located on river left on a short off-channel slough, with a boat ramp and parking. In low water, it is not accessible for trailered boats. Because the boat ramp is off the main channel, it is easily missed, but a large granite tablet commemorating "The Last Timber Raft" is conspicuous on the bluff adjacent to the slough. Canoes, kayaks, and other lightweight vessels can take out on the slope adjacent to the tablet.

DIRECTIONS From Scuffle Bluff Landing, return to Ga. 117. Turn right and proceed 11.2 miles. Turn right on County Road 185 and proceed 0.3 mile to the boat ramp.

Alternative Take Out Sites Trips of 2, 4 and 10 miles can be created by using the Rocky Hammock, Stave, and Burkett's Ferry landings, respectively. Note, however, that the shuttle distances for trips to Rocky Hammock and Burkett's Ferry are lengthy.

DIRECTIONS TO ROCKY HAMMOCK AND BURKETT'S FERRY LANDINGS From Scuffle Bluff Landing, return to Ga. 117. Turn left and proceed 6.9 miles to Jacksonville. Turn left on U.S. 441 and proceed 3.7 miles. Turn left on Ga. 107 and travel 10.0 miles. Turn left on Rocky Hammock Road and travel 2.0 miles. Turn right on Rocky Hammock Landing Road and proceed 3.4 miles to the boat ramp.

To reach Burkett's Ferry Landing: From the intersection of Ga. 107 and Rocky Hammock Road, continue on Ga. 107 for 2.9 miles. Turn left on Union Springs Church Road and travel 2.9 miles. Turn left on Burkett's Ferry Road and continue 4.9 miles. Turn left on Burkett's Ferry Landing Road and proceed 1.2 miles to the boat ramp.

DIRECTIONS TO STAVE LANDING From Scuffle Bluff Landing, return to Ga. 117. Turn right and proceed 1.5 miles. Turn right on CR 213 and travel 3.0 miles to the landing.

Outfitters Three Rivers Outdoors provides canoe and kayak rentals and shuttle service.

Three Rivers Outdoors, 612 McNatt Falls Road, Uvalda, 30473, 912-594-8379, www.explorethreerivers.com

Description As the Big Bend of the Ocmulgee turns northeast, the river changes slightly. Rock outcroppings along riverside bluffs—and even riverside sandbars—along with rock reefs (visible only in low water) interrupt the Ocmulgee's typically sandy bottom and its path through meandering oxbows and cut banks. This difference is most obvious at the aptly named Rocky Hammock. Cut-throughs and oxbow lakes are still common. The section's first 5 miles flow through the Horse Creek and Flat Tub Wildlife Management Areas, and the section ends at the historic McRae's Landing, just upstream of Lumber City.

Points of Interest

MILE 29.6 (31.814457, −82.824120) Rocky Hammock Landing. Located on river right in the eddy of a significant rock outcropping, this picturesque Georgia Department of Natural Resources landing provides a paved boat ramp and unpaved parking. The rock outcropping comes at the end of a long terrace, nearly 200 feet in elevation, that slopes sharply to the riverbank here. During the 1800s, the site served as a steamboat landing. An account of a voyage of the *City of Macon* steamer that appeared in the *Macon Telegraph* on February 17, 1898 speaks to how the river connected communities along its banks. The report details Macon merchandise being delivered to downriver landings, including Jacksonville (40 sacks of flour and 10 boxes of tobacco), Flat Tub (45 sacks of guano, 20 sacks

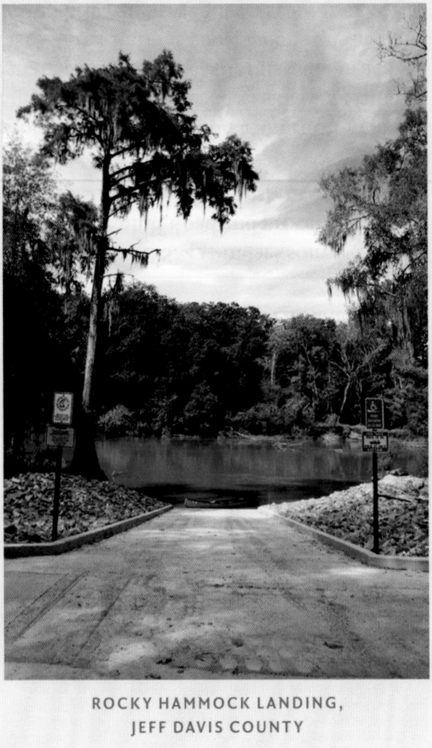

ROCKY HAMMOCK LANDING, JEFF DAVIS COUNTY

of cotton seed, and 5 sacks of acid), Rocky Hammock (20 sacks of guano), and Brunswick (75 casks of "Famous American Queen" bottled beer).

MILE 27.9 (31.828227, −82.809626) Montgomery Lake. On river left here, hidden by the riverside forest, is this famous oxbow lake. Here in 1932, George Perry, a 20-year-old farm boy from Telfair County, landed the world-record largemouth bass—a 22-pound, 4-ounce behemoth that anglers have been chasing ever since. In an interview years after the catch, Perry told *Sports Afield* that his first thought upon landing the fish was "how nice a chunk of meat" it would be to take home. Indeed, after measuring the fish at a store in nearby Helena-McRae and weighing it at the town's post office, he took it home, where his mother fried up one side of the fish for dinner that night to feed the family of six and did the same with the other half the following night. In addition to getting two good meals from the fish, Perry won a *Field & Stream* big-fish contest worth $75 in merchandise, and later his likeness was used in magazine ads for Hiram Walker's blended whiskeys. He also earned a lifetime of fame. Perry moved to the Georgia coast, where he operated a shipyard crane, ran a bait shop and marina, became a certified aircraft mechanic, earned his pilot's license, and managed Brunswick's airport. In 1974, he died when a plane he was flying from Brunswick to Birmingham crashed on Shades Mountain during inclement weather. In 2009, a Japanese fishing guide equaled Perry's catch, landing a 22-pound, 5-ounce largemouth on Japan's Lake Biwa. The latest big fish is considered a co-world-record holder because the international sanctioning body requires record fish weighing less than 25 pounds to surpass the existing record by at least 2 ounces. The oxbow lake may be accessible in high water.

MILE 27.5 (31.831849, −82.804200) Stave Landing. Located about 400 feet up the slough on river left, this public boat landing provides a concrete boat ramp and an unpaved parking area. In low water, it may not be accessible for all boats.

MILE 27.1 (31.830731, −82.800482) Haddock Landing. Along the high bluff on river right was a historic steamboat landing. During low water, numerous rock outcroppings and shoals interrupt this straightaway, the next bend, and the following straightaway. Noted in surveys of the river conducted in the 1880s, they were collectively identified as Haddock's Ledge.

MILE 25.0 (31.847125, −82.792312) Horse Creek. On river left is this tributary, which, despite its relatively small size, carried massive timbers to the Ocmulgee River during the 1800s. John Clements, who owned a prosperous plantation along Horse Creek in Telfair County before the Civil War, used the creek to float logs on the first leg to Darien. Even as late as 1898, locals were dependent on this natural transportation corridor. The July 29 issue of the *Macon Telegraph* that year noted after a heavy rain in the area: "The mill men, too, are now hopeful of an opportunity to get their lumber to market out of the creeks. Some of them have not been able to run their timber out for nearly a year on account of low water." In fact, low water was the bane of many a lumberman during this era. In 1877, the Georgia Land and Lumber Company reported some 360 rafts being detained due to low water on the river. The company's rafts would often get hung up and

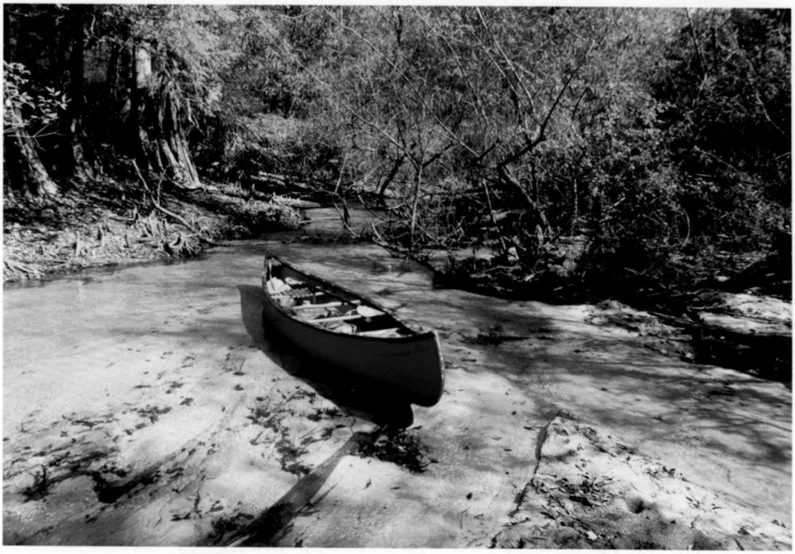

MOUTH OF HORSE CREEK, TELFAIR COUNTY

further complicate river navigation. By 1880, the company had become so frustrated by conditions that it offered, free of cost, "twenty or more hands" to the U.S. Army Corps of Engineers to remove obstacles from the river channel, including a raft of sunken logs near the mouth of Horse Creek, known as "Horse Creek snags."

MILE 24.6 (31.852372, −82.790796) Orianne Society Indigo Snake Preserve. On river left here is a 640-acre parcel of land that is part of this nearly 49,000-acre preserve of private and public land aimed at protecting habitat of the federally protected eastern indigo snake and the gopher tortoise, currently a candidate for the federal endangered species list. The nonvenomous eastern indigo snake is North America's longest snake, reaching lengths of up to 7 feet. It is known for its lustrous blue-black body and the reddish-orange hue on its chin, throat, and cheeks. It needs lots of room to roam. A single snake can range over a territory as large as 805 acres, and they like feeding along the edges of wetlands. In Georgia especially, it depends heavily on the gopher tortoise. Gopher tortoises dig extensive burrows that the snakes then use for shelter during the winter. Both species are partial to longleaf pine habitat, but that habitat has all but disappeared in the last 150 years. Once the dominant forest of the southern Coastal Plain, stretching from Virginia to Texas, longleafs covered some 90 million acres. Today only about 4.5 million acres remain; much of Georgia's longleaf pines were cut and floated down the Ocmulgee and Altamaha during the 1800s and early 1900s. The Orianne Society is a nonprofit organization dedicated to conserving critical ecosystems for imperiled reptiles and amphibians.

MILE 22.9 (31.862997, −82.774464) Dodge's Bluff. This spot along the river was once a bustling hub of the Georgia Land and Lumber Company, which established a sawmill along the east bank of the river in the 1870s. Beginning in 1878, the mill was serviced by the company's Ocmulgee and Horse Creek Railroad, bringing lumber from the interior while a boom on the river collected logs floated downstream. Some 250 men and 60 mules worked to keep the timber flowing to the sawmill. Owned by William E. Dodge and William P. Eastman, the Georgia Land and Lumber Company brought industrial-scale timber harvesting to this part of Georgia. The company cut the available timber along the Ocmulgee and Horse Creek Railroad in short order and then moved further north and west, establishing a similar railroad (the Normandale and Ocmulgee River) and mill along the river at Wilcox Lake in the mid-1880s. According to Mark Wetherington's history of the area, *The New South Comes to Wiregrass Georgia*, "At its height during the late 1880s, the company's timber colony controlled almost 345,000 acres of land, maintained 50 miles of railroads of various gauges, employed 700 hands at mill sites worth $350,000, and paid out from $8,000 to $10,000 per month in wages." Today, nothing of note remains to attest to what once was here. Even the river has changed significantly, having eliminated two large oxbows located just upstream and downstream of the bluff.

MILE 21.2 (31.858555, −82.762813) Backwater Slough & Mussels. On river right here, sandwiched between the sandbar and the riverbank, is a large slough. These sloughs, which are common on the back sides of the river's sandbars, are often excellent locations to find some of the river's freshwater mussel species. The Altamaha River basin is home to 18 species of mussels, including 7 that are endemic. Among those often found in these backwater sloughs are the Altamaha lance, the Altamaha pocketbook, and the Altamaha slabshell. Of these, the lance is the most easily identified. As the name implies, its shell resembles a long narrow blade several inches long but little more than an inch wide. You will find them buried in the silt. These mostly immobile creatures depend on fish to disperse and spread their populations. Gravid females release their glochidia (fertilized eggs) into the river, where they attach to the gills and fins of fish. In some cases, the female mussels display elaborate lures outside their shells to attract host fish and improve the chances of their young properly attaching to the fish. After developing for a time on the fish, the young mussels fall to the riverbed and grow into adult mussels. In many cases, specific mussels depend upon specific host fish. Studies conducted by Jason Wisniewski, a biologist with the Georgia Department of Natural Resources, and others have found that the Altamaha lance prefers two species of bullhead catfish; the slabshell prefers bluegills; and the pocketbook depends on bluegill or largemouth bass for its life cycle.

MILE 20.7 (31.857423, −82.756932) Lower Winslow Point. Here the river bounces off a high bluff on river right and then narrows before flowing around a pair of rock reefs over the next half mile. An 1880 survey of the river noted this location as "very dangerous for rafts." At low water, modern powerboats should use caution around these shoals.

MILE 19.7 (31.869178, –82.751715) **Burkett's Ferry Landing.** On river right is this public boat ramp. The ramp is on the site of a former steamboat landing and, before that, a ferry dating from the early 1800s, when William Burkett and his family settled in the area and established this important crossing. William was the subject of a fanciful tale retold in multiple publications during the late 1800s. Under the headline "A Visitation of God," news stories told how the backwoods ferryman had been paralyzed by the hand of God for tempting the Almighty with the words "I hope that God may paralyze me." As documented in the *Waycross Headlight*: "He was of giant physique, with long gray locks, and especially noted because of the brace of revolvers which he kept strapped to his waist. He was a great hunter and the ferry being in the midst of the swamp, he was convenient to an abundance of game. From those that lived around him it is learned that he was fearfully profane. Whenever he sighted game and was called off from it by alarm from the ferry, he would pour out such a volley of oaths as would make the flesh of ordinary men crawl. It was while in one of these profane spells that he cursed his Creator and wound up with the expression above quoted." The account of this visitation ended with the notation that "preachers in the neighborhood have used the incident in their sermons to great effect."

MILE 19.5 (31.871957, –82.747741) **Ashley's Landing.** On river right are a series of dwellings and fish camps that mark the approximate location of this historic steamboat landing, where, in the early 1890s, the U.S. Army Corps of Engineers constructed a pair of "snag dams." In the first four years of that decade, the corps spent about $55,000 on river improvements that included, among other things, the removal of 6,766 snags and stumps and 20,551 overhanging trees. Additionally, some 600 cubic yards of rock were removed from the river with the help of 73 pounds of explosives.

MILE 18.2 (31.883285, –82.730640) **Brewer's Oxbow.** On river left is the outlet of this oxbow, which once curved to Brewer's Landing, a 19th-century riverboat landing. Since the late 1800s, the Ocmulgee has cut off two sizable oxbows here. Slaughter Bluff, once a cut-bank bluff on the river's mainstem, is now an oxbow lake that is home to the Walker's Camp community.

MILE 16.1 (31.894824, –82.706621) **Timberlands.** On river right and for the next 5 miles are signs identifying the property on the Jeff Davis County side of the river as belonging to 4S Timberlands. In fact, much of the land along the Ocmulgee consists of privately owned forests that support Georgia's top-ranked forestry industry. No other state in the nation has more private, commercially available timberland than does Georgia, and no other state harvests more timber than Georgia. The state is the top exporter of pulp, paper, paperboard products, wood chips, and wood pellets. Locally, more than 10 percent of the workforce in Jeff Davis County in 2017 was employed at the county's three wood mills.

MILE 15.3 (31.904038, –82.699535) **McRae's Landing.** On river left, hidden off-river in a short slough, is a public boat ramp that marks this historic riverboat landing, which was named for Murdock McRae, a prominent Telfair County planter during the mid-1800s. On the bluff adjacent to the boat ramp is a marker

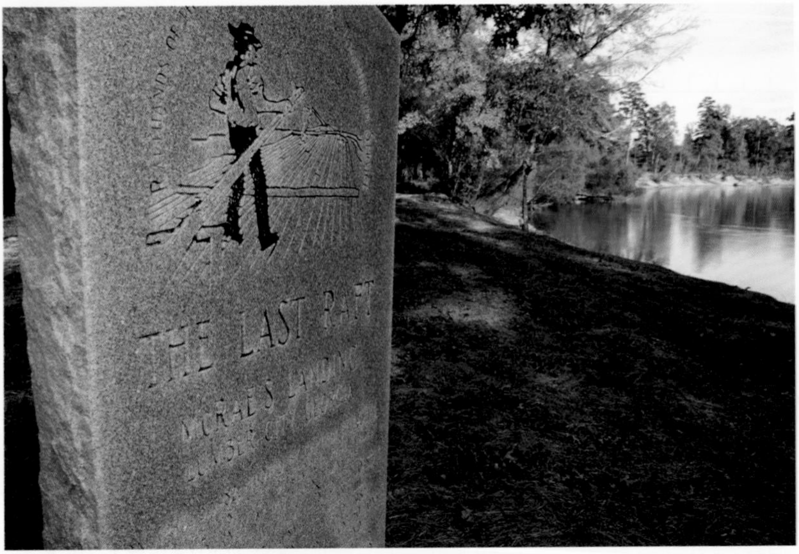

MCRAE'S LANDING, TELFAIR COUNTY

commemorating the "Last Raft." In 1982, Dr. Delma Presley, an English professor at Georgia Southern University, organized an expedition to reenact the log-raft voyages that took place on the Altamaha River system from the mid-1800s through the 1930s. "Project RAFT" and its crew of eight raft hands, piloted by the 90-year-old Bill Deen, who had worked as a raft hand as a young adult, launched from this landing on April 3 and completed the journey to Darien 17 days later. The purpose of the trip was to celebrate the area's culture, which was strongly linked to the woods and waterways of the Altamaha and the life of the raft hand.

Before the dawn of the industrial logging of Georgia's Wiregrass in the late 1800s, the rafts were typically manned by farmers who cut timber in the winter and then floated the trees to Darien in the early spring. With the advent of large-scale harvesting of the region's longleaf pines in the 1870s, rafting became a profession and a way of life for many. These men—and some women—were, as an 1898 *Atlanta Constitution* report from Darien described them, "hardworking," but also "a peculiar factor in the make up of the river counties." The newspaper story detailed the rafters' "peculiar" nature: "A party of these chaps passed through the city last evening, and had every mark of the raft hand so plainly stamped on them that none could fail to know them. First and foremost, they still carried the soot and smoke marks on their faces, caused from hovering over a little fire built on the rafts to keep them warm; second, the ever present ax, long auger and piece of rope used in tying their rafts; and third, a strong love for 'red eye,' and when full of this latter they become boisterous and make their fellow travelers wish they had taken some other way home." The way back to their Middle Georgia homes in 1898 was usually via railroad or steamboat, which exposed more refined travelers to these hardy bands of river rats.

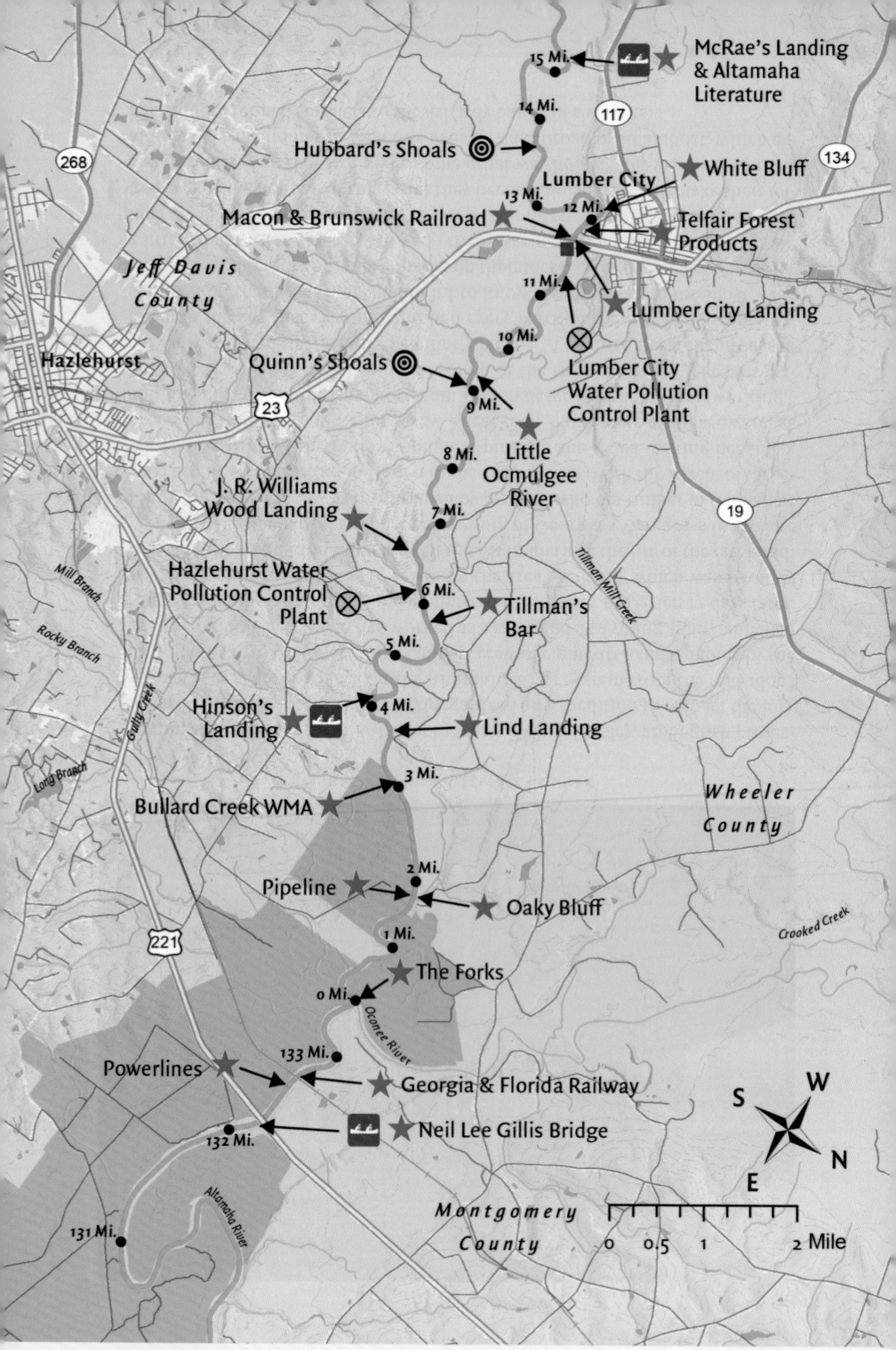
McRae's Landing & Altamaha Literature
15 Mi.
14 Mi.
117
Hubbard's Shoals
268
134
White Bluff
Lumber City
13 Mi.
12 Mi.
Macon & Brunswick Railroad
Telfair Forest Products
Jeff Davis County
11 Mi.
Lumber City Landing
10 Mi.
Hazlehurst
Quinn's Shoals
Lumber City Water Pollution Control Plant
23
9 Mi.
8 Mi.
Little Ocmulgee River
J. R. Williams Wood Landing
7 Mi.
19
Hazlehurst Water Pollution Control Plant
6 Mi.
Tillman's Bar
Tillman Mill Creek
Mill Branch
Rocky Branch
5 Mi.
Hinson's Landing
4 Mi.
Lind Landing
Gully Creek
Long Branch
3 Mi.
Bullard Creek WMA
Wheeler County
2 Mi.
Pipeline
Oaky Bluff
Crooked Creek
221
1 Mi.
The Forks
0 Mi.
Oconee River
133 Mi.
Powerlines
Georgia & Florida Railway
Neil Lee Gillis Bridge
132 Mi.
S
W
N
E
Altamaha River
Montgomery County
131 Mi.
0 0.5 1 2 Mile

The Forks

Length 17 miles (McRae's Landing to U.S. 221 on the Altamaha River)

Class I

Time 8–11 hours

Minimum Level Navigable year-round.

River Gauge The nearest river gauge is located at the U.S. 341 bridge in Lumber City, downstream of the launch site for this section: https://waterdata.usgs.gov/ga/nwis/uv?site_no=02215500.

Launch Site McRae's Landing is located at the end of County Road 185, 0.3 mile off Ga. 117, with a boat ramp on the slough off the main river channel and a parking area. In low water, the ramp is not accessible for trailered boats. Canoes, kayaks, and other lightweight vessels can launch from the sloped bank on the main channel near the boat ramp.

DIRECTIONS From the intersection of Ga. 117 and U.S. 341 in Lumber City, travel west on Ga. 117 for 2.2 miles. Turn left and proceed 0.3 mile to boat ramp.

Take Out Site The U.S. 221 boat ramp and parking area are located on river left just upstream of the bridge.

DIRECTIONS From McRae's Landing, return to Ga. 117. Turn right and proceed 2.2 miles to U.S. 341. Turn right and proceed 0.2 mile. Turn left on Ga. 19 and travel 2.3 miles. Turn right on Bells Ferry Road and proceed 9.0 miles. Turn right on U.S. 221 and travel 2.0 miles to the entrance to the boat ramp, on the left.

Alternative Take Out Sites Trips of 4 and 11 miles can be created by using the Lumber City and Hinson Landings, respectively.

DIRECTIONS TO LUMBER CITY AND HINSON'S LANDINGS From McRae's Landing, return to Ga. 117. Turn right and proceed 2.2 miles to U.S. 341. Turn right and proceed 0.8 miles to the entrance to the Lumber City Landing, on the right. To reach Hinson's Landing, continue straight on U.S. 341 another 3.6 miles. Turn left on Marcor Drive and proceed 0.2 mile. The pavement ends and the road becomes Yankee Paradise Road. Continue for 1.8 miles. Turn left on McEachin Landing Road and proceed 0.7 mile. Turn right on Towns Bluff Road and proceed 1.2 miles. Turn left on Hinson's Landing Road and travel 1.0 mile to the boat ramp.

Outfitters Three Rivers Outdoors provides canoe and kayak rentals and shuttle service.

Three Rivers Outdoors, 612 McNatt Falls Road, Uvalda, 30473,
912-594-8379, www.explorethreerivers.com

Description The final and historic miles of the Ocmulgee have a little bit of everything. Soaring, picturesque bluffs and historic railroad bridges at Lumber City, a beautiful blackwater tributary in the Little Ocmulgee at the Telfair-Wheeler county line, rock outcroppings along high forested bluffs in Jeff Davis County, navigational dikes dating to the late 1800s, and the confluence of the Oconee and Ocmulgee. The final mile and a half is on the wide Altamaha.

Points of Interest

MILE 15.3 (31.903968, −82.699467) McRae's Landing & Altamaha Literature. McRae's Landing is significant in the literary works of the Altamaha River basin's most celebrated writers, both of whom are members of the Georgia Writers Hall of Fame. In 1982, 81-year-old Brainard Cheney, the author of four novels set in the Altamaha basin, took part in the festivities here that launched the "Project RAFT" expedition downriver; in 2002, Janisse Ray, best known as the author of the memoir *Ecology of a Cracker Childhood*, launched from this same spot, retracing that 1982 logging raft journey. Ray's kayak journey informed her book *Drifting into Darien: A Natural and Personal History of the Altamaha*. Cheney, who grew up in Lumber City and dreamed of becoming a steamboat captain, instead preserved the history and culture of raft hands and hardscrabble farmers along the Oconee, Ocmulgee, and Altamaha Rivers in his novels: *River Rogue*, *Devil's Elbow*, *Lightwood*, and *This Is Adam*. Ray, a naturalist, poet, essayist, and farmer, is a strident defender of the natural areas of her home state, most especially the Altamaha River.

MILE 13.7 (31.907210, −82.684517) Hubbard's Shoals. Noticeable only in extreme low water, these shoals were worked over extensively by the U.S. Army Corps of Engineers between 1880 and 1901. In 1881, the Corps scraped and plowed this shoal to remove rock and deepen the channel, and in 1901 it used explosives to blast off a "clay point."

MILE 12.2 (31.920934, −82.681716) White Bluff. This picturesque bluff hides some of Lumber City's industrial past that adversely affected the Ocmulgee River. Just beyond the bluff are the decaying remains of Amercord, a facility that produced steel belts for radial tires; it ceased operation in 2001, putting some 400 employees out of work. During its time, the facility repeatedly violated its pollution-control permit by dumping excessive amounts of zinc, copper, and cyanide into the river. Altamaha Riverkeeper sued the facility for this pollution, and in 2003 it won a $1 million settlement. But the defunct company had no money. Today, the Amercord site awaits further cleanup; it continues to contaminate groundwater with a host of toxins, including lead. But with Amercord gone and no responsible party able or willing to pay for the cleanup, the work has fallen to the state's taxpayers and the Hazardous Waste Trust Fund, a multimillion-dollar trust created by the Georgia General Assembly in the 1990s. That trust is funded by fees that citizens and businesses pay to the state when, for example, they dump trash at landfills. Through 2019, the trust had generated more than $500 million for hazardous-site cleanups, but unfortunately, it has been repeatedly looted by leg-

WHITE BLUFF, TELFAIR COUNTY

islators who use the funds to pay for other portions of the state's budget. More than 40 percent of the funds collected have been diverted, resulting in a backlog of hazardous-waste sites awaiting state-funded cleanups. At the base of the bluff, look for the rusting hulks of antique cars and other debris left over from the time when it was common practice to dump trash over this high bluff at the edge of the city.

MILE 11.9 (31.919883, −82.678366) Telfair Forest Products. Though you may not see this facility, which is hidden by the wooded riparian buffer on river left, you will undoubtedly hear it. It is the roar of machinery turning pine logs into pine flakes and pellets. The flakes are dried and used primarily for animal bedding, and the pellets are used for energy production.

MILE 11.7 (31.919605, −82.675091) Macon & Brunswick Railroad. A railroad has crossed the river here since 1869, with the completion of this early Georgia railroad from Brunswick to Macon. Like the river, this railroad, which essentially paralleled the river, stitched together the river communities along its route, and like the Ocmulgee's steamers and rafts, it was instrumental in the industrial-scale exploitation of the area's longleaf pine forests for timber and naval stores during the late 1800s and early 1900s. The Macon and Brunswick was absorbed into the East Tennessee, Virginia and Georgia Railway in 1881. Today, trains still run on this line, part of the Norfolk Southern system. The 1928 bridge, one of the iconic structures on the Ocmulgee, features a center-pivot draw and a crow's nest from which the bridge keeper operated the draw mechanism. The Ocmulgee Depot, which was located on the south bank of the river,

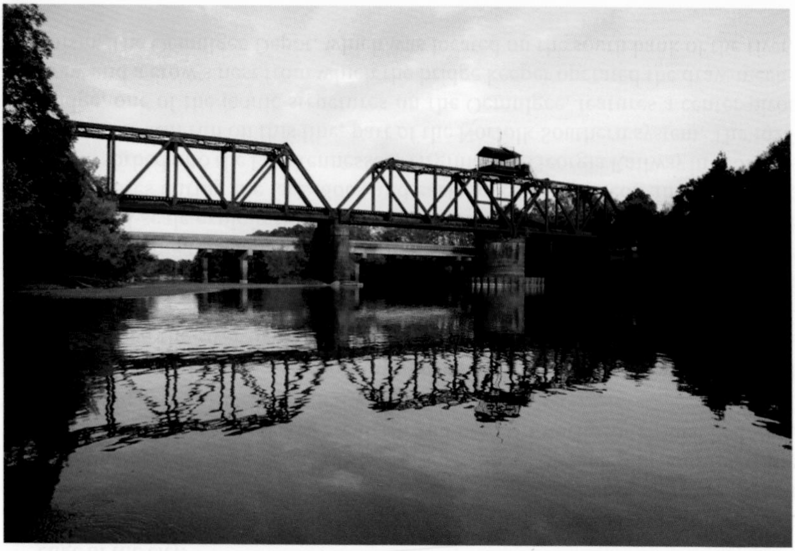

MACON AND BRUNSWICK RAILROAD, TELFAIR COUNTY

served as an important port; goods were exchanged from railroad to river steamers, and vice versa. The location also served as an important shipyard. From 1886 to 1913, no less than 14 steamers were built here, including the *Tommie* (1886), *Ocmulgee* (1887), *Dixie* (1903), *Nan Elizabeth* (1906), *Osceola* (1907), *B. T. Phillips* (1909), and *Altamaha* (1913).

MILE 11.6 (31.919990, −82.674690) Lumber City Landing. On river left, between the railroad bridge and the twin U.S. 341 bridges, is this Ocmulgee River Water Trail boat ramp and parking area. The access point sits at the site of the Lumber City Ferry, which operated until 1926, when a steel Pratt truss bridge consisting of two 100-foot spans and one 210-foot swing span (to allow the passage of river steamers) was opened. The bridge-building project cost $245,000 and took two years to complete. Like many bridge dedication ceremonies during this era, the occasion was one of great public interest. The *Atlanta Constitution* reported that "probably ten thousand persons attended the event," which feature two brass bands, a barbecue, and speeches from Governor Clifford Walker and local dignitaries. The existing bridges, built in 1986 and 2005, were named in honor of Dr. Comer Roger Youmans, a prominent physician from nearby Hazlehurst, who died in 1965.

MILE 11.4 (31.921941, −82.669371) Lumber City Water Pollution Control Plant. On river left is the discharge from Lumber City's sewage treatment plant, which services the city's more than 1,200 residents. The facility is permitted to discharge up to 500,000 gallons of treated wastewater into the river daily.

NEAR THE LITTLE OCMULGEE RIVER, TELFAIR COUNTY

MILE 9.3 (31.919500, −82.645709) Little Ocmulgee River. On river left, adjacent to the riverfront cabin, is the mouth of the blackwater Little Ocmulgee River. Originating in the northernmost portions of Telfair County, it flows some 30 miles, forming the county line between Telfair and neighboring Wheeler. A true blackwater river, its flow is oxymoronic. The water is clear but opaque: clear because blackwater rivers have such low gradients that they do not pick up much suspended material, but opaque because the dissolved organic matter from vegetation is not absorbed by the sandy soils and remains dissolved in the water column, creating the "tea-colored" water. Thus, in shallow water you can see the river bottom through the stained water, but in deep water, the river appears impenetrably black. The Ocmulgee itself is an alluvial river flowing out of Georgia's Piedmont and is thus highly turbid, carrying much suspended material. Where the rivers' flow mix, these differences are striking. Wheeler County is unique among Georgia's 159 counties in that it is bound by rivers in three directions—the Ocmulgee to the south, the Oconee to the east, and the Little Ocmulgee on the west.

MILE 9.1 (31.919808, −82.643216) Quinn's Shoals. Nothing to speak of remains of these historic shoals—a rock ledge that once stretched across the river. In 1890, the U.S. Army Corps of Engineers recommended removing some 250 cubic yards of rock from the river channel here to improve steamboat navigation—a project the corps estimated would cost $1,250. In 1902, the corps reported to Congress that the rock ledge at Quinn's Shoals was "entirely removed." The process sometimes involved drilling holes in the rock, inserting dynamite, and dredging the remains from the river bottom.

MILE 6.5 (31.927378, −82.613445) J. R. Williams Wood Landing. In the late 1800s, a steamboat landing occupied this rocky bank and high bluff on river right. In the mid-20th century, had some boosters been successful (and Congress been foolish), the backwaters of an Altamaha River reservoir would have lapped at these shores. In the late 1950s, after more than seven decades of dredging, blasting, and snagging the Ocmulgee and Altamaha by the U.S. Army Corps of Engineers to improve and maintain a navigational channel to the coast, the corps concluded that to maintain this channel, the construction of upstream reservoirs would be required. To that end, Congress appropriated funds to study the Altamaha River basin and the feasibility of taming it through a series of dams and reservoirs. The study recommended the construction of 12 locks and dams on the Altamaha and Ocmulgee Rivers—and even a short canal—with the goal of bringing "the ocean into the heart of . . . Georgia." The proposed Ohoopee-Goose Creek dam would have cost a projected $145 million in 1963 ($1.2 billion today) and would have backed the Altamaha and Ocmulgee up to this bluff. Those plans persisted into the 1970s, but by then the costs, to the taxpayer and the environment, were more fully understood, and none of the proposed dams were ever built.

MILE 6.2 (31.931363, −82.608934) Hazlehurst Water Pollution Control Plant. On river right here is the discharge from this sewage treatment plant, which services Hazlehurst and its more than 4,000 residents. The facility is permitted to discharge up to 1.5 million gallons of treated sewage into the river daily.

MILE 5.7 (31.935345, −82.605090) Tillman's Bar. In low water, the lengths to which the U.S. Army Corps of Engineers went in the late 1800s and early 1900s to make the Ocmulgee navigable are clearly evident. Beginning just beyond the

TRAINING DIKE AT TILLMAN'S BAR, JEFF DAVIS COUNTY

discharge from the Hazlehurst Water Pollution Control Plant are the remains of training dikes, jetties, and bank stabilization projects that stretch nearly a half mile downriver, all built in an effort to mitigate this shallow run of river. Work began as early as 1882, when the corps reported building 2 jetties. By 1893, the corps had completed extensive work here, including the construction of 12 jetties and a length of bank protection. For river boosters in Macon, this was exciting news. Under the headline "Direct Route by Water to the Sea," the *Macon Telegraph* on December 5, 1893, reported the tally at Tillman's Bar: 124 piles driven and filled with 832 cubic yards of stone, along with 1,163 cubic yards of brush mattresses for the jetties. The bank protection project used 309 pounds of explosives to quarry 972 cubic yards of stone, which was then used to fill two parallel lines of foot-square timbers stretching more than 270 feet. "With the opening of business in 1894," the paper wrote, "this river route . . . will be a busy scene, and once more the steamboats will snort and puff at their wharves, once more the deep whistle will be a familiar sound, and . . . the song of the stevedore will enliven the banks of the Ocmulgee . . . within the boundaries of Macon." Despite those high hopes, the river proved uncooperative, and steamboats remained undependable. The last steamer plied to Macon around 1909.

MILE 4.2 (31.935074, −82.589479) Hinson's Landing. On river right near the mouth of a large slough is this Ocmulgee River Water Trail landing, with a boat ramp and parking. The bluff that rises on river right is known as Round Bluff.

MILE 3.5 (31.940502, −82.585919) Lind Landing. Archeological work done near this site has uncovered Native American pottery dating from 1350 to 1600, along with middens that provide clues to the diet of these early dwellers along the Ocmulgee. Among the items found were corn, bean-like seeds, mussel shells, and deer bones. Also in the ancient trash was a glass bead, indicating contact with the Spanish during that time—a period that corresponds to Hernando de Soto's expedition through the region in 1540. Historians also believe that the Spanish mission of Santa Isabel de Utinahica was located near the confluence of the Ocmulgee and Oconee during that time, though the exact location remains a mystery.

MILE 3.0 (31.945252, −82.578881) Bullard Creek WMA. Most of the land on the south side of the river from this location to U.S. 1 north of Baxley on the Altamaha River is part of the state-owned Bullard Creek Wildlife Management Area. The WMA encompasses 14,000 acres and protects more than 17 miles of riverfront. This is one of the many parcels encompassing more than 165,000 acres of land that have been permanently protected in the Altamaha River corridor from here to the coast. These lands protect both the scenic view from the river and the more than 120 rare or endangered plant and animal species found in the Altamaha River basin.

MILE 1.8 (31.957656, −82.564865) Oaky Bluff. On river left here an extensive training dike stretches along the riverbank for about 1,000 feet. The U.S. Army Corps of Engineers, using contract labor and the U.S. steamer *Sapelo*, along with another hired steamer and barge, completed this work in 1899 and 1900.

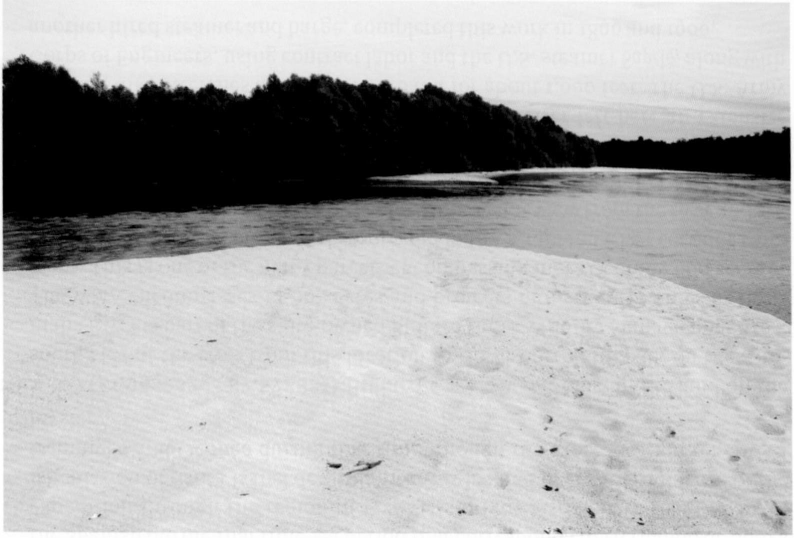

THE FORKS, WHEELER COUNTY

MILE 1.8 (31.957491, −82.564817) Pipeline.

MILE 0.0 (31.959517, −82.543373) The Forks. At this spot, the Ocmulgee collides headlong with the Oconee, forming Georgia's largest river—the Altamaha. The Altamaha is the third-largest contributor of freshwater to the Atlantic Ocean on North America's eastern shore. It flows 137 miles from here to its mouth, between Wolf Island and Little St. Simons Island. Just as the rivers gather at The Forks, so have people. Among the most famous to reside or do business near here was Mary Musgrove, the Pocahontas of Georgia. Around 1745, Musgrove and her third husband, the Reverend Thomas Bosomworth, established a trading post in this vicinity. By that time, Musgrove, the daughter of an English trader and a Creek woman, had made a name for herself by serving as an intercessory and interpreter for General James Oglethorpe and the Creek. In that role, she played a pivotal part in the new colony, keeping the Creek loyal to the English and limiting Spanish influence. In her later years, she became embroiled in a bitter legal battle with England over debts owed to her for serving as interpreter and over her claim of ownership of several barrier islands granted to her by a Creek leader. In the end, the colonial government granted her some back payments and the title to St. Catherines Island, where she died in 1763. The Ocmulgee's sister river, the Oconee, likewise has its origins in Georgia's Piedmont. The North and Middle Forks of the Oconee join on the south side of Athens to form the Oconee, which flows 220 miles to this spot.

MILE 132.7 (31.958661, −82.526829) Georgia & Florida Railway. This abandoned railroad bridge, built in 1909 at a cost of about $140,000, carried freight and pas-

DEER ON SANDBAR, WHEELER COUNTY

sengers on the Georgia & Florida Railway. On river right is visible the bascule drawbridge mechanism, which allowed the passage of river steamers. This type of drawbridge was known as the Scherzer rolling lift bridge, a concept developed and patented by William Scherzer. When engaged, counterweights on the end of the bridge would lift the 102-foot-long rail span vertical. Scherzer died in 1893 at age 35 from complications of typhoid fever, but his brother continued his work, building 175 of these kinds of drawbridges, including this one, before 1916.

MILE 132.6 (31.958379, −82.524790) Powerlines.

MILE 132.2 (31.957883, −82.517178) Neil Lee Gillis Bridge. Built in 1952, this half-mile-long bridge spans the Altamaha and its expansive floodplain. On river left is the first public boat ramp on the Altamaha. The bridge is named for the patriarch of one of South Georgia's most influential political families. Neil Lee Gillis is known as the father of Treutlen County, since he campaigned tirelessly for its creation in 1917. For his efforts, voters elected him the first state senator to represent the newly created county. Gillis's son, Jim L. Gillis Sr., served as chairman of the State Highway Board during the 1950s and 1960s; in turn, Jim Gillis Sr.'s son Hugh Gillis served 56 years in the General Assembly. Finally, Donald W. Gillis, Hugh's son, in 2009 was appointed by Governor Sonny Perdue to be a superior court judge in the state's Eighth District Court, in Dublin. Despite the family's fame, the Gillis patriarch's first name was misspelled "Neal" on the 1952 dedication plaque attached to the bridge. Subsequent Department of Transportation road signs have repeated the error.

Animals and Plants along Georgia Rivers

Species are arranged, as best as possible, into groups similar to one another. Mammals move from aquatic toward terrestrial; birds from water birds to birds of prey and wild turkey; fish from cold-water to warm-water species; reptiles and amphibians from smallest (frogs) to largest (alligators), with snakes and turtles grouped together; and plants from largest to smallest, with large trees first, then smaller flowering trees, shrubs, understory vegetation (ferns, canes, wildflowers), and finally aquatic vegetation.

Mammals

Beaver (*Castor canadensis*)

Reaching lengths of up to 4 feet (including the iconic paddle-shaped tail) and weights of up to 60 pounds, beavers are North America's largest rodents. On Georgia rivers they usually live in burrows in the banks, rather than in constructed dens. They are rarely seen during daylight hours, but along the shore, "bleached" sticks that they have stripped of bark are a sign of beaver activity. Beavers are keystone species for clean water, as the wetlands they construct serve as natural filters that capture sediment and other pollutants and provide habitat for many other species.

Muskrat (*Ondatra zibethica*)

This common aquatic rodent grows to lengths of 2 feet (including its foot-long, hairless tail). Though primarily nocturnal, muskrats can sometimes be seen foraging for food during the day. Its riverbank dens are concealed via an underwater entrance. Among its more notable attributes: lips that close behind its teeth to allow underwater feeding, and a prodigious reproductive cycle. They commonly bear four litters of five to seven young each year. They eat primarily plants but also consume mussels, frogs, and crayfish. If you come across a pile of small mussels, it's likely the site of a muskrat feast.

Otter (*Lutra canadensis*)

Reaching lengths of over 4 feet (including its long fur-covered tail), river otters are long and slender compared to muskrats and beavers. They commonly commandeer abandoned muskrat or beaver dens for their homes, but unlike their aquatic neighbors they are carnivores, using their swimming skills to capture fish, crayfish, frogs, salamanders, snakes, and turtles. They also partake of mussels and even birds. Although they are rarely seen during the day, you sometimes hear their barks and squeals and see them in the early morning or at twilight.

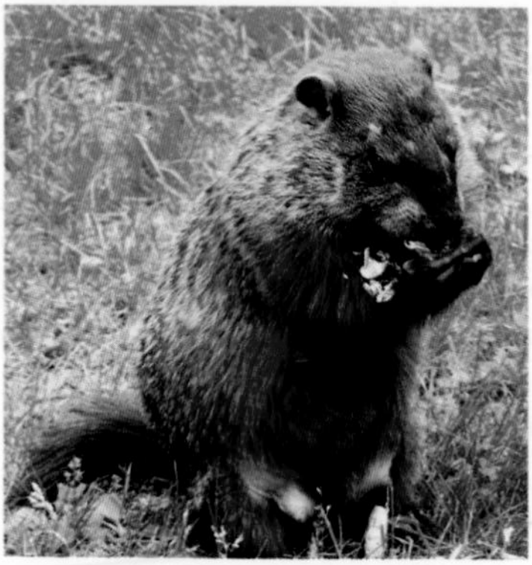

Groundhog (*Marmota monax*)

Often mistaken for an otter or beaver, groundhogs (also known as woodchucks) frequent areas where woodlands meet open spaces—like along rivers—where they forage on grasses, plants, fruits, and even tree bark. Yes, woodchucks do chuck wood. Though they are not aquatic, they do swim . . . and climb trees, but den in the ground, lending them their common name. Groundhogs grow to about 2 feet in length and have a short (7–9 inches) furry tail.

Raccoon (*Procyon lotor*)

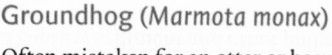

Known for its black mask and black-ringed tail, raccoons are riverside foragers. While they are highly adaptive and opportunistic, they prefer habitats near water (for food) that are filled with mature hardwoods (for shelter). The Latin *lotor* means washer—a reference to the raccoon's penchant for washing its food before eating. Theories abound about this practice, but to date scientists have not reached any conclusions. Raccoons feed on crayfish, fiddler crabs, fish, and even some snakes as well as fruits and acorns. They grow to lengths of 3 feet and can weigh as much as 20 pounds.

Opossum (*Didelphis virginian*)

About the size of your average house cat, opossums are North America's only marsupial. After birth (following a gestation period of just 12 days), infants crawl into a pouch on their mother's abdomen, where they are suckled for about 70 days. They are unique for additional reasons . . . they have more teeth (50) than any other land mammal in North America, and they are immune to snake venom and kill and eat venomous snakes.

Coyote (*Canis latrans*)

A nonnative species to Georgia, coyotes have filled the ecosystem niche vacated by the red wolf, which is a critically endangered species. In the late 1960s, coyotes were reported in only 23 Georgia counties, but in 2010 they could be found in all 159 counties. Their success in the state is attributable to their adaptability: they'll eat anything and live anywhere.

Armadillo (*Dasypus novemcinctus*)

Originally restricted to Texas, nine-banded armadillos have pushed steadily east during the past century and are now found throughout Georgia except in the far north. Their preferred habitat is along streams, and they cross water either by swimming or by walking on the stream bottom while holding their breath. Their primary food is insects, which they forage from the ground, employing a sensitive nose, a sticking tongue, and feet adapted for digging.

Gray Squirrel (*Sciurus carolinensis*)

The most commonly seen native mammal in Georgia, adaptable gray squirrels survive in many habitats but prefer hardwood forests, where nuts and acorns provide the bulk of their pound-a-week dietary requirements. Cracking the forest masts requires specialized equipment—namely incisor teeth that are continuously ground down but also continuously grow—up to 6 inches per year. Fossil records show that the gray squirrel roamed North America 50 million years ago.

White-tailed Deer (*Odocoileus virginianus*)

A species nearly lost to Georgia, white-tailed deer survive now because of restocking and wildlife management programs initiated during the mid-20th century. In 2002, Georgia's Department of Natural Resources estimated the state's deer population at 1.2 million. Hunting season in Georgia for white-tailed deer runs from September to January, depending on the area.

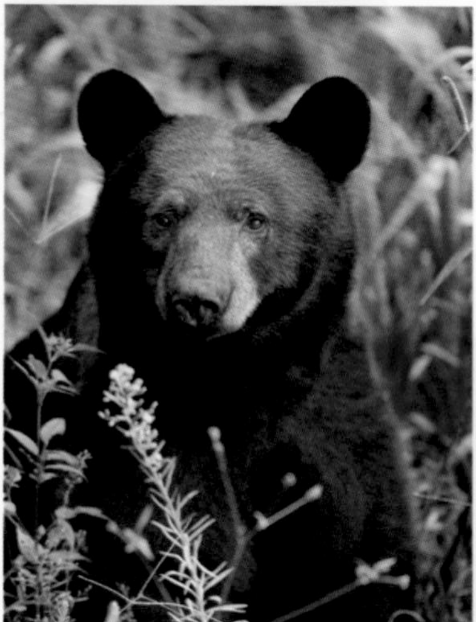

Black Bear (*Ursus americanus*)

Prior to the 19th century, black bears were abundant in Georgia, but habitat loss and overhunting dramatically reduced their population. Restrictions on hunting and other management practices implemented during the 20th century have allowed the species to recover. Georgia's Department of Natural Resources estimates a population of more than 5,000. Their range is mostly restricted to the North Georgia mountains, the bottomland forests along the Ocmulgee River, and the Okefenokee Swamp. Reaching weights of up to 500 pounds, black bears are the state's heftiest land mammals, but their weight doesn't slow them down. They are excellent climbers, swim well, and can run at speeds up to 30 miles per hour.

Red Fox (*Vulpes vulpes*) and Gray Fox (*Urocyon cinereoargenteus*)

The gray fox is Georgia's only remaining native member of the canine family, but along Georgia rivers you're more likely to encounter the red fox, a species introduced from Europe by early settlers. That's because the red fox is more common along forest edges, fields, and river bottoms, whereas the gray stays primarily in wooded areas. Grays are distinguished by a mottled gray coat, a black-tipped tail, and the unique ability (for canines) to climb trees. Reds have a rust-colored coat and a white-tipped tail.

Birds

Kingfisher (*Megaceryle alcyon*)

A slate-blue back, wings, and breast belt along with a white belly and crested head distinguish this patroller of riverbanks. Feeding mostly on fish, the kingfisher spends its time perched in trees over the water. In the spring, they construct nest burrows in riverbanks, and mating pairs produce five to eight offspring. Kingfishers, which have a distinctive cry (a loud, harsh rattle usually delivered in flight), are among the most common birds sighted along Georgia rivers.

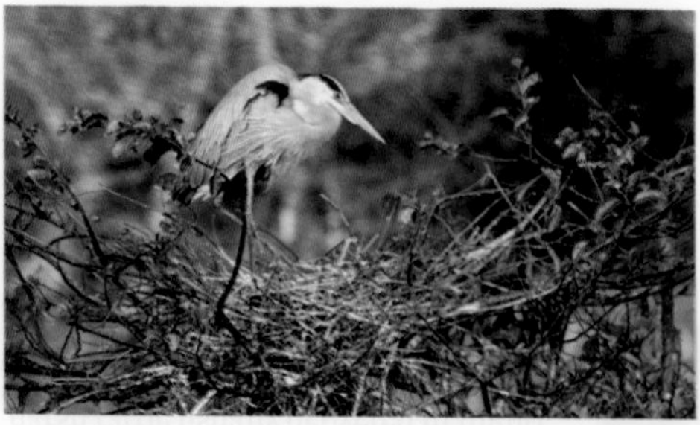

Great Blue Heron (*Ardea herodias*)

The largest North American heron, great blues grow to almost 4 feet in length and have a 6-foot wingspan. Silent sentinels along riverbanks, they wade slowly but strike with their bill with lightning quickness, feeding mostly on fish, frogs, and crustaceans, which they swallow whole. Herons engage in elaborate courtship displays and nest in colonies located high up in trees along rivers and lakes. When disturbed, they sometimes let out a loud, distinctive squawk as they flee.

Green Heron (*Butorides virescens*)

A small, stocky wading bird reaching lengths of 18 inches, the green heron is one of the few tool-using birds. It commonly drops bait onto the surface of the water and grabs the small fish that are attracted. It uses a variety of baits and lures, including crusts of bread, insects, earthworms, twigs, or feathers. It feeds on small fish, invertebrates, insects, frogs, and other small animals.

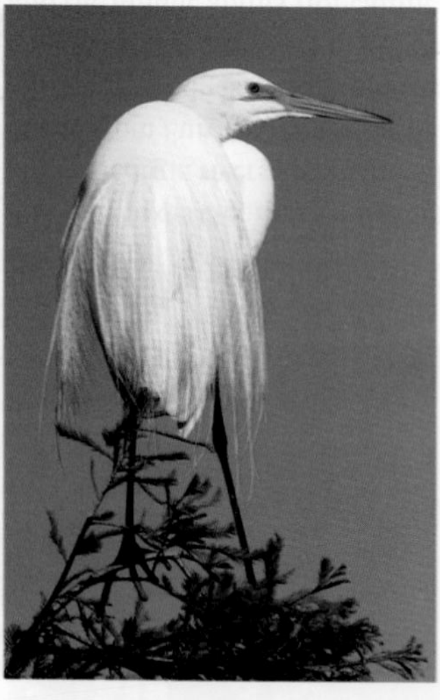

Great Egret (*Ardea alba*)

Like the great blue heron, this large wading bird reaches lengths of close to 4 feet, but it is distinguished by its all-white plumage and black legs and feet. It is more commonly seen along the Georgia coast. It has the distinction of being the symbol of the National Audubon Society because when the society was founded in 1905, the egrets were being hunted into extinction for their plumes, which were used to decorate hats and clothing.

Osprey (*Pandion haliaetus*)

Known as fish hawks because they feed almost exclusively on live fish, ospreys glide above open water and then dive-bomb their prey, sometimes completely submerging themselves to secure their quarry. Studies have shown that ospreys catch fish on at least 25 percent of their dives, with some kill rates as high as 70 percent. The average time they spend hunting before making a catch is about 12 minutes. Ospreys have a wingspan of 4–6 feet and can be confused with bald eagles because of their white head and brown wings. In flight, however, the white underside of their wings gives them away as eagle imposters. They build large nests of sticks in trees and artificial platforms high above open water.

Bald Eagle (*Haliaeetus leucocephalus*)

The bald eagle has been emblazoned on the Great Seal of the United States since 1782 and has been a spiritual symbol for Native people far longer than that. Once endangered by hunting and pesticides, bald eagles have flourished under federal protection. Though regal-looking birds, their behavior is often less than noble. While they do hunt and capture live prey, they more often obtain their food by harassing and stealing it from other birds (like the osprey) or by dining on carrion. They can be found on rivers throughout Georgia.

Turkey Vulture (*Cathartes aura*)

This large, black bird with a bald, red head can often be seen along Georgia rivers feeding on carrion that has washed onto sandbars or become stranded on strainers. Turkey vultures soar to great heights searching for food, and unique among birds, they have a strong sense of smell, which helps them locate it. They have a wingspan of 4–6 feet and are easily identified in flight by their two-toned wings—silvery to light gray flight feathers with black wing linings.

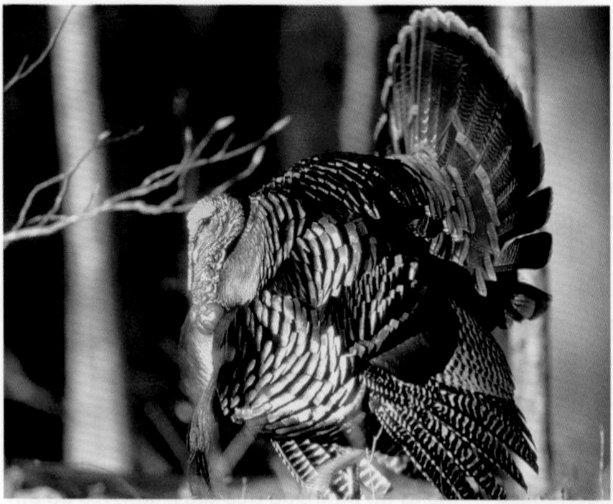

Wild Turkey (*Meleagris gallopavo*)

Wild turkeys were almost hunted to extinction by the 20th century, but conservation efforts implemented after the 1930s have resulted in a dramatic increase in populations. Benjamin Franklin lobbied for the wild turkey to be featured in the national emblem instead of the bald eagle. He thought the turkey a more noble and beautiful bird than the thieving, carrion-eating bald eagle. Turkeys feed on nuts, seeds, fruits, insects, and salamanders and are commonly seen in floodplain forests along the river. And, they do fly . . . on wingspans of more than 4 feet.

Fish

Brook Trout (*Salvelinus fontinalis*)

The East Coast's only native trout species, brookies require cold, clear water to survive and as such are found only in the highest headwaters of the North Georgia mountains. Aquatic insects, like mayflies, caddisflies, and stoneflies, as well as fish and crayfish, make up the bulk of their diet. There are 5,400 miles of trout streams in Georgia. Nonnative rainbow and brown trout can be found in all those streams, but only 142 miles support native brook trout.

Longnose Gar (*Lepisosteus osseus*)

This prehistoric fish is known for its long, cylindrical body and pointed snout filled with many sharp teeth. Little changed since the day of the dinosaur, its body is armored in thick hard scales that Native Americans employed as arrowheads. Its evolutionary longevity might be attributed to its unique ability to acquire oxygen from air. During summer months, when oxygen levels in water decrease, it can often be spotted just beneath the surface and surfacing to "gulp" air—a trait that makes it well adapted for surviving in warm, shallow water.

Striped Bass (*Morone saxatilis*)

Easily identified by rows of dark horizontal lines on their flanks, striped bass are one of Georgia's native anadromous fishes, meaning they move from saltwater to freshwater to spawn. Female stripers can carry as many as 4 million eggs. Once fertilized by males, the eggs need at least 50 miles of free-flowing river to hatch. Less than 1 percent survive to adulthood. Dams have interrupted most migratory routes along the Atlantic and Gulf Coasts, but stocking programs maintain populations on inland lakes and rivers.

Channel Catfish (*Ictalurus punctatus*)

One of 20 catfish species found in Georgia, channel cats are the most commercially important catfish species in North America and are commonly raised in large aquaculture operations. In the wild they are nighttime hunters, feeding on everything from small fish to algae and insects. They aren't fazed by low-visibility situations thanks to their distinctive whiskers and skin being covered in "taste buds." These external sensors help them locate food by taste rather than sight.

Reptiles and Amphibians

Green Tree Frog (*Hyla cinerea*)

Georgia's official state amphibian, the green tree frog primarily resides along South Georgia rivers. A green back, a white belly, and a white, yellow, or iridescent stripe down each flank distinguish this frog among the state's 30 native species. Protecting riparian vegetation along water bodies helps ensure the survival of this and other frogs.

Snapping Turtle (*Chelydra serpentine*)

Snapping turtles are not commonly seen on Georgia rivers because they rarely bask. Instead, they spend much of their lives on the river bottom under cover of vegetation and mud, where they feed on aquatic vegetation and ambush fish, crayfish, frogs, and anything else that happens to cross their paths. They are most often spotted from May to June, when females leave the water to lay eggs in nearby sandbars or loamy soil. Young hatch out from August through October.

River Cooter (*Pseudemys concinna*)

The consummate baskers of Georgia rivers, you may often spot river cooters sunning themselves on logs or rocks. At the first sign of danger, they plunge into the water, often creating loud splashes. They grow to 12 inches in length, feed mostly on aquatic vegetation and algae, and lay their eggs in sandbars along riverbanks. A pile of broken white shells on a sandbar in August and September is a likely indication of a cooter nest. Georgia limits the wild harvest of river cooters and other turtles that have come under increasing pressure due to demand in Asian food markets.

Spiny Softshell Turtle
(Apalone spinifera)

Sometimes described as a pancake with legs, the spiny softshell turtle sports a flat leathery shell. Males and young have dark spots on the shell that are absent in females, which can grow to lengths of 17 inches (males top out at 9 inches). Unique in the turtle world, softshells have the ability to obtain oxygen from adaptations on their throats and anuses, enabling them to remain submerged for up to 5 hours. They are carnivorous, ambushing unsuspecting prey while lying partially covered on the river bottom.

Banded Watersnake
(Nerodia fasciata)

The most common snake of Georgia's coastal plain rivers, streams, lakes, and wetlands, banded water snakes are often spotted basking on rocks, logs, and limbs overhanging the water's edge. They vary in color from light brown or reddish to black in ground-color with darker crossbands, and hunt for fish and amphibians in shallow water. A similar species, the northern watersnake (*Nerodia sipedon*), is restricted to North Georgia.

Water Moccasin
(Agkistrodon piscivorous)

Georgia is home to 11 species of water snakes; only the water moccasin is venomous. Unfortunately, five species of water snakes are similar in appearance to water moccasins, making positive identification of moccasins tricky. Moccasins are best differentiated from other snakes by their behavior and habitat preference. They are restricted to Georgia's Coastal Plain and southern portions of the Piedmont. In these regions, they bask on land, stumps, or logs near the water's surface and prefer slow-moving streams, swamps, and backwaters. Common water snakes, on the other hand, bask on limbs and shrubs overhanging the water and prefer large, open reservoirs and rivers. Finally, swimming moccasins hold their heads above the water and their bodies ride on the surface of the water; water snakes swim below the surface. It is illegal to kill nonvenomous snakes in Georgia.

Alligator (*Alligator mississippiensis*)

The largest predator in the state, alligators can grow to 16 feet in length and weigh as much as 800 pounds. They are found only in South Georgia, below the fall line running from Columbus to Augusta. Once a federally protected species, alligators have rebounded in population, and they are now common within their range. During warm weather, they can be spotted basking along riverbanks or patrolling the water with only their snouts visible above the water's surface. Since 1980, there have been only nine confirmed alligator attacks on humans in Georgia, only one of which was fatal.

Macroinvertebrates

This group of animals includes mollusks (mussels and snails), arthropods (crayfish and sowbugs), and aquatic insects (mayflies, stoneflies, etc.). Though usually small, they form the base of the aquatic food chain and play critical roles in clean water. Their life cycles and adaptations are among the most interesting in nature, and their presence, or lack thereof, can be an indicator of the health of a water body.

Native Freshwater Snails

Georgia is home to 67 species of freshwater snails that range in size from 0.1 inch to more than 1 inch in length. Easily overlooked because they dwell on the river bottom, they play an important role in river ecosystems. They scour rocks and other debris of algae, helping maintain healthy water and providing suitable habitat for aquatic insects. Snails, in turn, are an important food source for other wildlife.

Native Freshwater Mussels

Historically, Georgia was home to 126 species of freshwater mussels. However, many have become extinct due to habitat changes wrought by the construction of dams and water pollution. The state is currently home to 14 federally protected species. Because they are filter feeders, meaning they remove nutrients from the water, they play a critical role in clean rivers. They come in various colors, shapes, and sizes, with some species growing to the size of dinner plates. Because their unique life cycle involves fish carrying young mussels on their gills, the loss of some fish species has contributed to declining mussel populations.

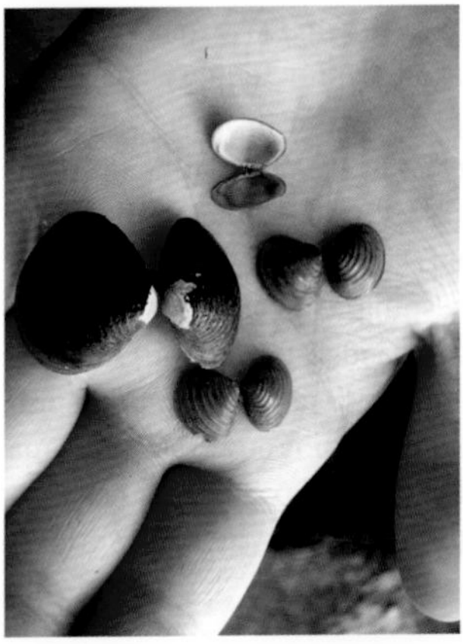

Asian Clams (*Corbicula fluminea*)

This nonnative, invasive clam is the most commonly seen mollusk in Georgia rivers. Corbicula entered the United States in the Pacific Northwest and are now found in 38 states. Prolific reproducers and adaptable to many habitats, corbicula have flourished where native mussels have struggled. In doing so they have filled a food void. Numerous species of fish as well as crayfish, raccoons, muskrats, and otters feed on them. They are distinguished from native mussels by their size, rarely growing to more than 1 inch in length.

Crayfish

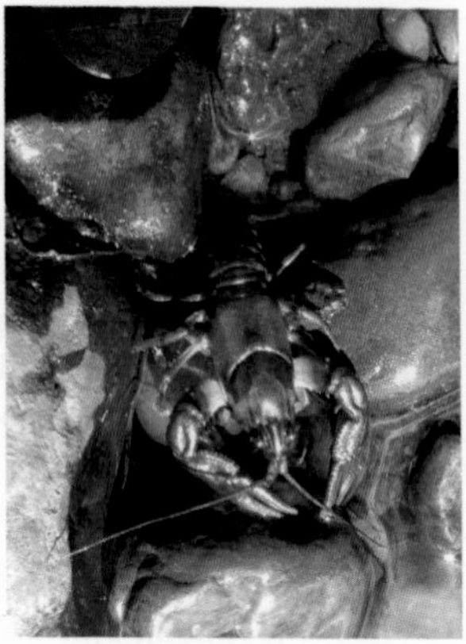

Georgia is home to 73 species of crayfish, many of which are restricted to isolated populations in specific regions of the state. On Georgia rivers, you'll find them beneath rocks and debris on the river bottom, though some species create extensive burrows in the soil near wetlands areas. They are protected by a hard exoskeleton that, as adults, they outgrow and molt once or twice each year. In combination with diminishing stream health because of pollution, the introduction of nonnative crayfish used as bait by anglers poses a serious threat to Georgia's native crayfish.

Hellgrammite (Dobsonfly Larvae)

Flip over a rock in a healthy to moderately healthy stream in Georgia, and you'll find these frightening-looking creatures that are distinguished by two large mandibles. Reaching up to 3 inches in length, the hellgrammite is a predator of other aquatic insects and is a favorite food of popular game fish species. Dobsonfly larvae develop for one to three years in the water, crawl from the water, dig a cavity to pupate, and emerge 14–28 days later as adults. The adults survive just long enough to mate and lay eggs. The females deposit their eggs, encased in a white covering, on overhanging leaves, logs, tree trunks, or rocks so that when the larvae hatch they fall into the water.

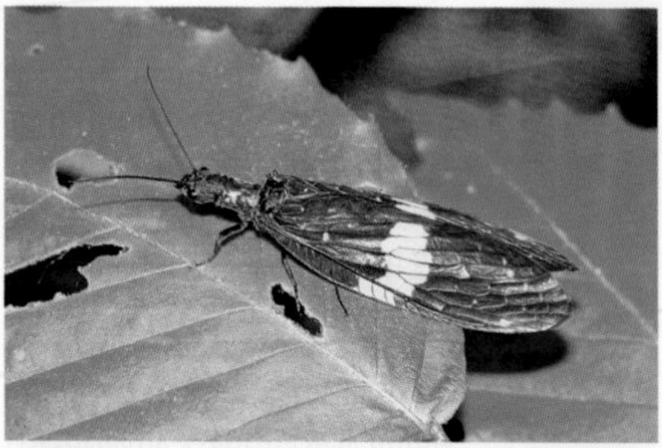

Dragonfly Nymphs

While adult dragonflies are always associated with water, by far most of a dragonfly's life is spent in the water, not hovering above it. Dragonfly nymphs live in the water for up to four years before crawling out for their final molts and becoming adults. The skin (exuvia) left on rocks and plants along the water can be found long after the molt has occurred. Adult dragonflies generally survive less than two months. Dragonflies are appreciated for their efforts in mosquito control. Nymphs eat mosquito larvae from the water, while adults can consume hundreds of flying mosquitos daily, earning them the moniker "mosquito hawks."

Mayfly Nymphs

Because all mayfly nymphs in an area commonly transform to adults at the same time, mayflies are known for their massive swarms that occur during the summer months. Their life underwater in Georgia rivers consists of clinging to the underside of rocks, where they feed mostly on algae. After a prolonged period (in some cases more than two years), they crawl out of the water to transform into adults. Nymphs are easily identified by their three hairlike tails (though sometimes only two). With fossil evidence confirming their existence more than 300 million years ago, they are believed to be the oldest living winged insects.

Trees and Plants

Sycamore (*Platanus occidentalis*)

A dominant deciduous tree of river corridors, sycamores are easily identified by their dark-brown to gray bark that peels and flakes, revealing a white inner bark. Sycamores also sport large, multilobed leaves that turn yellow and then tan in the fall, as well as conspicuous fruits—a round woody ball that in the winter breaks into many soft, fluffy seeds. Native Americans fashioned the large trunks of sycamores into dugout canoes; beaver, squirrel, and muskrat eat the fruits; juncos and finches eat the seeds. They grow to 80–100 feet tall with a spread of 40–50 feet.

River Birch (*Betula nigra*)

The deciduous river birch is known for its reddish brown to cinnamon-red bark that peels back in tough papery layers, giving the trunk a ragged appearance. In the winter, its fruits and flowers are conspicuous. Male flowers, dangling woody tubes (catkins) that are 1–3 inches long, can be seen on the ends of stems, along with the remnants of the previous year's fruit—1-inch woody cones. In the spring, the male flowers release pollen, fertilizing the emerging female flowers that produce the fruit. Growing to heights of 80 feet, birch play an important role in stabilizing stream banks with their extensive root system. Extracts from the tree are used in herbal treatments for gout, rheumatism, and kidney stones.

Black Willow (*Salix nigra*)

The deciduous black willow is a dominant tree of Georgia's coastal plain rivers, especially along sandbars. Distinguished by its long, lance-like leaves, willows are perhaps most conspicuous in the midsummer, when their cottony seeds are borne on the wind, falling to the river and sometimes forming large floating mats of white fluff. Their fibrous roots play a critical role in stabilizing stream banks, and a compound derived from their bark is known for its fever-reducing and pain-killing effects. A synthetically produced variety is found in modern aspirin. Willows can attain heights of up to 60 feet.

Black Walnut (*Juglans nigra*)

Because it thrives in full sunlight, the black walnut is often found in the open, well-lit spaces afforded by riverbanks. In the fall, after dropping its leaves it then drops its golf-ball-sized fruits, and it is not uncommon to find them floating down the river. After removing their husk (which stains hands and clothes), the hard, brown corrugated nut can—with considerable work—be broken to obtain the meat. Walnuts are high in antioxidants and beneficial fats and have more protein than any other nut—thus they are prized by squirrel, deer, and people. Walnuts typically grow to 60–70 feet, but specimens over 100 feet are common.

Red Maple (*Acer rubrum*)

Aptly named because its buds, winged seeds, leaf stems, and leaves (in the fall) are all brilliant red, the red maple is one of the earliest flowering trees of the spring. Its buds sprout long before vegetation appears, and once pollinated, these buds mature to bright red, winged seeds that twirl off, helicopter-like, in the wind. Red maples also change color in the fall long before other trees have begun their transformation. Because of its tolerance for moist soils, it is commonly referred to as swamp maple.

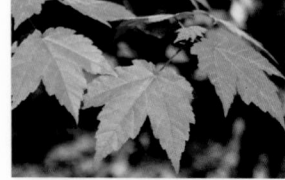

Water Oak (*Quercus nigra*)

A dominant oak of bottomland forests and riparian buffers, water oaks sport leaves that resemble a small kitchen spatula—narrow at the base and widening at a lobed end. Though deciduous, young water oaks are known to hold their leaves through the winter, while leaves on older specimens persist well into the winter. The tree's acorns are important food for squirrel, deer, and wild turkey. They commonly grow to a height of 50–80 feet.

American Hornbeam (*Carpinus caroliniana*)

A tree of the bottomland forest understory, hornbeams grow to 20–30 feet in height and thrive in the shade beneath larger trees. Leaves are egg-shaped with distinct veins radiating from the main stem, ending in toothed leaf edges. The tree's fruit is conspicuous, as the nutlets are contained within a three-winged, narrow, leaflike bract. The leaves turn yellow, orange, and red in the fall and sometimes persist on the tree into the winter, causing confusion with the beech tree, which also holds its leaves in the winter.

Tag Alder (*Alnus serrulata*)

Fibrous roots and flexible stems make this a favorite species for stream bank restoration projects. A shrub-like tree, it grows to heights of 8–12 feet and tends to form thickets along rivers and streams. Like river birch, during the winter months it is easily identified by the presence of last year's fruit (0.5-inch woody cones) and dangling catkins, which though brown in the winter bloom bright yellow in the early spring. The bark and leaves of the alder have historically been used as an astringent to treat internal bleeding as well as external wounds.

Catalpa (*Catalpa bignonioides*)

Perhaps the showiest bloomer of Georgia's river corridors, the catalpa produces large clusters of white bell-shaped blossoms with purple spots and two large orange markings at the throat. In the summer, these fertilized blooms produce long (up to 16 inches) bean-like pods that hang beneath the tree's heart-shaped leaves. The pods ripen and turn brown in the fall, eventually splitting to release paper-thin fringed seeds that float off in a breeze. Catalpas are best known as the sole host for catalpa sphinx moth larvae—a black-and-yellow, horned caterpillar highly prized by anglers as fish bait.

Mountain Laurel (*Kalmia latifolia*)

A showy shrub of the Georgia mountains and Piedmont (and occasionally the Coastal Plain), mountain laurel produces abundant clusters of white-to-pink honeycomb-shaped blooms in the early spring. It is commonly seen along Georgia rivers at rocky outcroppings. Its evergreen leaves are conspicuous in the winter but can be confused with rhododendron, another evergreen flowering shrub. Rhododendron leaves are larger and more elongated. The leaves of the mountain laurel, as well as those of rhododendron and azalea, are toxic if consumed in quantity.

Piedmont Azalea (*Rhododendron canescens*)

In 1979, the Georgia General Assembly designated wild azaleas as the state wildflower, and with good reason: Georgia is home to 10 of North America's 16 native azalea species. Almost all are partial to moist woodlands and stream banks, thus traveling Georgia's rivers you are likely to encounter many, from the hammock sweet azalea on the coast to the sweet azalea of the mountains. Piedmont azalea is among the most common. Its pink-to-white flowers appear from March through early May and emit a sweet, musky fragrance. Azaleas are considered shrubs and rarely grow taller than 15 feet.

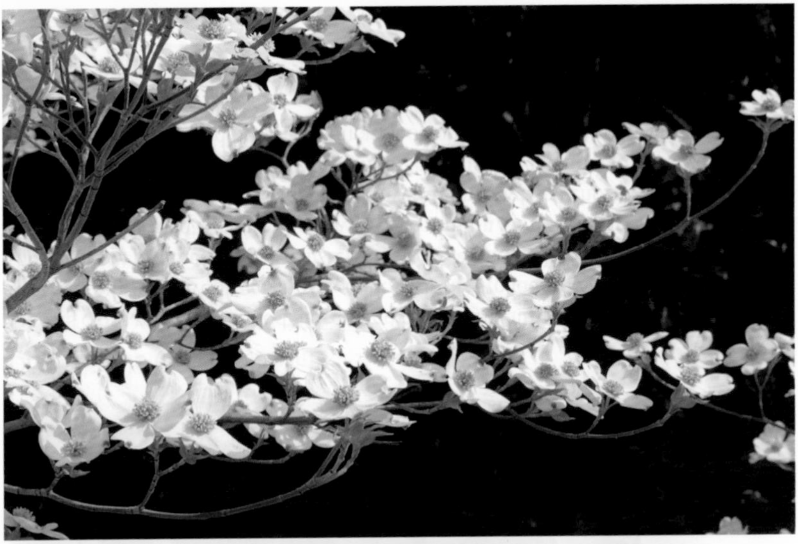

Dogwood (*Cornus florida*)

Perhaps the best known of North America's native flowering trees, dogwoods are common understory trees in floodplain forests along Georgia's rivers. The iconic four-petal, white flower blooms from March through April. In the fall the leaves turn scarlet red and the red berries become very conspicuous. Songbirds, wild turkeys, and a host of mammals—from chipmunks to bears—feed on these berries. Historically, humans have employed the root bark as an antidiarrheal agent, fever reducer, and pain reliever. Dogwoods grow up to 20 feet in height with a spread of up to 30 feet.

Persimmon (*Diospyros virginiana*)

A lover of bottomland forests, persimmons can be found growing along streams and rivers in Georgia, and occasionally the prized fruit can be plucked from branches overhanging the water in the late fall. The plum-sized pulpy fruit filled with large seeds is very sweet, but only after it is fully ripe (usually after a hard frost). Unless the fruits are fully orange to black—and soft—avoid them. Unripe persimmons can leave you puckering and longing for a drink of water. Birds, deer, and hogs eat the fruits and thus help distribute the seeds throughout the forest. Persimmons can grow to 80 feet in height.

Dog Hobble (*Leucothoe fontanesiana*)

Like its close relatives rhododendron and mountain laurel, this member of the heath family is an evergreen shrub, making it easy to identify during the winter. In the spring, it produces showy clusters of small, white bell-shaped blossoms that are often concealed beneath the leaves. Its common name is derived from its dense tangle of arching branches that make traveling through it a chore. Hunters say that bears run through stands of dog hobble to distance themselves from pursuing hounds. The leaves and flower nectar are poisonous to both humans and animals.

Yellowroot (*Xanthorhiza simplicissima*)

A streamside dweller throughout the state, this unique shrub derives its common name from the color of its roots and inner bark. In the early spring before its leaves appear, it puts out 2-to-4-inch clusters of purple star-shaped flowers. The leaves are unique, their deeply toothed edges giving them a lacey appearance. In the fall they turn yellow, bronze, or red. It has long been recognized for its medicinal properties in treating ulcers of the mouth and stomach. It tends to grow in dense thickets and reaches no more than 3 feet in height.

Elderberry (*Sambucus nigra*)

Common along streams, springs, and swamps, the elderberry is a favorite of songbirds and humans thanks to its abundant purple berries that appear in the late summer and early fall. More than 50 birds are known to feed on elderberries, and humans transform the berries into wines, jellies, and pies. The plant was an important food and medicinal source for Native Americans, who also fashioned the stems into flutes and arrow shafts. Elderberries tend to form thickets that commonly reach heights of 12–15 feet. The flower and berry clusters sit conspicuously at the top of the foliage.

River Cane (*Arundinaria gigantean*)

Arundinaria is the only genera of bamboo native to North America. Growing in expansive, dense stands known as canebrakes, it was once the dominant plant along Georgia's rivers, but today scientists believe that it occupies less than 5 percent of its original range due to agriculture, grazing, fire suppression, and urbanization. It propagates primarily through rhizomes, with these spreading roots leading to the impenetrable canebrakes. The demise of river cane has likely contributed to the pollution of our streams, as it plays a critical role in slowing stormwater and filtering pollutants. Native Americans used the plant for nearly everything, fashioning it into spears, arrows, baskets, homes, mats, knives, torches, rafts, tubes, and drills.

River Oats (*Chasmanthium latifolium*)

This 2-to-4-foot-tall native grass is distinguished by its seed head clusters that resemble flattened oats. In the summer, these clusters are bright green, but with the fall they turn brownish tan along with the plant's grasslike leaves. Like other riparian vegetation, it plays a critical role in stabilizing stream banks and minimizing erosion. It also serves as food for many songbirds.

Sensitive Fern (*Onoclea sensibilis*)

This shade-loving fern is found in floodplain forests along rivers and streams as well as in swamps and marshes. To the untrained eye, the fronds of this fern may look very unfernlike because of the generous space between lobes. By late summer, fertile fronds arise that resemble an elongated cluster of dark brown beads on a stalk. Like many ferns, the leaves of the sensitive fern contain toxins that dissuade grazing by deer.

Cinnamon Fern (*Osmunda cinnamomea*)

Cinnamon fern flourishes where its roots remain wet; thus it is a common fern along the river's edge. A large fern, it sends up several fronds in a palmlike whorl that reach 5 feet in length. The fertile fronds (cinnamon-colored stalks bearing the plant's spores) rise from the center of the whorl. In early spring, the young, hairy fiddleheads are a culinary treat for both humans and beasts, and hummingbirds are known to line their nests with the "hair" that covers this early growth. Fossilized fern specimens resembling cinnamon ferns date back 220 million years.

Privet (*Ligustrum sinense*)

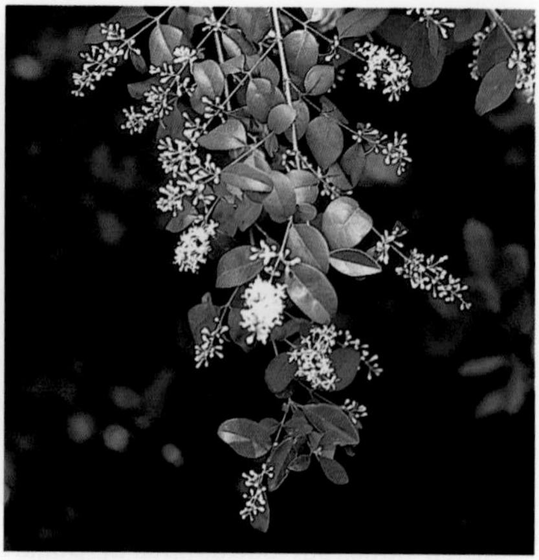

Next to kudzu, perhaps no other invasive plant has done more to alter Georgia's woodlands. A native of China, privet was introduced into the United States in 1852 for use as an ornamental shrub. By the mid-20th century, it had escaped domestic cultivation and spread throughout Georgia. It can grow to 30 feet in height and, owing to its ability to spread via seeds and sprouts, it forms dense thickets, outcompeting native species like river cane. Once established, it is very difficult to remove. Its berries are eaten by many songbirds (which unfortunately further disperse the seeds), and beavers like the bark. Privet sports sickly-sweet-smelling white blooms in the spring and summer, which produce blue-black berries that persist on the plant into the winter.

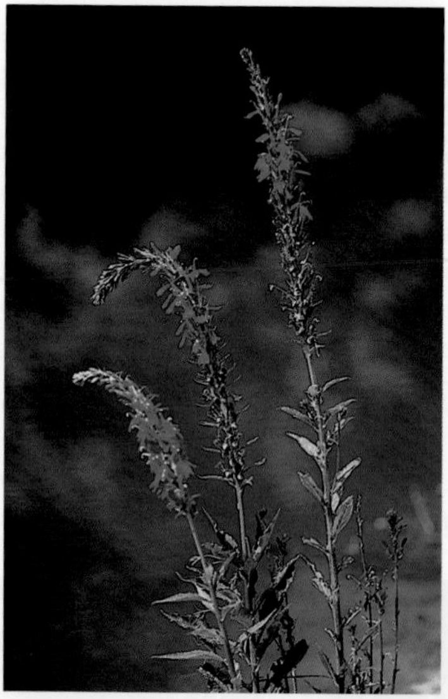

Cardinal Flower (*Lobelia cardinalis*)

From July through September, it is difficult to find a Georgia river that does not have the tall slender green stalks of cardinal flower topped by a cluster of brilliant red blooms along its banks. The stalks can grow to up to 4 feet in height and are common along the base of the riverbank. A lover of moist soils, some have even been seen growing in cavities of partially submerged logs. Their common name is derived from the colored vestments worn by cardinals of the Roman Catholic Church. That color makes the plant irresistible to hummingbirds, which, along with bees and butterflies, are the flower's primary pollinators.

Aquatic Plants

Riverweed/Threadfoot (*Podostemum ceratophyllum*)

This inconspicuous and highly specialized aquatic plant grows on rocks and boulders on the river bottom in swift-moving shoals, rapids, and waterfalls of Georgia rivers above the fall line. Its threadlike masses have an unusual rubbery, seaweed-like texture sporting many narrow olive-green leaves. It plays an important role in stream ecology by providing habitat and food for aquatic insects that form the base of a river's food chain.

Water Willow (*Justicia americana*)

This perennial aquatic wildflower is common along river, stream, and lake margins and is often seen in large, dense colonies. Grasslike, its has leaves very similar to those of the black willow tree, but its white-to-pale-purple orchidlike blooms with purple streaks on the lower petals make this plant easy to identify. The blooms that appear throughout the summer are borne at the top of long (up to 3 feet) slender stems. Another important plant for the river's macroinvertebrate community, mammals also make use of it. Deer browse the leaves, while beavers and muskrats consume the plant's rhizomes.

Pennsylvania Smartweed (*Polygonum pensylvanicum*)

There are more than a dozen native species of smartweed in Georgia, with Pennsylvania smartweed being one of the most important for waterfowl, songbirds, and mammals. Stands of smartweed provide cover for young waterfowl, and the shiny black seeds produced in the late summer provide food for those waterfowl and dozens of other birds. Muskrats, raccoons, and fox squirrels also feast on the seeds and the plants themselves. The white-to-light-pink blooms of smartweed are borne on spikes at the end of stems.

Species of Special Interest in the Ocmulgee River

Below are highlighted some of the Ocmulgee River system's rare or notable aquatic critters. For more information about Georgia's rare species found in the Ocmulgee River, visit www.georgiabiodiversity.org.

Altamaha Shiner (*Cyprinella xaenura*)

Found only in the upper reaches of the Ocmulgee and Oconee River basins, in north-central Georgia (and no where else in the world), the Altamaha shiner is a small minnow that grows to lengths of about 4 inches. Dusky olive in color along its back, it usually sports a black spot at the base of its caudal (tail) fin. Males develop yellow or orange fins and prominent bumps, called "tubercles," on their heads and scales during the spring and summer spawning season. Listed as a threatened species by the state, they have seen much of their habitat destroyed by the construction of small dams. They are very susceptible to sediment pollution because the sediment can cover the rocky river-bottom crevices where they lay their eggs.

Robust Redhorse (*Moxostoma robustum*)

A member of the sucker family, the robust redhorse was once thought extinct, but in 1991 the fish was rediscovered in the Oconee River. Since then, specimens have been found in several Atlantic Coast rivers in Georgia, South Carolina, and North Carolina, and a coordinated effort among state and federal agencies has attempted to reestablish healthy populations of the fish. It is now listed by Georgia as an endangered species. Growing up to 30 inches in length and reaching weights of up to 18 pounds, it feeds exclusively on freshwater mussels, using molar-like teeth to crush the shells of its bivalve prey. Declining native mussel populations have likely contributed to its demise, though the rise of nonnative Asian clams during the later half of the 20th century has provided the native fish with needed food. In addition to its sucker-like mouth, its bronze-colored back and sides and red fins (in juveniles) are distinguishing characteristics.

Atlantic Sturgeon (*Acipenser oxyrinchus oxyrinchus*)

This federally protected fish makes annual spawning runs up the Altamaha, and is believed to spawn in the Ocmulgee and the Oconee Rivers too. Scientists estimate that before 1890 there were some 11,000 spawning females in Georgia rivers. Today, the Altamaha River system's female population is estimated at less than 400 individuals. Overharvesting during the last two centuries, dams that block spawning paths, poor water quality, and dredging activities are believed to be the primary causes of the declining populations. They are distinctive fish, having a long, slender, scale-less body with rows of bony plates, called scutes, running along the back, sides, and belly. In Georgia rivers, they can reach lengths of up to 8 feet and weigh more than 300 pounds while surviving for decades. But their slowness in reaching spawning age (5–19 years) makes recovery of this rare and once commercially important fish all the more difficult.

Altamaha Bass (*Micropterus sp. cf. cataractae*)

This dweller of the upper reaches of the Oconee and Ocmulgee River basin doesn't yet have an official scientific name, but state wildlife biologists believe it is a distinctive species of black bass. It differs from all other bass species in that the caudal (tail) fin is darkly spotted with narrow orange upper and lower margins. The fish grow to lengths of 16 inches. There are 11 species of black bass in Georgia, many of which, like the Altamaha, are found only in specific river systems.

Altamaha spinymussel (*Eliptio spinosa*)

Federally protected, the Altamaha spinymussel is among the most unusual-looking mussels in Georgia, thanks to the spines or spikes that grow up to an inch long from the tops of their shells (3–4 inches wide). This feature makes them look something like an alien spacecraft. It is believed that the mussel survives only in the lower portions of the Ocmulgee River and the Altamaha River—and nowhere else on Earth. Like other mussels, it depends on host fish to carry fertilized young, known as glochidia, during the early stages of life. Thus, mussel populations often depend on robust fish populations. The host for the spinymussel's glochidia is still unknown—determining its identity could help restore populations of this rare invertebrate.

Protecting the Ocmulgee

If you have put this book to use by exploring the Ocmulgee River and its tributaries, you can cite dozens of reasons to protect it. Aside from providing nearly 500 miles of recreational opportunities, the Ocmulgee and its main tributaries (the South, Yellow, and Alcovy Rivers) provide drinking water for hundreds of thousands of Georgians; assimilate the waste of residents in more than 30 counties; provide water for countless businesses, industries, and farms; support a robust riverine ecosystem; and contribute freshwater to important coastal fisheries. It is a workhorse of a river.

Unfortunately, like all of Georgia's rivers, it faces challenges. After years of neglect, sewer infrastructure in Metro Atlanta is slowly getting needed upgrades, which will help restore the South River. Those projects must be completed, maintained, and continually upgraded to fully restore this critical Ocmulgee tributary.

Likewise, stormwater pollution from all the rivers in urbanized locales must be minimized through innovative green infrastructure, especially in the watersheds of the Yellow and Alcovy, which continue to see rapid development. Polluted runoff from industrial and agricultural operations must be mitigated to maintain the health of the river and the streams that feed it.

Hydropower dams that no longer provide a significant amount of electricity or serve any useful purpose, such as those at Juliette, Porterdale, Milstead, and Snapping Shoals, should be considered for partial or complete removal in order to restore habitat for fish and mussels and to open the river for more recreational boating opportunities and the corresponding economic development.

Plastic pollution, which plagues all of Georgia's rivers and our oceans, must be dramatically curtailed.

LITTER AT PANOLA SHOALS, DEKALB COUNTY

You can protect the Ocmulgee River by getting involved with Altamaha Riverkeeper and one of the organizations listed below. Make a contribution to support their efforts, volunteer as a water monitor, get involved in a river cleanup, learn about Georgia laws protecting our rivers, report problems when you see them, engage elected officials in supporting laws that protect our rivers, and tell your friends and neighbors about the treasure that is the Ocmulgee.

Can one person make a difference? You bet, and the river teaches us how. The springs that give birth to the South, Yellow, and Alcovy are but trickles of water, yet by the time these rivers merge, a significant force has been created. The gathered energies of these waters, temporarily held back at Lloyd Shoals Dam, go on to carve a nearly 250-mile path from Butts County and Jackson Lake to the river's confluence with the Oconee, creating a mighty movement in Georgia's largest river—the Altamaha.

Similarly, the cumulative actions and choices of many people can create a mighty movement—one that cherishes and protects the Ocmulgee River.

Altamaha Riverkeeper
127 F Street
Suite 204
Brunswick, GA 31520
855-902-4040
www.altamahariverkeeper.org

Ocmulgee River Water Trail
Telfair Chamber of Commerce
9 East Oak Street
McRae-Helena, GA 31055
www.ocmulgeewatertrail.com

Yellow River Water Trail
P.O. Box 560
Porterdale, GA 30070
www.yellowriverwatertrail.org

South River Watershed Alliance
P.O. Box 1341
Decatur, GA 30031
404-285-3756
www.southriverga.org

Georgia River Network
126 South Milledge Avenue
Suite E3
Athens, GA 30605
706-549-4508
www.garivers.org

American Rivers (Atlanta office)
108 Ponce de Leon Avenue
Decatur, GA 30030
404-373-3602
www.americanrivers.org

Georgia Water Coalition
www.garivers.org/gawater

Georgia Sierra Club
743 East College Avenue
Decatur, GA 30030
404-607-1262
www.georgia.sierraclub.org

Georgia Wildlife Federation
11600 Hazelbrand Road
Covington, GA 30014
770-787-7887
www.gwf.org

Nature Conservancy
100 Peachtree Street
Suite 2250
Atlanta, GA 30303
404-873-6946
www.nature.org

Georgia Conservancy
230 Peachtree Street NW
Suite 1250
Atlanta, GA 30303
404-876-2900
www.georgiaconservancy.org

Trust for Public Land
600 West Peachtree Street, NW
Suite 1840
Atlanta, GA 30308
404-873-7306
www.tpl.org

Rivers Alive
Georgia Department of Natural Resources
2 Martin Luther King Jr. Drive
Suite 1462, East Tower
Atlanta, GA 30334
404-463-1529
www.riversalive.com

Georgia Adopt-A-Stream
Georgia Department of Natural Resources
2 Martin Luther King Jr. Drive
Suite 1462, East Tower
Atlanta, GA 30334
404-651-8515
www.georgiaadoptastream.com

Photo Credits

All photos are by Joe Cook except the following, for which the author thanks the photographers:

Brett Albanese, Georgia DNR: 304 bottom
R. D. Bartlett: 306 bottom
Steven J. Baskauf, http://bioimages.vanderbilt.edu: 312 left and right; 313 left and right; 314 left and right; 315 right; 316 right; 317 left and right; 318 left and right; 319 bottom right; 321 top and bottom right
Giff Beaton: 301 bottom; 302 top and middle; 311 top and middle
Alan Cressler: 327 top
EIC, used under Creative Commons license 3.0: 298 middle
Kevin Enge: 307 bottom
Arlyn W. Evans: 327 bottom
Georgia DNR, Wildlife Resources Division: 329 bottom
Brian Gratwicke, used under Creative Commons license 2.0: 328 bottom
Cris Hagen: 308
Matt Hill, Georgia DNR, Wildlife Resources Division: 328 top
Ty Ivey: 302 bottom
John Jensen: 299 bottom
Steven G. Johnson, used under Creative Commons license 3.0: 305 middle
Phillip Jordan: 298 bottom; 299 top; 300 bottom; 303 middle and bottom; 304 top; 315 left
Colton Lockaby, South Carolina DNR: 329 middle
Thomas Luhring: 306 top
Linda May, Georgia DNR: 319 top and bottom left
James H. Miller: 323 bottom
James H. Miller and Ted Bodner: 320 top, middle, and bottom; 322 bottom; 324; 326 top and bottom
Hugh and Carol Nourse: 322 top left, center, and right; 323 top; 325 top; 327 middle
Richard Orr: 310 middle; 311 bottom
Robert Potts, © California Academy of Sciences: 297 top
Todd Schneider, Georgia DNR, Wildlife Resources Division: 316 left; 321 bottom left; 325 middle and bottom
David E. Scott: 305 top and bottom
Terry Spivey, USDA Forest Service, Bugwood.org: 299 middle
David Stone: 310 bottom
Robert Wayne Van Devender: 307 top and middle
Jess Van Dyke: 309 top
Daniel F. Vickers: 297 bottom; 298 top; 301 top left and top right; 303 top
Whatcom County Noxious Weed Board: 309 bottom
Wikimedia Commons: 329 top
Tom Wilson: 300 top and middle
Jason Wisniewski: 309 middle
Robert T. Zappalorti: 306 middle